Grave Words

Notifying Survivors about Sudden, Unexpected Deaths

Grave Words

Notifying Survivors about Sudden, Unexpected Deaths

Kenneth V. Iserson, M.D.

Galen Press, Ltd.
Tucson, AZ

This publication is designed to provide comprehensive information in regard to the subject matter covered. It is not intended as a substitute for professional, legal, or medical advice and is sold with the understanding that neither the Author nor the Publisher is engaged in rendering such services through this book. If legal advice or other expert assistance is required, the services of a competent professional person should be sought.

Galen Press, Ltd.
P.O. Box 64400
Tucson, AZ 85728-4400
Phone: (520) 577-8363 Fax: (520) 529-6459
Orders: (800) 442-5369 (U.S./Canada)

ISBN: 1-883620-02-3

Library of Congress Cataloging-in-Publication Data

Iserson, Kenneth V.
Grave words : notifying survivors about sudden, unexpected deaths / Kenneth V. Iserson.
p. cm.
Includes bibliographical references and index.
ISBN 1-883620-02-3 (pbk.)
1. Sudden death--Psychological aspects. 2. Counseling. 3. Bereavement--Psychological aspects. 4. Grief. I. Title.
BF789.D4I84 1999
155.9'37--dc21 99-21208
CIP

Printed in the United States of America.

9 8 7 6 5 4 3 2 1

Table of Contents

List of Tables

Acknowledgements

Many people provided assistance during the writing of this book: I would like to thank them for their input.

The reference librarians at the University of Arizona Health Sciences Library, Tucson, AZ, continue to amaze me with their ability to find obscure (and not-so-obscure) information. Special thanks to Hannah Fisher, R.N., M.L.S., AHIP, Associate Librarian–Reference; Nga T. Nguyen, B.A., B.S., Senior Library Specialist; and Mary L. Riordan, M.L.S., Associate Librarian–Reference. Also thanks to an ingenious researcher, Robert Fisher, M.L.S., Tucson, AZ.

I would like to thank the following people for taking the time to review the book and for their excellent advice concerning the content: Reverend Patrick Andresen, M. Div., Chaplain, Univ. Medical Center, Tucson, AZ; Vicki Began, R.N., M.N., Director, Women & Children's Services, Univ. Medical Center, Tucson, AZ; Kate Christenson, M.D., Internist and Director of the Regional Ethics Dept. for Kaiser Permanente, Martinez, CA; Liz Criss, R.N., Prehospital Services, Univ. Medical Center, Tucson, AZ; Myra Christopher, President, Midwest Bioethics Center, Kansas City, MO; Colleen Anne Ducke, Child Life Specialist/Volunteer Coordinator, Emergency Dept., New England Medical Center, Boston, MA; Ellen Fox, M.D., Adjunct Assistant Professor, Center to Improve Care for the Dying, George Washington Univ., Washington, DC, and Clinical Assistant Professor of Medicine, Univ. of Illinois at Chicago; Anna Graham, M.D., Pathology Dept., Univ. of Arizona College of Medicine, Tucson; Larry Graham, Deputy Sheriff, Pima County (AZ) Sheriff's Department; Joseph Hanss, M.D., Phoenix, AZ; Patricia Ruth Hastings, D.O., LTC, MC, Deputy Director, Center of Excellence in Disaster Management and Humanitarian Assistance, Tripler, HI; Andrew R. Iserson, M.S.B., North Potomac, MD; Lawrence S. Iserson, Freehold, NJ; Mary Lou Iserson, Tucson, AZ; Jay A. Jacobson, M.D., Div. of Medical Ethics, Internal Medicine Dept., LDS Hospital & Univ. of Utah School of Medicine, Salt Lake City, UT; Tammy Kastre, M.D., President, First Correctional Medical, Inc., Tucson, AZ; Ruth Kimmons, R.N., Recovery Coordinator, Donor Network of Arizona, Tucson, AZ; Steve Kohler, M.D., Emergency Physician, Kaiser Permanente Hospital, San Diego, CA; Gary H. Lambert, M.D., FACEP, Medical Staff Executive Secretary, Cottonwood Hospital Medical Center, Murray, UT; Cendra Lynn, Ph.D., GriefNet Founder & Director, Ann Arbor, MI; Mary Ann Matter, R.N., Prehospital Services, Univ. Medical Center, Tucson, AZ; Kyle Nash, D.Min.(c), Associate Faculty in Clinical Thanatology/Humanistic Issues in Ethics & Medicine, MacLean Center for Clinical Medical Ethics, Pritzker School of Medicine, and Consulting Thanatologist, Univ. of Chicago Hospitals, Chicago, IL; Steve Nash, J.D., Executive Director, Pima County Medical Association, Tucson, AZ; Sue Ogden, R.N., John Corey Ogden, and Randy Ogden, EMT-P, Tucson, AZ; Tammie E. Quest, M.D., Assistant Professor of Emergency Medicine, Emory Univ., Atlanta, GA; Alan Reeter, M.S.E.E., President, Medfilms, Inc., Tucson, AZ; Ron Salik, M.D., Assistant Professor of Clinical of Surgery (Pediatric EM), Univ. of Arizona College of Medicine, Tucson; David

L. Schiedermeyer, M.D., Associate Professor of Medicine, Dept. of Medicine, Medical College of Wisconsin, Milwaukee, WI; Terri Schmidt M.D., M.S., Associate Professor & Vice Chair, Emergency Medicine Dept., Senior Scholar, Center for Ethics in Health Care, Oregon Health Sciences Univ., Portland, OR; Mary Jo Villar, D.O., Section of Hematology-Oncology, Jackson Memorial Hospital, Miami, FL; Donald Witzke, Ph.D., Associate Professor, Pathology & Laboratory Medicine, Univ. of Kentucky School of Medicine, Lexington, KY; and Robert Wrenn, Ph.D., Professor of Psychology, Univ. of Arizona, Tucson.

For their stories: Vicki Alexander, R.N., Emergency Dept., Univ. Medical Center, Tucson, AZ; Ken Briggs, EMT-P, Tucson, AZ; Jennifer G. Gilbert, Tucson, AZ; Joshua Helman, M.D., Resident, Emergency Medicine Dept., Detroit Receiving Hospital, Wayne State Univ., Detroit, MI; Mark Ivey, M.D., Payson, AZ; Sam Keim, M.D., Sec. of Emergency Medicine, Univ. of Arizona College of Medicine, Tucson; Fran D. Kunz, Pima County Search & Recovery Divers, and Southern Arizona Rescue Association, Tucson, AZ; David Lebiner, M.D., Associate Professor, Neurology Dept., Univ. of Arizona College of Medicine, Tucson; Robert Orr, M.D., Bioethics and Family Medicine Depts., Loma Linda Univ. School of Medicine, Loma Linda, CA; Joseph W. Rossano, Medical Student, Univ. of Arizona College of Medicine, Tucson; Alan Taplow, M.A., Plainfield, VT; and Charlotte Yeh, M.D., Emergency Physician & Medical Director, Medicare Policy, National Heritage Insurance Company, Charlotte, NC.

For indicating how important this topic is and how little good information is available, as well as for providing some excellent information: Mr. Bill Byrnes, Regional EAP Representative, United Airlines, Chicago, IL; Commander Gilbert D. Gibson, Office of the Navy Chief of Chaplains; Mrs. Alicia Gonzalez, Emergency Medicine, Univ. of Arizona College of Medicine, Tucson; L. Wayne Harris, Senior Mortician, Pathology Dept., Univ. Medical Center, Tucson, AZ; Sara Pace Jones, Public Affairs, Donor Network of Arizona, Phoenix, AZ; Herbert L. Lawrence, Director, Field Support, Armed Forces Emergency Services, American Red Cross; Betty McEntire, Ph.D., Executive Director, American Sudden Infant Death Syndrome Institute, Atlanta, GA; Richard Nelson, M.D., FACEP, Professor & Vice Chair, Emergency Medicine Dept., Ohio State Univ. College of Medicine & Public Health, Columbus, OH; Robin Perin, R.N., J.D., University Physicians, Inc., Tucson, AZ; Suzanne F. Sawyer, Executive Director, Concerns of Police Survivors, Camdenton, MO; Lt. Col. Michael C. Whittington, USAF Chaplain Service Institute, Maxwell AFB, AL; and Jennifer Wolpert, M.S.W., Victim Service Project Specialist, National Organization for Victim Assistance, Washington, DC.

I also want to thank the folks at Galen Press, Ltd., especially Christopher W. McNellis, Jennifer G. Gilbert, and Mary Lou Sherk, as well as Lynn Bishop Graphics of Tucson, AZ, for the great cover design.

INTRODUCTION: The Problem

Mortality tables fractionate the certainty of death into a variety of separate causes . . . but the statistics about death itself are easy to remember—100%.

Weisman, Avery D., Coping with untimely death. Psychiatry. 1973 Nov;36(4):366-78

1: The Problem

Directness, truth, consistency, and clarity are the key factors when delivering information about a sudden, unexpected death. These points were driven home for Jennifer Gilbert, a Galen Press editor, while she was reading this manuscript for the first time. She encountered sudden death one evening and describes the experience:

> Hearing Kathy scream my name, I rushed next door. "My baby is dead," she moaned in disbelief as she met me at the door. She had just returned from work to find her 40-year-old fiancée lying face down on the kitchen floor. It was obvious from his coloration that he had been dead for hours. I hugged her hard while I tried to swallow my own mounting panic, fear, and grief. Instinctively, I knew there was nothing I could say—just being there, hugging her, was enough.
>
> "He's asthmatic," she had me relay to the 911 operator as she leaned over his body, "He'd just discovered that the inhaler he was using could cause his heart to stop." Within minutes (it seemed much longer) the room began to fill with paramedics and policemen. Somehow Kathy was pushed out onto the front porch as they proceeded to do something to his now lifeless body. "They're going to take him away from me," she cried. "Why are they working on him? He's not coming back." A paramedic rushed past carrying syringes. "Is he breathing?" she asked. "No, he's not," the young man answered quickly, without pausing or turning his head.
>
> I rubbed Kathy's back as she crouched by a phone, trying to remember people to call. I asked if there was someone I could notify and she had me telephone a nearby relative. "Don't say he's dead," she cautioned, "Say there's been an accident and to meet us at the hospital." I will always remember how clear she was—still thinking about others in the midst of her terrible shock and sadness.
>
> A couple of men brought in a gurney in preparation for the short ride to the hospital emergency room. "I want to go with him. I have to go with my baby,"

> Kathy sobbed. My role had been to hug her whenever she needed support, inform the professionals entering the yard that the dogs were harmless. Now I rushed out to the ambulance and made sure she would be allowed on board. Everyone seemed extremely busy, absorbed in the tasks they no doubt performed efficiently several times a day, but they nodded a brief affirmative.
>
> By the time her fiancée's body was placed in the ambulance, a young policeman, who told her she needed to answer some questions, had stopped Kathy in the living room. "I have to go with the ambulance," she pleaded. But three minutes later the ambulance sped away, carrying his lifeless body and leaving Kathy to follow behind in my truck. This created a lasting (and unnecessary) memory of callousness and pain for Kathy, who needed to spend those last moments with her partner's body. At no time did any of the professionals involved in the response take a personal interest in the one person who would remember this evening forever—Kathy, the survivor.[1]

Death has replaced sex as the major taboo topic in Western culture. Imaginary death—such as cartoon-like violence on television and in movies—has replaced reality for most people. When death strikes, as it must, and especially if it strikes suddenly and unexpectedly, we respond with discomfort, distress, and dismay.

A sudden death is one that is unforeseen, unexpected, gives little or no warning, and leaves survivors unprepared for their loss. It comes from an unexpected injury or suicide, or from a medical cause such as heart attack, stroke, overwhelming infection, poisoning, or massive bleeding. Death might even result from fear.[2,3] We have no ingrained cultural responses to tell us how to deal with these crises.

Survivors are victims. Their reactions separate them from life, from reality, and often from caring about themselves, their future, or those around them. When a person learns of the sudden unexpected death of a loved one (*bereavement*), they experience "a sense of being lost and not knowing what to do. Their sense of being suspended from life, inability to concentrate, indifference to immediate needs, disbelief that the decedent is really gone, and feeling that life can never be worth living again hinders their ability to arrange for the funeral and to make plans for other ongoing life needs."[4] This is *grief.*

No one likes to deliver the news of a sudden, unexpected death to others; it is an emotional blow, precipitating life crises and forever altering their worlds. Yet many health, law enforcement, religious, and social service professionals must repeatedly do this as part of their daily work. In fact, nearly every adult will eventually be in this position within his or her own family, acting not only as the messenger of grief, but also as an initial support system for the distraught recipients. Even for skilled professionals, this can be an emotionally draining and even harrowing experience. This book is designed to help us perform these duties with more skill, aplomb, and assurance.

Perceptive survivors can easily tell which notifiers care and which are only "going through the motions." It often takes imagination to put oneself in the position of a grieving survivor, especially when wide cultural or age differences exist. Imagination, studying people, advance planning, and learning from experienced mentors is the only way to successfully perform this necessary, but tragic, task. Young physicians, nurses, police, chaplains, EMS personnel, and other notifiers, in particular, may not have enough life experiences to empathize with the elderly woman who has just lost her husband of fifty years or with the recent-immigrant couple whose child has just died from SIDS.

But, even if you cannot learn to empathize with survivors, you can learn to behave appropriately, speak correctly, and assist them in their time of grief. Using death-notification protocols and, hopefully, being accompanied by more experienced partners may be the only way to positively affect these survivors.

Why Sudden, Unexpected Death Notification Is Unique

Sudden, unexpected deaths severely shock survivors. These deaths, whether they occur in the young or the old, the healthy or the infirm, strike blows to the very essence of life for those left behind. The decedent's sudden transition from being very alive to being very dead shocks all observers, both professionals and lay people alike. The degree of this shock is related to how independent, autonomous, and distinctive the decedent was when he or she died.[5] For example, the death of someone confined to a nursing home with Alzheimer's Disease generally affects survivors less than a 40-year-old executive and father suddenly dying of a heart attack.

Some sudden deaths can even be considered "calamitous" when victims die unexpectedly from violent, destructive, demeaning, or degrading causes such as from murder or by suicide. These deaths can profoundly affect the victim's community (some deaths more than others).[6] Victims' relatives often have a much more difficult time dealing with the aftermath of these acts.

Once a person is dead, the survivors become the victims, the patients—those in need. Sudden deaths often represent major life transitions for the survivors. In an instant and with no warning, women go from wives to widows, children become orphans, and friends survive alone. They need someone to deliver the news to them sensitively and in the right context, support them through their time of shock and bewilderment, and direct them toward continued assistance.

In modern societies, people often don't witness the events that bring them grief. Survivors need someone to communicate this news to them. That is the primary role of the death notifier: to "break the bad news." At some point, nearly everyone fulfills this role in his or her private life. Both the occasional notifier and their professional counterparts, who must perform this function as a regular part of their jobs, often anguish over how to do this correctly and how to assess their own performances. This book provides a yardstick with which to measure performance, tools to use in training, and examples of both good and bad death notifications and practices.

A word must be said here about the commonly used terms, "breaking/giving/delivering bad news." As death educator Kyle Nash says,

> These negatively value-laden phrases imply one-sided communication, which should never be the goal of any notifier-survivor relationship. If the communication is thought of in that manner at the outset, notifiers will tend to feel awkward, anxious, and uncomfortable about what they will be or are

communicating. When notifiers feel uncomfortable, the type of communication that occurs in these situations does become one-sided.

While it may seem obvious that death notification will indeed be interpreted as negative (i.e., bad), I believe that only the survivors can determine what the information means to them. Preferable terms that I use when teaching are "initiating or engaging in difficult conversations." These phrases clearly express two-way communication and are value neutral.[7]

Survivors' first reaction when they hear the news is often, "It can't be true! It can't be happening!" But it is true, and the professionals around them must give all the support that they can. One of the hardest things for health care professionals to do, and certainly for other professionals tasked with this job as well, is to face someone whose loved one has just suffered a sudden, tragic death. Despite this reluctance, it is vital that these notifications be done correctly to attempt to lessen survivors' subsequent distress and pathological grieving behaviors. Family members of those who die suddenly and unexpectedly, either in the emergency department or in the hospital (and also presumably outside the hospital) do much more poorly than do those whose deaths are expected. This may be because there is no time for psychological preparation.[8-10]

Who are the Survivors?

The "primary" survivors addressed in this book are the people with close emotional, social, and cultural ties to the decedent. Primary survivors are, in most cases, a spouse, parent, sibling, children, "significant other" or domestic partner, or grandchildren. Less often, they may be other relatives, friends, neighbors, baby sitters, or housekeepers.

While the most readily accessible survivors are notified first, all notifiers generally try to contact at least the decedent's closest next of kin, which is usually defined in this order: current spouse, adult children, parent(s), and sibling(s). If a domestic partner or very close friend appears to have been the decedent's closest relation, then they are usually notified. Once notified, family members can make notification calls to others.

Although it is considered more common in the elderly, even young survivors occasionally die when hearing the news of a loved one's death. Engel cites two cases: a 14-year-old girl dropped dead upon learning of her brother's death and an 18-year-old girl died when she heard that the grandfather who had raised her had died.[11] Appropriate notification techniques may lessen the frequency of immediate adverse incidents. Notifiers may have a profoundly beneficial effect on survivors' future lives if they approach them with caring, knowledge, and professionalism.

Who are the Notifiers?

In the United States and Canada, approximately 70% of deaths occur in health care institutions, so their staff is usually responsible for making these notifications. In the other 30%, however, this job falls to the police, ambulance or fire department personnel, chaplains, medical examiners or coroners, or co-workers. In nearly all cases, whether or not the death occurs in a health care facility, family members and friends of the decedent must then notify others.

Custom, not law, defines who should be the notifier and who should be notified. Generally, this depends upon where and how the death occurs. For example, when death occurs outside of medical facilities, the police usually do the notification.

Resuscitations in Progress

Within most medical facilities, protocols determine who is considered to be the notifier. If a family arrives at the hospital while resuscitation attempts are still ongoing, a chaplain, social worker, or nurse may be delegated to inform the family of the patient's status. These individuals may be more inclined to use non-medical words to explain what is occurring than would a physician. This is vital because, despite its wide use in the media, the "lingo" commonly used in hospitals is still unfamiliar to most people. To avoid any miscommunication, health care workers who act as notifiers should use "heart attack" rather than "MI," "injury" rather than "trauma," and "breathing machine" rather than "ventilator."

These notifiers should continually update the family. When things are going badly, the same person, or at least one person from the group who initially spoke with them, should progressively inform the family "that things are not looking good." This alerts them to the grave situation and gives them at least a little time to prepare for the bad news. Often disparagingly termed "hanging crepe," survivors usually view this as "being gentle." Technically, the strategy is called "presaging," or allowing survivors time for "anticipatory grief" and psychologically preparing them to lose their loved one. Some have also referred to these updates as "successive pre-announcements" and "preliminary suspicion announcements," suggesting that it is a gradual buildup to what is expected to be tragic news.[12] Even if the outcome changes for the better (which, unfortunately, it seldom does in these situations), experienced notifiers think it best to tell potential survivors what they really expect to happen. As one notifier said, "I prefer to paint it as black as I can because it is, and if it changes, then I would go back and tell them differently."[13] And when the bad news finally arrives, as it nearly always does in these situations, it is only a confirmation of what those individuals awaiting news have been anticipating.

In a typical emergency department scenario, a nurse, chaplain, or social worker acts as the liaison between the resuscitation team and the family. They meet family members as they arrive and guide them to a waiting area. Having already been into the resuscitation room, the liaisons have a sense of or have been explicitly told about the patient's condition and what chance the clinicians think the patient has of making it out of the emergency department and the hospital alive and functional. They in turn deliver this news to the family. Initially, they may say, "The medical (surgical) team is working very hard, but he is very ill (badly hurt)." On subsequent visits, they will reassure the family that the team is still working, but will say "Things are not looking good" or "They are not sure they will be able to save him." Ultimately someone, usually the physician in charge, will tell the family that the effort was unsuccessful. By that time, it is news they are expecting to hear.

In some instances, the physicians or surgeons only need to stop, shake their heads, and say "I'm sorry" for survivors to get the news they expect. In these instances, the physicians clearly mean they are sorry for the survivors' loss as well as for their own inability to change the outcome. (Hopefully, after delivering the news in this fashion, they take the time to sit with and assist the survivors for at least a short period of time.) When these non- or minimally verbal announcements fail, clinicians must fall back on their standard death notification methods.

Occasionally, interactions between the clinician and survivors during resuscitation attempts convey important clinical information, as Dr. Bob Orr relates: "Things weren't going well during an emergency department resuscitation and I had 'hung crepe' a few times with the potential widow. Finally, I told her that we were only continuing with CPR because his pupils had not dilated, so that we thought his brain still might have some function. 'But he has two glass eyes,' she said. We stopped."[14]

The Notification

Once death has occurred, especially within the emergency department, the physician usually has the task of delivering the news, often accompanied by a chaplain, a nurse, or a social worker. Most survivors, however, have no objection if more timely notifications can be made by other professionals, such as the nurse, chaplain, or social worker, as long as they have subsequent contact with the physician.[15] What survivors want most is a notifier who seems to care that their loved one has died—someone who will inform them in a warm, sympathetic tone of voice. As a survivor who didn't have that experience said,

> I could not believe that a death that was so important to me was so unimportant to the people in that emergency room. I left thinking that there must be something wrong with me, that somehow I should not be feeling the way I was feeling. I felt as though I was abnormal.[16]

Some professionals avoid this responsibility and pass the job to others. This is usually because they have difficulty dealing with one or more aspects of death or the interaction with survivors. This task, however, should never be relegated to the unit assistant, medical or nursing student, or other untrained or partially trained person. (The exception to this is when a student or resident, who is in the process of being educated to the death-notification process, is accompanied by an experienced, supervising mentor.) When these reluctant notifiers must speak with survivors, they often use a standard, rapid, unconcerned approach as a defense. Others, even those who try to do a good job, just "wing it," using whatever method seems best. For professionals, these can be career-crippling strategies.

A key psychological response that often diminishes notifiers' effectiveness is identifying too closely with survivors, thus becoming entangled in their emotions. This may be due to the notifier having experienced a similar event or closely matching the key survivor's age, cultural background, and social or professional position. Such close identification may produce a sense of awkwardness or inadequacy in notifiers, causing them to rush through the process to hide their own emotions. Consequently, their presentation may seem callous or insensitive, and the exact opposite of what they desired.

Telling survivors about sudden unexpected deaths poses difficulties for those individuals responsible for doing it because they often:

- Lack training and experience.
- Fear being blamed.
- Do not know how to cope with survivors' reactions.
- Fear expressing their emotions.
- Fear not knowing the "right" answers.
- Fear their own death or disabilities.[17]

The qualities of a good communicator are genuineness, warmth and respect for the survivors, active listening, empathy, and openness.

Survivors' Perspectives

Understanding survivors' perspectives helps notifiers realize the importance of their task, how they can do it better, and the lasting impact notifications have. The following are notifications from survivors' perspectives:

> On arrival at the hospital just after 10:15 P.M. no one was expecting us. "Everybody has gone now, and I should have gone too by now," a social worker said. My friend and I were put in a small anteroom and the door was closed. We had been put into a box with the lid closed to spare us the sight of panicky people rushing to and fro, telephone calls being made, etc., while the system was being reassembled for us. I wouldn't have that. I behaved myself for three to four minutes, and then I opened the door. I still couldn't see anything but felt better. What would have made me feel much better was to have seen and shared the panic. That would have been human: being put in a small, quiet, impersonal room behind a closed door was not. . . .
>
> [I had to be] interviewed by the coroner's officer, who, not knowing I was to arrive, was somewhere else. Eventually he arrived. By now I was getting nicely institutionalized. I was behaving myself. I put him at his ease while he asked his questions—well, I tried. He, poor man, knew the formula and knew each question had to be put with a sympathetic preamble. He was unctuous. He was sorrowful. And I wanted to see my son. He knew what to do with grieving relatives. He knew the formula, so he did it—to the end. He had no idea whom, in reality, I was.[18]

No more support was available to Betty Jane Spencer, who came to the emergency department after her four sons were killed.

> "Oh no, it can't be." Nurses were staring at me. "What happened?" I was having trouble making sense of it all. I didn't want to think of the boys and what had happened to them. I was alive, so I reasoned they were too, even though I had

seen them killed. Words hung in the air while I tried to make sense of them. Words like 'dead' and 'autopsy' floated through. I didn't want to hear them. But all I could say out loud was, "Please don't tell me how many of them are dead."[19]

A nurse who observed a survivor's (John) struggles in both the emergency department and the intensive care unit relates his story:

He had been summoned from work to learn that his wife, Lisa, and two of their children had been killed in a car accident outside a shopping mall. Only his 16-year-old son survived the accident. When John arrived at the hospital, he had been taken to the emergency department (ED) to identify the body of his 7-year-old daughter. The chaplain then accompanied him to the pediatric intensive care unit where John's other daughter, who was only five, lay brain-dead. Within hours, cardiac arrest would end her short life. John was spared the awful task of identifying Lisa, who had suffered several facial injuries in the crash. A family friend offered to do this for him. His son was critically injured. John had only a brief moment to tell him how much he loved him before the boy was taken to the operating room for orthopedic surgery.[20]

This is a survivor's description of a home notification she endured:

Being awakened out of a sound sleep in the early hours of the morning by an insistent knocking on the door, you finally get to the door and open it to find two strangers with radios, notepads, and maybe flashlights in hand. They introduce themselves by name, one being from the police department and the other, a chaplain. Their questions denoted their seriousness in making certain that they have the right person; their questions also reflect the fact that they are there to give you some information about a member of your family. You start wondering who is in trouble. Your mind begins to race down the checklist of family members: your husband is at work; your son has been staying out too late recently; your daughter is expecting her first child, and she and her husband have been arguing a lot recently.

As this stranger, these 'intruders,' continues asking questions, your own questions start flashing though your mind. Your world begins crumbling in on you. You are brought back to the present moment by an insistent voice gently, but firmly, calling your name. "Are you all right?" You look at the speaker's face, trying to read what is being said. You hear your own voice, as from a distant point saying, "Yes, I'm all right." Those probing, insistent voices then ask, "Is your husband at home?" You feel yourself beginning to feel faint. The voices urge you to go inside and sit down. As you sit, they ask about your husband again. You take a deep breath, trying to clear some of the cobwebs from your thoughts. Finally, you realize your husband is at home. He traded nights off with a friend and is sleeping. You call him several times before he answers, and you ask him to come downstairs.

Taking the stairs two at a time, he hurries to his wife's side. "Who are you?" he asks, as he puts his arm protectively around his wife's shoulder. You introduce your husband to these strangers who are bringing obviously bad news, although they radiate a calmness and a genuine friendliness which help you feel a little less anxious. Icy fingers of fear clutch your throat as you hear the question, "Do you have a son named Tom? He has wavy blond hair and a mustache?" Your hands move to your throat as though to seek release from that stranglehold of fear. The questions continue. "Is your son about eighteen years old? Does he drive a blue antique pick-up truck?"

Almost at the same instant as you say, "Yes," the pent-up fear erupts as you cry out in anguish, "Oh my God, what has happened?" It seems an eternity before you hear those dreaded, but not unexpected words, "I'm sorry, your son has been involved in an accident." The words, even though spoken softly and compassionately, shatter your world. Though dazed by this news, you feel compelled to strike out against its reality. With your heart pounding and aching, blinded by the tears that gush uncontrollably from your eyes, you jump up from the chair to vent your anguish by beating on these people who have torn your little world asunder. Your husband, stunned by this news, now moves to your side. One of the intruders gently but firmly has been holding your wrists, saying, "It's all right, go ahead and vent your anger and hurt." You feel your husband's arm around you, and he leads you back to your chair. As you sit, your husband asks, "How bad is it? Is he hurt bad?" "Yes," comes the reply, "it is very serious." Looking at the intruders, and wanting them to deny the next question, you and your husband ask in a single voice, "Is he . . . dead?" Stepping closer to where they can touch both of your shoulders, the intruders answer very softly, "Yes."

The dam of restraint can no longer hold back the deluge of tear-filled anguish. The intruders silently, and understandingly, wait with patience until the sobbing subsides. After a while, you and your husband look at them as sources of guidance, strength, and information. You ask "What happened?" The intruders, now companions in this sorrow, review the incident with sufficient detail for you to understand what happened. They answer, to your satisfaction, the questions of who was involved, where it happened, how it happened, and where your son's body is now. They ask if they can contact your own clergy. As you look at your husband, he nods his head and says, "Yes, we would appreciate that. His number is ___."

You begin to focus on the details, the arrangements for Tom's funeral. A flood of questions begins to come into your mind. So many details to see to. What should you do first? "What should we do now?" you ask. They reply, "At your convenience, contact a funeral director, give him your son's name, tell him that he was fatally injured in an automobile accident, and that he is at the General Hospital. The funeral director will lead you through the other steps. If you don't have a funeral home in mind, we have a list of all those in the local area. If you want, we can call them for you."

They then ask, "Are there family members or special friends you would like us to call for you?" You have a brother who is very close to you and you ask them to call him. After the call, one of the notifiers, the policeman, says that he must go back on patrol, but that the chaplain will stay with you. He gives you his card and says to contact him if you have additional questions he can answer. The chaplain then sits and begins talking with you about your family, home, jobs, and hobbies. He is interrupted when your clergyman arrives. Now that your own clergy is here, the chaplain quickly reviews the details of the event, including specifics that you will need to know later, such as where your son's truck is and how to contact him later, if necessary. He promises to revisit within the week.

As she shakes hands with you and your husband, you find a smile of gratitude working its way through the tears as you thank her for coming and telling you about your son's accident. As she walks out the door, you think, "Less than two hours ago, she came in as a stranger; intruded into and tore up our world. Now, as she leaves, she leaves as a friend." [Modified from Reference 21. Used with permission.]

Expected versus Sudden, Unexpected Deaths

Most people's deaths can generally be anticipated. Those who die are usually elderly people with chronic, often obviously progressive, diseases. Even if the exact day, week, or even month when the death occurs comes as a surprise, no one is surprised when it happens. The differences between these expected deaths and the sudden unexpected deaths highlighted in this book are illustrated in table 1-1.

This story from Mark Ivey, M.D., a general practitioner in Payson, Ariz., illustrates a case in which the death started out as unexpected, but progressed into an expected one.

Fifteen years ago, a previously healthy 67-year-old woman presented to the emergency department at our local rural hospital with an obvious cerebral vascular accident (stroke) affecting her speech, swallowing, and the ability to move her arms and legs. I expected that she would soon die, so I asked her husband, son, and minister to stay by her bedside. But she didn't die.

For days this forlorn assemblage huddled by her bed, discussed her fate, prayed, and cried. After several days it seemed clear to everyone that she would die if disconnected from life supports. As they watched, I removed her from the ventilator and waited. The next 45 minutes as we clustered around that dying woman's bed were the longest of my professional career. While we stood a deathwatch, I questioned whether I had made the correct decision based solely on clinical grounds (without transferring her to another hospital for an EEG, CT scan, etc.). I wondered whether the family thought I had made a mistake.

Table 1-1: Expected versus Sudden, Unexpected Deaths

	Sudden, Unexpected Death	Expected Death
Approach of death	Immediate or over very short time.	Gradual.
Nature of illness or injury	Acute process or acute worsening of a stable chronic illness.	Chronic—usually an illness or combination of illnesses.
Causes of death	Disease, suicide, homicide, accidental, disaster, unknown cause.	Usually disease or a result of aging processes.
Age of decedent	Any age, commonly young or middle-aged adults, fetuses, and neonates.	Usually elderly but can occur at any age.
Place of death	Usually in public, emergency department, ICU, or at home or work.	Usually home, hospital, or nursing home.
When death occurs	At the time of or shortly after the acute event.	Months to decades after diagnosis of chronic disease, or in old age.
Survivor reaction	Disbelief, shock, grief, dismay, disorganization, hostility, and fear.	Grief.
Survivor involvement	Usually not present at time of death; appear gradually at death scene or ED.	Often present at time of death or aware of impending death.
Site of last contact with medical personnel	Public space, home, or emergency department.	Hospital, home, hospice, nursing home.
Resuscitation procedures	Often performed.	Rarely performed. Advance directives often available.
Patient identity	Known or often, at least initially, unknown.	Usually known.
Autopsy	Frequent and done by medical examiner or coroner.	Rare, and when done, usually by hospital pathologist.
Family's immediate after-death rituals and requirements	Usually not pre-arranged.	Often pre-arranged by individual or family in anticipation of death.

Then she died—calmly and quietly. I still wondered whether what I thought was compassionate care had been correct. The minister reassured me and the family of my wisdom, the family thanked me, and, after an autopsy, the pathologist congratulated me on my astute diagnosis. The family still sees me professionally—and I still think about that case. What was it that made me do the right thing and involve the family in this decision?

Why Use Protocols?

It's been claimed that "effective grief support cannot be reduced simply to a protocol-driven response."[22] It is true that no protocol can anticipate every eventuality; every notification will differ in some way. Neither can it enable notifiers to break bad news painlessly. It can, however, help notifiers prepare for their task and help them understand what to expect. Protocols combined with staff education have made significant differences in how survivors perceive and respond to sudden-death notifications.[23]

Obviously, optimal survivor notification, especially in cases of sudden unexpected deaths, includes individuals' emotional commitment to and a personal investment in the process. There must be a place to start learning the process and a way to measure the quality of notifications. Protocols fulfill these two goals.

For many in the healing professions as well as other professionals tasked with notifying survivors of sudden, unexpected deaths, protocols have become a standard method of learning complex material. Certainly, as they become more experienced in the process, these professionals will deviate from the protocols to meet the needs of individual situations. But protocols provide both notifiers and death educators a framework to build on.

References

1. Gilbert J: Personal communication with author, January 1999.
2. Harvey WP, Levine SA: Paroxysmal ventricular tachycardia due to emotion—possible mechanism of death from fright. *JAMA*. 1952;150:479-80.
3. Engel GL: Sudden and rapid death during psychological stress. folklore or folk wisdom? *Ann Intern Med*. 1971 May;74(5):771-82.
4. Silverman PR: Services to the widowed: first steps in a program of preventive intervention. *Comm Mental Health J*. 1967;3:38-44.
5. Weisman AD: Coping with untimely death. *Psychiatry*. 1973 Nov;36(4):366-78.
6. *Ibid.*
7. Nash, Kyle: Personal communication with author, April 1999.
8. Tolle SW, Bascom PB, Hickam DH, et al.: Communication between physicians and surviving spouses following patient deaths. *J Gen Intern Med*. 1986 Sep-Oct;1(5):309-14.

9. Parkes CM, Brown RJ: Health after bereavement. a controlled study of young Boston widows and widowers. *Psychosom Med.* 1972 Sep-Oct;34(5):449-61.

10. Levinson P: On sudden death. *Psychiatry.* 1972 May;35(2):160-73.

11. Engel GL: "Sudden and rapid death."

12. Glaser BG: *Time for Dying.* Chicago: Aldine, 1968; As cited in: Clark RE, LaBeff EE: Death telling: managing the delivery of bad news. *J Health Soc Behav.* 1982 Dec;23(4):366-80.

13. Clark RE, LaBeff EE: Death telling: managing the delivery of bad news. *J Health Soc Behav.* 1982 Dec;23(4):366-80.

14. Orr R: Personal communication with author, March 1999.

15. Tolle SW, Bascom PB, Hickam DH, et al.: "Communication between physicians and surviving spouses."

16. Jones WH, Buttery M: Sudden death: survivors' perceptions of their emergency department experience. *J Emerg Nurs.* 1981 Jan-Feb;7(1):14-7.

17. Modified from: McLauchlan CA: ABC of major trauma. handling distressed relatives and breaking bad news. *Br Med J.* 1990 Nov 17;301(6761):1145-9.

18. Awoonor-Renner S: I desperately needed to see my son. *Br Med J.* 1991 Feb 9;302(6772):356.

19. Lord JH: *Trauma, Death, and Death Notification: A Seminar for Professional Counselors and Victim Advocates.* Washington, DC: Mothers Against Drunk Driving and the U.S. Dept. of Justice for Victims of Crime, 1996, p. 32.

20. Coolican M, Vassar E, Grogan J: Helping survivors survive. *Nursing.* 1989 Aug;19(8):52-7.

21. Cunningham WA: *Thoughts on Making Death Notifications.* Presented to the International Conference of Police Chaplains, July 1980.

22. Wolfram RW, Timmel DJ, Doyle CR, et al.: Incorporation of a "Coping with the Death of a Child" module into Pediatric Advanced Life Support (PALS) curriculum. *Acad Emerg Med.* 1998 Mar;5(3):242-6.

23. Adamowski K, Dickinson G, Weitzman B, et al.: Sudden unexpected death in the emergency department: caring for the survivors. *CMAJ.* 1993 Nov 15;149(10):1445-51.

SECTION 1: Notifications

Dealing with death . . . You have to be aware of your own feelings and biases because if you don't, you'll wind up dealing with yourself first and the other people second. This isn't the best way to do it.

Clark RE, LaBeff EE: Death telling: managing the delivery of bad news. *J Health Soc Behavior.* 1982;23:366-80.

2: Communicating With The Living

Excellent communication skills represent the basis for correctly delivering tragic news of sudden death to survivors. But the ability to empathetically communicate is rarely taught and is an even rarer natural gift. How to correctly deliver bad news is thus often left to practitioners' intuitions, rather than to skills they learned and practiced during their education. Poor clinician-patient communication disappoints both the patients and the clinicians. Often, this failure occurs when clinicians

- Use highly technical language.
- Don't show appropriate concern for problems voiced by patients.
- Don't pause sufficiently to listen.
- Don't verify that the listener has gotten the information presented.
- Take a generally impersonal approach to the interaction, which includes their manner of speech.[1]

Emergency situations demand excellent communication skills. This is especially true when sudden unexpected deaths occur within emergency medical services (ambulance systems), emergency departments, and trauma centers, or when police, coroners, or chaplains must make home notifications. In these situations, the notifiers and the survivors rarely enter into their relationship by choice, do not know each other, and may view each other with mutual distrust and negative stereotyping. Given the stress inherent in these situations, the potential for miscommunication is enormous.

Delivering the news about sudden unexpected death provokes strong emotions in both the notifier and survivors. Communication is improved if the notifier acknowledges those emotions. Notifiers must be prepared to vocalize and demonstrate their sadness, and to recognize and acknowledge it in the survivors.

Para-verbal and Verbal Communication

Using the voice to communicate does not always mean talking. In some instances, para-verbal behavior is preferred. Para-verbal communication means the sounds we make, such as mmmmm, ahhhh, or mhmmm. These are often sufficient to show that a person is listening and understands if they are accompanied by appropriate non-verbal cues, such as nodding the head.

Beyond that, it often helps to use "facilitative listening." This has three components:

1. **Echoing:** repeating back key words, often as questions, from what the person has just said. This prompts them to continue in a specific direction. For example, when a survivor says "I feel so sad every time I think about her," a response of "Sad?" prompts him or her to talk about that feeling.
2. **Reflect Content:** summarizing what the survivor has just said, with interpretation, if necessary. This helps survivors focus and clarify their thoughts. If they feel uncomfortable talking about important issues, this helps them do it. For example, after a rambling discourse about the stresses of having to face the various monthly bills, children's demands for expensive toys, and the need to reciprocate for a gift received from a neighbor, the listener might say, "It sounds as if you are concerned about how to make ends meet."
3. **Reflect Feeling:** to help a person label the emotions they are expressing. This requires the listener to put into context both the survivor's words and their sentiments. This should be done in a non-critical and non-dogmatic way, such as by saying, "You sound as if you are frightened to return to work."

The combination of reflecting content and feeling is the basis of what we often call "empathy." Some phrases to use when actively listening that both summarize and reflect content and feeling include:

- I'm picking up that you . . .
- I gather . . .
- To me you're conveying a sense . . .
- I wonder if you're saying . . .
- If I'm hearing you correctly . . .
- It seems that you are concerned with . . .
- Listening to you it seems that . . .
- Let me check to see if I understand . . .
- I really hear you saying . . .
- It sounds as if you're concerned about . . .
- You often feel . . . ?

- Sometimes you . . .?
- You seem to be saying . . .
- So your world right now is a place where . . . [2]

The following open-ended questions and requests perform similar tasks. Be careful when asking questions that may sound critical of the survivor, such as "How did you decide that?" They can be either helpful or hurtful, depending on the speaker's tone of voice and the context in which they are asked.

- Can you tell me more about how you see this?
- How do you perceive the situation?
- Help me understand the situation.
- Can you tell me more about . . . ?
- What alternatives have you considered?
- How did you decide that?
- What do you mean by . . . ?
- How can I help you do something about that?
- In what ways is this important to you?
- What other possibilities are there?
- Where would that lead?
- What might be some of the consequences if . . . ?
- What have you done so far about that?
- Explain this to me again . . . I'm having a hard time understanding.
- What are some other ways you've thought about doing it?

I could write many more words about effective verbal communication and active (facilitative) listening, but the following poem from the ubiquitous "anonymous" seems to say it best:[3]

PLEASE LISTEN

When I ask you to listen to me and you start giving advice,
You have not done what I asked nor heard what I need.

When I ask you to listen to me and you begin to tell me
That I shouldn't feel that way, you are trampling on my *feelings*.

When I ask you to listen to me, and you feel [that] you have to do something
To solve my problems, you have failed me—strange as that may seem.

Listen, please!
All I asked was that you listen. Not talk nor "do"—*just hear me*.
Advice is cheap. A quarter gets both "Dear Abbey" and astrological
Forecasts in the same newspaper. That I can do for myself,

I'm not helpless, maybe discouraged and faltering—but not helpless.

When you do something for me *that I can and need to do for myself,*
You contribute to me seeming fearful and weak.

But when you accept as a simple fact that I do feel what I feel,
No matter how seemingly irrational, then I can quit trying to convince
You and can get around to understanding what's behind what I am
Saying and doing—to what I am feeling.

When that's clear, chances are so will the answers be,
And I won't need any advice. (Or then, I'll be able to hear it!)

Perhaps that's why, for some people, prayer works, because God is mute,
And doesn't give advice or try to fix what we must take care of ourselves.

So, please listen and just hear me.
And if you want to talk, let's plan for your turn,
And I promise I'll listen to you.

Non-verbal Communication

In addition to verbal communication, notifiers also need to be aware of their non-verbal communications We often think of communication simply as the words we speak. At least as important are the non-verbal cues we generate, including bodily contact, physical proximity, posture, gestures, facial expressions and eye movements, and appearance.

Non-verbal communication becomes especially important in the highly charged atmosphere surrounding sudden-death notification. Notifiers may inadvertently send incomplete, erroneous, or distorted non-verbal messages, especially if they have been involved in the resuscitation, are simultaneously dealing with personal or professional stress, or have personal issues surrounding the decedent or the survivors. Table 2-1 illustrates common non-verbal cues among most, but not all, Western Europeans and North Americans. They may need to be adjusted for other cultures.

Touching is the most obvious communication between notifiers and survivors. Hold their hand with a firm, but friendly, grip. Physical contact demonstrates that the survivor is still part of the community despite the devastation he or she has suffered, eradicating what has been called the "leper complex."[4] As one nurse described, "A man, a big man, told me how a staff nurse held his hands when his wife died. 'I didn't want her to take them away,' he said."[5] Feelings and signals from the survivors should guide staff. If you err and unintentionally do something a survivor seems to feel is inappropriate, remain calm, explain why you acted as you did, and apologize.

Table 2-1: Non-verbal Messages

Bodily Contact	Generally, touching the key survivor's shoulder, hand, or arm is welcomed as a sign of closeness, no matter what the gender or age of the parties involved. The circumstances and following the survivor's lead should govern any additional contact.
Body Posture	The way the torso is positioned delivers the most obvious message. Sitting forward connotes empathy. Sitting too relaxed, e.g., sitting back or with arms draped over the furniture, connotes disinterest, fear, or anger.
Eye Movements	One of the most culturally unique factors, direct eye contact, suggests that the speaker is listening to the other party. Persistent eye contact suggests that you are in control—a necessity when survivors are threatening to act violently. (In some cultures, however, direct eye contact is a sign of disrespect.)
Facial Expressions	How the mouth is held and how the eyebrows and nose move during speech or in response to another person says volumes about what the person really feels. We commonly use our eyebrows to express disbelief, surprise, puzzlement, or anger.
Hand & Foot Gestures	Other than when making bodily contact, hands and feet should be comfortably at rest. Sitting on one's hands or having fidgety hands or feet suggests disinterest or deceit.
Head Position	Anything other than a neutral position connotes disinterest. (This means that the chin should be centered over the chest—not turned away from the survivor.) Nodding the head reinforces survivors' statements and suggests that they should continue speaking.
Physical Proximity	Sitting next to the key survivor, or crouching in front or beside them suggests empathy.
Relative Position to Survivors	Positioning oneself on the same level, usually sitting, as the key survivor eliminates any suggestion of an imbalance of power. (The uniform or white coat is enough of a power statement.)

Being aware of the non-verbal signals we send is the easiest way to control this part of the message. One excellent method for both teaching and learning the impact of non-verbal messaging is to test out various positions, expressions, etc. with a partner or in front of a mirror while simply saying, "I'm sorry." Note the enormously different impacts you make, depending on your facial expression, head and body position, and tone of voice.

One other aspect, actually a part of verbal communication, is *how* we say our words. Whether they are said with sorrow, anger, or ambivalence greatly affects the way survivors hear and interpret our words.

Working through Interpreters

As worldwide mobility grows and increasing numbers of people don't speak the majority's language, interpreters are frequently needed to help relate the news of sudden unexpected deaths to survivors. For example, the 1990 U.S. Census found that almost 14 million people living in the United States have "limited English proficiency." (The U.S. Department of Health and Human Services Office for Civil Rights uses "Limited English-proficient" to define the non-English speaking or limited-English speaking portion of the population.) In five states (California, Hawaii, New Mexico, New York, and Texas), more than 10% of the population has such limited English skills, and in three more (Arizona, Florida, and New Jersey), it is at least 8%.[6]

The Deaf

Another commonly necessary "translation" is that of verbal language to communication for the deaf. In the United States, American Sign Language (ASL) is commonly used. Not all deaf people read lips and, even when they can, frequent feedback is necessary to be sure that the spoken message is what they have received. Written communication is usually possible, but it can be very slow and laborious, especially in the highly charged atmosphere surrounding a sudden death. When possible, it is best to have a fluent ASL interpreter to assist with communications. In December 1998, Arizona's Attorney General warned all hospitals that under the 1990 federal Americans With Disabilities Act (ADA), they must have sign-language interpreters available to help patients or family members. This ruling stemmed from a case in Sun City West, Ariz., in which a deaf woman was unable to communicate with the staff while her husband was dying in the emergency department.[7]

The Interpreter's Job

Medical interpreters must translate three different things simultaneously. This is a difficult job, especially when dealing with such complex issues as the medical and social events surrounding an unexpected death. First, they must *translate medical terms and procedures* into language that their listeners can understand. How difficult this is depends upon the events surrounding the death, the amount of medical intervention that took place, and the listeners' knowledge of medicine—which may vary immensely depending upon when and from where the listeners came. Survivors may have a high level of sophistication and knowledge of medical terms, may be baffled by most of what is said, or fall somewhere between these extremes. If the listeners do not know much about the medical system, the translator must take the time to completely describe the context as well as what is being said.

Second, the translator must *interpret the clinician's view of events* into the survivors' cultural perspective. Survivors from other cultures may view the world and the events being described through a window quite different than the one the notifiers use.

> They tried to explain to Mui, a recent Vietnamese immigrant, that she could neither personally prepare her husband's body for burial nor dress him in his best clothes, as was their custom. He would need to have an autopsy, the doctor tried to explain. She didn't understand how this could happen and the refugee workers doing the interpreting weren't very good at providing an explanation. They told her that she would have to perform prefuneral ceremonies at the mortuary, rather than at home—and they would be delayed—imperiling the spirit. She was sure that the doctor's words and the strange culture were denying her husband a peaceful last rest.[8]

It is incumbent upon the translator to "translate" the cultural view as well as the words. This has been called being a "clinical broker," grasping two often opposing backgrounds and immediately taking them into account while interpreting concepts and content.[9] Therefore, someone from the survivors' culture should be used for this duty, if possible. One role of a good interpreter is to help "interpret" survivors' cultural norms as well as the language. These norms include their use of non-verbal messages. Knowing survivors' cultural backgrounds greatly facilitates using non-verbal messages correctly.

Third, translators must *use the common words and phrases that survivors will understand.* For example, just because someone speaks Chinese does not mean that they speak the same dialect as another Chinese speaker. Likewise with Spanish, it may be difficult for native Spanish speakers to understand speakers from another country, especially if both are used to talking in their own region's vernacular.

Basic Forms of Interpreting

Three basic methods can be used for interpretation, depending upon the situational needs and the interpreter's skills. Often the most difficult, but most rapid, is *simultaneous* translation. Using this method, the interpreter translates words almost as soon as they are spoken. The second method is *consecutive* translation. This method allows the speaker to pause after speaking several phrases to allow the interpreter to translate. While better rapport can be established between the caregiver and the survivor using this method, its success depends, in part, upon how well the interpreter can remember what was said. The third method, most often used by inexperienced interpreters, is *paraphrasing*. After several sentences or paragraphs are spoken, the interpreter translates what they understand to be a summary of the information. It does, however, allow the interpreter to change the message, if necessary, to account for cultural amenities.[10]

Who Interprets?

Specially trained and certified translators are often used for diplomatic, legal, and even business translation. However, in both the medical arena and during home notifications, interpreters are often members of the family, especially young children who have learned the common language in school. At other times, they will be friends or "interpreters of convenience"—people who can translate and who happen to be available, such as neighbors, strangers who are accompanying other patients, or non-clinical ancillary personnel. Professional translators are rarely used, partly because their services are expensive, but also because this need is so intermittent.

The problem with using *ad hoc* interpreters in emotional or complex situations is that the quality of the translation is usually unknown and the amount and type of information transmitted may be unclear. Many of these individuals have been found to omit, add, substitute, or otherwise edit professional communications, leading to seriously distorted messages.[11] Part of the problem is that many of these individuals have an incomplete knowledge of one or both languages, and this results in mistranslating up to half of the professional's words or phrases.[12] Unbeknownst to the notifier, the translator may be unsuccessfully transmitting all necessary information or transmitting it in a manner that is unprofessional, erroneous, or insensitive.

Another problem with *ad hoc* translators is that confidentiality is compromised. If sensitive issues are being discussed with survivors, such as events surrounding murder, suicide, or illicit drug use, third-party translators may limit what survivors wish to say. It may also disclose more information to the public than either the survivors or the notifiers wish.

Children and ancillary workers are often used as translators. In the case of children being used as translators, this inverts family roles and exposes them to information that they often do not understand, that may be sensitive, or that they or their relatives may not want them to hear. Non-professionals dragooned into interpreting may have the same problems as other *ad hoc* interpreters, with the added strains that they are being pulled from their jobs and are not normally compensated for this valuable skill.[13] Yet children and ancillary workers may be more aware of the cultural milieu than a professional who tries to "wing it" using inadequate language skills and without any knowledge of the survivors' cultural background.

The inadequate funding for translators in the United States will not be remedied any time soon. Medicare does not pay for outpatient translation services and (foolishly) presumes that the general payments cover inpatient translations. Medicaid payments are variable and usually non-existent, although Washington State does have specific billing for these services. The three best methods for finding adequate interpreters are: (1) by training and rewarding staff members, volunteers, and retirees who have tested excellent language and people skills to work as on-call translators, (2) doing the same among the immigrant community, and (3) using on-line translation services, such as those provided by some phone companies, although this method lacks the non-verbal cues that are usually present in conversations.[14]

In all cases, notifiers should spend a few minutes with interpreters before they speak with survivors. This gives them the opportunity to smooth over at least the major language difficulties that might occur. No matter who is used as a translator and how much preparation goes into it, a notifier must be aware that words and ideas may not flow smoothly from him to the survivors.

Dealing with Anger

Anger is a common response to death—especially sudden unexpected death. It is a form of communication survivors use when they have no words to convey their depth of feeling, feel a great deal of guilt about the death, or are unprepared to accept the death. Some individuals may also strike out at others as a routine method for dealing with stress. Survivors manifest anger after a sudden, unexpected death in several ways (table 2-2).

Managing the angry survivor is similar to managing anger in anyone. The key to dealing with this situation is to remain quiet and calm. The goal is to quietly set limits on the survivor, both verbally and with non-verbal cues, without getting defensive about his or her words.

Speaking quietly rather than in a loud voice often helps. Use phrases such as "Yes, and . . ." to show agreement, rather than "No, but . . ." which tends to inflame the situation.

Acknowledge the anger. If they verbally abuse notifiers or other survivors or clearly have pent-up anger, they may respond to this gesture and talk about their concerns. Gently touching the person may help, but it is often too dangerous a technique for caregivers to use.

At some point, it may be best if the angry individual "takes it outside" and leaves the premises. No longer confronted by reminders of the death and by solicitous family members and staff, these people normally settle down.

Sometimes the anger is clearly directed at the situation and quickly dissipates, as Joshua Helman, M.D. relates from his days as a plastic surgery fellow at a New York County hospital's burn unit:

> A 16-year-old teenager was brought in after a car crash. He did not appear to have any internal injuries, but had third-degree burns from head to toe (covering 100% of his body). I knew that his prognosis was grim and that the burn would kill him from infection over the next few days. He was able to communicate his extreme pain, which I relieved with morphine. His mother arrived at the hospital about 10 minutes after he did. We sat down and I explained what had happened. As gently as possible, I told her that he had an inevitably fatal injury. She turned on me with pointed anger, reached into her purse, and pulled out her son's picture—a handsome young man dressed in a tuxedo. She thrust it in my face, shouting, "This is what my son looked like this morning. I want you to see this. Look at him now. Look at him! Look at him!"

Table 2-2: Ways Survivors Express Anger

Verbal Demands	• Sense of impatience. "Where is the doctor? He should have been here to meet us!" • Inappropriate expectations. "Your ambulance should have been able to get here much faster!" • Sense of irritation, frustration. "Would you have done more if he had been White?"
Verbal Abuse	• Incriminations of incompetence. "You should have been able to save him!" • Incriminations of neglect or abuse. "If this had been a teaching (non-teaching) hospital, they would have recognized the problem right away!" • Slanderous comments. "Just as I always thought; nobody here has a clue what they're doing!"
Physical Acting Out	• Speaking in a loud voice or screaming. • Throwing objects, either with or without a specific target in mind. • Striking objects with the intent of damaging them. • Physically striking another person.

Adapted, in part, from: Poster EC, Betz C: When the patient dies: dealing with the family's anger. *Dimens Crit Care Nurs.* 1984 Nov-Dec;3(6):372-7.

> After a painful and protracted silence and tears from everyone in the room, I somehow managed to bring up treatment options with her. The anger subsided and, understanding the inevitable outcome, she agreed to let us place him on a morphine drip without [attempting] heroic measures. Within a few hours, he died painlessly with his mother at his side. Before leaving the hospital, the mother stopped by to thank me.[15]

If survivors are acting out and becoming physically abusive, destructive, or dangerous, advise them of appropriate, *enforceable consequences* you will implement. Tell them that you will have them physically restrained if they don't "settle down." Simply saying, "You can't do that" does not help eliminate the threat. If the angry individual is armed, is much larger than you, or there are several angry people in the group, immediately exit and get help. Safety outweighs other considerations at this point. Sam Keim, an emergency physician, had an experience that clearly illustrates this.

> One night a nurse suggested that I use the chapel ("We have a chapel?" I said.) to tell a group of survivors about a death. She offered to show me where it was. I became bewildered as she led me far from the maddening crowds of the ED through a maze of dark hallways to a small chapel. She opened the door to let me enter—alone. As I heard the door close behind me, I found myself facing a small mob of very angry gang members. They wanted to know why I "had killed their friend," as they advanced menacingly toward me. Even though I am a triathlete, I think I garnered some kind of record as I escaped from the room. If I hadn't been that quick, I'm sure I would have been badly hurt, if not killed.[16]

Dr. David Lebiner, now a neurologist, describes an incident that happened when he was a resident. The issue here was the safety of the survivors.

> As a resident in an Atlanta hospital, we heard that we were getting a young man with diabetic ketoacidosis (a severe metabolic abnormality) transferred from a small distant hospital. He was in critical condition, and hadn't received enough care to stabilize him before he was transferred via an ambulance staffed with basic EMTs, who couldn't administer the fluids or medications necessary to keep him alive. The boy's family was following in a car.
>
> When he arrived belatedly at the hospital five hours later (the ambulance broke down about the time the boy went into cardiac arrest), he was dead. The family assembled and, when told that he had died, reacted violently. One brother ran into the hall and began pounding the wall so hard that he cut his hand badly. The boy's mother then passed out, hitting the floor rather hard. A sister then began seizing. So, instead of having one patient who arrived DOA, we now had three patients and a grieving father who also needed to care for his injured family.[17]

If the survivor is very intoxicated or is obviously being affected by drugs, calming the person may be a futile effort and physical restraint may be the safest course of action. In these cases, experience is the best guide, but security or police backup should be in attendance—even if not in plain sight.

Using Humor

Humor, laughing, and any jocularity is generally considered out of place either when informing others of a death or during the grieving process. Yet as George Bernard Shaw said, "Life does not cease to be funny when people die any more than it ceases to be serious when people laugh."[18]

Those closest to the survivors may usefully interject humor in such a way that a survivor may feel comfortable expressing some joy, in order to help him or her. Recalling humorous episodes in the decedent's life does this best; it's a way to celebrate the life of a loved one who has died. For example, relatives, friends, co-workers, or fellow students can help others by retelling funny (not cruel or demeaning) incidents about the decedent, especially those that the person had retold while alive. "Remember when . . ." and "Were you there when . . ." are not only acceptable, but also a traditional part of the mourning process and were often a formal part of the wake. Storytelling recalls the person's memory in a kind and loving way while allowing survivors to smile or even laugh about the anecdote.

Even survivors may use humor to lessen the impact of the news they receive. Terri Schmidt, an emergency physician and author of a number of works cited throughout this book, relates:

> Just before Valentine's Day a man was brought in to our ED in cardiac arrest. He had been on his way to meet his wife and buy her a gold, double-heart necklace. Shortly after being told of his death, his widow said, "He always did go to great lengths to avoid buying me jewelry."[19]

References

1. Korsch BM, Negrete VF: Doctor-patient communication. *Sci Am.* 1972 Aug;227(2):66-74.
2. Adapted from: Federal Bureau of Investigation Employee Assistance Unit: *Critical Incident Survival Manual.* Washington, DC: FBI, 1997 (no page numbers).
3. Quoted in: Federal Bureau of Investigation Employee Assistance Unit: *Critical Incident Survival Manual.* Washington, DC: FBI, 1997 (no page numbers).
4. Graham JR: Touching and imparting of bad news. *Lancet.* 1991 Jun 29;337(8757):1608-9.
5. Waters V: First impressions of grief . . . nurse's attitude has a profound effect on bereaved relatives. *Nurs Times.* 1987 Feb 4-10: 83(5):46-7.
6. Kirkman-Liff B, Mondragon D: Language of interview: relevance for research of southwest Hispanics. *Am J Public Health.* 1991 Nov;81(11):1399-404.
7. Mendoza M: Interpreters for deaf must be available at hospitals, state says. *Arizona Daily Star.* 1998 Dec 24; Sect. B:1.
8. Adapted from: Reade R: Harsh transition to a new way of death. *Soc Work.* 1981;12:11-12.
9. Rios J: *Converse in español: Español pais personal medico.* Tucson, AZ: Rios Associates, 1988.
10. *Ibid.*
11. Putsch RW: Cross-cultural communication: the special case of interpreters in health care. *JAMA.* 1985 Dec 20;254(23):3344-8.
12. Ebden P, Carey OJ, Bhatt A, et al.: The bilingual consultation. *Lancet.* 1988 Feb 13;1(8581):347.
13. Woloshin S, Bickell NA, Schwartz LM, et al.: Language barriers in medicine in the United States. *JAMA.* 1995 Mar 1;273(9):724-8.
14. *Ibid.*
15. Helman J: Personal communication with author, December 1998.
16. Keim S: Personal communication with author, December 1998.
17. Lebiner D: Personal communication with author, December 1998.
18. Shaw G B: *The Doctor's Dilemma*, Act 5.
19. Schmidt, Terri: Personal communication with author, March 1999.

3: A Protocol For Sudden-Death Notification

Death notification can be divided into four stages: *Prepare*, *Inform*, *Support*, and *Afterwards*. The mnemonic "PISA" can be used to remember them. (It's as easy as pie— or precarious as the Leaning Tower of . . .) Each stage is divided into a number of substages:

Prepare: Anticipate, Identify, Notify, Organize

Inform: Introduce, Tell

Support: Reassure, Relieve, Assist, Answer, Communicate, View, Protect, Provide, Conclude

Afterwards: Debrief, Follow up

Table 3-1 identifies key elements for notifiers to perform in each of these four stages. The list is composed of sequential activities. Not all the actions will apply to all notifiers or all notification situations. Notification methods and procedures often differ in emergency departments, inpatient medical facilities, public spaces, and homes. But this protocol provides a good checklist to use before a death notification or when educating others about death notification.

Supplemental protocols are listed in the chapters, or sections, for Emergency Departments, Chaplains/Clergy, Emergency Medical Services, Children, Students, Obstetrics, Prisons, Police, and the Military. Telephone notifications are unique, see chapter 5 for that protocol.

Table 3-1: Protocol for Delivering News of Sudden, Unexpected Death

****Modify to allow for medical facility, in-home, and field notifications*****

PREPARE	
Anticipate	• Have a non-clinical room available for bereaved survivors. Have comfortable places to sit, tissues, a "panic button" with which staff can summon help, and a telephone available. • If possible, have a special room in which survivors can view the body. Have tasteful, non-denominational décor. • Have a policy regarding relatives being present during resuscitation. This may vary, depending upon the resuscitation team's leader, whether it is a medical or trauma resuscitation, and the relatives' emotional states. • Have a list of agencies (and 24-hour telephone numbers) to be notified about different types of deaths, such as medical examiner/coroner, organ/tissue procurement organizations, public health department, police, medical school anatomy department (for bodies that have been donated), child welfare agencies, etc. • If your facility or agency has a written protocol for death notifications, get it and review it.
Identify	• Positively identify the individual who has died. • Identify by name and relationship those who will be notified. • Will other survivors be arriving who must also be told? When? • Obtain complete information about the circumstances of death and anything else pertinent to the notification (What? Where? When? How? To whom?).
Notify	• Experienced individual should contact key survivor(s) if they are not present. • If there are multiple fatalities in one incident, attempt to notify all primary survivors at the same time. • Medical examiner or coroner should be contacted in appropriate cases. • Notify patient's physician.

Continued on next page

Table 3-1: continued

	PREPARE, cont.
Notify, cont.	• If possible, those assigned to meet the survivors should discuss their own reactions to the death and resuscitation attempt (if any) before the survivors arrive. • Have one or more staff members meet survivors when they arrive and escort them to a private area. If the group is large or if there are both adults and children, some staff with special skills may be needed, such as Child Life Specialists. • If a survivor arrives by ambulance with the decedent (or critical patient), have someone guide them to the family room. If resuscitation is still in progress, someone can meet them there and ask if they want to view the resuscitation procedures.
Organize	• If there are groups of survivors for more than one victim, assign at least one staff member to each group. • Get survivors out of the corridor and into a comfortable, quiet room—preferably a spacious room with windows, where both you and the survivors can sit. Sitting allows you to symbolically join their group. • Have tissues, blankets, drinks (coffee, soft drinks, and water), telephones, ashtrays, and bathrooms available for the survivors. It is useful to have toys for any small children. • If survivors arrive inebriated, intoxicated, or violent, call security or the police immediately. Be aware of safety issues for all staff and patients. • Clean yourself up! Be sure your clothes do not have blood or other bodily fluids on them. Change any soiled clothes. Have someone else help you identify any soiled areas you may have missed. • If you were not the primary individual involved in the case, get as much information about the case as possible before meeting the survivors. • Have that staff member tell you which survivors are present so that you can better prepare to meet the family and will be able to identify the right family. • If possible, wear your uniform or badge of authority such as scrubs, white coat with your name on it (or an ID badge), clerical collar, or identification tag.

Continued on next page

Table 3-1: continued

	PREPARE, cont.
Organize, cont.	• Be accompanied by one or more staff people (social worker, chaplain, nurse) who have already interacted with the survivors—for your own, as well as the family's, support. This also shows that a team was involved in the patient's treatment and supplies a "bridge" person to be with survivors when the primary notifier leaves. • Have the information about any lab tests or radiographs available in case survivors want to know more specific details. • Ascertain from those who escorted them what the family knows, expects, or suspects. Family may already have been notified by unskilled individuals or by accident (such as through news reporters' questions). • Give yourself a moment to think about what you are going to say. If you have not done this often, practice with another staff member for a few minutes.
	INFORM
Introduce	• Identify parties and their relationship to the patient with a phrase such as, "Are you ____'s wife?" (Don't tell the wrong family.) • If little children are present, ask the survivors if they would prefer that the children wait outside initially. If so, have another staff person take them to someplace with a television or toys. • Introduce yourself and the support personnel. Identify who was involved in the resuscitation attempt and what role they played. • Address the key survivor by name. For adults, use their last name and title, such as "Mr.," "Mrs.," "Dr.," etc. For children and teenagers, use their first name.
Tell	• Sit down next to the person you will be speaking to, if possible. If the family does not wish to sit, remain standing. • Arrange for enough time so that you do not appear rushed and won't be disturbed for at least the initial notification. Even if you have other critical matters to attend to, try to appear unhurried. If necessary, delay meeting the family until you can spend at least a few uninterrupted minutes with them. If you can, turn off your pager or radio for a few minutes.

Continued on next page

Table 3-1: continued

INFORM, cont.	
Tell, cont.	• Don't dash in and out of the room or hang by the half-open door as if ready to flee at any moment—preparing to "hit and run." • Be aware of non-verbal communication and make good eye contact with the family. Physical contact is often helpful. • Take cues from the survivors by watching their reactions. • Address the closest relative or the one who looks most composed. • If still not completely certain of decedent's identity, describe the decedent (key identifying characteristics) or show them a photograph (of cleaned face only). • Ask, "Can you tell me what you know about what happened today?" This allows the person to briefly tell their story if they want to do so, and gives notifiers an opportunity to correct any misunderstandings. • Briefly (30 seconds or less) describe the prehospital and hospital events that led up to the death, including resuscitative efforts. (See p. 43, "Deliver the News Quickly," for the reasons to do this quickly—and when to go a bit slower.) • Use the deceased person's name rather than "decedent," "victim," "your son, daughter, husband, etc.," "our patient," "him or her," or "he or she." • Use clear, non-technical language to explain what occurred. It should be in terms the survivors will understand. Don't use medical jargon. • Do *not* describe all the injuries in detail, but be willing to answer any questions about the injuries or the person's condition—including the odor of alcohol and the presence of drugs. Say that the death *may* have been a suicide if that is very clear from the evidence and the police are treating it that way. (This must await the medical examiner's/coroner's ruling, however.) • Use a "D" word— "Died," "Death," or "Dead" (including "Dead by brain criteria"). Don't resort to euphemisms such as "passed away," "left us," "didn't make it," "fatally injured," "lost him," "gone," or "expired." If they don't seem to understand, repeat another "D" word in a different context.

Continued on next page

Table 3-1: continued

	INFORM, cont.
Tell, cont.	• Pause for a moment and remain quiet so survivors can have time to react. • Be prepared for any possible reaction to the news, including disbelief; guilt; anger (at the patient, those responsible for the death, or the medical staff); exacerbation of medical conditions (such as angina); and for reactions suggesting the need for psychiatric intervention, such as absolute denial. • Do not be afraid to show your emotions, but avoid false sympathy and platitudes. • Allow periods of silence so family members can react to the news. Wait for the family to break the silence. • If survivors want to speak, *listen*. Do not simply continue on with your prepared remarks. • Attentively listen to what survivors say about their understanding, about the circumstances surrounding the death, and about the decedent. • Parents of deceased children may want to describe their version of the circumstances surrounding the death to demonstrate (to themselves or others) that they were not negligent. • Be certain that the family understands the key point—that the patient is dead. • Do not apologize for the death, since this may make survivors incorrectly think that more could have been done. • Do not argue with survivors. Be prepared to field angry comments without considering them a personal attack. • Be prepared to answer more difficult or complicated questions as survivors accept the situation or as other survivors arrive. • If in a medical facility and the physician did not deliver the news about death, advise the survivors when they will be able to talk with the physician.

Continued on next page

Table 3-1: continued

SUPPORT	
Reassure	• Reassure the family that everything that could have been done was done. • Give survivors enough information so that they can feel assured that everything reasonable was tried to resuscitate the individual. • Assure family that the staff will, if possible, follow the religious customs they specify.
Relieve	• Assuage the family's guilt and mental anguish. State (unless it is very obvious that this is not true) that the event was not their fault. • Challenge any unrealistic expectations parents raise about their roles. Reinforce that there was no way to protect their child from this death (if not patently obvious that this is incorrect). • Help parents recognize that they must grieve not only for their child, but also for their hopes and dreams for that child. • If it is possibly true, reassure them that the patient did not suffer. Couch the information in such phrases as "Most people with a bad head injury never have a memory of the accident" or "Death comes almost immediately after ____." • Avoid philosophical statements and clichés (table 4.2). • Tell them about some common grief reactions they may experience. (See tables 10.1 and 13.1.)
Assist	• Keep someone with the key survivors, unless they expressly ask to be left alone. It may be a staff person, family member, or friend. If that person must leave, notify other staff so someone can stay with the survivors. • Answer all questions you can answer. • Listen to survivors' descriptions of events surrounding the death and of the deceased person. • If they do not volunteer the information, ask about the deceased person. (See table 4-1 for some helpful phrases.) It may help them start a healthy grieving process and establishes a connection between notifier and survivor. • Ask survivors what needs they have (phone, transportation, specific information).

Continued on next page

Table 3-1: continued

	SUPPORT, cont.
Assist, cont.	• Avoid telling them what to feel or do. But do give them suggestions about how to proceed with the grieving process. • Do not change the subject when survivors speak of the decedent by name. • Give verbal and non-verbal permission for survivors to openly express their grief and to discuss their memories of the decedent. • Be aware of special needs of some survivors (children, elderly, breast-feeding mothers, etc.). • Be aware of the needs of the parents of a deceased adult, since most of the support will be given to the decedent's spouse and children. • If they want periods of privacy without outsiders present (for a brief religious service, for example), provide that opportunity. • Don't appear in a hurry to end the discussion. Signal that the immediate discussion will shortly end and ask if there are additional questions • Following the initial meeting with the survivors, tell them that you will return after a short period to answer any additional questions. • Help the survivors contact their friends, clergy, and relatives. • Provide the survivors access to long-distance telephone services.
Answer	• Provide written materials answering the most common questions. • Have someone explain how the decedent's belongings will be returned to the family. (It may be immediately or be delayed if they go to the police or medical examiner.) Belongings should be returned in something other than a plastic garbage bag. • Give them a preprinted list of the local and national telephone numbers and addresses for various support groups, such as SIDS, murder victims, elderly survivors, etc. Tell them that they may need them during this time of intense grief. (Chapter 11 lists many national and regional support groups.)

Continued on next page

Table 3-1: continued

	SUPPORT, cont.
Answer cont.	• Explain the routine involvement of the police in cases of sudden unexpected deaths. (This explanation is especially important in SIDS cases.) If survivors ask to speak with the police, help them arrange that. • Have someone provide survivors with any additional information they need (how to contact funeral homes, medical examiner information, and death certificate procedures).
Communicate	• Contact a chaplain or the patient's religious support if they request it. Suggesting that this support is available often helps. • State that you will attempt to contact (or have contacted) their physician. • Provide a way for the family to contact you (such as through your pager, secretary, or dispatcher) if they have questions or need additional assistance.
View	• Ask survivors if they wish to "view (decedent's name)," rather than "(decedent's name)'s body" or "the body." • Clearly explain any visible injuries from trauma or resuscitation attempts or postmortem changes (e.g., facial blueness or *livor mortis*) before the family sees the body. • Describe any equipment that remains on the body (such as an endotracheal tube) and why it is still there (generally because of medical examiner requirements). • Allow time for the survivors to see the decedent (after the body and the area have been cleaned as much as possible). Sometimes this may be mandatory so that they can make positive identification. • Ask parents if they want to help bathe or clean their dead child. In messy or disfiguring situations, at least a small part of the cleaning can be left for parents. (Other survivors, especially those from specific religions, may also do this for adults.) • Encourage the family to touch and, in the case of young children, hold the body. • Allow families to cut off a lock of hair, if requested.

Continued on next page

Table 3-1: continued

SUPPORT, cont.	
View, cont.	• Offer a Polaroid® photograph of the decedent to survivors. If not desired, put it with their medical records; they may want it later. • Consider using "memory boxes," even if some mementos are taken at the time of death. (See "The Memory Box" in chapter 12.) • Be respectful of different customs after death. • Allow the family to be alone with the body if there are no legal constraints to doing this.
Protect	• If survivors are seriously injured, consult the family or other survivors as to the timing of notifying them. Generally, even if they are injured, if they are alert and competent enough to say they "need to know," it is best to tell them of the death. Until or unless they do this, they are not ready for the news. • Protect survivors from the media. Brief them in advance if the media wants to speak with them. • Warn them that graphic footage and any interviews may be replayed many times in the future. • Offer to speak with the media for them, but only after you clear the information with the family. The only exception to this is if the public's "need to know," usually on the basis of safety or control of dangerous rumors, is more important. • Be prepared for violence, even though interpersonal violence is unusual. Property damage (hitting a wall, for example) and subsequent survivor injury is more common. • Do not permit violence. Protect the survivor and the staff from harm. Use the security staff or police as needed. • If a survivor is suicidal or homicidal, get a formal psychiatric consultation. If you believe they may be, ask them whether they are. (Asking the question does *not* cause someone to act if they were not going to anyway.)

Continued on next page

Table 3-1: continued

	SUPPORT, cont.
Provide	• If asked, do not automatically prescribe anti-anxiety medications for survivors. Mild sedation for a key survivor may be necessary. This requires a physician's evaluation of that individual. If clinical indications warrant, dispense for a *very* limited time. • Have a written list of the local and national numbers and addresses for various support groups, such as SIDS, murder victims, elderly survivors, etc. (See chapter 11.) • If requested, be prepared to supply limited amounts of survivors' prescription medications—especially if they are from outside the local area. • If autopsy is an option, return (or have the institution's designated person come) to ask about autopsy permission. Explain why an autopsy is required if it is a medical examiner/coroner case. • Unless they broach the issue during the first meeting, return to discuss organ and tissue donation after survivors have had a chance to emotionally accept the death. Consider using specially trained people for this task. • Arrange overnight accommodations for survivors, if necessary. • If there are complex issues surrounding family housing and basic support, contact social services.
Conclude	• Ask one more time if there are any questions. • Give survivors a copy of all papers they signed. Most recall "signing something," but without these copies they won't know what they signed. • Give survivors those personal effects and clothing not still on the body and not required by the medical examiner or police. Tell them the condition of any clothing (i.e., torn, bloody). Put in a paper bag or box—not a garbage bag. • Give the key survivors, in writing, your name and contact numbers that they can call for additional information in the next few days. (See tables 6-1 and 6-2.) • Get phone numbers and addresses for recontacting survivors over the next few days or weeks.

Continued on next page

Table 3-1: continued

	SUPPORT, cont.
Conclude, cont.	• Advise survivors of any updated information or where they can obtain additional information, as it becomes available. • If they are alone, call to have someone take them home and, if possible, stay with them overnight. • Inform the survivors when everything they need to do in the hospital/facility/agency is complete, and that they may leave whenever they like. • Accompany survivors to the exit.
	AFTERWARDS
Debrief	• Make time for the staff who participated in the resuscitation and in the death notification to safely share both medical and personal information about the resuscitation and death and vent their feelings. Note: it is also important for physicians to express their own feelings. • No death notification is perfect. It can always be to improved and the process is best discussed immediately after the event. • Take a little time to regain your composure before continuing with your next tasks. • Notify staff that they can release information that the individual has died to callers. (For deaths of well-known individuals or during criminal investigations, this information may be temporarily withheld.)
Follow Up	• Make a follow-up call the next day to ask if the survivors have any additional questions. • When the autopsy results become available, call the family again to answer any questions. Ask how they are doing and if they have contacted the referral they were given or another support group. • Be prepared to answer survivors' common questions. (See chapter 27.) • Send a sympathy card and additional contact, support group, or community resource information.

Adapted from many sources, including References 1 through 6.

Deliver the News Quickly

When considering how quickly to deliver the news about a death, notifiers should consider whose needs are being met by going slowly. Usually, going slowly only serves to calm the notifier's nerves. Nearly 80% of the respondents in one Gallup Poll preferred that they be informed about a sudden unexpected death immediately or very soon after the start of the conversation, when the news is delivered in person.[7] Not to do this has been described as "making a slow surgical incision on a patient who cannot be anesthetized. Although the intention may be to limit pain, it actually increases it."[8] The only exceptions to this were respondents who were not born in the United States or Canada, who often prefer that notifiers slowly unfold the events before delivering the news of the death.[9]

One way to get to the news in a sensitive and caring fashion might be to say, "I'm afraid that I have some very bad news for you . . . (Person's name) has been in a bad car crash and s/he died despite everything we could do. I'm so sorry." The pause between the two phrases allows the survivors to anticipate what is coming and psychologically prepare for it. They are probably somewhat prepared already, either because of the circumstances (being called to the hospital, having police come by the home, etc.) or from "crepe hanging" (dribbling out bits and pieces of bad information over a very short period of time) done by the hospital staff.

Use the "D" Word

Although to some it may seem cruel and to others obvious, notifiers must use one of the "D" words when informing survivors about a death. "D" words include: "Died," "Death," and "Dead." For many reasons, including their own discomfort, many notifiers prefer to use euphemisms instead. The more common ones include such phrases as "passed away," "passed on," "left us," "gone to a better place," "didn't make it," "lost him," "gone home," "no longer with us," "checked out," "fatally injured, "gone," "deceased," or "expired." But it is better for the survivors if you use a "D" word. A nurse describes how she learned this lesson during a telephone notification.

> . . . she died. And I had to call him. I did not say she was dead. I said she was gone. I said, "Do you have anybody with you?" and he said, "No, I don't need anybody." I wouldn't say she was dead . . . at the time, I think I was out of school about four months. "But, do you understand what I mean when I say she's gone?" And he says, "Yeah, I know." And then I said, "You know for sure?" He said, "You're telling me she's dead." And that made me realize right then that my function was to tell him that she was dead, not that she was gone. It was his function to believe that she was gone. Since then I always use . . . when I'm talking to the family . . . she's dead or he's dead.[10]

Even when a "D" word is almost used (such as "brain death" in the following case), it may not be sufficient, as this emergency physician recounts:

> Evidently, an older gentleman had had a heart attack and was found in his bathtub. I don't know how long he was not breathing, but he had turned blue. The ambulance brought him to the hospital in that condition . . . [It was] at least 40 minutes from the time he was found, transported in, until we got him . . . I said, "Evidently, from what I understand, when your husband was found lifeless, he hadn't been breathing because he was blue in color. They couldn't get any oxygen into him. He essentially had brain death before he arrived." The wife asked me, "Is he all right now?"[11]

I discovered the need to explicitly use a "D" word in a much more dramatic misstep as a new emergency medicine resident.

> My patient had died from a gunshot wound after a long and grueling resuscitative attempt. I was already physically drained, but felt that I had to quickly tell the family that had gathered. Entering the room set aside for this purpose, I noticed that it didn't seem to be large enough. I had difficulty just opening the door because of the number of people who had crowded in. Having gained entrance, I was uncomfortably plastered against the door. The clamor that had roared only moments before calmed. I rapidly searched for the key survivor—who would obviously be one of the few able to sit. There she was—the clan's matriarch and my patient's mother.
>
> With a heavy heart I carefully explained what happened, what we did, and that "we were not successful." Still there was quiet. "I'm sorry we were not able to save him," I continued. No one responded. "He had an irreparable injury." Still, only silence. Finally, she cleared her throat and asked, "When will he be coming home?" Emotionally drained, I could barely utter, "He won't be coming home. I'm sorry, he died." Only then did the grieving begin.

Saying the "D" word is the pivotal step in notifying survivors about a death. Up to that point, the notifier is in charge and in control. Once the "D" word is uttered, the deliverer should remain silent and await the survivor's response—verbal or non-verbal. The survivor essentially determines what happens next.

The Final Steps

The elements listed under "Conclude" in the protocol can be very important to survivors. These statements tell them that they have done everything possible at that point and that they have "permission" to leave. It gives a sense of completion. Without this, survivors often describe themselves as being "lost," "set adrift," or "waiting to be called back because we forgot to do something."

Once a death has occurred, it is public information. At that point, staff should be informed that they can release a confirmation to callers who identify the decedent by name. No information should be released about the circumstances, as this may be the subject of a police investigation.

An activity that is often omitted is the debriefing. A debriefing should occur for both the resuscitation team, if there was an attempted resuscitation, and the death notification group. When the team has been traumatized because of the nature or circumstances of the death, it is often best to have trained personnel formally do a "critical incident stress debriefing (CISD)." Teams familiar with this process are often found associated with fire and police departments and in major teaching hospitals, but may also be associated with psychiatric facilities in larger communities. (See chapter 26 for more information about CISD.)

Follow-up with the survivors should be done later.

Cultural Differences

All cultures must deal with death, survivors' bereavement, grief, and mourning. Everybody makes attachments to others, has them broken through death, and has to deal with the pain these losses cause. While death is important to all, "how it is regarded, the values, explanations, beliefs, fears concerning it, and the ways of managing the reactions to death depend to a large extent on the norms of one's particular culture."[12] Throughout the world and even within each country, many different behaviors and postmortem rituals exist to handle these inevitable occurrences.[13]

This suggests that any standard protocol may need to be modified when notifying survivors from other cultures or who were raised in other traditions. In times of great stress, individuals will gravitate toward their own culturally acquired way of dealing with bereavement. Yet if survivors have moved to a new "host" society, some of their traditional mourning, body preparation, and disposition rites may not be permitted. This may increase survivors' grief. Table 23-2, for example, lists some differences among religions. Some cultures may not be as different in dealing with death as one might believe. For example, Black and White Americans seem to have the same level of death anxiety.[14] Yet any generalization about a culture is just that—a stereotype that may or may not be applicable to individual survivors. The key is to listen closely to what the survivor says, take a lead from the key survivor, and whenever possible, include a member of the notification team (staff member, neighbor, friend, minister) who belongs to that culture.

Some survivors experience not only cultural differences, but also language difficulties. (See "Working through Interpreters" in chapter 2.) As this story from Fran Kunz, of the Pima County (Ariz.) Search and Recovery Divers, demonstrates, cultural sensitivity may overcome language difficulties.[15]

> There had been a flash flood in the normally dry Santa Cruz River. A father had tried in desperation to hold on to his little girl, but the current tore them apart and she was lost downstream. We searched for a couple of days, with divers searching deep pockets of water. The father, who only spoke Spanish, was out searching with Search and Rescue every day. He could not communicate verbally with the English-speaking teams, but spoke volumes about his grief with his body language. The teams allowed him to participate fully and tried to indicate to him

what they were doing and why they were doing it. On the third day of the search, approximately six miles from where he lost her, the father found his little girl. He was visibly upset, but I believe he knew what the outcome of the search would be and found some peace in being the one who found her. The sensitivity of the search team sustained him through the arduous search and our wordless support after locating his daughter expressed that we also grieved. I believe he felt responsible for 'losing' her, and being the one to find her helped him assuage his guilt.

Implementing the Protocol

Implementing death-notification protocols has occasionally been difficult, because, to follow the protocol, experienced notifiers often must change how they perform a difficult and unpleasant task. The best way to implement death-notification protocols is to enlist the help of the key people involved (e.g., supervisor, administrator).[16] They need to "buy into" the concept and the specifics of the protocol before it is unveiled for the entire team. Once a team has adopted and used the protocol for a while, it can be modified based on the team's experiences.

References

1. McLauchlan CA: ABC of major trauma. handling distressed relatives and breaking bad news. *Br Med J.* 1990 Nov 17;301(6761):1145-9.

2. Schmidt TA, Tolle SW: Emergency physicians' responses to families following patient death. *Ann Emerg Med.* 1990 Feb;19(2):125-8.

3. Hamilton GC: Sudden death in the ED: telling the living. *Ann Emerg Med.* 1988 Apr;17(4):382.

4. McQuay JE, Schwartz R, Goldblatt PC, et al.: "Death-telling" research project. *Crit Care Nurs Clin North Am.* 1995 Sep;7(3):549-55.

5. Creek LV: How to tell the family that the patient has died. *Postgrad Med.* 1980 Oct;68(4):207-9.

6. Marrow J: Telling relatives that a family member has died suddenly. *Postgrad Med J.* 1996 Jul;72(849):413-8.

7. Viswanathan R, Clark JJ, Viswanathan K: Physicians' and the public's attitudes on communication about death. *Arch Intern Med.* 1986 Oct;146(10):2029-33.

8. International Chaplains' Ministry: *Introduction . . . Death Notification for Emergency Service Chaplaincy.* Edmonds, WA: ICM, 1993.

9. Viswanathan R, Clark JJ, Viswanathan K: "Physicians' and the public's attitudes."

10. Clark RE, LaBeff EE: Death telling: managing the delivery of bad news. *J Health Soc Behav.* 1982 Dec;23(4):366-80.

11. *Ibid.*

12. Krupp GR, Kligfeld B: Bereavement reaction: a cross-cultural evaluation. *J Relig Health*. 1962 Apr;1:222-46.

13. Iserson KV: *Death to Dust: What Happens To Dead Bodies?* Tucson, AZ: Galen Press, Ltd., 1994.

14. Pandey RE, Templer DI: Use of the death anxiety scale in an inter-racial setting. *Omega*. 1972;3(3):127-30.

15. Kunz FD: Personal communication with author, December 1998.

16. Collins S: Sudden death counseling protocol. *Dimens Crit Care Nurs*. 1989 Nov-Dec; 8(6):376-82.

4: "Helping" Phrases: The Good, The Bad, and The Ugly

When speaking with survivors, use comments that are helpful and that are more supportive than directive (table 4-1). Avoid using common clichés that sound trite and will only make them angry (table 4-2). (Clichés are overused expressions or ideas that have lost their originality or force through overuse, and are often referred to as platitudes or truisms.) In some cultures, especially if *survivors* begin using these phrases, notifiers may also wish to employ them—carefully.

Helpful or facilitative phrases are person-centered, encouraging, supportive, and caring. They are focused on feelings, acknowledge what the survivors are experiencing, and indicate that the speaker understands, accepts, and respects them and their feelings. These phrases require words describing feelings or emotions, such as "You're uncertain about what to do next" and "You're feeling confused and angry." Similarly helpful are phrases that disclose how the notifier or supporter is feeling, such as "I'm feeling terrible" or "I want to cry with you."

Only slightly less helpful are statements that clarify and summarize what survivors say, such as "If I'm following you, you plan to move in with your in-laws" and "Correct me if I'm wrong, but it sounds like you want to discuss your plans with your attorney first." Simply rephrasing and interpreting the survivors' ideas shows them that the person is listening closely and that they can be used as a "sounding board." Survivors report that only about one in five phrases that notifiers or "consolers" use are of the "helpful" type.[1] Table 4-1 contains phrases that survivors find helpful.

Questions can either help or hurt, depending upon the assumptions that lie behind them and the way they are said. "Can I help prepare the children's dinner?" can be seen either as very supportive or as accusatory, depending upon the tone. This is also true of some of the seemingly innocuous phrases to avoid in table 4-2. If said in a kind and loving tone, some could be seen as not harmful (and even helpful).

Table 4-1: Helpful Phrases

I can't imagine how difficult this is for you.
I know this is very painful for you.
I'm so sorry for your loss (inclusive, rather than pitying).
It's harder than most people think.
It's okay to be angry with God.
It must be hard to accept.
You must have been very close to him/her.
How can I be of help?
Let's spend some time together.
People really cared for her/him.
I'm praying for you.
You are not alone; I'm here to help you.
I know this must feel like a dream to you.
Tell me how you're feeling.
I know you will miss him/her.
S/he was very special to you.
I know you are feeling totally overwhelmed right now.
I'd give anything to be able to make it better for you, but I know I can't.
Most people who have gone through this react just as you are.
Tell me about (decedent's name) and your life with him/her.
When did you last see (decedent's name)?
What special memories do you have?
May I just sit here with you?
Is there anyone I can call for you?
We cannot afford to have you lose control. We need to keep you and those around you safe.
Were you there when (decedent's name) died? What was that like for you?
I'll call you tomorrow. In the meantime, if you need me, here is my number.

Developed from multiple sources, including References 2 and 3.

Table 4-2: Comments to Avoid

God Clichés

It was God's will.
God picks the most beautiful flowers first.
This will make your faith stronger.
God needs him/her more than you do.
Now you have an angel in heaven watching over you.
You can talk to her/him anytime you want. S/he hears you.
God relieved his/her pain.
It was actually a blessing because . . .
God has a reason for this.
Only the good die young.
God never gives us more than we can handle.

Unhealthy Expectations

You shouldn't feel/act that way.
Death happens. Get over it!
Be grateful that you still have your (can have) other children.
Aren't you lucky that at least . . .
You must be strong for your (other) children, spouse, etc.
You must get hold of yourself.
The healthy must go on.
S/he's gone and you'll just have to make the best of it.
Don't take it so hard.
You'll get over this
You're young . . . you'll find someone else.
So you think you'll get married again?
You must focus on your precious memories.
You can always find someone worse off than yourself.
It's time to buck up and get on with life.
Go back to work. It will distract you.
I don't want to make you cry.
You have to keep busy.

Disempowering Statements

You don't need to know that.
What you don't know can't hurt you.
I can't tell you that.

Table 4-2: continued

Ignorance

Let's not talk about it.
S/he died because . . .
It must have been his/her time to go.
His/her death was for the best.
Things always work out for the best.
This will make you a better/stronger person.
He/she was really holding you back.
You're young enough to have more children.
The kids are young, so they'll most likely forget him (her).
Something good always comes out of tragedy.
You're not the only one who suffers.
At least you have a long life ahead of you.
Losing a second spouse later in life must not be as painful.

Basic Insensitivity

I know just how you feel. My ____ died last year.
We all have to deal with loss.
S/he never knew what hit her/him.
Time heals all wounds.
At least you're young enough to remarry.
S/he had a very full life.
It could have been worse if . . .
At least your children are grown.
Everything is going to be okay.
You must go on with your life.
Did s/he make peace with God before s/he died?
Things will be better.
It's too bad you're not pregnant.
It's better to have loved and lost than never to have loved at all.
Let me know if there's anything I can do.

Developed from multiple sources, including References 4 through 6.

The most commonly used phrase, "I'm sorry," is another example. If it is said so as to imply "I'm sorry for you," survivors see it as non-helpful and it may make them angry. Survivors generally don't want to be pitied. If, however, it is said as the more inclusive, "I'm sorry and sad for all of us," survivors find it helpful. The best course, however, is to indicate your support for survivors by using the "helpful" phrases. When physicians use the phase, "I'm sorry," they often engender even more confusion. Many, at least implicitly, use the phrase to mean, "I'm sorry I failed." It then becomes a negative emotion for both the physician and the survivors.

Unless they have been trained to do so, few death notifiers and even fewer supporters of survivors use "helping" phrases. Rather, 80% of the time they fall into the trap of using the non-helpful clichés.[7] This may be due to their own discomfort with death or their unease when dealing with bereaved survivors. Although well intended, inappropriate interactions may leave survivors feeling hurt, misunderstood, and alienated.

Non-helpful comments can be categorized as God Clichés, Disempowering Statements, Unhealthy Expectations, Ignorance, and Basic Insensitivity. Interestingly, although the clergy is the one group best trained to use helpful comments, this group is also the one who most commonly resorts to using God clichés. Perhaps this is done to pass on their strong faith during a time of crisis, but unless the survivors are strong believers of that faith, and willing to believe even in their time of grief, it is best to avoid these statements. (While most people perceive God Clichés negatively, some cultures, such as those in the Arab world and those in fundamentalist sects of some religions, expect condolences to be phrased that way.)

References

1. Davidowitz M, Myrick RD: Responding to the bereaved: an analysis of "helping" statements. *Death Education*. 1984;8(1):1-10.
2. McQuay JE: Support of families who had a loved one suffer a sudden injury, illness, or death. *Crit Care Nurs Clin North Am*. 1995 Sep;7(3):541-7.
3. Davidowitz M, Myrick RD: "Responding to the bereaved."
4. McQuay J: "Support of families."
5. Davidowitz M, Myrick RD: "Responding to the bereaved."
6. Lord JH: *Trauma, Death, and Death Notification: A Seminar for Professional Counselors and Victim Advocates*. Washington, DC: Mothers Against Drunk Driving and the U.S. Dept. of Justice for Victims of Crime, 1996, p. 87+.
7. Davidowitz M, Myrick RD: "Responding to the bereaved."

5: Telephone Notification

One of the least preferred notification methods is the telephone call. (The most impersonal are e-mail and television/radio notifications.) Hospital staff members are often reluctant to notify survivors immediately when an acute unexpected death occurs. They often say, "Why don't we let them (the survivors) get a good night's sleep; we'll call them in the morning." Yet families overwhelmingly want to be notified immediately. One study showed that 90% of respondents want to be contacted immediately (but not told of the death by phone) when a loved one dies.[1]

Even when deaths are unexpected, physicians use the telephone to notify survivors about 25% of the time; when death is expected, they use it nearly two-thirds of the time.[2] For deaths occurring in the emergency department and for trauma deaths, survivors who live close enough to be told in person are rarely told over the phone unless they demand that information immediately.

The question always arises whether to notify the individual via telephone or wait (at least with survivors who live nearby) until they arrive. In cases of unexpected deaths, most people want to wait until they arrive at the hospital to be notified of the death. Among the general public, 70% prefer to wait to hear the news, as would 60% of physicians when they must receive this type of news. Most people prefer that hospital personnel only tell them that their relative is "critically ill" and that they should "come to the hospital." Nearly 90% of all women, and both men and women born outside of the United States or Canada, do not want to be told of unexpected deaths over the phone. Males born in the United States or Canada are most likely to want this news via telephone, although this varies greatly.[3]

No matter what method is used to relay the news of death to survivors, an obviously uncaring attitude and sloppy procedures should not be accepted. The U.S. Department of Justice's Office of Victims of Crime collected the following three examples of inappropriate telephone notifications:[4]

One family in Hillsborough County, Florida, was notified by phone that their son had been killed, but didn't learn until the next day when they went to the funeral home that he had lived for eight hours after they were notified. They felt they missed the opportunity to say good-bye.

Jack Baughman's daughter was one of the Chi Omega girls Ted Bundy killed. At 7 A.M. one morning, he went to the door and was handed a note to call a Tallahassee phone number . . . that's all. It took a number of calls for him to discover what had happened.

A police officer called to inform a man that "his son" had been killed at another location. The officer didn't know the boy's name. The man had three sons, and it took several hours to find out which one had died and how.

There are also good legal reasons to notify survivors in a timely manner. In several cases, survivors have sued (at least once successfully) for not being notified of their loved one's demise. During World War II, Western Union was sued when they delivered messages about battle deaths (the method at that time) to the wrong people, not only disrupting one family, but also delaying the news to those really affected. In a more recent case, the Appellate Division of the New York Supreme Court ruled that not notifying a spouse of her husband's death was malpractice. (In that case, the hospital failed to notify because they misidentified the patient.)[5] In another case, a family brought suit when only the injured spouse, but not the waiting relatives, was notified. The California Court of Appeals ruled against the family because there was no malice involved. In fact, the primary physicians were attending another patient in surgery soon after the patient's unexpected demise.[6] In both instances, the medical personnel were dragged through long court battles which wouldn't have occurred if there had been timely notification.

The courts themselves may delay notification.

Fearing a mistrial, a Hastings, Minnesota, judge refused to tell a juror that her father had a heart attack and was very ill. In November 1997, a juror's husband asked Judge Rex Stacey to release a juror so that she could be with her dying father in a hospital about twenty miles away. The news came during deliberations in the case of a 14-year-old boy's murder. Since the alternate jurors had already been dismissed, letting the juror go would have caused a mistrial. "So we tried to wait and see what (her father's) condition was," said the judge. "We kept trying to determine if we were at a critical point where I've got to make a call." Later that day, the father died in surgery. Only after the jury reached a verdict was the juror escorted into the judge's chambers where her husband told her that her father had died minutes earlier.[7]

Dr. Bob Orr illustrates how easy it is to accidentally delay death notification.

After pronouncing an elderly man from a nursing home dead, he [Dr. Orr] called the contact number on the medical record. A woman answered and he told her that, as expected, her husband had died. "Yes," she replied, "he had been sick for some time." Several days later, another woman stormed into his office demanding to know why she hadn't been informed that her husband had died. "Who was your husband?" he asked. She said it was the man from the nursing home. "But I called this number and spoke to his wife," he said. "She hasn't been his wife for more than a decade. She has Alzheimer's Disease, though, and doesn't remember she got divorced."[8]

Luckily, he was able to explain the situation to her without involving attorneys.

What To Say

The best course of action is to avoid giving bad news over the telephone unless asked or unless the person is too far away to immediately come to the hospital. About 80% of physicians say only that the person is in "critical condition." Their reasoning is that survivors need personal support when they receive this news, that this gives the family time to psychologically adapt, that death notification over the phone can be too shocking, and that relatives may be involved in accidents if too distraught by such news. (If true, protecting survivors' lives may constitute sufficient reason to "lie" during these initial communications.)

Interestingly, other physicians use the possibility of survivors being involved in auto accidents as they rush to the bedsides of their "critical" loved ones as a reason to deliver the news over the phone.[9] These notifiers have also been shown to experience less death anxiety than those who say that a patient is "critical."[10] (Is this lack of anxiety also related to callousness?) Most experienced telephone notifiers, however, believe that the best tack is to make "critical notification" via the telephone and deliver the news about death in person. As one nurse said,

> You indicate on the phone how serious the situation is without having them fly to the hospital and be in an accident on the way. You would say, "so and so has taken a turn for the worse [for patients who suddenly die while in hospital] and the doctor is here" . . . do not tell them on the phone . . . always in person. Even if you know they are dead . . . you say "so and so has taken a turn for the worse. When can you get here?"[11]

On the other hand, a bit more information can be provided than was given by one neophyte medical student some years back. As the now more experienced Dr. Anna Graham reports:

> When I was just a medical student, I was standing in Mr. Deal's room when he went into cardiac arrest. He had had an uncomplicated heart attack (up to that point) and was about to be discharged from the hospital. The "code" team arrived and began resuscitative procedures. I was standing out of the way, and happened to be near the telephone when it rang. I answered it and the caller asked, "Can I speak to Mr. Deal?" After a moment of panic, and thinking that I shouldn't tell the unidentified caller what was going on, I simply said, "Mr. Deal can't come to the

phone right now." The code team members guffawed as they continued their efforts.[12]

When it is necessary to deliver death notifications via telephone, an experienced professional should deliver the news. Not only do they have the authority and knowledge to answer any questions, but their normal professional responsibilities ensures a measure of compassion and authority, especially if they have received training in delivering such news correctly. If done incorrectly, as in the case below, the recipient may dwell on the life-altering telephone call for many years.

> When the woman answered the telephone, an unidentified man's voice said, "Mrs. A, this is the police. About an hour ago your husband was killed by a truck. Can you come down to headquarters and identify the body?" Her reaction was bewildered disbelief, followed quickly by panic and then denial. "Are you serious?" she exclaimed. "Is this a crank call?" An interchange followed, and she was finally persuaded that the call was legitimate. She then waited alone for the police to arrive and take her to the mortuary.[13]

The incident above violates some of the cardinal rules used by police. (See chapter 19 on police and table 5-1 for telephone notifications.) The psychiatrist who related this incident considered that a better way to have relayed the same news more tactfully, although a bit more completely than is justified, might have been, "I am here because there was an accident, a bad accident. Some cars collided—your husband was in his car and was injured very badly. We took him to the hospital right away—but the doctors found that he was hurt too seriously—and I must tell you that he didn't survive."

Some coroners' offices handle telephone death notifications in much the same way. The coroner first asks the individual answering the phone if they have received any calls about their deceased relative. They then encourage the relatives to ask questions by delivering small bits of information that progressively relate the bad news. The following is an example:

> I tell them that he collapsed today while at work. They ask if he is all right now. I say slowly, "Well, no, but they took him to the hospital." They ask if he is there now. I say, "They did all they could do—the doctors tried very hard." They say, "He is dead at the hospital?" Then I tell them he's at the coroner's office.[14]

Coroners and medical examiners find that if they use euphemisms first, such as "fatally injured" or "passed away," they can manipulate the person on the phone to use a "D" word themselves. (They can often do this because, unlike other notifiers, everyone knows coroners and medical examiners only deal with the dead.) This helps them to make the transition to understanding that their loved one is dead. Then, in concert with their need to get families to assume responsibility for the costs of disposing of the body, they wait for the survivors to ask, "What do I do now?" They then respond, "All you need to do is to call your local funeral director and he'll direct you."[15] They have now completed their two tasks for the call: notification and transferring financial liability.

Even when the call is made with kindness, knowledge, and understanding, the recipient can be confused, as I was in the following instance.

> Not having seen Barbara, an older cousin, for some years, I was delighted that she could collect me at the airport and take me to a conference site in her city. We reminisced about old times, discussed her husband Jerry who had a severe disease (but seemed to be tenuously stable at the time), and made plans to have dinner together two days later. I remarked how fit she appeared at 50 years of age. Of course, this was no surprise, as she had always exercised regularly, practiced yoga, and carefully watched her diet.
>
> During the conference, I got an emergency phone call from home. "Your cousin just died," said my wife, calling me from Arizona after receiving the news. "Who?" I asked. "Jerry?" "No, Barbara," she answered. "You mean Jerry," I said. "No, Barbara," she responded. "You mean I should call Barbara?" I asked really confused. "No. Barbara died. Call Jerry." It took several minutes to receive, process, and believe this message. Then I called Jerry.

If the person answering the phone identifies himself as a child (such as, "My mother isn't home right now" when the caller asks for her) or even sounds like a child, notifiers should give only identifying information, despite the person's requests for more information. Just as in other situations, young children should not be saddled with the responsibility of informing their family of a death, as happened to my neighbors.

> When Dr. Michael Cummins' father was instantly killed and his mother critically injured in a motor vehicle collision in another state, the emergency department where they were taken called the Cummins' home. The only person home when the ED called was their teenage son, the victims' grandson. He identified himself as the teenage son of the person the hospital was trying to reach, but pressed them for information. Despite knowing that he was a child, they told him of the collision, the death, and the injuries. Over the next two hours, he became more and more distraught over not being able to reach either his parents or any other relative. This memory still haunts him—his inability to do anything or get any help for himself or for his grandmother while he was alone.[16]

Telephone Notification Protocol

Protocols, such as the one in table 5-1, are useful when making death notification calls or when teaching others how to make them. When making these difficult calls, callers should speak in a calm voice, consciously trying not to use a high-pitched voice that will sound alarming to a listener. Allow brief periods of silence during the conversation so the recipient can digest the information. When possible, an experienced person should make the call. If new personnel are present who may need to make these calls in the future, they should listen in so that they can learn how it is done.

Table 5-1: Telephone Notification Protocol

Before Making the Call	
Get Identifying Information	• Patient Name • Patient Age • Male/Female • Skin color • Eye color • Distinguishing marks • Patient social security number or other ID numbers
Get Event Information	• Type of event (accident, sudden illness, injury, etc.) • When did event occur? • Where did event occur? • How did the person arrive at the hospital? • When did the person arrive?
Get Survivors' Contact Information	• Name Address Phone number Alternate phone numbers/pagers Relationship to decedent Time(s) contact attempted Time contacted • Second Name Address Phone number Alternate phone numbers/pagers Relationship to decedent Time(s) contact attempted Time contacted
Prepare	• Calm down. • Find a quiet area with a phone. • Get any long distance access numbers. • Review what you will say.

Continued on next page

Table 5-1: continued

Making the Call	
How Will You Say It?	• Concentrate on the telephone conversation. • Speak distinctly and slowly so you can be understood. • Repeat the message, especially the directions if the recipient hesitates when asked if they have the location/directions. • When the recipients say something, do not interrupt them. Wait until they are finished to add to or clarify the information. • If you cannot reach the person, leave a message. Clearly pronounce your name (and spell it), the name of your health care facility or agency, the name of person you are trying to contact, *a return telephone number that will be answered by a person who knows how to quickly locate you,* and the date and time you called. (**Note:** Only leave this message on a phone machine or with an answering service if you are sure that the individual you called is the person you are trying to contact.)
What Will You Say?	• Hello. This is (your name) from (name of health care facility or agency). Is this (name of person you are trying to contact)? Are you the (relationship) of (name of decedent)? • (Name) has been in a serious accident. We would like you to come to the hospital. (This can be used for any type of injury.) • (Name) has had a (name of illness). We would like you to come to the hospital. • Can you arrange to get here? Do you know where it is?
Tell Them Your Location	• Ask the person to get a piece of paper and pencil to write down the information. • Location (including address, parking, specific area—such as the emergency department—and a contact phone number). • Directions to facility. • Who to contact on arrival. • Are they alone? If so, can they get someone to transport them?

Continued on next page

Table 5-1: continued

Making the Call, cont.	
Contact Information	• Give them your name or a person who they can call back, if necessary. • Give them a working telephone number and any other specific instructions about how to contact the individual (pager, badge number, extension, etc.). • If applicable, tell them the hours that the contact person is available. • Be sure they write down all information you give them. • Have them repeat back all information. (**Note:** Detailed contact information is especially important for long-distance notifications.)
If They Say/Ask:	**Response:**
The person you want is not here.	• "Do you know how to contact them? When they will return?" (Be certain that they have your *accurate* contact information.)
I am their son, daughter, etc.	• "How old are you?" If s/he is a child, give only the contact information. If s/he is an adult, give the same responses as if you had reached the individual.
How is s/he?	• "S/he's in critical condition."
Can't you tell me any more?	• "The (physician, surgeon, trauma team) is here with him/her. It's probably best if we discuss other specifics when you arrive." *OR* • "S/he just arrived at the hospital and we will know a lot more by the time you get there."
Is s/he dead?	• "S/he's in critical condition. We can discuss his/her condition when you get here."
Is s/he dead? (2nd time) Tell me now.	• "I'm sorry. Yes, s/he died (on arrival, despite our attempts at resuscitation, etc.)."
Who did it? (Or other details of the event).	• Briefly give only the details that are listed above in "Event Information." For any others say: "I don't have those details. We can find some of them out when you arrive."

Continued on next page

Table 5-1: continued

If They Say/Ask:	Response:
How will I tell them (other emotionally close survivor)?	**For Local Calls:** • "Would you like me to call them and: (1) ask them to come to the hospital also *or* here so I can speak with them? or (2) tell them what I have told you?" **For Long-distance Calls:** • "Would you like: (1) me to call them and tell them what I have told you? or (2) discuss the best way to do it?"
I can't come in right now.	• "I think that you need to come in right now."

Making these calls correctly not only helps survivors, but also can be good risk management. At least one egregiously bad telephone notification after an unexpected infant death resulted in a civil suit.[17]

There are limitations to this protocol. An obvious one is when the caller lacks all pertinent information. Another is when the survivor needing to be notified is a professional who knows the "code words." This can lead to confusion.

> A nurse with twin teenaged sons was awakened one night by the call every parent dreads. "Your son Michael has been in a bad accident," said the caller from the local trauma center. "He may need to go to the operating room, so we think that you should come to the hospital." "But, but . . ." she stammered, trying to think of what to say while her mind was reeling with the similar calls she had made during her career. She had two fears. She was concerned about Michael's condition, but more than that, she worried about her other son. Both twins had been in the car that night. Not mentioning the other meant—to her—that he must be dead. She was certain of that. But did she really want to ask? No! She would wait and be told at the hospital.

As it turned out, the caller was completely unaware that there had been another passenger. Twenty minutes later the other twin arrived by ambulance, having only broken his wrist.

Local Calls

Two questions arise when making telephone calls to survivors who live nearby. First, should they be told that their loved one has died, and second, should this notification be altered if they are alone, in poor health, or appear unusually distressed?

In general, health care workers agree that, whenever possible, they should delay notifying survivors until they arrive at the hospital. This allows a more complete and personal interaction, helps to ensure that they are speaking with the correct people, and allows them to assess and assist those to whom they are delivering the news. In some instances, delivering the news over the phone may result in survivors not coming to the hospital or the dissemination of incorrect information. Some police departments and coroner's offices, however, routinely make these notifications by phone.

Yet when surveyed, some people believe that they would prefer being told over the phone, whether or not they are alone. They say that they would be angry if they later discovered that the caller had known of the death but hadn't told them, although even the survey's author has never found this to be true in real situations.[18]

What if the contacted survivor specifically asks to be told whether or not the patient is alive? This is not unusual, especially when survivors receive calls from emergency departments, police, or military personnel. In those situations, notifiers should confirm that survivors really want to know the information immediately. This confirmation could consist of a response such as, "Wouldn't you like to discuss this in person?" If a survivor insists on knowing immediately, it is prudent to gently and briefly relay the news. Then offer to discuss it with them in greater detail when they arrive. In general, however, family members usually appreciate being informed as a group so that they can mourn together. Callers should tell survivors not to drive themselves to the hospital whenever it can be avoided.

A typical telephone call to survivors from the physician of a hospitalized patient who unexpectedly died might be:

> This is Dr. Peters. I am at the General Hospital with your wife. She has taken a sudden turn for the worse. Could you come here as soon as possible? I will meet you here.
>
> Do you know how to get here? Do you have a way to get here? Please drive carefully, there is no need to rush.

Subsequent notifications, such as those to more distant (emotionally and geographically) relatives, friends, co-workers, etc., can usually be made by phone. These individuals usually have less emotional investment in the decedent than do the primary survivors.

Long-distance Notification

Sometimes the only reasonable way to notify survivors is via telephone, such as when they live far from the death location. This is often the case when relatives must notify others, and for deaths among military personnel, after commercial transportation accidents, for deaths in retirement communities, for travelers, and for college students. In our extremely mobile society, long-distance notification has become routine.

When long-distance notification is necessary, it is best to have someone with the survivor when they receive the call. Unfortunately, that can be difficult to arrange. If possible, the notifier should ask the survivor who is alone to get a relative, friend, minister, or neighbor with them and then call back. As one experienced clinician said,

> I do not like to tell anyone over the phone that someone has died. Now, if we have a dead patient here from [a long distance away] and the family has to be notified, it is kind of hard to have them come all the way up here and tell them that and turn around and go right back. But I usually ask, "Are you alone? If you are, call your neighbor and call me back." I just don't like to tell anyone when they are alone. I don't know what their physical condition is, they may be a coronary patient.[19]

For many survivors, however, just making this suggestion to have someone with them will make them demand the information. In that case, the notifier should break the news with compassion. If other emotionally close survivors are in the same area as those receiving the initial call, they can then make subsequent in-person survivor-to-survivor notifications. That, of course, is at the discretion of those receiving such calls.

If long-distance notification must be made, inform the survivors using one of the "D" words: "died," "death," or "dead." It is important that this information be transmitted clearly. *Be certain* they have written down your contact information and the hospital or agency's address and telephone number. Ask them to repeat it back to you. If the two parties fumble in transmitting this information, the results can be frustrating, and sometimes tragic. For example, one man, in shock when he heard the news of his son's death on a cross-country trip, did not write down the information, and then could not remember who had called. His wife, also in the accident, died two days later, before he had found his way to the hospital. Be certain that survivors write down and correctly repeat back your contact information. Also, be certain that the contact information is operable, that the phone calls are not being "forwarded" or answered by a machine or voice-mail, and that someone will be available to speak with this or another survivor if they call back.

Occasionally, either because of an inability to make contact with survivors or because of the survivor's health or mental state, notifiers must contact local police, the Red Cross (for military or disaster deaths), local social service agencies, neighbors, or even the media to help make notifications. Usually, these agencies will only assist the survivor in returning a call from the notifier, but sometimes they will render any reasonable assistance that survivors need.

References

1. Leash RM: Death notification: practical guidelines for health care professionals. *Crit Care Nurs Quart.* 1996 May;19(1):21-34.

2. Tolle SW, Elliot DL, Hickam DH: Physician attitudes and practices at the time of patient death. *Arch Intern Med.* 1984 Dec;144(12):2389-91.

3. Viswanathan R, Clark JJ, Viswanathan K: Physicians' and the public's attitudes on communication about death. *Arch Intern Med.* 1986 Oct;146(10):2029-33.

4. Lord JH: *Trauma, Death, and Death Notification: A Seminar for Professional Counselors and Victim Advocates.* Washington, DC: Mothers Against Drunk Driving and the U.S. Dept. of Justice for Victims of Crime, 1996, p. 49.

5. *Smith v. St. Joseph's Hosp., Inc.* 619 N.Y.S. 2d 709 (1994).

6. *Aquino v. Superior Court (Reichman)* 26 Cal. Rptr. 2d 477-CA (1993).

7. Associated Press: Juror's father stricken; judge keeps quiet. *Arizona Daily Star.* 1997 Nov8;Sect. A:11.

8. Orr R: Personal communication with author, March 1999.

9. Viswanathan R, Clark JJ, Viswanathan K: "Physicians' and the public's attitudes."

10. Viswanathan R: Death anxiety, locus of control, and purpose in life of physicians. their relationship to patient death notification. *Psychosomatics.* 1996 Jul-Aug;37(4):339-45.

11. Clark RE, LaBeff EE: Death telling: managing the delivery of bad news. *J Health Soc Behav.* 1982 Dec;23(4):366-80.

12. Graham A: Personal communication with author, December 1998.

13. Weisman AD: Coping with untimely death. *Psychiatry.* 1973 Nov;36(4):366-78.

14. Charmaz KC: The coroner's strategies for announcing death. *Urban Life.* 1975 Oct;4(3):296-316.

15. *Ibid.*

16. Cummins M: Personal communication with author, December 1998.

17. *Muniz v. United Hospitals Med Center Presbyterian Hospital*, 379 A.2d 57 (1977).

18. Leash RM: "Death notification. practical guidelines."

19. Clark RE, LaBeff EE: "Death telling."

6: Survivor Information Forms

Families often cannot recall much of the information given verbally during in-person death notifications. In all such notifications, it is best to provide written information to guide them through the procedures they should do immediately. (See table 6-1.) This should include specific telephone numbers for important agencies or individuals. Some information may need to be filled in at the time of notification, since it will be family- or notifier-specific.

Many patients may not be able to understand these written instructions, due to reading or language difficulties.[1] Someone should verbally go over these instructions with survivors, item by item. These instructions should also be available in the common alternate languages used by patients at each medical facility. (Table 6-2 is a Spanish version of these instructions to use for survivors who feel more comfortable with that language.)

Reference

1. Jolly BT, Scott JL, Feied CF, et al.: Functional illiteracy among emergency department patients. a preliminary study. *Ann Emerg Med*. 1993 Mar;22(3):573-8.

Table 6-1: Survivor Information Sheet

Family members and friends. Make a list, with phone numbers, of those who should be contacted. Check them off when notified.

Minister, priest, or rabbi. If you have one, call him or her immediately. The chaplain will help you do this.

Funerary instructions. If (name of decedent) left any instructions for his/her disposition, find them and read them now.

Decedent's remains. The decedent's body is at (location).

Funeral director. Call your funeral director if one has previously been selected. If not, a list of local funeral homes, crematoria, and burial societies is attached.

Obituary. Usually placed through funeral homes. If you want something extra, the phone numbers for the local newspapers are (telephone number) and (telephone number).

Finances. If (name of decedent) left any detailed information about these or other important matters, find it and read it as soon as possible.

Insurance. Check all life and casualty benefits, including those from Social Security, employers, credit unions, trade unions, the military, and fraternal organizations. Contact your accountant, if you have one.

Insurance companies. Notify them.

Attorney holding the will. Notify him or her.

Debts. Check all of them. Some have insurance clauses that will cancel the debts. If there will be a delay in meeting payments, consult creditors and ask for extensions of time.

Death certificate. You probably will need a copy. To get it, call the medical examiner's office at (telephone number).

Police. If you have additional questions for the police, contact officer (officer's name), badge number (badge number), at (telephone number).

Physicians. If you have questions for the physician who took care of (name of decedent), contact (physician's name) at (telephone number) or (pager number). It is best to call between the hours of (____A.M./P.M.) and (____A.M./P.M.), (days of the week).

Other questions. If you have any other questions for (name and title of other notifier), contact me at (telephone number) or (pager number). It is best to call between the hours of (____A.M./P.M.) and (____A.M./P.M.), (days of the week).

Modified from "Guidelines for Volunteer Police Chaplains" developed by the International Conference of Police Chaplains.

Table 6-2: Hoja De Información Para El Sobreviviente

Haga una lista de los miembros de *la familia y amigos* que deben ser notificados, y sus números de teléfono. Indique cuales se han notificado ya.

Llame al *ministro, sacerdote, or rabino* inmediatamente. El capellán ayudará en todo lo posible.

Si (nombre del difunto) dejó instrucciones para la disposición de su cuerpo y arreglos *funerarios*, búsquelos y léalos inmediatamente.

El difunto se encuentra en (la dirección).

Llame al *director de la agencia funeraria*, si se ha escogido uno. Si no, le podemos dar una lista la funerarias locales, crematorios, y asociaciones de entierros.

Generalmente *la esquela de defunción* es publicada por medio de la funeraria. Si quiere agregar algo mas, llame a los periódicos locales: (número de teléfono) y (número de teléfono).

Si (nombre del difunto) dejó información detallada sobre sus *finanzas*, o de otros asuntos importantes, búsquelos y léalos lo más pronto posible.

Revise todos las policias de *los seguros*, incluyendo el Seguro Social, seguros de vida, seguro de gastos médicos, de empleo, de uniones de crédito, de comercio, fraternal, militar, etc. Notifique al contador, si tiene uno.

Comuniquese con *los seguros*.

Averique con el abogado encargado del *testamento*.

Revise todas *las deudas*. Hay deudas que contienen cláusulas de seguro que cancelan la deuda. Si hay una deuda sin esta cláusula, y va a tardar en dar el pago, consulte con el acreedor y pida una extensión de tiempo (prorroga).

Si se necesita copias del *acta de defunción*, llame a la oficina del Examinador Médico al teléfono (número de teléfono).

Si tiene preguntas para *la policia*, comuniquese con el oficial (nombre), número de escudo (número de escudo), a (número de teléfono).

Si tiene preguntas para *el médico* que atendió a (nombre del difunto), llamar a (nombre del doctor), a (número de teléfono), o (número de biper). Llame entre las horas (____A.M./P.M.) y (____A.M./P.M.), los (dias de la semana).

Si hay *otras preguntas* para (nombre y título de otro notifador), llame al (número de teléfono), entre las horas (____A.M./P.M.) y (___A.M./P.M.), los (dias de la semana).

7: Requesting Organ/Tissue Donations and Autopsy Permission

Physicians are generally reluctant to request organ or tissue donations and autopsy permission. They request organ or tissue donations in only about 7% of acute unexpected deaths. They discuss autopsies about 38% of the time.[1] These requests are part of the always-distasteful paperwork that accompanies sudden unexpected deaths. As one physician said,

> Although it is somewhat impersonal, you have to get the paperwork done . . . to get them [the bodies] where they have to go, the morgue or whatever. They [survivors] have to sign some releases so you have to approach those topics, too, which is impersonal but necessary. You can't leave the body on the ward for a day or so. They have to be put somewhere, so you have to talk about those sorts of things.[2]

Organ or Tissue Donations

Federal law (Public Law 99-5-9; Section 9318) requires hospitals to offer survivors an opportunity to donate their loved one's organs and tissues. Department of Health and Human Services rules require that to get Medicare reimbursement, hospitals must have procedures in place for reporting all deaths and imminent deaths to their Organ Procurement Organizations (OPOs) and local eye and tissue banks, and for approaching families about donation. Some states have even stricter requirements.

It may seem intuitively obvious, but organ or tissue donation and autopsy requests should be separated emotionally, if not in time, from the death notification. While it may be ideal to wait a period of time and then return to discuss these issues, that is not always possible. It is vital, however, that survivors accept the death and verbalize that death has occurred before any requests are made. For example, University of Kentucky researchers found that delaying the request for organ donation until after the family has acknowledged the patient's death markedly increases the number who agreed to donate. If they waited until after the family had clearly articulated that their loved one was dead, 57% of the families agreed to donate. If the request accompanied the death notification, fewer then 18% agreed to donate.[3]

More than half of all survivors who donate organs do so either to help others in need or because they want some good to result from the death. As a young widow said, "I can remember thinking what a godsend to salvage something from an otherwise wasted young body." Another, voicing the belief of nearly all other donating survivors said, "She was always helping others and here was a chance for her to do so in death."[4] Another widow, expressing how the donation helped in her grieving process said, "You'll never know how good I felt knowing that part of my husband was helping a little boy to live a normal life."[5]

Children's sudden deaths deeply sadden most medical personnel, often making them reluctant to request organ or tissue donations. Yet most parents do not find this request offensive. In some cases, the parents may be bothered that they were not asked.[6] As one mother said, "The nurses and doctors, in their attempt to make my daughter's death as painless as possible, did not approach me about organ and tissue donation. However, their good intentions denied me an important option, causing more pain than their asking."[7] About 85% of U.S. and Canadian parents said they are favorably disposed to donating their child's organs, with half of these being certain they would donate. Their willingness to donate is associated with the certainty that their child will die (or is dead), altruism, previous discussions of organ donation with a family member, knowledge of their adolescent or adult child's attitude toward donation, and empathy toward children in need of an organ transplant. The child's age does not enter into the decision.[8] Commonly, parents will also achieve a sense of comfort from their child's donation. This is reflected in the comments of one mother whose 14-year-old son committed suicide: "Dan was a special boy and, to me, so are those people [organ and tissue recipients] because they have a part of him living and growing inside of them."[9]

It is important to know, before approaching survivors, whether regional organ/tissue procurement organizations will want an individual's organs and tissues. Nowadays, in most cases *some* organs and tissues from nearly anyone can be used for research, if not for transplantation. To ease survivors' concerns about organ and tissue donations and to increase the number willing to donate, those requesting organ or tissue donation must be able to answer this question as well as others that survivors commonly raise, such as:

- Can we donate organs, tissues, or the whole body?
- How are organs and tissues procured?
- How are tissues donated?
- Which can be donated?
- What happens after donation?

- Can the whole body be donated to a medical school?
- What costs are involved in body disposition?

Brief answers to these questions are in chapter 27. (See also, Iserson KV. *Death to Dust: What Happens to Dead Bodies?* Tucson, AZ: Galen Press, Ltd., 1994.)

While many larger centers now have specific individuals trained to request organ and tissue donations, this is not universally true. Using such trained requesters, who are separate from the notifiers, increases the donation rate. Most survivors want this request to be made, although they can have negative reactions if it is not done correctly.[10]

When notifiers ask about organ and tissue donation, the moment has clearly arrived when the survivors have to admit to themselves that the person is dead. Chaplain Pat Andresen describes his and many of his colleagues' experiences with making these requests.

> In-laws and extended family often have very harsh opinions that sway the already overwhelmed next of kin. I feel it is more ideal to pull the person or a small number of the people making the decision aside and discuss the issue in private. At that point the goal is to help them have the accurate information they need to make the right decision for them. If they choose to donate, the notifier can then go to the larger group and explain the decision and ask for the group's support of this very important issue. This limits how family members with distorted views and other emotional baggage can influence the decision and leave the next of kin later regretting they had been talked out of something that was important to them. Typically I have seen relatives and friends confuse this process for very misguided reasons that subsequently makes the grieving process more difficult for the closest survivors.[11]

Table 7-1 is a protocol that can be used to request organ and tissue donation. It can be modified if the patient is a candidate for organ donation ("brain dead" and still on "life" support systems) or for tissue donation (already or soon-to-be heart-lung dead).

Autopsy Permission

Those requesting autopsy permission need sensitivity, education, and most importantly, a willingness to ask. In cases of sudden unexpected deaths, when medicolegal autopsies may be performed without permission or despite survivor reluctance, the physician should at least be familiar with the local regulations governing which bodies must go to the medical examiner's or coroner's office for examination. If possible, they should also know whether that official is willing to do "limited autopsies" (e.g., examining only a part of the body, only taking needle specimens, or otherwise modifying the standard technique), and how to make this request.

Table 7-1: Discussing Organ and Tissue Procurement with Survivors

Notify	• Ensure that medical personnel have advised them of the death or the hopelessness of the situation. If the same clinician will both notify them and request organ/tissue donation, separate the events emotionally and in time.
Meet	• Meet the family as soon as the possibility of "brain death" has been raised.
Support	• Help the family gather the support (clergy, other family, friends) they need.
Understand Death	• Be sure that survivors understand that the patient is or will soon be dead—especially if the patient is dead by brain criteria ("brain death").
Visitation	• Allow survivors (including children) to visit with the decedent's body as soon and as often as possible.
The Situation	• Talk to survivors about their perception of the accident or illness and how the patient's death may affect them individually and as a family.
Organ Donation	• Introduce the subject of tissue and organ donation. Asking "Did s/he ever mention organ donation?" may be enough.
Agreement	• Even if they immediately agree to or request organ and tissue donation, make certain that the person has the legal right to agree. Continue supporting the family even after they have agreed to the donation.
Information	• Provide answers to survivors' questions about donation and the aftermath. Repeat information as needed for clarification or as new people arrive to assist the family. (See chapter 27.)
Discuss	• Encourage survivors to discuss donation, even after they have made a decision.
Paperwork	• Complete the regional- and institutional-specific paperwork necessary for the donation (or documenting the refusal). But do not overburden survivors with the paperwork. Make it as simple as possible for them and get as much information as possible from secondary sources (medical records, license) or other people (friends, minister).
More Information	• Give survivors as much information as they want about the process of donation, organ and tissue distribution, and subsequent possibilities for funerary rites. (See chapter 27.)
Good-byes	• Help survivors say good-bye to the patient before the donation.

Some of this information was adapted from: Gideon MD, Taylor PB: Kidney donation: care of the cadaver donor's family. *J Neurosurg Nurs*. 1981 Oct;13(5):248-51.

When bodies will or may go to the medical examiner's office for an examination or autopsy, survivors should be told about it and about the legal requirements. The experience should not be similar to that of this surviving husband:

> We [my son and I] followed the ambulance down and I went in the emergency room and the doctor was in there before long. They wanted to know who would take care of the body and I told them [about] the mortuary and I walked out and talked to the doctor . . . I went out and talked to the mortician and the doctor was standing there and I asked him once again if there was anything I had to sign or had to do and he said, "No, we've got everything taken care of." I did this three times before we left.
>
> We came at 9:30 the next morning [to the mortuary] after she had been taken care of. They were going to take the body out too and get the casket and stuff . . . You could tell something wasn't right. I said [to the mortician], "What is the matter?" [I found out that] my wife's body was on the way to Salt Lake [City] to do an autopsy. I was never notified. They never said a word about ever taking her body to Salt Lake to do an autopsy . . .
>
> My concern is that if you got to do this, I think I'm the first one that should know what's going on. I mean it ain't your mother, it ain't your wife, it's mine and I should have the say-so.[12]

Physicians often fail to request autopsy permission. Usually they believe that they know the cause of death and do not need an autopsy. Yet even in these days of modern medical techniques, physicians misdiagnose many causes of death.[13-15] Other reasons physicians may not request autopsies include: their belief that the findings will only be used to "put them on the hot seat" in departmental conferences, the autopsy rate is more important for hospital accreditation than for education, they feel anxiety and guilt related to the deceased patient and the survivors, they don't know how to ask, and they had no education about it in medical school.[16]

The behavior of the medical staff has been shown to increase survivors' acceptance of autopsies. For example, when Australian physician-administrators at one hospital met with relatives of patients who died there the day after a death to simply answer the survivors' questions and generally assist them, the rate for non-medicolegal autopsies increased from 16.3% to 26.5% in the first year.[17]

If physicians both think of the autopsy as "an examination after death" and explain it that way to families, everyone would be better informed. Non-medicolegal autopsies are most commonly requested when the patients are young, when clinicians are not sure why the patient died, and when relatives seemed favorably disposed to such a request.[18]

When they do ask, physicians occasionally lack sensitivity, as the vignette below demonstrates.

> The family was sitting in the head nurse's office, unaware that their 23-year-old daughter had just died of a subarachnoid hemorrhage. There was a knock at the door, which opened slowly. A doctor slid into the room, keeping close to the wall. He gradually came to a halt and said, "I'm sorry to have to tell you that your

> daughter has just died I am sure that this is a great shock we did all that we could and I need to ask you whether we might have permission to do a postmortem. You don't have to decide this minute but I have been beeped to see someone else and I will send my colleague with the form." Having delivered this breathless statement to the family, the doctor slid back toward the door. As the door closed he was heard to say, "I'm very sorry."[19]

This episode is one of the reasons that specially trained personnel now often request permissions for both autopsies and organ or tissue donations.

The need for an autopsy is not always immediately obvious to the family. Later they may realize that they may never have the answers to important questions, either because they refused to permit an autopsy or because they were never asked. Autopsies, whether done for forensic or non-forensic reasons, may detect (or remove the suspicion of) unsuspected trauma, environmental hazards, or infectious and genetic disorders of importance to surviving family members and contacts.[20]

Survivors usually refuse autopsy permission because they lack information. Common beliefs that cause survivors to refuse autopsy permission include:

- Medical diagnosis is excellent and diagnostic machines almost infallible; an autopsy is unnecessary.
- If the physician could not save the patient, he or she has no business seeking clues after that failure.
- The patient has suffered enough.
- They are worried about objections from other survivors.
- Autopsy is not accepted in their religious or cultural group.
- Body mutilation occurs.
- An autopsy takes a long time and delays final arrangements.
- Autopsy results are not well communicated.
- The decedent had said they did not want an autopsy.
- Religious objections, such as an autopsy will result in an incomplete body, and so life in the hereafter cannot take place.[21, 22]

Each of the first eight points has just enough truth to make it almost believable. Item Nine is a plea for allowing the decedent to retain his or her decision-making influence after death. In cases where survivors may be harmed (psychologically or physically) by not learning the causes of death, it may be inappropriate. Item Ten addresses religious objections. While individuals from several religious traditions may have concerns about autopsies, except in a few instances, religious teachings do not prohibit autopsies. In medical examiners' cases, this objection will often be overridden by legal necessity, although they make every effort to conform to religious restrictions. Generally, college-educated young adults are most likely to approve autopsies on their relatives.

Appropriate information often assuages these concerns.[23] Therefore, those seeking autopsy permission must be able to clearly explain: (1) why they are requesting the procedure, (2) that autopsies are similar to surgery, (3) that autopsies generally don't interfere with funeral arrangements, and (4) that they help advance medicine, reassure families, and help society. Specifically, requesters must be able to answer the questions survivors commonly ask, such as:

- Is an autopsy required? Possible?
- Will I get the results?
- If there is an autopsy, can there be an open casket?
- When can we hold the funeral?

Brief answers to these questions can be found in chapter 27. (For additional information on these topics, see Iserson KV. *Death to Dust, What Happens to Dead Bodies?* Galen Press, Ltd., 1994.)

Somewhat surprisingly, while the general hospital autopsy rate has declined from 50% of all deaths in 1950 to less than 10% today in teaching hospitals (and as low as 5% in community hospitals), there is a much higher rate for pediatric autopsies.[24] Many pediatric medical centers now autopsy over 60% of the children who die there. Experienced physicians ask for autopsies more often and are more successful at getting permissions.[25] In part, especially for children who die suddenly and unexpectedly, autopsies may answer "why" the child died, helping parents to begin their grieving process with less guilt or animosity than they otherwise might have.

References

1. McQuay JE, Schwartz R, Goldblatt PC, et al.: "Death-telling" research project. *Crit Care Nurs Clin North Am.* 1995 Sep;7(3):549-55.
2. Clark RE, LaBeff EE: Death telling. managing the delivery of bad news. *J Health Soc Behav.* 1982 Dec;23(4):366-80.
3. Randall T, Marwick C: Physicians' attitudes and approaches are pivotal in procuring organs for transplantation. *JAMA.* 1991 Mar 13;265(10):1227-8.
4. Morton JB, Leonard DR: Cadaver nephrectomy: an operation on the donor's family. *Br Med J.* 1979 Jan 27;1(6158):239-41.
5. Bartucci MR: Organ donation: a study of the donor family perspective. *J Neurosci Nurs.* 1987 Dec;19(6):305-9.
6. Ahrens WR, Hart RG, Maruyama N: Pediatric death: managing the aftermath in the emergency department. *J Emerg Med.* 1997 Sep-Oct;15(5):601-3.
7. Savaria DT, Swanson MA: Organ and tissue donation: rights and responsibilities. *Crit Care Nurs Clin North Am.* 1995 Sep;7(3):569-75.
8. Walker JA, McGrath PJ, MacDonald NE, et al.: Parental attitudes toward pediatric organ donation: a survey. *CMAJ.* 1990 Jun 15;142(12):1383-7.
9. Bartucci MR: "Organ donation."

10. Morton JB, Leonard DR: "Cadaver nephrectomy."
11. Andresen, Patrick: Personal communication with author, 2 April 1999.
12. Jacobson JA, Francis LP, Battin MP, et al.: Dialogue to action: lessons learned from some family members of deceased patients at an interactive program in seven Utah hospitals. *J Clin Ethics.* 1997 Winter;8(4):359-71.
13. Prutting J: Lack of correlation between antemortem and postmortem diagnoses. *NY State J Med.* 1967 Aug 1;67(15):2081-4.
14. Burton EC, Troxclair DA, Newman WP 3rd: Autopsy diagnoses of malignant neoplasms: how often are clinical diagnoses incorrect? *JAMA.* 1998 Oct 14;280(14):1245-8.
15. Kajiwara JK, Zucoloto S, Manco AR, et al.: Accuracy of clinical diagnoses in a teaching hospital: a review of 997 autopsies. *J Intern Med.* 1993 Aug;234(2):181-7.
16. Katz JL, Gardner R: The intern's dilemma: the request for autopsy consent. *Psychiatry Med.* 1972 Jul;3(3):197-203.
17. Dreher GH, Osborne LW: Talking with relatives about a kinsman's death in hospital. *Med J Aust.* 1980 Dec 13;2(12):653-5.
18. Katz JL, Gardner R: "The intern's dilemma."
19. Speck P: Communication skills. breaking bad news. *Nurs Times.* 1991 Mar 20-26;87(12):24-6.
20. Beckwith JB: The value of the pediatric postmortem examination. *Pediatr Clin North Am.* 1989 Feb;36(1):29-36.
21. Brown HG: Lay perceptions of autopsy. *Arch Pathol Lab Med.* 1984 Jun;108(6):446-8.
22. Sherwood SJ, Start RD: Asking relatives for permission for a post-mortem examination. *Postgrad Med J.* 1995 May;71(835):269-72.
23. *Ibid.*
24. Marwick C: Pathologists request autopsy revival. *JAMA.* 1995 Jun 28;273(24):1889, 1891.
25. VanMarter LJ, Taylor F, Epstein MF: Parental and physician-related determinants of consent for neonatal autopsy. *Am J Dis Child.* 1987 Feb;141(2):149-53.

8: Viewing The Body

Health care providers hold strong views on whether adults and children should view the bodies of deceased individuals. This is especially true for bodies that have suffered acutely disfiguring trauma and for disfigured stillborns. Survivors' potential reactions to the body, especially to a disfigured one, induce anxiety in the medical staff. But many survivors have an overwhelming need to view the body, as Sheila Awoonor-Renner wrote after her 17-year-old son had died in a car crash:

> Permission was finally granted for me to see Timothy on the condition that I "didn't do anything silly." As they watched, I presumed that meant I was not to touch him or disturb anyone . . . Timothy was my child; he had not ceased to be my child. I desperately needed to hold him, to look at him, to see his wounds. These instincts don't die when the child dies. I needed to comfort and cuddle him, to examine and inspect him, to try to understand, and most of all, to hold him. But I had been told "not to do anything silly." So I betrayed my instincts and my son by standing there and "not doing anything silly." If I did, I feared my watchers would rush in, constrain me, and lead me away. . . We are tearful and sympathetic when an animal refuses to leave its offspring when it dies, nuzzling him and willing him to live again. That is exactly what a mother's human instinct tells her to do. If a mother is not able to examine, hold, and nuzzle her child, she is being denied motherhood in its extreme.[1]

Even more telling is the following story from an emergency nurse:

> Little Mike was the worst. While riding his bike on a warm summer evening, he somehow slid under a bus. His body was perfect, with not a mark on it, but the

> bus had crushed his head so severely that it was flattened. A horrified police officer brought the brain matter to the hospital separately. We all agreed that Mike's parents simply couldn't see him—we could hardly look at him ourselves and we were nurses. But John, an emergency department technician and the father of three boys, felt differently. He asked us: if our child had died, was there any situation in which we wouldn't want to see him and we had to say no. So John did what he could for Mike. He used washcloths to fill out Mike's empty, flattened head and he reshaped his skull as best he could. With almost half of his face and the top of his head covered with gauze bandages, Mike once again looked like a nine-year-old boy. Mike's parents sat with him quietly for hours. They held each other and they touched Mike gently, tenderly. They talked about how he loved his bike and how he was riding on a forbidden street. They reminisced about his birth and his toddling antics. At times, they smiled and almost laughed. Their grief was so deep, so moving, we felt awed by it. Once again we were glad that we hadn't sent the parents home without a chance to be with their child and express their grief.[2]

Some notifiers welcome survivors' requests to see the body. They see it as a sign that they have accepted the death and are ready to begin grieving. As one clinician said,

> You know . . . in your mind . . . accepting the fact that this person is dead is a way of finalizing it. And they go in and see the patient lying there and they see that they're not breathing, and they've turned blue. Sometimes, they'll touch the body. They'll put their hand on the chest to see that they're not breathing. If they see this they accept that, you know, "my loved one is gone." Some of them want to see that before they will be able to accept and make plans for the funeral home and things like that.[3]

Families may *need* to view the body, but are often reluctant to ask for "permission" from health care workers.[4] As for bodies disfigured by trauma, most survivors regret not seeing the decedent. If they view the body, they find that their fantasies are often worse than reality, they have the important confirmation that their loved one is dead, and they have an opportunity to "say good-bye." For example, eighteen months after a terrible train accident with many deaths, twenty-two of the thirty-six relatives who had not seen their loved one's body wished that they had done so.[5] Dissuading survivors from viewing a body because it is disfigured may later cause them to question whether it really was their loved one who died. That may make resolution of their grief prolonged, difficult, and perhaps impossible.

Surprisingly, survivors often act very calmly if they are permitted to see the bodies of their loved ones, even if disfigured.

> A woman's son was killed in a car crash. He ran head-on into a telephone pole and his head was split in two. She wanted to go to the medical examiner's office to see him. She was told "no" initially, but she insisted. After more persistence, she was allowed to see his body, but his head was covered. She mourned

> appropriately. She then said that she wanted to see his head. Again, she was told "no" at first, but she insisted. So they removed the towel from his head. She looked just a couple of seconds, then looked away. The mother displayed no traumatic outcry or loss of control.[6]

Even when families initially decline to view the body, they often wish to see it after they have spent more time coming to grips with the death.[7] Those who continually decline, however, should not be coaxed into doing so. In these situations they make comments such as:

- I just want to remember her as she was.
- I'll see her at the funeral.
- If I see him again, I'll start to cry.
- He looked so awful when I saw him; I couldn't bear to look again.

Often, after talking about the decedent for twenty to thirty minutes with the nurse- or chaplain-notifier, they change their minds and wish to see the body.

Most families find that it is important for at least one member to see the body. After their child is killed in a war, for example, one of the biggest regrets many parents have is that they did not get to view the body. Some centers now offer survivors several alternatives. They show them Polaroid pictures of the (cleaned) face of the decedent. They also offer them several opportunities to see the body, even if it is disfigured.

Notifiers and those accompanying families during these viewings should be aware that some survivors really do not want to view the body, but feel a social pressure to do so. This attitude may be reflected in their behavior, to which notifiers should be sensitive. Although survivors can be encouraged to view, touch, and sometimes hold the decedent's body, they should never be forced to do so.

Even when survivors want to view the body and the health care workers are willing, they may face another obstacle. Some zealous police officers now try to forcefully prevent families from seeing the body if the death was due to a potentially criminal activity. That includes victims of homicides, deaths that occurred in the course of a felony, and probable suicides where the circumstances are a little hazy and the police are investigating. Police officers may have a reason to prevent survivors from removing anything from the body (if they died in a trauma center it is unlikely that there is anything remaining on the body that the medical staff did not put there) or touching the body, but this can be easily prevented. The standard I use when faced with this situation is that the hospital is medical "turf" and the medical staff rightfully controls what occurs there. Since survivors are also our "patients" needing help and since part of that help is to let them view the body, we permit that despite any police objections. In cases where they have concerns, police officers can be present in the room during the viewing.

Viewing Procedures

Survivors should be asked if they "wish to view (decedent's name)," rather than "the body" or "(decedent's name)'s body." To them, that person is still socially alive, and may not cease to be a person in their minds for some time—usually at least not until after the funerary ceremonies.

Some hospitals have family members view bodies in smaller rooms where they can spend significant time and will be undisturbed. In many emergency departments, though, families view the body in the resuscitation room. Both methods have their advocates. Private rooms give survivors additional time and privacy, while the resuscitation room setting demonstrates that the medical team made significant resuscitative efforts before declaring death. Each may have its place in differing circumstances.

Survivors should be prepared for what they will see. If the viewing is in the resuscitation room, it should not, except for blood on the floor, be cleaned too much. The sight of resuscitative equipment surrounding the body may comfort some survivors, assuring them that everything possible was done. As one writer said, survivors are not shocked by the equipment—they are shocked by the death.[8] Yet some cleaning of the area is in order, as Dr. Glen Hamilton related:

> [I have] painful memories of more than twenty years ago when my mother and I were allowed to view my grandmother after her death in the hospital. She was in a bed with her eyes open, staring far beyond us. The residual debris of the "code" was still scattered about the room and the sheets were rumpled with what looked to us as some sign of a struggle. Two or three minutes of preparation for our viewing could have made my vivid recall of that scene considerably different than what it is.[9]

In all cases, whether it is in a hospital, a home, or elsewhere, notifiers *must* explain to survivors what the body and the room will look like. This "softens the sight" so survivors can steel themselves for what they will see.[10] Although the body will usually be cleaned as much as possible, the tubes used during the resuscitation attempt will normally remain in place. (Medical examiner and coroner rules usually preclude removing these from the body after sudden, unexpected deaths.) Also, some injuries cannot be hidden. When bodies are badly disfigured, it is best to cover as much of the body as possible before survivors visit by using clean sheets and covering exposed wounds with clean dressings.

Some survivors, especially the parents of children who die, feel that they need to bathe their child's body themselves. Kyle Nash, a death educator, says:

> They see this as an important task, part of their role as parent—their duty, their right, their responsibility—a final act of love and care. Participating in their child's death in this way often aids parents during the grieving process. Being denied this opportunity often causes distress during bereavement. Therefore, I teach that all parents be offered this option.

> In truly horrific (messy or disfiguring) situations, staff can do most of the cleaning and adjusting of the body, but a small amount should be left uncompleted. If parents want to be involved in the cleaning/bathing, they still can. However, should they decline the invitation to participate in this way and want to see their child immediately, they can then either go right in, or wait a few minutes for the staff to finish the job.[11]

Survivors may only want to hold a hand or touch the head. However, with a staff member in attendance, they can make their own decision about how much they wish to view.

Questions that should be addressed before the family views the body are:

- Why is his mouth hanging open?
- Why aren't her eyes closed?
- What is the frothy stuff coming out of his nose and mouth?
- Will those marks go away?
- Why doesn't she look the same?

When families enter the room to view the body, they are often reluctant to touch it. This is part of our culture's abhorrence of death. As one nurse said, "The relative may have lived with the decedent for fifty years but still, within this setting, may not be sure if it is all right to touch the dead person's hand. The person is not theirs any more."[12] The accompanying staff member should make the first move toward the body, touching the hand or head, implicitly giving survivors permission to do likewise. It helps if at least the hands and arms are left exposed so that they can be touched.

One question that may need to be addressed is whether, especially in cases where blood or other body fluids remain on or around the body, survivors should use universal precautions. This may be moot for spouses or other intimate contacts. Many survivors may even be offended by the suggestion—although others may appreciate it.

Survivors may want to leave personal items with the body, such as rings, necklaces, or watches. Or they may wish to leave religious or other sentimental items. To ensure that valuable or irreplaceable items will remain with the body, notifiers should encourage survivors not to leave these items, but rather to give them to the mortician or put them in the casket or the urn later. (The body may be in relatively insecure areas at times.)

Children: Bodies and Viewings

The attitude about perinatal deaths has changed markedly over the last several decades. Where parents were once dissuaded from viewing miscarried fetuses or stillborns with any disfigurement, parental viewing is now a standard part of most obstetric and emergency department practices. While staff may perceive a fetus or stillborn baby as being badly disfigured or macerated, parents may not see that much damage.[13] Their fantasy of any damage may be worse than reality, and their grieving may be aided by holding the child. Some medical centers now hold funerals and burials for miscarried fetuses. (See chapter 27 for more information.)

In prior generations, most deaths occurred at home and children routinely viewed bodies after death. They no longer generally do. While many children who may wish to see the body hold back because of the stress they sense from adults, those who explicitly request to see the body should be allowed to do so. But they should not be coerced into viewing the body if they show any reluctance.

Parents often fear that viewing a body will cause children nightmares, although more often it is not seeing the body and fantasizing about what happened that causes them later distress. Parents can minimize problems by carefully explaining what the child will see: the body, the room, and how other survivors might act. After viewing the body, they can prepare the child for their classmates' inevitable questions by asking, "What will you tell your friends when they ask you about this?"[14] This also gives the child a chance to discuss the experience.

Viewing Photographs

If, rather than viewing the body, survivors prefer to view photographs of the body, that too can be an option. Many emergency departments, neonatal nurseries, and all police departments have photographic capability. What is shown to survivors and how it is done is important.

Parents of Murdered Children, a support group, has developed a viewing procedure that seems to work well, especially if the body has been disfigured (through the injury or decomposition).[15]

1. A trusted support person who is also willing to view the photographs accompanies the person wishing to view the photographs.
2. Each photograph (even if there is only one) is placed either in a separate envelope or in one large envelope with the photographs separated by pieces of paper.
3. The photographs are arranged in order, with the least offensive on top and the most offensive at the bottom.
4. One by one, the support person views a photograph and describes it to the survivor.
5. If the survivor wishes to view the photograph given their support person's reaction to and description of the picture, they can.
6. The session generally ends with the photograph that the survivor does not wish to view.

It is often helpful to give survivors a set of the pictures. These may be Polaroid pictures from the hospital or crime photographs from the medical examiner's office or the police department.

References

1. Awoonor-Renner S: I desperately needed to see my son. *Br Med J.* 1991 Feb 9;302(6772):356, as rewritten in: Lord JH: *Trauma, Death, and Death Notification: A Seminar for Professional Counselors and Victim Advocates.* Washington, DC: Mothers Against Drunk Driving and the U.S. Dept. of Justice for Victims of Crime, 1996, p. 35.
2. Selder F: *Enduring Grief: True Stories of Personal Loss.* Philadelphia: Charles, 1997, p. 28.
3. Clark RE, LaBeff EE: Death telling: managing the delivery of bad news. *J Health Soc Behav.* 1982 Dec;23(4):366-80.
4. Schultz CA: Sudden death crisis: pre hospital and in the emergency department. *J Emerg Nurs.* 1980 May-Jun;6(3):46-50.
5. Singh B, Raphael B: Postdisaster morbidity of the bereaved. a possible role for preventive psychiatry? *J Nerv Ment Dis.* 1981 Apr;169(4):203-12.
6. Lord JH: *Trauma, Death, and Death Notification: A Seminar for Professional Counselors and Victim Advocates.* Washington, DC: Mothers Against Drunk Driving and the U.S. Dept. of Justice for Victims of Crime, 1996, p. 36.
7. Collins S: Sudden death counseling protocol. *Dimens Crit Care Nurs.* 1989 Nov-Dec;8(6):376-82.
8. *Ibid.*
9. Hamilton GC: Sudden death in the ED: telling the living. *Ann Emerg Med.* 1988 Apr;17(4):382.
10. Von Bloch L: Breaking the bad news when sudden death occurs. *Soc Work Health Care.* 1996;23(4):91-7.
11. Nash, K: Personal communication with author, April 1999.
12. Wright B: Sudden death: aspects which incapacitate the carer. *Nursing (Lond).* 1988 Nov;3(31):12-5.
13. Savage W: Perinatal loss and the medical team. Part 1. *Midwife Health Visit Community Nurse.* 1978 Sep;14(9):292-5.
14. Cathcart F: Seeing the body after death. *Br Med J.* 1988 Oct 22;297(6655):997-8.
15. Lord JH: "Trauma, Death, and Death Notification," p. 39.

9: Follow Up With Survivors

Survivors need, and usually want, follow-up contact with those who notify them of sudden, unexpected deaths. After emergency department deaths, for example, 92% of survivors found a follow-up telephone call helpful. Most commonly, they appreciated the caring, warmth, and understanding the callers expressed, and their ability to give them additional information about community resources.[1]

Medical personnel rarely attend their patients' wakes or funerals. Even among specialists with large numbers of dying patients, few attend. For example, less than 15% of cardiologists and 9% of oncologists ever attend their patients' funerals.[2] However, when they do, the result can be meaningful for both the survivors and the clinician, as this physician's story shows.

Attending the Funeral

It was during the busy Christmas season when I turned my car into the parking lot of the funeral home. This patient was my third to die in the past few weeks and tonight was my second wake in three days.

It was not easy to make the stop that evening. The holiday season is a difficult time for me to practice medicine; patients are more lonely and depressed, families are under greater stress, and tonight, the bittersweet juxtaposition of holiday joy and the sorrow of death were stressful. I had second thoughts as I got out of my car, but I continued up the steps to the front door and went inside.

As I walked into the viewing room, I could hear a loud whisper, "Dr. Irvine is here!" Whether because of my imagination or innate shyness, the situation felt like the television commercial for an investment firm in which everyone stops to look and listen. Close family members recognized me immediately and came over to greet me, saying, "It was nice of you to come." Then they introduced me one by one to sons, daughters, grandchildren, neighbors, friends, and clergy. "Tell the priest to wait with the prayer," I overheard a voice say. "This was Dad's doctor."

It wasn't easy for them either. My presence brought tears to many eyes. Perhaps I was a painful reminder of the events of the past week in the intensive care unit. Indeed, it did not take long before they asked their questions: "We really shouldn't have ___. What do you think about that catheter? Did we do the right thing? Do you think he would have had a chance if we had ___?" Most were careful questions, but they were clearly laden with hints of self-doubt, guilt, curiosity, and fear.

This was a rather typical visitation for me. I started attending them a few years ago; why, I can't even remember. In those years my experiences convinced me that my participation was essential, and for many reasons. It gives families an opportunity to talk about their experiences surrounding the death. They have questions about what happened in the last days. Second thoughts need to be discussed when the pressure is off. They want to know about the autopsy. They need reassurance and help with their guilt; no one can do that like the physician.

The doctor's visit does two other things that I have come to believe are very important. Our presence adds credibility to the sense of worth that family members gather about their loved one. (He was important enough that his doctor came to his funeral.) It is a very consoling thought. And secondly, family members regard the physician's attendance as a demonstration of caring for the person who died—that the doctor views his or her patients as more than a business client, consumer, or scientific curiosity with an unusual disease; that the patient had value as another human being.

The visitation is also personally important to me. My feelings need resolution just as the family's feelings do, and society's rituals help me with that as well. Interestingly enough, family members often console me, as when I hear myself say, "I'm sorry we couldn't do better," and they respond, "But you did your best doctor, thank you." They are so appreciative.

I am reluctant, almost embarrassed, to bring this up with colleagues. When I do, they look a bit distant and become quiet. They haven't thought about it much, or so they say. Few with whom I have talked have ever attended patients' funerals, and those that have attended have usually done so under special circumstances. A prominent clergyman friend told me that among literally hundreds of funerals he has conducted, he could "count on one hand" the number of physicians who attended the visitation or funeral. In one recent survey of physician behavior toward death, only 6 percent reported that they routinely contacted the family after the death.[3] Fewer than 10 percent reported that they sent cards or flowers or attended the funeral.

Does our behavior reflect the objective approach toward patients that we learned in our training? Does it remind us of our own eventual death or of our professional failure? Or are we simply insensitive to family needs? I doubt that it is any of these, but rather our failure to appreciate how important physician participation is to the process. Perhaps the lack of education about dying patients in our medical schools and continuing medical-education courses is partly responsible. Somehow, we must come to realize that our responsibility does not end with the pronouncement of death.

Most of all, the funeral helps me bring "living" and "medicine" into proper perspective. In a special way, it gives me perhaps my best understanding of how that person fit into his or her community, and how medical care fit into that life—on the patient's own ground rather than my medical ground—away from the demeaning patient gowns, the sterile professional uniforms, and the white lights of the intensive care unit. The funeral brings that person back home to the community to rest; we are part of that community too.

Reprinted with permission: Irvine P: Attending the Funeral. *N Engl J Med.* 1985 Jun 27;312(26):1704-5.

At the time of notification, many survivors are directed toward religious or specialized support groups such as those for parents of SIDS babies, survivors of victims of violence, or elderly survivors. (See chapter 11 for information on support groups.) Yet they often find that they need additional information after the notifiers leave.

In addition to giving survivors written materials for follow-up contacts (see table 6-1), some centers recontact key survivors within two weeks of the death. Some also have found that routinely sending a condolence card along with a package of literature is useful. This package normally contains information about the grieving process, lists of physical and emotional symptoms the survivor might be experiencing, a list of general or specialized support groups and telephone help-lines, and a list of helpful books available in local libraries.[4]

Many emergency departments have tried to follow up with survivors. But the nurses often are reluctant to participate. In one intensive program of telephone follow-up by emergency department nurses, for example, about half of the nurses were intensely resistant and unwilling to make calls to the patients they initially helped in the emergency department. A "grief committee" now makes these calls.[5] (Few physicians do this type of follow-up, although their doing so would be extremely helpful.)

Survivors can often use this follow-up assistance. Surviving spouses have been the best-studied group and probably exemplify many "primary" survivors. In general, they have difficulties readjusting to a normal life, with those surviving their spouses' sudden unexpected deaths having the most difficulties. Many surviving spouses have significant unresolved (often medically related) questions, even a year after the death.[6] These unresolved questions, however, can also be found among surviving parents, children, and friends. The following story demonstrates the depth of one survivor's strife over unanswered questions.

Mrs. Ryan's 17-year-old son, Billy, had died from a severe head injury after a car crash. He was airlifted to a distant trauma center, which delayed his mother

> getting to his bedside. When the trauma support team volunteer called her three months later, Mrs. Ryan "told her she was having trouble sleeping. . . [S]he was having nightmares in which she heard Billy calling for her as he lay in the ED. Because of the time that had passed between Billy's injury and her arrival at the hospital, Mrs. Ryan feared that Billy had needed her and wondered why she hadn't been with him, why she'd taken so long to get to the hospital. Those fears tormented her throughout the night." The volunteer and the flight nurse who had cared for him "assured her that he'd been unresponsive from initial care to his death . . . [They] were able to assure Mrs. Ryan that he hadn't been aware of her absence and hadn't been in pain. Her nightmares stopped."[7]

Alcohol and drug use is common among surviving spouses, with alcohol use being greatest in the younger survivors and tranquilizers being the most-abused drug. This reaction in younger spouses may occur because they often have experienced fewer crises in their lives, and may not have developed sufficient coping mechanisms to deal with the situation.[8] Yet follow-up contact seems to have a positive impact on all survivors' readjustments.

The exception is when follow-up is done in a crass and unfeeling manner. A letter that a grieving mother received from a Utah hospital typified this. She wrote back:

> When my child died here at ______ Hospital, and I don't know who writes these letters, I got the tackiest letter. Please review your letter! What it basically said was we are sorry your son died here, but we want you to know we have the best technology available. It sounded like an ad.[9]

Two models for hospital bereavement programs can be successfully used. One is from the Oregon Health Sciences University and the other from Hartford (CT) Hospital. To develop their program, the Oregon team appropriately started by getting institutional, survivor, and medical staff support. When they began their program in 1988, they targeted for change seven areas that are still problematic in many hospitals:[10]

1. Physician procedures in reporting the news of death.
2. The family's access to autopsy information.
3. Nursing procedures at the time of death.
4. Staff expressions of concern to survivors.
5. Patient accounts—completing financial obligations.
6. Survivors' needs for ongoing supportive communication from staff.
7. Staff need for ongoing education and support regarding the bereavement process.

They went on to develop a seven-step bereavement program with an estimated non-staff cost of about $5 per patient death.

1. Two sympathy cards: One for hospital staff (housestaff, nurses, chaplains, and social workers) and one for the attending physician. These are pre-addressed by the Admitting Office and sent to the appropriate staff within hours of a patient's

death. The cards are tasteful, non-religious, concise, and supportive. Many different people often write messages on the staff card. The cards are sent only if the staff or physician want them sent.

2. Packet of materials, including supportive letter, community support list, and pamphlets on grief. This packet, with an explanatory cover letter, is mailed to the survivors two weeks after the patient's death. Some of the material is provided by the local funeral industry. Separate packets were designed for infant, child, and adult deaths, since the survivors' needs differ.
3. The nurse who had the most contact with the family generally contacts the survivors by phone (making these calls is voluntary). Calls are made at the intervals below. The nurse uses a color-coded card that identifies the time interval and contains specific questions related to that time period (based on work at the Talbot Hospice Foundation).[11]

   Call 1: within the first two weeks.

   Call 2: at three months.

   Call 3: at six months.

   Call 4: on one-year anniversary.
4. Explanation of autopsy findings.
5. Family conference with medical staff on request or as necessary.
6. Educational programs for physicians and nurses.
7. Ongoing research with health care professionals to modify the program, as required.

Hartford Hospital's Trauma Support After-Care Program exemplifies another well-thought-out, on-going, longitudinal method of assisting survivors whose loved ones had sudden unexpected deaths. At the time of death, personnel explain the program to survivors, provide them with descriptive pamphlets, and complete a short information form to use as a follow-up tool. Survivors are placed into categories for the type of follow-up depending upon the decedent's age and where the survivors live. They receive either regular telephone or mail contacts from trained program members if they live within the state or a referral to a local bereavement support program if they live outside the state.

Initial follow-up is made one month after the death because that is when support from other family, friends, and neighbors often slackens. The support program supplies additional information on the grieving process, helpful literature, referrals to other community resources, access to hospital personnel, and assistance in obtaining autopsy results. There also is an annual gathering of survivors, volunteers, and hospital staff at which survivors have an opportunity to share their experiences and to memorialize their loved ones. Families are discharged from the program after two years.[12]

References

1. Williams M, Frangesch B: Developing strategies to assist sudden-death families: a 10-year perspective. *Death Stud.* 1995 Sep-Oct;19(5): 475-87.
2. Bates DW, Tolle SW, Elliot DL: Subspecialty differences in responding to patient death–comparing cardiologists with oncologists. *West J Med.* 1988 Apr;148(4):471-3.
3. Tolle SW, Elliot DL, Hickam DH: Physician attitudes and practices at the time of patient death. *Arch Intern Med.* 1984 Dec;144(12):2389-91.
4. Collins S: Sudden death counseling protocol. *Dimens Crit Care Nurs.* 1989 Nov-Dec; 8(6):376-82.
5. Williams M, Frangesch B: "Developing strategies."
6. Tolle SW, Bascom PB, Hickam DH, et al.: Communication between physicians and surviving spouses following patient deaths. *J Gen Intern Med.* 1986 Sep-Oct;1(5):309-14.
7. Coolican M, Vassar E, Grogan J: Helping survivors survive. *Nursing.* 1989 Aug;19(8):52-7.
8. Jacobson GF, Strickler M, Morley WE: Generic and individual approaches to crisis intervention. *Am J Public Health Nations Health.* 1968 Feb;58(2):338-43.
9. Jacobson JA, Francis LP, Battin MP, et al.: Dialogue to action: lessons learned from some family members of deceased patients at an interactive program in seven Utah hospitals. *J Clin Ethics.* 1997 Winter;8(4):359-71.
10. Moseley JR, Logan SJ, Tolle SW, et al.: Developing a bereavement program in a university hospital setting. *Oncol Nurs Forum.* 1988 Mar-Apr;15(2):151-5.
11. Guthrie E, Jennings PK, Parrott M, et al.: The Talbot Hospice Foundation bereavement program: a history. *Am J Hosp Care.* 1987 Jan-Feb;4(1):24-7.
12. Coolican MB, Pearce T: After care bereavement program. *Crit Care Nurs Clin North Am.* 1995 Sep;7(3):519-27.

10: Acute Grief Reactions

Survivors are victims. Their reactions separate them from life, from reality, and often from caring about themselves, their future, or those around them. When people learn of the sudden unexpected death of a loved one (*bereavement*), they experience "a sense of being lost and not knowing what to do. Their sense of being suspended from life, inability to concentrate, indifference to immediate needs, disbelief that the decedent is really gone, and the feeling that life can never be worth living again all hinder the survivor's ability to arrange the funeral and to make plans for other ongoing life needs."[1] This is *grief*. Expressing one's grief through behavior, wearing certain clothing, and other conventional signs is *mourning*.

Immediately upon hearing the news, survivors may experience a brief (15-30 minutes) period of acute psychic pain during which little, if any, information can be imparted to them. After that, they begin the grieving process, which provides a moratorium from the routine tasks of life—but they eventually must reintegrate themselves to life.

Not surprisingly, after sudden unexpected deaths the survivors often have more anger than do survivors after other types of deaths. After unexpected deaths, survivors feel they have lost control of a world in which, only a short time before, they had placed their faith and trust. They feel frustrated and helpless, and use anger as a response to the meaninglessness of death.[2]

Grief reactions can take many forms, although few appear immediately. These forms have been divided into ten types:[3]

1. "Normal" grief.
2. Anticipatory grief.
3. Inhibited, delayed, and absent grief.

4. Chronic grief (perpetual mourning).
5. Depression.
6. Psychophysiologic reactions.
7. Development of medical symptoms and illness.
8. Hypochondriasis and exacerbation of pre-existing somatic conditions.
9. Acting-out (psychopathic behavior, drugs, promiscuity).
10. Specific neurotic and psychotic states.

Life stressors simply add intensity to the grieving process. Any ongoing stress, such as from family illnesses, job or financial worries, or interpersonal strife, do not abate for long, if at all, following a sudden death. Often, the death simply increases the intensity of these stressors. Acute deaths also bring additional costs and responsibilities, for example, ambulance or hospital bills, identifying the body, notifying other family and friends, preparing and paying for the funeral, hosting friends and relatives and, in some cases, dealing with the media or the police.

Deaths also bring on role changes for family members. Spouses may become the sole support for themselves and their children. Especially in the elderly, survivors may be alone for the first time in decades, needing to readjust their lives completely yet lacking the primary support system they had come to rely upon. Adjusting to the death may take a long time.

Losing Someone Very Close

A loved one's death is one of life's major stressors. On average, a person suffers a loved one's death once every twelve years.[4] The Social Readjustment Rating Scale, a measure of how likely life stressors are to cause a major illness or depression within one year, rates a spouse's death as the highest stressor, with 100 points. Death of other family members rates 63, and that of a close friend is 37. In contrast, divorce rates only a 73, a jail term rates 63, and being fired from work rates 47.[5] (These, of course, are generalizations. Some couples find that their child's death is their most stressful life experience.) The acute, sudden loss of a loved one can be equated with an emotional amputation. A loved one, because of the affection, the shared memories, and the usual mutual reliance, is almost as much a part of a person as are their arms and legs. When they lose this "part," they feel the same pain, suffering, and sense of loss as do those who lose limbs. Our language even gives expression to this, as in "I would give my right arm if. . . ."

Both widows and widowers usually exhibit marked deterioration in their health, often with the exacerbation of underlying medical conditions. When they heard "'Til death do us part" at their wedding, few actually imagined that death would actually intervene on their union.

At least among widows who experience declining health, a key factor seems to be their unhelpful interactions with people in their social network during the first three months after their spouse's death. For example, trying to push a widow into new activities or new romantic relationships for which she is emotionally unprepared.[6,7] More than 20% of widows less than sixty years old show marked health deterioration, including sleeplessness, general nervousness, excessive tiredness, depression, increased drug use, and a lessened ability to work after their husband's death.[8]

However, survivors' reactions may not actually be what might be anticipated. Many parents grieve more over the loss of a child than they do for their spouse. Some grieve more for their pets; some don't grieve at all. Professor Bob Wrenn warns us that regarding survivors, "You can't tell a book by its cover," and relates the following example from his death-counseling practice:

> A man died suddenly from a massive heart attack. Subsequently, his wife came to me for counseling. Her problem was that she was ecstatic that "this s.o.b. had finally 'corked off'" and she didn't have to go through the anticipated divorce. "What do I do with my friends," she asked, "when they come around trying to console me—and all I really want to do is party?"[9]

An oft-neglected group is the parents of adult children who die. No matter what their age, parents continue to think of their offspring as children, as the following story shows.

> While working on the Wheaton Rescue Squad in the Maryland suburbs of Washington, D.C., we were called for a "baby with difficulty breathing." With only two of us on the ambulance and several flights of stairs to climb carrying our oxygen bottles and other equipment, we tried to be efficient—bringing in only our infant-child airway equipment, which was in a separate box. Unfortunately, the "baby" was a 35-year-old woman, an only child, who had been living at home with her doting mother. The woman, who had a known terminal illness, was already developing *rigor mortis* when we arrived. We sat with the distraught mother until relatives arrived.

Nearly all parents of adult children who die suddenly continue to grieve for years after the event, although they may not demonstrate evidence of depression. Nearly all continue to dwell on thoughts of their deceased children and to feel a sense of profound loneliness. Parents suffering the deepest depression and having the most psychiatric distress include those whose deceased children were experiencing problems at the time of death, mothers whose children had been living at home, and those with fewer prior bereavement experiences.[10] While it may seem logical to use short-term psychiatric crisis intervention for survivors, it does not seem to benefit them.[11]

Individuals who lose loved ones through suicide have the double burdens of loss and shame. Although suicide usually stems from severe depression, society often unjustly stigmatizes the survivors by providing awkward silence rather than support. Since the person who committed suicide is already being "blamed" by society for their act, survivors may direct their anger at doctors, the police, and anyone else involved, rather than toward the deceased individual. They must also "make sense" of what is usually an irrational act—an impossible task. (In a ploy to exploit yet another market, in 1996 Hallmark introduced a sympathy card for those who lost someone to suicide. Since they

Table 10-1: Acute Grief: Actions, Attitudes, and Coping Strategies

Actions/Attitudes Denoting Grief

- Anger (rage; screams; shakes)
- Self-harm (e.g., pounding on wall)
- Anxiety
- Helplessness
- Hopelessness
- Relief/Giddiness
- No reaction
- Shame
- Guilt
- False calmness
- Fear (terror)
- Numb, mechanical responses
- Confusion/Aimless activity

Coping Strategies

- Denial
- Blame (self or others)
- Cry
- Disbelief
- Use drugs or alcohol
- Resolve to "go on living"
- Get on with life
- Acceptance
- Talk with others
- Intellectualization
- Work through pain
- Seek physical exercise
- Adjust to new environment

---

couldn't think of anything else, it uses a "God cliché" to reassure the reader that "our compassionate Creator" has "already welcomed" the loved one home.)

The ways people cope with acute grief vary according to individual and cultural factors (table 10-1). Coping methods can be divided into the way survivors think about a death (coping strategies) and the actions they take. Because the death notifier inevitably triggers strong reactions, even if they aren't immediately evident, it is important to recognize the reactions to grief. The notifier's task is to help as much as the survivors will permit and to not take any of their reactions personally.

Unfinished Business

The most serious complications during the grieving process occur when the decedent and the survivor have intense unfinished personal business. This often surrounds interpersonal conflict—usually just before the death. This sets the stage for an extremely complicated grieving process that the survivor may not be able to mature through. In other words, this person never finds healing, but rather adopts new unhealthy coping skills that compensate for or avoid their pain. Chaplain Pat Andresen describes two such incidents, the first much more common than the second.[12]

> After a mother and son fought, he left home vowing to never return. Soon afterwards, he was in a car crash and suffered a bad head injury. About thirty hours later he was declared dead by brain criteria. All that his mother could think about was that she killed her son—that if she had done things differently he would not have died. She was so overwhelmed by her angry words that she could no longer remember that the angry words had occurred because her son had started abusing alcohol and drugs and had been stealing from their home. Eventually it took three years of intensive therapy [for her] to overcome her anger at herself.
>
> The morning of his death, a farmer and his wife had had a serious fight, yelling unkind words at each other. These were the wife's last words to him. Six months after his death, she continued to make him breakfast every day. Each morning she would set the table for two and cook his favorite eggs, something she rarely cooked when he was alive. At noon, she would clear the table and then set one place for her lunch. During this time, she talked about him as if he was just in another room. She finally had to be institutionalized for her own safety, never getting beyond that point in her grief.

Medication for Acute Grief Reactions

Survivors will often ask for anti-anxiety medication—usually for someone else rather than for themselves. Some people recommend never prescribing any sedative, since they believe that it will delay the onset of grieving. Given that anti-anxiety medications and drugs (alcohol, for example) are readily available to nearly everyone, I use a different approach.

If asked by someone to prescribe this type of medication for another survivor, I usually first ask that survivor if that is what they want. While I do not automatically prescribe anti-anxiety medication for survivors, mild sedation for a key survivor may be necessary. If that seems to be the case, a physician should evaluate that individual. If clinical indications warrant it, such medication should be dispensed for a *very* limited time with appropriate follow-up arranged.

Relationships after a Death

Survivors change after the death of a person who was significant in their life. For better or worse, the issues that affect them are based on what relationship they had to the decedent. The most common feelings are listed in table 10-2.

Table 10-2: Issues that affect Different Relationships after Death [13]

	Relationship of Decedent to Survivor				
	Spouse/Partner	**Child**	**Sibling**	**Parent**	**Friend/Peer**
Survivors Generally	Loss of companion, or connection to life. Sexual changes. Social isolation.	Immortality. Identity crisis. Social isolation. No chance for life.	"Special one died." Love/hate. New roles.	Orphan. Time to grow up. New roles.	Non-family. Isolation.
Men	Long-term health problems. Workaholic. Abandon family. Angry outbursts.	Failure to protect. Weakness. Lack of control. Avoids other children.	If gender of sibling: Male: may take on role. Female: may interfere with male/female relationships.	Loss of role model. Jealous of siblings. Regret over relationship.	Loss of confidante. Loss of generation.
Women	Short-term health problems. Income issues. Feel abandoned.	Break in family circle. Inability to nurture. Failure to protect.	Male: may interfere with male/female relationships. Female: may take on role.	Loss of role model. Jealous of siblings. Regret over relationship.	Loss of peer support. Loss of generation.
Children	N/A	N/A	Death anxiety Ghosts. Forgetting. Survivor guilt	Dependency. Abandonment Betrayal of trust. Anger.	Death anxiety Ghosts. Forgetting.

Table 10-2: continued

	Relationship of Decedent to Survivor				
	Spouse/Partner	**Child**	**Sibling**	**Parent**	**Friend/Peer**
Adolescent	Depression or despair. No one understands. Immortalize loved one. Suicide. Intellectualization. Sublimation. Risk-taking behaviors.	N/A	Death preoccupation. Suicide. Substance abuse. Jealousy/competition with decedent. Anger. Risk-taking behaviors	Instability. Low self-esteem. Judgmental. Anger. Move to adulthood. Risk-taking behaviors.	Death preoccupation Isolation. Sense of abandonment.
Young Adult	Psychological symptoms. Death anxiety. Compulsive self-reliance.	Loss of hope. Loss of future. Shattered dreams.	Breaking of alliance. Survivor guilt.	Loss of friendship. Loss of past. No one to turn to.	Similar to spouse or sibling.
Middle Age	Sleep disorders. Abandonment Overwhelmed by new role. Amputation.	Loss of family Acquisition of grandchildren. No chance of grandchildren.	Death anxiety. Loss of generation.	The aged orphan.	Similar to spouse or sibling.
Elderly	Physical symptoms. Loss of hope: Often die soon afterwards. Loss of connection with life	Similar to above.	Similar to spouse.	Mixed relief. The aged orphan.	Similar to spouse or sibling.

Crisis Characteristics

After sudden unexpected deaths, survivors could generally be said to be in "crisis." A crisis has been described as "the unpleasant psychological and social feelings/ sensations, which result from the onset of a perceived insurmountable stressful life event, disrupting stability, and accompanied by an inability to adjust or cope."[14] This has also been termed a "crisis syndrome." The characteristics of this constellation of symptoms are that the:[15]

- Stressful event presents a problem or perceived threat that is seen as insoluble in the immediate future.
- Situation taxes the individual's emotional resources, since it is beyond his or her traditional problem-solving methods.
- Person's marked behavioral changes make him or her less efficient than usual, diminishing prior levels of functioning.
- Person feels helpless, ineffective, anxious, fearful, guilty, numb, overwhelmed, and defensive.
- Individual sees the event as a threat to his or her life goals.
- Person feels a generalized physical tension, symptomatic of anxiety.
- Situation awakens unresolved problems from the near and distant past.

Grief increases in proportion to our closeness to the decedent—how important he or she was to us in our daily life, thoughts, and actions. It is the price we pay for loving or feeling close to others. In some instances, such as when a famous individual suddenly dies, many people who never even met the person will grieve. Yet they grieve because that individual was an important element in their life. Such was the case, for example with John F. and Robert Kennedy, John Lennon, Martin Luther King, and Princess Diana.

Patterns of Grief

Following the tragic Coconut Grove nightclub fire, Erich Lindemann did groundbreaking work by analyzing hundreds of survivors' grief experiences. He found that these survivors demonstrated sensations of physical distress occurring in waves lasting from twenty minutes to an hour at a time, often precipitated by visits or by mentioning the deceased person's name.[16] The sensations almost universally included five elements:

1. Bodily Distress

- A feeling of throat tightness and choking with shortness of breath.
- An intense feeling of distress, described as tension or mental pain.
- A marked tendency to have sighing respirations. Hyperventilation may occur.
- Exhaustion. A feeling that they lack strength and are profoundly exhausted to the point of difficulty climbing stairs, lifting objects, or walking normal distances.

- An empty feeling in the abdomen and an inability to eat or enjoy food, and sometimes diarrhea.
- Headaches.
- Insomnia.

2. *Preoccupation with the Deceased Person's Image*

- A slight sense of unreality, a feeling of increased emotional distance from other people (sometimes they appear shadowy or small), and an intense preoccupation with the image of the decedent.

3. *Guilt*

- Self-blame. Marked guilt feelings, with a search of the time just prior to death for evidence that they failed the deceased person in some way. They usually accuse themselves of negligence and exaggerate minor omissions.

4. *Hostile Reactions*

- Lack of warm relationships with others. They respond with irritability and anger, and a desire not to be bothered during a time when friends and relatives are making a special effort to relate.

5. *Loss of Normal Patterns of Conduct*

- Restlessness, an inability to sit still, aimless movement, and a continual search for something to do. They have pressured speech, especially when speaking of the deceased person.
- Inability to concentrate.
- Depression.

Lindemann found that the bereaved often learn to avoid these episodes by shunning contact with others and deliberately refusing to think of the deceased person. Yet this behavior only prolongs the grieving process.

Complicated Grief: Psychosis, Guilt, and Hostility

Emotions and reactions that can psychologically or physically harm the survivor or others can complicate grief. These complex reactions can be divided into three reactions: (1) altering the way survivors view and react to the world, (2) internalizing self-destructive ideas, and (3) externalizing self-destructive behavior.

Psychoses

Grief reactions are, in many ways, similar to the combat-induced syndrome sometimes termed "shell shock," "battle shock," "war neurosis," or "combat exhaustion," but now usually referred to as Post Traumatic Stress Disorder (PTSD). Many of the symptoms (see table 10-3) closely parallel reactions seen in survivors after a loved one has died suddenly and unexpectedly. As might be expected, symptoms of acute combat reactions are most common soon after the death; chronic reactions occur in the subsequent weeks, months, and years.

Unusual reactions after a sudden death can suggest the development of pathological grief, but may also be the result of lack of sleep, acute agitation, anxiety, and drug or alcohol use. This is amply demonstrated in the following story from Fran Kunz, a long-time member of both the Southern Arizona Rescue Association and the Pima County (Ariz.) Search and Recovery Divers.[17]

> A body recovery that I will remember forever was that of a young man at Peña Blanca Lake near Nogales, Ariz. He had been on a high-school outing. This boy and a number of others ran down to a well-known rock outcropping and jumped into the water. The student never surfaced. We were called out and quickly located his body. The boy's father was notified and, after initially going to the wrong lake, arrived at the boat ramp where we were standing with the body. He appeared intoxicated. Once he saw his son, he could not contain his sorrow. Upset and crying, he told us he was going to take his boy home so he could spend one last night with his "mama." Eventually the police and victim witness personnel convinced him that that was not the right thing to do.

It is important to understand that grief may recur throughout an individual's life when something stimulates key memories. This is a normal reaction. It only becomes pathological if these memories and the resultant mourning behavior are frequent and dominate the survivor's life.

Pathological grief may take the form of obsessive-compulsive behavior, anxiety, hysteria, manic-depression, or psychosis. One example of how severe pathological grief can become after a sudden death is described in the case history below.

> A 30-year-old man had just recovered from a serious illness and his six-months-pregnant wife was jubilantly planning a party to celebrate it [when] the man suddenly dropped dead. The [wife] was acutely shocked. She screamed and cried and then withdrew and denied the occurrence. She was heavily sedated . . . [Although] the reaction of apathy and denial continued, it was insisted that she attend the funeral where she wept bitterly. During the mourning period which followed, she remained in bed, refused religious ministry or any other attempt at solace but was not averse to being seen by [a psychiatrist] daily. She was withdrawn from her children, but was able after a few weeks to be up and about. She abjured cosmetics and ate poorly.
>
> Three months after her husband's death, she gave birth to a daughter [and moved in with her parents. After she was "abandoned" again when her relatives took a vacation], she again stopped eating—with suicidal intent, and became more emaciated. She was then admitted to the psychiatric hospital for intensive treatments.[18]

Table 10-3: Signs and Symptoms of Psychological Reactions to Combat

Acute Combat Reaction

- Reluctance to leave a secure setting.
- Difficulty comprehending and following instructions.
- Unintentional body movements.
- Life-threatening behavior.
- Overwhelming fear.
- Hyperactivity, agitation, rapid heart rate.
- Psychosomatic paralysis, seizures.

Chronic Combat Reaction

- Loss of sense of humor.
- Psychomotor retardation.
- Excessive complaints.
- Sleep disturbance, weight loss, constipation.
- Excessive alcohol or drug use.
- Paranoia.
- 2000-yard stare.
- Lowered frustration tolerance.

Adapted from: Rahe RH: Acute versus chronic psychological reactions to combat. *Mil Med.* 1988 Jul;153(7):365-72.

In their grief, relatives feel a great deal of guilt. They play the "if only . . ." game. It's a sophisticated form of torture used by mourners to castigate themselves. This practice should be actively discouraged, since such self-recrimination serves no purpose and is self-destructive. Some "if only . . ." statements and the variations I have heard include:

- If I hadn't bought him that car (gun, snowmobile, dirt bike, horse) he would still be alive.
- Why did I let him eat that steak for dinner? (Her husband suffered a fatal heart attack.)
- I should have come home sooner and found him.
- Why did I let him go to the dance? (Son killed in a car crash on his way home.)
- I should have made her go to the doctor when she first complained of a headache. (Wife died of a stroke soon after first having symptoms.)
- If I had been there I could have saved his life. (From medically trained parents of a son with inevitably lethal injuries.)

- If I hadn't agreed to go on vacation this weekend, she would still be alive. (Daughter drowned in a hotel swimming pool.)

Hostility

Many notifiers fear that survivors will become hostile. This rarely occurs, but when it does, it only reinforces any (normally) unfounded guilt the notifiers have about whether they could have done more to save the life. Survivors' hostility is often a way for them to demonstrate to others their guilt and fear. (See also "Dealing with Anger" in chapter 2.) Occasionally, younger men will pound on a wall or, without thinking, on a glass door, leading them into the role of patient—to repair the resulting fractures or lacerations. On occasion, entire families strike out physically in their grief.

> A nurse was aghast when a whole family, the mother and two daughters, became hysterical as she told them of their father's death. They had walked into her ward and, as she came toward them, had said, "He's dead, isn't he? He's dead. Why didn't you do more?" The three of them began to weep and the two daughters struck out at anything within reach, much to the consternation of the patients and staff in the ward. "What could I have done?" asked the nurse. She could have done very little . . . The family needed to blame someone, probably anyone, possibly because of their own desperate deep emotional need.[19]

Notifiers should be particularly wary in the situations below. It is usually a good idea to seek additional assistance in such instances.

- Suicide threats. Following a sudden unexpected death, survivors may not simply threaten suicide, but may actually kill themselves.
- Extreme guilt. If a survivor feels that he or she greatly contributed to the death, such as after a suicide, they may themselves be a suicide risk.
- Survivor contribution to death. Most common after motor vehicle crashes where a friend or family member dies, Survivors may feel enough guilt to need psychiatric intervention—often quite soon after the event.
- Psychotic symptoms. Some survivors, often because of underlying problems, exhibit hallucinations, delusions, or uncontrolled behavior. They need acute psychiatric intervention.
- Gang-related deaths. Threats may be directed at survivors or medical personnel. Police assistance is mandatory.
- Elderly surviving spouse. After a long marriage and decades of a symbiotic relationship, surviving spouses are at high risk for serious illness and death. Significant supportive services are needed.

Aspects of Grief

There is a difference between grief and mourning. Grief is the emotional reaction to the loss, while mourning is the process of withdrawing the emotional capital that has been invested over a prolonged period. Grief is the shorter process, gradually merging into the mourning stage, which may take years to resolve—and in some cases, lasts a lifetime. These different aspects of grieving (table 10-4) can take varying amounts of time to develop and occur in varying order (if at all), depending on people's psychological makeup, their preparation for the death, and their prior experiences with death and dying. In addition, the grief reaction may be complicated by many factors, such as the loss of the family's main provider and a lack of outside support for the family. Table 10-5 lists additional factors that complicate grief reactions.

How long does the "normal" grieving process last? It's been suggested that this question is akin to the question, "How high is up?"[20] It depends upon one's vantage point. Specifically, it depends on one's cultural, religious, and community expectations, and on one's personality.

Denial, an element of what is often an early grief phase, may play a large part during the notification process. Survivors may use it to initially cope with overwhelming catastrophes—when a person is abruptly confronted with the prospect of a perilous or markedly altered future. In the short term, it is not only a feasible coping mechanism, but also prevents overwhelming despair and is often necessary for survival. Denial may also reappear later, interspersed with the other grief phases. Those most likely to use denial for long periods are people who are "lifelong deniers, chronic optimists who euphemize existence, or chronic complainers who blame misfortune upon the malevolence or indifference of others." [21]

More recent research suggests that we may need to rethink the paradigms often used to define time-limited grief stages and bereavement recovery. A three-year study of individuals who lost friends and family members during the 1980 Mount Saint Helen's volcano explosion demonstrated that recovery is a lengthy and dynamic process influenced by numerous events, including personal and social factors. The most significant of these factors was how close the decedent was to the bereaved individual. The closer the decedent was, the less chance of recovery from grief, even after three years![22]

Not only survivors, but also notifiers, may find comfort in denial, and many professionals use it to disown any relationship to the events they must describe or to those they notify.

Helping Survivors Deal with their Grief

Helping grieving survivors cope with their grief primarily involves encouraging them to maintain social interactions and as healthy a lifestyle as possible. The four goals for grief recovery are:

1. Believing that the death really occurred.
2. Willingness to experience the pain of loss.
3. Adjusting to the environment and activities associated with the loved one.
4. Saying good-bye to the relationship that was and can never be again.

Table 10-4: Aspects of Grief *

	Lindemann[23]	Caplan[24]	Brown[25]
Phase I	**Shock & Disbelief**	**Impact**	**Shock**
	Distress, guilt, denial, failure, self-accusing	Stress, confusion, denial, bewilderment, coping	Numbness, sighing, crying, throat tightness, abdominal emptiness, sense of unreality, denial, disbelief
Phase II	**Developing Awareness**	**Recoil**	**Preoccupation with the Decedent**
	Disorganization, despair, helplessness, identification	Disorganization, incompetence, fatigue, shame, anger	Anger, sadness, insomnia, anorexia, weakness, fatigue, guilt, dreams, thoughts of the dead, anhedonia, introversion
Phase III	**Resolving the Loss**	**Adjustment & Adaptation**	**Resolution**
	Reorganization, object relationships discovered, fond memories	Problems reduced or removed, acceptance	Can think about the past with pleasure, regaining interest in activities, forming new relationships

* We now know that survivors may experience these grief phases in different orders, simultaneously, or not at all.

To accomplish these goals, New Hampshire's Office of Victim/Witness Assistance offers eight suggestions to survivors:[26]

1. Express their feelings. When survivors are feeling grief they need to cry, to get angry, to share their guilty and unacceptable feelings with someone they trust. The important thing is to seek and find the outlet that helps them. Feelings are not right or wrong. They simply are. Their feelings are their feelings with no "should" attached.
2. Accept help from those who offer it. Understanding and support can make difficult moments easier.
3. Ask for help when they need it. Relatives and friends want to help, but often don't know quite what to do until survivors make their needs known to them. Professional help is also available.

Table 10-5: Factors That May Complicate the Grief Reaction

- Loss of the person (people) who provided emotional and actual support and companionship.
- Loss of financial support.
- Loss of home or housing.
- Children or adolescents to be cared for.
- Elderly, handicapped, or sick dependent family members.
- Reluctance to acknowledge the death.
- Conflict with decedent just prior to death.
- Marital or family discord.
- Difficulty in dealing with previous losses.
- Lack of spiritual support.
- Lack of community support.
- History of mental illness.

Adapted from: Yates DW, Ellison G, McGuiness S: Care of the suddenly bereaved. *Br Med J.* 1990 Jul 7;301(6742):29-31.

---

4. Keep social contacts.
5. Be kind and patient with themselves. Some days will be more difficult than others will.
6. Get plenty of rest, eat right, and exercise.
7. Seek support from their support groups or victim advocates.
8. Be conscious of the increased grief responses associated with holidays, birthdays, death anniversaries, etc.

Although prayer seems only to help those whose faith endures through crises, the ideas in this invocation may be useful when speaking with survivors.

O God, help me to live with my grief!
Death has taken my beloved, and I feel that I cannot go on.
My faith is shaken; my mind keeps asking: Why?
Why does joy end in sorrow?
Why does love exact its price in tears? Why?

O God, help me to live with my grief!
Help me to accept the mystery of life.

Help me to see that even if my questions were answered,
Even if I did know why, the pain would be no less,
The loneliness would remain bitter beyond words.
Still my heart would ache.

O God, help me to live with my grief!
Help me to endure this night of anguish.
Help me to walk through the darkness with faith in tomorrow.
Give me comfort; give me courage; turn me to deeds that bless the living.
O God, help me to live with my grief![27] (Used with permission.)

References

1. Silverman PR: Services to the widowed: first steps in a program of preventive intervention. *Comm Mental Health J.* 1967;3:38-44.
2. Sanders CM: Effects of sudden vs. chronic illness death on bereavement outcome. *Omega.* 1982;13(3):227-41.
3. Peretz D: Reaction to loss. In: Schoenberg B, et al., eds.: *Loss and Grief: Psychological Management in Medical Practice.* New York: Columbia Univ. Press, 1970, pp. 20-35.
4. Haglund WD, Reay DT, Fligner CL: Death notification. *Am J Forensic Med Pathol.* 1990 Dec;11(4):342-7.
5. Holmes TH, Rahe RH: The social readjustment rating scale. *J Psychosom Res.* 1967 Aug;11(2):213-8.
6. Maddison D: The relevance of conjugal bereavement for preventive psychiatry. *Br J Med Psychol.* 1968 Sep;41(3):223-33.
7. Epstein G, Weitz L, Roback H, et al.: Research on bereavement: a selective and critical review. *Compr Psychiatry.* 1975 Nov-Dec;16(6):537-46.
8. Raphael B: Preventive intervention with the recently bereaved. *Arch Gen Psychiatry.* 1977 Dec;34(12):1450-4.
9. Wrenn, R: Personal communication with author, March 1999.
10. Shanfield SB, Swain BJ: Death of adult children in traffic accidents. *J Nerv Ment Dis.* 1984 Sep;172(9):533-8.
11. Williams WV, Lee J, Polak PR: Crisis intervention: effects of crisis intervention on family survivors of sudden death situations. *Community Ment Health J.* 1976 Summer;12(2):128-36.
12. Andresen, P: Personal communication with author, April 1999.
13. National Organization for Victim Assistance: Death and dying. In: *Community Crisis Response Team Training Manual,* 2nd ed. Washington, DC: NOVA, 1997, pp. 4.30-31.
14. Byers BD: Uses of clinical sociology in crisis intervention practice. *Clin Sociol Rev.* 1987;5:102-18.

15. Eastham K, Coates D, Allodi F: The concept of crisis. *Can Psychiatr Assoc J.* 1970 Oct;15(5):463-72.
16. Lindemann E: Symptomatology and management of acute grief. *Am J Psychiatry.* 1944;101:141-8.
17. Kunz FD: Personal communication with author, December 1998.
18. Lehrman SR: Reactions to untimely death. *Psychiat Quart.* 1956;30:564-78.
19. Waters V: First impressions of grief . . . nurse's attitude has a profound effect on bereaved relatives. *Nurs Times.* 1987 Feb 4-10: 83(5):46-7.
20. Weisman AD: Coping with untimely death. *Psychiatry.* 1973 Nov;36(4):366-78.
21. Weisman AD: On the value of denying death. *Pastoral Psychol.* 1972;23:24-32.
22. Murphy SA: Mental distress and recovery in a high-risk bereavement sample three years after untimely death. *Nurs Res.* 1988 Jan-Feb;37(1):30-5.
23. Lindemann E: "Symptomatology and management of acute grief."
24. Caplan (1964): as cited in Hendricks JE: Death notification: the theory and practice of informing the survivors. *J Police Sci Admin.* 1984;12:(1)109-16.
25. Brown JT, Stoudemire GA: Normal and pathological grief. *JAMA.* 1983 Jul 15;250(3):378-82.
26. Modified from: New Hampshire Office of Victim/Witness Assistance: *Coping skills.*
27. Stern C, ed.: After a tragic loss. In: *Gates of Prayer: The New Union Prayerbook: Weekdays, Sabbaths, and Festivals, Services, and Prayers for Synagogue and Home.* New York: Central Conference of American Rabbis, 1975, p. 624.

11: Support Groups

Support groups help survivors share experiences and access other resources. They also provide survivors with a method of getting their lives "back together." Often it is the ability to find that one is not alone in one's grief that helps a person transition into continuing with his or her life.

Survivors want . . .

to be able to retell their story repeatedly.

to have all their feelings accepted and believed.

to be with others who have been through the same experiences.

Survivors do not want . . .

to be prematurely referred to support groups. They want those they select to listen. They do appreciate having the information, so that if they decide to go, they know how to contact them.

to be encouraged to take medication for anxiety.

to be told "not to think about it."[1]

Many, but not all, survivors benefit from connecting with support groups after sudden unexpected deaths. Survivors should be counseled that they should not make a decision about whether to continue with the group until after they have attended several meetings. The group dynamics and social norms of support groups may be different than other discussion groups adults typically attend. Some groups may "fit" an individual, while others do not. Nearly all groups have some aspects that prove unhelpful for some people. Groups may even drift into periods of diminished usefulness, especially when members begin simply exchanging non-helpful clichés with one another. All support groups, however, offer a safe haven for expressing grief and act as a source of tools to aid survivors in their own recovery.

Even if they don't wish to attend (or communicate on-line with) a support group immediately after the death, survivors may find one useful if they (or if others recognize that they):

- Begin to feel isolated.
- Are "coming apart."
- Begin having symptoms such as persistent crying, continued difficulty sleeping, repeated angry outbursts, abusing alcohol or drugs, or abstaining from social situations or usually pleasant activities.
- Generally cannot face life's daily tasks.
- Would like to talk to others about their experience.

Listed below are some organizations with support groups for survivors throughout the United States and, in some cases, other countries. This should provide a good starting point for learning about appropriate local meetings. Other resources can be provided by local religious, family service, mental health, and victim witness agencies. Community crisis help lines can also provide the names of local support groups. If all that fails, check the mental health section in the telephone directory's yellow pages.

National Support Group Organizations

Air Crash Support Network

1594 York Ave., Box 22
New York, NY 19928
http://www.aircrashsupport.com/

Provides links to incident-specific support groups for the families of air crash victims, and to useful government agencies. Match survivors with others with similar experiences.

American Foundation for Suicide Prevention

120 Wall Street, 22nd Floor
New York, NY 10005
Tel. (212) 363-3500 or (888) 333-AFSP (toll-free) Fax (212) 363-6237
http://www.afsp.org

Provides support to survivors after a loved one's suicide.

American Self-Help Clearinghouse

Northwest Covenant Medical Center
Denville, NJ 07834-2995
Tel. (201) 625-9565 Fax (201) 625-8848
E-mail: asch@buttercup.cybernex.net
http://www.cmhc.com/selfhelp/

Provides worldwide information on local self-help group clearinghouses that have information on starting groups and keep updated information on hundreds of local self-help support groups that are not affiliated with national organizations.

The Compassionate Friends

National Office
PO Box 3696
Oakbrook, IL 60522-3696.
Tel. (708) 990-0010 Fax (708) 990-0246
http://www.compassionatefriend.org

Founded in 1969, this non-sectarian and multicultural support group has over 600 chapters in United States and publishes a quarterly newsletter. They assist parents and siblings after children's deaths, miscarriages, and stillbirths. They also provide information about bereaved parents and siblings to employers, co-workers, and professionals.

Concerns Of Police Survivors, Inc. (COPS)

COPS National Office
PO Box 3199
Camdenton, MO 65020
Tel. (573) 346-4911 Fax (573) 346-1414

COPS directly supports survivors of law enforcement officers killed in the line of duty and assists law enforcement agencies in interacting with and supporting survivors. They contact each of over 7,300 surviving families at least six times a year. Special programs are offered for surviving parents and for their children, including education, counseling, and volunteer support during trials and parole hearings.

Griefnet

Rivendell Resources
PO Box 3272
Ann Arbor, MI 48106-3272
Email: rivendel@falcon.ic.net *or* griefnet@griefnet.org
http://rivendell.org *or* http://www.griefnet.org

The web site contains an extensive list of support groups for different losses. Includes groups for those who have lost: a spouse or significant other; children; a twin or multiple-birth child during gestation or subsequently; neonates; only children; children through accidents, suicide, SIDS deaths, or substance abuse; grandchildren; a sibling; adult parents; and someone through violence or AIDS. It has a kids-to-kids support group. Request an optional donation of $5/mo. for each support group joined.

In Loving Memory

1416 Green Run Lake
Reston, VA 22090
Tel. (703) 435-0608

Helps parents cope with the death of their only child or all their children by providing information on relevant bereavement newsletters and support groups.

The International THEOS Foundation (THEOS)
322 Boulevard of the Allies, Suite 105
Pittsburgh, PA 15222-1919
Tel. (412) 471-7779 Fax (412) 471-7782

With a system of over 120 U.S. chapters and over 70 chapters outside the United States, they help recently widowed men and women work through their immediate grief and cope with day-to-day practical concerns.

Invincible Summer
http://www.drizzle.com/~hall/invsum/

This web site contains practical information for those who have lost their only child or all their children, and provides access to their scheduled chat room.

M.A.D.D. (Mothers Against Drunk Driving)
511 E. John Carpenter Freeway, Suite 700
Irving, TX 75062-8187
Tel. (214) 744-6233 or (214) 869-2206
Victim Hotline: (800) GET-MADD

With over 600 local chapters, it offers support to family and friends of drunk driving victims. It also helps develop local support groups.

National Donor Family Council
30 E. 33rd Street
New York, NY 10016
Tel. (800) 622-9010 (toll-free) Fax (212) 779-0068
http://www. Kidney.org/donor/

With 52 affiliated groups, it provides support for families who donated the organs or tissues of a loved one who died.

National Sudden Infant Death Syndrome Foundation
Metro Plaza, Suite 103
8200 Professional Place
Landover, MD 20785
Tel. (301) 459-3388 or (800) 221-SIDS (toll-free)

With over 70 chapters in the United States, it supports parents after SIDS deaths.

Parents of Murdered Children (POMC)

100 East 8th Street, B-41
Cincinnati, OH 45202
Tel. (513) 721-5683

Interdenominational, POMC provides ongoing emotional support through self-help groups for parents and other survivors whose children have been murdered. Fifty local chapters. Provides information about the grief process and the criminal justice system as it pertains to survivors of a homicide victim.

Pregnancy and Infant Loss Center

1421 East Wayzata Boulevard, Suite #30
Wayzata, MN 55391
Tel. (612) 473-9372 Fax (612) 473-8978

Provides information to individuals and families who have experienced the death of their baby. Offers connection to others with a similar loss, and makes referrals to support groups and counselors.

Rainbows

1111 Tower Road
Shaumburg, IL 60173-4305
Tel. (800) 266-3206 (toll-free) Fax (847) 310-0120

Provides curricula and training for establishing peer support groups for children, adolescents, and adults who are grieving a death.

Ray of Hope, Inc.

P.O. Box 2323
Iowa City, Iowa 52244
Tel. (319) 337-9890

A national self-help organization for coping with suicide, loss, and grief. It organizes suicide postvention programs and support groups for survivors after a suicide.

The Sudden Infant Death Syndrome Alliance (SIDS Alliance)

1314 Bedford Avenue, Suite 210
Baltimore, MD 21208
Tel. (410) 653-8826 or (800) 221-SIDS (toll-free) Fax (410) 659-8709

A non-profit national voluntary health organization. Local affiliated chapters offer support groups, one-on-one contact and/or educational guidance.

S.O.S. (Survivors of Suicide)

http://www.thewebpager.com/sos/

This on-line site provides survivors of a loved one's suicide with an extensive state-by-state listing of support groups.

SHARE

National SHARE Office
St. Joseph Health Center
300 First Capitol Drive
St. Charles, MO 63301-2893
Tel. (800) 821-6819 (toll-free) Fax (314) 947-7486
http://www.NationalSHAREOffice.com

Provides support for parents and siblings after miscarriages, stillbirths, or newborn death. Over 200 chapters worldwide. Offers parents and caregivers a state-by-state printout of perinatal bereavement support groups and resources.

Society of Military Widows (SMW)

5535 Hempstead Way
Springfield, VA 22151
Tel. (703) 750-1342, x3007 Fax (703) 354-4380

Affiliated with the National Association for Uniformed Services (NAUS). State chapters provide assistance to women whose husbands died on active duty military service or during retirement from the Armed Forces.

TAPS (Tragedy Assistance Program for Survivors, Inc.)

2001 S Street, NW, Suite 300
Washington, DC 20009
Tel. (800) 959-TAPS (toll-free) Fax (907) 274-8277
E-mail: tapsak@aol.com

Provides peer support through a national network of military survivors (parents, children, spouses, and friends) to those affected by an in-line-of-military-duty death. Operates national toll-free crisis/information line. Provides caseworkers to support families in tracking information/benefits after the death of a military service person. All services are provided free to military survivors.

Twinless Twins Support Group International

11220 St. Joe Road
Fort Wayne, IN 46835-9737
Tel. (219) 627-5414 Fax (219)-627-5414

Supports parents and siblings who have experienced the death of a twin (or other multiple birth children) via education and publications.

Unite, Inc.

7600 Central Avenue
Philadelphia, PA 19111-2499
Tel. (215) 728-3777

Provides grief support following the death of a baby, including miscarriage, ectopic pregnancy, stillbirth, and infant death. Local chapters are predominantly in Pennsylvania and New Jersey.

Widowed Persons Service

c/o American Association of Retired Persons
601 E Street, NW
Washington, DC 20049
Tel. (202) 434-2260 Fax (202) 434-6474
E-mail: astudner@aarp.org

Provides assistance for widows and widowers of all ages, including individual peer support and information on starting support groups

Reference

1. Adapted from: Lord JH: *Trauma, Death, and Death Notification: A Seminar for Professional Counselors and Victim Advocates*. Washington, DC: Mothers Against Drunk Driving & the U.S. Dept. of Justice for Victims of Crime, 1996, p. 20.

SECTION 2: The Survivors

This, as I see it, is the capital fact about the relationship between living and dying. There are two parties to the suffering that death inflicts; and in the apportionment of this suffering, the survivor takes the brunt.

Toynbee A. *Man's concern with death.*

12: Telling Parents

Death among otherwise healthy children is now so rare in much of the population that, when it occurs, it comes as an overwhelming shock to parents. Unfortunately, sudden deaths in childhood are on the increase. In the United States, for example, each year about 8,000 children under the age of 15 die from homicide, suicide, and unintentional injuries. Many thousands more die between the ages of 15 and 21. For example, we know that nearly 26,000 Americans between the ages of 15 and 24 die annually from unintentional injuries, homicide, and suicide.[1] Of those children aged 5 to 17 years old who die, more than half succumb to sudden violent ends (41% die from accidents).[2] Each year, more than 18,000 infants under the age of 1 year die from prematurity, SIDS, obstetric complications, or infections.[3]

Sudden, unexpected deaths of children are possibly the most painful and poignant for everyone involved. Losing a child seems "generationally wrong." That is, it is a deviation from nature's plan for children to die before their parents—an "untimely" death. (Before the mid-twentieth century, it was common, at least for infants and young children. Parents were prepared through an almost constant expectation of their children's deaths. In some parts of the world, it is still the norm.) A child's death permanently alters and often destroys families. Family members normally help each other repair damage from devastating events. After a child's death, however, this system often fails, leading to extreme isolation and the inability to cope.

The death of children who have developed their own personalities evokes a special kind of tenderness, and damages our belief in a future with fulfilled potential. Their deaths make us feel as if we have failed to protect those who are blameless, innocent, and vulnerable.[4] These deaths are seen not only as unnatural, but also unfair—to the child, to survivors, and to the community they would have joined as adults.

Over the past few decades, notifiers increasingly have had to deliver tragic news to separated or divorced parents. After a child's sudden unexpected death, it is usually best to deliver the news to the parents together if they are both present. In cases where parents, for whatever reason, are not able to be physically present shortly after a child's death, it is best to tell the parent who has arrived first. If the other parent arrives at the hospital (or home) later, it may be better for medical personnel (or notifiers at the home), rather than the other parent, to deliver the news. Notification from official notifiers lends credence to the information, can be more complete than when coming from the other grieving parent, and avoids distorting the message.

It is often left to residents, the most inexperienced physicians, to notify parents that their child has died. Yet most emergency medicine and pediatric residency (postgraduate specialty training) programs spend little time on education in this area.[5,6] Practitioners, though, consider this one of their most difficult and stressful professional activities. As one physician said, justifying his emotionalism after a child's death:

> You always get to feel the loss of the kid—you get subjectively involved. It used to be embarrassing to shed a few tears and get involved but I don't feel I get unprofessional by getting involved, and I don't think the family feels it is unprofessional and thinks of me as an old softy. I think it is a plus for me.[7]

Two-thirds of emergency physicians reported that communicating with the family of a child who had died was the most difficult experience in emergency medicine and was much more difficult than communicating with the family of an adult who had died. Nearly two-thirds feel guilty or inadequate after an unsuccessful pediatric resuscitation attempt, and nearly half feel impaired for the remainder of their shift.[8] Nurses, of course, feel the same way, as one expressed:

> the situation for me personally changes because I tend to identify the children with my own children and it makes it very, very hard for me. I tend to become more personally emotional . . . because I see my own children there when I do it and it makes it very difficult.[9]

Experienced clinicians can also advise parents about ways to tell other children in the family about what happened. (See chapter 13 for more information.)

Sudden Infant Death Syndrome (SIDS)

> When a mother finds her previously healthy baby dead in its cot, she screams. In the first minutes and hours after the baby's death, the parents simultaneously know and deny the baby's death. They may attempt to resuscitate it. They may immediately blame themselves for the death.[10] (See also "What is SIDS?" in chapter 27.)

Notifying parents about deaths from Sudden Infant Death Syndrome (SIDS, also called Crib Death or Cot Death) often presents unique problems. These are deaths of previously healthy infants who die suddenly for no apparent reason. This syndrome has been known since at least biblical times, although it was long thought that mothers accidentally crushed or smothered the infants during sleep: "And this woman's child died in the night, because she overlaid it." (I *Kings* 3:19)

Prevalence of SIDS

About 3,000 SIDS deaths occur in the United States each year, even though the numbers have dropped more than 42% since 1992 when physicians learned that putting babies to sleep on their backs greatly reduces the SIDS risk. (As of 1998, however, more than 20% of mothers were still putting their infants to sleep on their stomachs.)[11] In Western countries, it strikes one in 500 babies between 8 days and 2 years of age, with most occurring between 4 weeks and 8 months, and with a peak incidence between 2 and 3 months.[12] African-American babies are 2.4 times more likely and Native American babies are 2.8 times more likely than are Caucasian babies to die of SIDS.[13] Nearly all pediatricians believe that SIDS deaths differ from other pediatric deaths, citing the "mysterious" nature of the death, the shock, lack of anticipation, and the increased guilt parents feel.[14]

Usually these deaths occur at home, so that police and EMS (ambulance) personnel are involved. Hospital personnel only become involved if the child is not clearly and irretrievably dead, e.g., in *rigor mortis*, when the situation is recognized. Even then, when paramedics bring the child into the emergency department, unless they have regained a heartbeat by the time they arrive, their prognosis is very grim. Fewer than 15% of children arriving in the emergency department without a pulse from any cause survive, and only about 3% are in anything other than a vegetative state.[15]

It is not unusual for survivors to show more overt grief, anger, and guilt following the sudden death of an infant than with any other death. The support that notifiers and others give to these families may be more stressful, yet more important, than that given to any other group.

Emotions commonly expressed immediately following SIDS notifications include:

- This really can't be happening to me . . . I think it must be a nightmare, and I just wish I would wake up.
- Why can't I just take my baby home?
- She can't be dead; I love her so much she just can't be.
- Please don't let him be dead!
- I just want my baby back again.
- Please let this be a dream.[16]

Parents often express the same emotions following other sudden childhood deaths.

Investigation

Complicated dynamics surround SIDS deaths. On the one hand, there are extremely distraught parents upon whom has been visited an unexpected disaster of the greatest proportions, while on the other hand, police are justifiably interested in investigating a possible homicide. Both sides have needs that must be served, so a compassionate balance is necessary.

Those in attendance must, no matter what their suspicions, support the grieving family. For example, parents should be allowed to hold their child. This leave-taking ritual helps parents accept the death and symbolizes, in part, a sense of closure. Some parents will lie on the stretcher with their child, while others, especially parents of infants, may carry the dead child around the room. One mother, who was not allowed to hold her dead infant, described both her resentment and her overwhelming impulse for months after the death to dig up the grave to see if her baby was really dead.[17] Parents may be comforted if the staff gives them mementos of the baby, such as a lock of hair, a picture (taken after cleaning the baby as much as possible), a footprint, or the clothes or blanket in which the baby arrived. (See "Memory Boxes" below.)

About 40% of the U.S. population is now served by multidisciplinary and multi-agency child-death-review teams. Originated in Los Angeles, Calif., in 1978, and promoted by the American Academy of Pediatrics, these teams investigate unexpected deaths, generally of children less than six years old. They coordinate and integrate data and resources from medical examiners, law enforcement, courts, child protective services, and health care providers.[18]

Guilt and Depression

Parents of SIDS infants feel tremendous guilt. They often "know" that it was something they did or didn't do that caused the death. It becomes even worse when one parent starts to blame the other. Notifiers (often the first police or EMS personnel to arrive) need to be willing and able to help explain what SIDS is and that no one is to blame, while at the same time communicating that there will be investigators present and, most probably, a forensic autopsy.

Mothers may be at risk for a prolonged and morbid mourning period following either the death of an infant or the delivery of a stillborn baby. Those at highest risk may be those mothers with a surviving twin of the dead child in the home or those who quickly become pregnant again. They find it difficult to manage their conflicting feelings: joy at a new birth and sadness for the lost child. Some statements these mothers make demonstrating this reaction are:

"Even now it's hard. I want to kill myself, I feel so bad."

"I can't get close to my new [subsequent] baby. I'm building up a little wall in case anything happens to him."

"I don't plan on ever getting over it."[19]

Parents often have serious marital problems following a child's death. These may begin immediately, as a paramedic responding to a SIDS death noted: "The husband removed the daughter [sibling] from the room. As he left, he and his wife looked at each other. It was a hateful glance—as if they had already begun to assign blame."[20]

Parents, especially mothers, also exhibit increasing anxiety toward remaining children, often holding or hugging them more than previously. In some cases, they begin to "baby" the surviving siblings. When a new baby is born, parents often spend inordinate amounts of time hovering over the crib, especially up to the time when the prior infant succumbed to SIDS.

Grandparents commonly blame the mother for the death.[21] Yet the grief responses of grandparents may actually be delayed mourning for prior, and nearly repressed, unresolved deaths.[22]

Occasionally, SIDS deaths occur with baby sitters or other caretakers in attendance. This increases the guilt parents feel (neglect) and emotionally scars the caretaker involved. Parents are often quick to blame these third parties and police often take an added interest in such cases. Physicians should consider an automatic referral for psychiatric counseling for such individuals.

The use of emotional supports by parents varies widely. Normal support systems, such as relatives, clergy, and friends must be brought in to help. In most communities, there are SIDS support groups and they can often send someone to aid the family. But all these support systems may fail. Many parents complain that they were treated like criminals and subjected to intense police scrutiny. Others are put off by their friends' and relatives' cool reactions. Religious support varies. For example, one distressed mother, after looking to religion to help her, said, "I was a Catholic until the priest refused to bury my child."[23] Even when support systems are available, some parents find them onerous.

SIDS deaths may also provoke extraordinary guilt feelings in the physicians who deal with the family, especially the child's pediatrician. They may worry that in some way they were "unknowing culprits" by not recognizing a life-threatening condition. This may lead to prolonged resuscitative attempts, difficult subsequent interactions with the family, or increased anxiety about their own children's welfare.[24]

Many parents do not understand why their child died and about the risk of recurrence in other children. Their understanding markedly increases if they have a follow-up discussion, either in-person or by telephone, with their physician several weeks after the death. This type of discussion, however, is not routine, and non-psychiatrist physicians are rarely seen as a part of the support system.

Parents of SIDS infants ask relatively predictable questions, either at the time of notification or during subsequent counseling sessions with health care providers:[25]

- Did the baby suffer pain?
- Did the baby suffocate, choke, or overheat?
- Did the baby die quickly or over a period of time?
- At what point did the baby slip into unconsciousness?
- How long was the baby dead?
- Would the baby have had brain damage had s/he survived?
- Why did it happen if the baby was well cared for?
- Would breast-feeding have prevented it?
- What were the autopsy findings?

- Need we be frightened that this will happen to any future children or to surviving brothers and sisters?
- Is there any special test we should get for future babies we may have?

In-Hospital SIDS Deaths

On rare occasions, apparently normal newborns die of SIDS or for another reason before they ever leave the hospital. This affects not only the parents (as does any infant death), but it also has a dramatic effect on the medical and nursing staff attending those children.

For example, an apparently healthy infant girl in a hospital's normal newborn nursery was discovered fifteen hours after birth to be on her abdomen, very blue, without a pulse, and not breathing. Nothing in her examination, history, or behavior indicated a problem. Yet, less than an hour after being found, and after resuscitative attempts, she was dead. The parents experienced the grief reaction typical in a SIDS death, with their anger directed at the medical team. The medical team's reaction was complicated by memories of a similar death about two years previously. In both cases, the clinicians involved experienced feelings of guilt, self-doubt, fear, anxiety, and sadness. Nurses caring for the infant, similar to cases involving baby sitters in SIDS deaths, received the brunt of the anger and criticism. The nurse who found the infant felt she could no longer work in the nursery, and she resigned. The stress encountered by the resident who responded to resuscitate the infant hindered his performance for several months thereafter.[26]

Unfortunately, while counseling was provided for the parents, the grief reactions of the medical staff went unattended. Apparently not recognizing their grief at the time, they experienced some of the reactions of any caregiver attending a SIDS death. When events like this occur, even in a medical setting, care should be taken to counsel the medical personnel as well as the parents. In these cases, they are both "survivors." (See "Handling Disasters: Critical Incident Stress Debriefing" in chapter 26.)

Child Abuse Deaths

One of the most difficult notifications is after a child's death from suspected abusive treatment by adults. Notifiers must consciously remember their professional role, and not give in to their passion and anger.

For health care providers, anger at families is not usually part of their daily experience. It appears most frequently, however, when they must notify suspects after a child's death from what appears to be abusive treatment. While righteous indignation may be appropriate in some circumstances, it is not appropriate in this one.

Notifiers must consider several things. First, although it may appear that the child died from abuse, it may turn out that abuse was not the cause. Second, even if the child died from abusive treatment, the perpetrator(s), whoever they turn out to be, may still feel a great deal of remorse over the child's death. Third, some of the survivors most likely were not involved in the child's death and they feel the same emotions as any survivor.

Finally, health care providers are not criminal investigators. They have a professional role to play and must do it—even under trying circumstances. That role is to sensitively notify and support the survivors. (They should, of course, also notify authorities as to their suspicions.)

Police also have to restrain themselves in these situations. They may have dual roles—of notifier and of initial investigator. "Losing one's cool" does not enhance either of these roles.

Death in Childhood

Children's deaths burn into the memories of everyone involved. One example is this anecdote of a British physician, recalling an occurrence from the 1960s:

> I was twenty-five years old and working in an accident and emergency department. A young lad was brought in with severe head injuries following a road traffic accident. We tried to resuscitate him, but it was obviously useless. I had to go out and tell his parents. I'd never told anyone before that their child was dead and didn't have a clue what to say. I just blurted it out and the mother started screaming—I didn't know how to handle the situation. I just said "Sorry" and ran out of the room. I can still hear that woman's screams. That was over thirty years ago and I don't think things are really much better in terms of helping young doctors learn how to break bad news.[27]

One mother's memories are little better: "My son was at the hospital an hour before he died. A nurse came out and abruptly said, 'He's gone,' and I was totally shocked. I'm sitting in the waiting room thinking he probably broke a leg, wondering how long he's going to be out of school and, well, they come out and just dump it on you and go home."[28]

Adult and children's deaths are usually handled differently. For example, in many EDs, paralleling how parents want to act toward their offspring, children's bodies are usually not left alone until they are taken to the morgue. Parents tend to be comforted by this show of affection and support.

The process of telling parents about their child's sudden unexpected death generally follows the model described in table 3-1. Specific items in the protocol (those discussing parents, children, and SIDS) address key points to remember when notifying survivors after a child's death. The main elements that must either be stressed or performed in these cases are to:

- Assuage the parents' guilt.
- Allow them to hold, or get into the stretcher with, their child.
- Offer to give them a memento, such as a lock of hair or a hand/foot inkblot.
- Arrange for follow-up with a support group, religious group, or social worker.
- Be sensitive to the needs of the decedent's siblings.

Parents may experience profound grief over the part of them that has died, sadness for the lost potential the child represented, and guilt over the event.

Viewing and Holding the Child

Parents should be encouraged to see their dead child—often multiple times—even if the body has been mutilated or disfigured. They often find some relief in holding the body, and most centers now encourage this.

Staff should first shorten or remove as many of the tubes and lines as is legally possible and wrap the child in a sheet or blanket. If there are disfiguring injuries, these should be covered as much as possible, leaving out the face and hands. Parents should then be allowed to hold the child. Usually, parents will sit in a comfortable chair to do this. If the child is too large to actually hold, such as with an adolescent, they may get into a (cleaned) stretcher with the child to say their good-byes. Older siblings should also be encouraged to participate in this leave-taking ritual.

When parents are prevented from holding the child, they may feel deprived of the opportunity to say "good-bye" as was this mother:

> A woman's three-year-old child drowned in her pool. Paramedics were called and initiated advanced life support, which emergency department personnel continued for over an hour and a half after arriving at the hospital. The child was intubated and ventilated, and numerous lines were placed. Eventually, when it was apparent that further resuscitative efforts would be ineffective, they were stopped. The child was pronounced dead.
>
> Hospital personnel told the child's mother that before she could leave with the body or have the body transported to a mortuary, someone from the medical examiner's office would have to examine the body. During the several-hour wait before the medical examiner's investigator arrived, the child was not disconnected from the now-idle resuscitation equipment. This prevented the mother from fully embracing or holding her child. The mother reported that when the investigator arrived he said something like "it looks like you've had a bad day" and proceeded to do what she thought was a rapid and rather superficial examination, after which he left.
>
> When the audience at one of our forums heard this story, both the lay persons and clinicians were aghast. A nurse commented that when she was faced with similar situations, she removed the patient from equipment and severed the lines close to the skin's surface so that survivors could feel closer to their relative. This left the decedent in a more natural state, while preserving the evidence needed by the medical examiner.[29]

Viewing usually breaks down any vestige of survivors' denial. But if it doesn't, the denial should not be reinforced. A young woman, brought in to view her dead baby, picked him up and announced, "I'm taking him home for a nap." She quickly ran out of the emergency department.[30] In such a case, the staff should follow her, reclaim the body, and treat the mother for, at least temporary, psychosis. In another case, "a man had come in, and we had to tell him that his 3-month-old baby was no longer living. [They used "D" words.] It took him an hour after we told him for him to accept it. And during part of that time, he was holding the baby."[31]

Delivering the News and Following Up

It may seem obvious, but a dead child's parents should generally be told before siblings or others are notified. The exceptions are when they cannot be reached or are themselves infirm. Young children should never be saddled with the burden of informing the rest of the family about their sibling's (or any) death. The following two cases illustrate this point. Unfortunately, this situation is all too common.

> In Miami, Fla., parents had gone out looking for their son and were not home when a police officer came by. The officer notified the victim's teenage sister—who was home alone and didn't know where her parents were.
>
> In Oregon, a family was aware that a crash had occurred down the road from their house, so they sent their son to see what had happened. He recognized his brother's car and walked up to the scene. An officer asked who he was and, when he gave his name, handed him his brother's billfold. The boy asked if his brother had been taken to the hospital. "No," the officer responded, "he's been taken to the morgue." The boy had to drive home to tell his parents to go to the morgue to identify the body. No one from the sheriff's office ever went to the parent's home. The boy underwent prolonged psychotherapy.[32]

Most parents of children dying suddenly and unexpectedly in emergency departments want the attending physician to deliver the news to them. However, if the delay will be extensive, they would prefer to have another staff person tell them and have the doctor available to answer their questions later. No matter who delivers it, telling parents their child has died often severely traumatizes the notifier. One chaplain who was tasked with relaying this news was incapable of voicing it, as he relates: "I had one family who had a 9-year-old son who drowned. I couldn't talk. I couldn't talk . . . The parents went crazy—started wailing, fell on the floor. It was a weekend when I was working in the emergency room. They just fell apart."[33] So did he.

Nearly all parents want to hold their child's body and would like a physical memento, such as a hand print or mold or a lock of hair. These mementos could be given to the parents either when they are ready to depart or two to three weeks after the death.[34] All newborn nurseries have the equipment to make ink prints and cutting a lock of hair is simple. Making a mold is a bit more complex.[35] The clothing the child was wearing also represents an important memento that parents usually want back. One hospital has developed the "Memory Box" described in the next section.

Most parents of children who die suddenly would also like a follow-up telephone call to re-emphasize that everything possible was done for their child and that they should have no guilt about the incident. Few ever receive this type of call.[36]

The horror and disbelief felt by parents receiving this news and of those delivering it is perhaps best expressed in a poem by Bonnie Salomon, M.D., an emergency physician.

Breaking the News

The spontaneous burst, the tears.
Fingers clutch the face.
Skin flushed and perfused.
The news injects his mother filling her, transforming her.
From this moment on, days and nights upside down,
Painful holidays, empty birthdays.
Photographs impossible to see.

She collapses on the couch
A different person.
The assassin in a white coat:
The best part of her life gone.

"It doesn't look good."
"He's not suffering anymore."
"We did everything we could."
She hears nothing.

She doesn't need to hear anything ever again.
Precious baby.
Ten years old.
Gone.

Ten-year-old boy
Chasing golf balls on an icy pond.
The ice breaks open.
He falls, freezes.

This priestly duty beyond me.
Make an MRI machine to tell her.
A blood test to confirm her grief.
A stainless-steel instrument to hold her hand.

She howls: I sigh.
Alone together in the family room.
In just enough pain
To know she's still alive.

Salomon B: Breaking the news. *Acad Emerg Med.* 1998;5(4):346. Used with permission.

Parental Grief

How Men and Women Differ

Men and women often grieve differently. Any attempt to define grieving patterns along gender lines, however, runs the risk of applying stereotypes that may not apply to specific individuals or couples. Simply knowing that differences may exist in the way parents grieve over the same event, though, may help notifiers to understand their behaviors and to help each of them more effectively. The following discussion (adapted from Buzz and Joanie Overbeck's seminar notes and used with permission.) provides an overview of possible similarities and differences between men's and women's grieving patterns.

Men may be uncomfortable dealing with their feelings and be reluctant to visit the cemetery. They often find ways to avoid showing their pain, particularly in front of strangers, and spend extra time on their work, hobbies, or other activities to keep busy, thus avoiding dealing with their pain. Men may want to make love for the comfort and reassurance that comes through intimacy, and openly wish for their life to return to the way it was before the tragic event. They may be angry with God, and feel that the tragic event invalidates their religion.[37]

Dealing with grief requires that men repudiate standard male stereotypes, that is, forget that men are supposed to hide their feelings and should never ask for help. Instead, men must allow themselves "to cry long and loud until you begin to recover. It won't be easy. Years of crippling training have to be undone. It takes tremendous courage to cry; almost as much courage as it took to *not* cry all these days."[38]

Women need to talk about the event, and may go over it time and again while trying to gather every possible detail to explain "why" and "how." They may take comfort in their faith: "God's will" may be the only explanation that gives the event any meaning. Women often seek out support groups as an outlet to express their grief, make repeated visits to the grave, and usually realize that their life is irrevocably changed and will never again be the same. Some women may withdraw, read books on grief, or write as a means of expressing their pain. They may have no interest in sex and, in fact, resent their husband's desire for it.

Other possible reactions parents have during this stressful time include trying to escape the event by taking a vacation, moving, or changing jobs and attempting to numb their pain through alcohol, drugs, shopping, extramarital affairs, or another child. Parents may become angry with the doctor or other authority figures involved and may discuss legal action, feel betrayed by their family and friends for a perceived lack of understanding and caring, or blame each other. Finally, one or both parents may become so absorbed in their own grief that they are unable to recognize or understand the grief experienced by their children or extended family members.[39]

Five Facts of Parental Grief

1. The intensity of His grief is dependent on his pre-death relationship with the fetus, baby, or child.

2. The intensity of Her grief is dependent on the place, the pregnancy, or child held in her hopes, dreams, future, self-esteem and self-worth.
3. Many fathers resolve (or make peace) with their grief in 3 to 6 months.
4. Many mothers need 9 to 24 months (or more) to resolve their grief.
5. Many men truly feel their spouse needs professional help after 3 to 6 months.[40]

Potential Relationship Problems

Because men and women deal with grief differently, spouses may come to resent each other during the grieving process. Men need space to grieve in their own way and may resent their spouse for imposing her feelings on him. Women also expect their husbands to grieve and behave the same as they do, and think he doesn't care when he doesn't. Parents will sometimes compete with each other to see who is grieving the hardest. [41]

How to Help Grieving Parents

Understanding common grief reactions parents may experience or exhibit allows notifiers to help survivors anticipate the difficult months and years to come. The following statement illustrates how helpful advance knowledge of grief reactions can be:

> The pediatrician told me I would probably visualize my child, and talk back to him. It happens at home, at the cemetery. I feel his presence. You gotta be prepared. Being informed was a help. I anticipated those reactions.[42]

Grief reactions that both parents may experience after a child's death (and particularly in SIDS cases) include:

- Difficulty concentrating.
- Fear of being alone in the home.
- Anorexia and insomnia.
- Time confusion.
- Despondency.
- Fear of the responsibility of caring for children.
- Failure to accept reality.
- Anger and guilt.[43]

Aside from recognizing the symptoms of grief, it is useful to have some tools to help grieving parents, both for the immediate notifier and for those who do follow-up, such as chaplains, social workers, grief counselors, and psychologists or psychiatrists. The following are some tips adapted from Buzz and Joanie Overbeck.[44]

1. Meet with the bereaved parents as soon as possible.
2. Explain the high likelihood of severe marital discord, and even separation, during the bereavement period.

3. Explain each other's grieving needs and expectations and the importance of recognizing and allowing each partner to grieve in his or her own way.
4. Encourage and help HER to find a local support group where she can meet others with whom she can share similar experiences.
5. Encourage HIM to attend some of these meetings with her, but only as an observer. Tell them both that there will be no pressure put on him whatsoever to actively participate. Most men will inevitably participate if you can just get them there.
6. Discourage making decisions that will affect any important area of their life *for one year.*
7. If there are other children, encourage them to openly and honestly express and discuss their grief. Ask how the child is coping with the experience and help them to recognize that the child is grieving too.
8. Help move them toward an awareness and acceptance of each other's grief using the following 4-step guide:
   - Separate the death from all other issues.
   - List and discuss those elements of grief unique to HER.
   - List and discuss those elements of grief unique to HIM.
   - List and discuss those elements of grief common to BOTH.
9. Encourage individual grief:
   - Help her give him permission to express his grief in his own way.
   - Help him give her permission to express her grief in her own way.
10. Encourage mutual grief.
11. Encourage them to establish periods during each week where they can express and share their common feelings.
12. Encourage them to establish periods during the week for intimacy and closeness when the loss is not discussed.
13. Encourage them to establish periods during the week or month for family activities that include the children, if any.

The Memory Box

Colleen Ducke, who began the Child Life Program at the New England Medical Center's (Boston, Mass.) emergency department in 1997 came up with the idea of using "Memory Boxes" in the ED for parents after a sudden death. Although many neonatal units use something like this, it is unusual for it to be used with older children. Normally she works with all children that come to the ED (as well as parents, siblings, and friends) to reduce the trauma and anxiety that arises from an ED visit. Her main tools are toys, which she uses for many different purposes. "I use them," she says, "to prepare and distract the children during their stay here. I prepare all the children who need it for their procedures and exams by showing them pictures and the actual medical equipment. I let them manipulate it and ask questions and hopefully clear up any misconceptions that the children have before their procedures. When a child dies, I generally will work with the siblings if there are any involved and explain to them what has happened and sit with them during this time."

After beginning to work in the ED, she decided to take courses in and get certified in Thanatology, the study of death and dying, and bereavement issues to better help people. Based on this, "I decided that parents who have a child die in the emergency department should have mementos to remember the last time their child was alive. So, I set out to find the proper items to be able to make this happen. I knew that I wanted to give the parents lockets with the child's hair and prints of their hand and foot. Depending on the individual case, I might take pictures of the children to give to the parents."

"I only start to prepare a memory box after the family has had a chance to say good-bye to the child and has left the hospital. I do this so that I don't intrude on their time together with their child. Only once have I prepared a memory box with the parent in the room. In that instance, I knew the parent and the child, and the mother asked that I do it with her present. If any parents make such a request in the future, I will prepare the box when and how they desire. In another case, a mother was so badly injured that she was not able to come to the ED to say good-bye to her child. Hopefully any guilt she felt was partly assuaged by having the memory box from the last time her child was alive."

How to Prepare a Memory Box

Says Ducke, "I have re-done the memory boxes several times because it seems like there are always different things that I come up with and different ways to improve what we give to the parents. Also I like to have a variety of things available, in case different situations arise. We have different ages and sizes of kids who die here and I like to do this for any child who dies, so I have to sometimes have bigger or smaller paper available.

"I have a big Tupperware™ box in which I keep all the items. I leave it out so that if I am not here the staff can prepare the memory boxes if they want. Nurses now frequently prepare them in my absence. Inside the box, I keep:

- Clear square or round small boxes (about the size of a ring box or a Petri dish) in which to put hair clippings.
- Pair of scissors to cut the hair.
- Nice pen to write the child's name on the top of the hair container and on the hand and footprint picture.
- Locket necklaces in which I put some of the child's hair so that the parents can have their child "with them."
- A faceless doll. These are dolls that we have people make for us to give to kids. They have many different purposes when working with children in the ED; one is for use with siblings after a child's death. If we have a child die in the emergency department, I often give their siblings dolls. They can decorate them by adding clothes, drawing faces, adding beads, or drawing in hair. They then have something personal to hold on to in a time of obvious stress, with the adults

around them in a somber mood and usually crying. It especially seems to help them when they enter the room to see their deceased sibling. Whether or not I use these dolls depends on each individual situation, but it is always an option in the memory box kit.

- Blank cards that have slots for Polaroid pictures. I write the child's name on the front of the card.
- Polaroid camera to take a picture if it is appropriate.
- Plain white paper for foot and handprints.
- Colored paper to frame these prints.
- Glue stick to put the frame around the hand or footprints.
- Paint and ink pads of different colors to do the hand and footprints.

"To make these prints, I take the paint or inkpad and use it on the child's hands and feet. I then press them on the white paper so that both are side by side. I used to do just one handprint, but lately I have started to take a print of both hands next to each other. I like the way the two handprints look. I keep paper of different sizes to accommodate different-sized children. For example, I had a teenage boy die last summer and his hands were too big to fit on the piece of paper that I had available for babies. So, I used an 8½ x 11-inch sheet of paper. I cut out his handprints after they were dry, pasted them on a different sheet of paper, and added his name and the date. After they dry, I frame the pictures and inscribe them with the child's name and the date. On the back of the framed prints I put a poem about handprints on the wall.

"After I have all these things prepared, I place them in a padded envelope. I do not have an actual box in the literal sense of the word. It is more like the idea of the memory boxes. We are currently looking for nicer packaging to give to the parents, but for now we use a padded envelope that I give to our hospital chaplains.

"I almost always make two of everything. We have had parents that are divorced and siblings who want them also. So I thought that there should be at least two memory boxes available.

"Three experiences using the memory boxes stand out for me—my first, my most recent, and the one I prepared in the morgue for a child I knew well:

> Shortly after I began my job in the emergency department, a 12-year-old boy was brought in after suffering a cardiac arrest in an ATV (all-terrain vehicle) crash. He was pronounced dead shortly after arrival. I had decided a short time before this happened that one aspect of my job was going to be to prepare memory boxes for the parents and siblings of the children who die in our ED. I knew exactly what I wanted to do, but was not sure exactly how to go about doing it. Because the child was 12, I thought that everyone was going to say he was too big or too old to have this done. I knew that a lot of neonatal intensive care units do some type of memory box for children who have died, but I had never heard of anyone doing it for older children. So, I decided to just go ahead and do it.

I was very scared to do this, as I was not sure how people would react. So I sort of did it quietly. I waited and waited for the right time to begin preparing the box. I found that for me the time was after the child's father had finished saying good-bye to him. I did not want to intrude on the family's time with the child. So, after they had left, I went into the room where a nursing tech was still cleaning up. I looked at the child; he looked as if he was just sleeping. I willed myself to remain calm, took a deep breath and continued with what I planned to do.

I asked her to help me cut some of the boy's hair to put in a plastic dish. She looked at me like I was crazy until I explained what I was doing, and then she gladly assisted me. However, it was summer and he had a very short buzz cut. So we were not able to get a lot of hair; but we got enough. Then I had to get his handprints.

I got the inkpad out of my box and I picked up his hand. It was very cold to the touch and his fingers were curled. I had to hold his hand and try to warm it up to be able to get his hands flat to make the handprint. I took the ink and blotted it all over his hand. Then I took his hand and the white sheet of paper and laid his hand down to make the print. It didn't work so well. So, we tried it again. This one worked better. Then I washed his hand and left the room with all my stuff.

The nurses started to come over to find out what I was doing. Once I told them, all were grateful that I had thought to do this for the family. Many of them have children of their own and expressed that it "hit too close to home" and that "they never could have done it"—but that they were glad that I had been able to do it.

I then cut out the handprint, glued it to a card, and wrote the child's name on it, as well as on the dish with the locks of hair. I put them in a manila envelope and gave it to the chaplain who would call the family a couple days later to, among other things, ask if they wanted her to mail it to them. When I gave it to her (the chaplain) she looked at the envelope and said, "His parents are divorced. We couldn't find his mother so she could come in and say good-bye to him. Could you make another one for her?" So I did. But from that experience I learned to always make two memory boxes. That way there is always another one for parents or siblings who may want one.

My most recent experience with the memory boxes was a little different. It was with an 8-year-old liver-transplant patient who had been a hospital patient for many years. He died unexpectedly while in the hospital. My co-worker asked me to come do a memory box for him. Because he spent most of his young life in the hospital, many of us knew him for years. I told her that I would be there after the family left, as this was my normal procedure. She informed me, however, that the mother wanted me to come and do it now because she wouldn't leave the room until the boy's father, who was away on a trip, arrived.

I went to the child's room with my supplies. I asked the mom what his favorite color was. She said green. So this time, instead of ink, I decided to use paint. I got everything out and ready to go. It was a very different situation for me because, as we were doing the memory box stuff, the child's mom was walking around the room and cleaning things up. And every so often there were people walking in and out of the room expressing their condolences. My co-worker was in the room with me and was helping me do the handprints. She held his hands for a few minutes to warm them up while I got the paints ready. Then we painted his right hand and pressed it on a full-sized sheet of paper. Then we did the same with the right. The prints were very nice. After we cleaned the paint off his hands, we took some locks of hair for the plastic dish, prepared them as we usually do and put them in the envelope. I gave it to his mom and she began to cry when she saw them, saying "Thank you for taking the time to do that."

A 7-month-old boy died. We had seen him often in his short life and I had, despite warnings, become attached to him. It is impossible in this job (Child Life Specialist) to not get involved. He died and his body was sent to the morgue when I wasn't there. I wanted to prepare a memory box for his parents, so I had to go to the morgue to do it. All kinds of thoughts ran through my head: Whom do I ask [for permission] to enter the morgue? Can I do this? I'm scared of what he will look like dead and in the morgue! God! What a scary thing to do! There are so many unknowns. Then I decided what the hell! I will regret it if I don't at least ask. And the worst they could say is no.

Lori (another Child Life Specialist) and I went down to the morgue with my memory box stuff to await Joe (a nurse) and security. Once he arrived, I was very nervous again. I wondered what it was going to look like, smell like, and feel like in there. We entered and they rolled the stretcher with the baby's body out of the cooler. We began to prepare the hand- and footprint pictures. Then came the part I was dreading—his face. To get to his hair, Joe had to uncover his face. Oh man, he had puffy cheeks, puckered lips—sweet baby! He still looked the same. What did I expect? Who knew? But he still looked like the same little boy. I wanted to cry. But no, I had to be strong. We finished and they opened the cooler door to replace the body. I couldn't look in. I had seen all the death I could stand at that point. Rest in peace, little guy!

"As mentioned in the first case, a few days after the death, the chaplain calls the family and asks them if they would like these things. The parents always have the right to refuse—but so far none of them have. The overall reaction to the memory boxes is positive. We take each case on an individual basis and do what we feel is appropriate for that case. So far, all the families that we have done this for have gladly accepted these mementos and thanked us for taking the time to do it. It allows them to have something nice and small to carry around, to keep under their pillow, or to just hang on to."

Charlotte S. Yeh, M.D., formerly head of New England Medical Center's emergency department, remembers a poignant result of preparing the memory boxes.

After one child's death, a nurse gave the mother a necklace with a dove and the father a matching pin that she purchased at a local jewelry store as part of the memory box. She gave the young sibling a stuffed bear. A year later, they came back to the ED with a large bag of bears for other grieving children. The parents said they always wear the jewelry, which reminds them of their lost child.

Absent a memory box, some survivors may be encouraged to develop a special memorial for the deceased person, such as planting a tree or a garden, creating a photo album, or beginning a scholarship fund.

References

1. National Center for Injury Prevention and Control: *Ten Leading Causes of Death by Age Group—1995, U.S.* Atlanta, GA: Centers for Disease Control, 1998.
2. Anonymous: Death and murder at a very young age. *Newsweek*. 1998;131(14):26.
3. National Center for Injury Prevention and Control: "*Ten Leading Causes of Death.*"
4. Weisman AD: Coping with untimely death. *Psychiatry*. 1973 Nov;36(4):366-78.
5. Greenberg LW: Death in the emergency department. (letter) *Pediatrics*. 1995 Feb;95(2):321.
6. Greenberg LW, Ochsenschlager D, Cohen GJ, et al.: Counseling parents of a child dead on arrival: a survey of emergency departments. *Am J Emerg Med*. 1993 May;11(3):225-9.
7. Clark RE, LaBeff EE: Death telling: managing the delivery of bad news. *J Health Soc Behav*. 1982 Dec;23(4):366-80.
8. Ahrens WR, Hart RG: Emergency physicians' experience with pediatric death. *Am J Emerg Med*. 1997 Nov;15(7):642-3.
9. Clark RE, LaBeff EE: "Death telling."
10. Cornwell J, Nurcombe B, Stevens L: Family response to loss of a child by sudden infant death syndrome. *Med J Aust*. 1977 Apr 30;1(18):656-8.
11. Centers for Disease Control and Prevention: Press release, 23 October 1998.
12. Randall B: *Death Investigation: The Basics*. Tucson, AZ: Galen Press, Ltd., 1997, pp. 114-29.
13. Centers for Disease Control and Prevention: Press release, 22 October 1998.
14. Mandell F, McClain M, Reece RM: Sudden and unexpected death. the pediatrician's response. *Am J Dis Child*. 1987 Jul;141(7):748-50.
15. O'Rourke PP: Outcome of children who are apneic and pulseless in the emergency room. *Crit Care Med*. 1986 May;14(5):466-8.
16. Smialek Z: Observations on immediate reactions of families to sudden infant death. *Pediatrics*. 1978 Aug;62(2):160-5.
17. Cornwell J, Nurcombe B, Stevens L: "Family response to loss of a child."
18. American Academy of Pediatrics Committee on Pediatric Emergency Medicine: Death of a child in the emergency department. *Pediatrics*. 1994 May;93(5):861-2.

19. Rowe J, Clyman R, Green C, et al.: Follow-up families who experience a perinatal death. *Pediatrics.* 1978 Aug;62(2):166-70.
20. Suslowitz B: The empty crib. *J Emerg Med Serv JEMS.* 1998 Mar;23(3):86-92.
21. Cornwell J, Nurcombe B, Stevens L: "Family response to loss of a child."
22. Smialek Z: "Observations on immediate reactions."
23. DeFrain JD, Ernst L: The psychological effects of sudden infant death syndrome on surviving family members. *J Fam Pract.* 1978 May;6(5):985-9.
24. Mandell F, McClain M, Reece RM: "Sudden and unexpected death."
25. Woodward S, Pope A, Robson WJ, et al.: Bereavement counseling after sudden infant death. *Br Med J Clin Res.* 1985 Feb 2;290(6465):363-5.
26. Sheagren TG, Puppala BL, Mangurten HH: Grief reaction to sudden unexpected cardio-orespiratory arrest in a normal newborn nursery. *Clin Pediatr (Phila).* 1987 Jul;26(7):369-71.
27. Fallowfield L: Giving sad and bad news. *Lancet.* 1993 Feb 20;341(8843):476-8.
28. Fischhoff J, O'Brien N: After the child dies. *J Pediatr.* 1976 Jan;88(1):140-6.
29. Jacobson J: Personal communication with author, April 1999.
30. Collins S: Sudden death counseling protocol. *Dimens Crit Care Nurs.* 1989;8(6):376-82.
31. Clark RE, LaBeff EE: "Death telling."
32. Lord JH: *Trauma, Death, and Death Notification: A Seminar for Professional Counselors and Victim Advocates.* Washington, DC: Mothers Against Drunk Driving and the U.S. Dept. of Justice for Victims of Crime, 1996, p. 52.
33. Clark RE, LaBeff EE: "Death telling."
34. Ahrens WR, Hart RG, Maruyama N: Pediatric death: managing the aftermath in the emergency department. *J Emerg Med.* 1997 Sep-Oct;15(5):601-3.
35. Brown CE, Kozick P: Impressioning: a way to preserve memories. *MCN.* 1994 Sep-Oct;19(5):285-7.
36. Ahrens WR, Hart RG, Maruyama N: "Pediatric death."
37. Adapted from: Overbeck B, Overbeck J: *He sighs/she cries; and some ideas on how you might help you neighbor.* Posted to Grief-Chat@Falcon.IC.Net.
38. Collenberger C: Men and grieving. In: Federal Bureau of Investigation Employee Assistance Unit: *Critical Incident Survival Manual.* Washington, DC: FBI, 1997 (no page numbers).
39. Overbeck B, Overbeck J: *"He sighs/she cries."*
40. *Ibid.*
41. *Ibid.*
42. Fischhoff J, O'Brien N: "After the child dies."
43. Pomeroy MR: Sudden death syndrome. *Am J Nurs.* 1969 Sep;69(9):1886-90.
44. Overbeck B, Overbeck J: *"He sighs/she cries."*

13: Telling Children

Nearly all children have an experience with a death. Often they first confront death in household pets. Later, it may be the deaths of their grandparents, parents, siblings, other relatives, personal friends, teachers, or family friends. In one children's grief counseling center, 49% of the children had lost a parent; 22%, siblings; 12%, grandparents; 10%, friends; and 7%, other relatives.[1]

Occasionally, children are present at a death. This may have disastrous consequences, as when preschool-age siblings witness their mother's discovery of an infant's death. The mother may, in panic, accuse the child of causing the death. This leads to subsequent mother-child interactions characterized by guilt and hostile dependency.[2]

Children's General Reactions to Death

It is nearly impossible to predict how any child will react to the news that a loved one has died. Some will have immediate strong emotions, while others will have many questions. Some will simply not want to discuss it. Children react to news of death in ways that reflect their own personalities. Although children often have many of the same feelings as adults, they may react to deaths differently (table 13-1). Children often tend to transform their own guilt feelings into the cause of the death. This has led, over the past half century, to shielding children from death.

Children often regress in their behavior after a death, acting as they did several years before. Part of this regression may be "acting out" to get attention and repeatedly testing the limits adults have set. They may also focus their guilt, anger, and aggression on themselves, becoming depressed, becoming obsessed with death, exhibiting accident-prone behavior, or developing psychosomatic complaints. The psychosomatic complaints

Table 13-1: Common Reactions Children Have to Death

Denial: Act as if the death didn't really occur. It is akin to children closing their eyes and pretending that they then cannot be seen.

Clinging or replacement: Children may be fearful of losing another close person in their lives and may try to replace the deceased person with someone else. They may cling to those around them and find separations difficult.

Panic: They worry that their emotional and physical needs won't be met. In the extreme, they fear that they will be separated from their family.

Preoccupation with the decedent: They may adopt the habits, likes, and attitudes of the decedent—especially of a sibling.

Anger: Acting out aggressively may be some children's only way of expressing their fears.

Hyperactivity: Similar to some adults, children may become hyperactive, talking incessantly and continually moving.

Guilt: Many children fear that they caused the death by doing or saying something. Unlike adults, they rarely verbalize this.

Withdrawal: This behavior is used to avoid coming into contact with others who may remind them of the deceased person.

Regression: A lack of coping skills may make the child begin behaving at an earlier developmental level.

Anxiety: This is often manifested by somatic complaints, such as sleep disorders, changes in eating patterns, and temper tantrums.

Adapted, in part, from: Mangini L, Confessore MT, Girard P, et al.: Pediatric trauma support program: supporting children and families in emotional crisis. *Crit Care Nurs Clin North Am*. 1995 Sep;7(3):557-67.

---

often include bedwetting, abdominal pain, headaches, nightmares, and other sleep difficulties. They also often develop separation anxiety (the fear of another loved one "leaving"), dread even minor illnesses (a harbinger, in their minds, of death), and hesitate to become close to either adults or other children (because they also may die).

After the death, the surviving siblings often have altered sleep patterns, usually characterized by a resistance to go to bed or to sleep, or nightmares. They also change their social interactions, becoming more quiet or aggressive when playing with other children.[3] Children may also adopt a dead sibling's mannerisms. A very effective method for dealing with this phenomenon is illustrated by the following episode.

> In the weeks that followed Josh's (19-month-old) sudden death, Toby (2½ years old) began to imitate all Joshua's mannerisms, including his baby-talk. It was as though, in a desperate attempt to make everything better for the grown-ups, he had decided to "be" his dead brother, a notion I find particularly heart-wrenching. It was very important then to let Toby know that we loved him for being himself, and that he did not have to "become" Josh to gain our approval. So we never admonished him for taking the role of Josh, but we did remind him often that we loved him very much.[4]

Children use these exposures to death to try to understand the concept of death—an important element in their maturation. During this process, however, they will do whatever is necessary to defend themselves against being overwhelmed by intolerable feelings. To adjust to a sudden death, children must know immediately that their parents (or other adult survivors) will support them. This means that adult survivors must do three things:

1. Provide the child with continuous and stable care. This may be difficult at a time when the adult is going through a mourning period. Yet for a child, this is the major factor in determining whether he or she will psychologically survive the event intact.
2. Talk with the child about the loss. When adults share and discuss their loss and grief with children, the children adapt quicker and better to the loss. These discussions must occur on multiple occasions, especially when the child gives verbal or behavioral clues that he or she wants to discuss it. Children want to talk about their experience with death and the events surrounding a death. Parents, however, frequently avoid these discussions. Because of this, the child often gets distorted concepts of illness, dying, hospitals, and religion, and develops a death phobia.[5]
3. Maintain familiar surroundings and behavior as much as possible. Children do better after a loss when they continue in their same home, school, and activities.[6] In some situations, this may be impossible, such as when an active-duty-military parent dies (see chapter 25) or with the death of the individual responsible for the family's financial support.

Children's Normal Responses to Death

For adults to support children effectively, they must understand what constitutes normal child behavior following deaths. Children's responses to death vary with their age, prior experiences, any preparation they have had, and the emotional support adults provide. They can be overwhelmed by an adult's grief reactions unless they are given an explanation of events and a secure supportive environment.

Basic Principles for Dealing with Children following a Death

- **Children can understand the concept of death as young as three years old**, and sometimes younger. They can most easily equate it to the deaths they have seen in their pets. Explain the death as "the end of life" or "no longer living." The explanation a two-year-old gave of a playmate's death is fairly typical: "When someone is dead and no longer alive, he will no longer eat or sleep or run or play or feel, or be sad, or happy, or angry, and (since this child speaking had just been toilet trained) then he won't do wee-wee or BM anymore either."[7]

- When possible, **tell siblings of the death simultaneously** so that they can immediately get mutual support and feel like they remain an integral part of the family.

- **Do not tell them or imply that the separation is temporary,** or that it is due to a reason they will most certainly misinterpret. Preschoolers already have a limited concept of time and often ask when the person is coming back. Using terms such as "went to sleep," "moved on," "gone," or "departed" suggests, in the concrete thinking of many young children, that the parting is only temporary.

- **Use real words to describe death,** such as: "Grandpa was very sick and his body stopped working. The doctors tried to help him, but his body just stopped working" or "A terrible thing happened (car crash, drowning, fall, etc.) and his/her body was badly damaged. It stopped working and the doctors couldn't fix it." Since children generalize from specific events to generalities, avoiding the truth by saying, "They are only asleep" only makes children fearful of sleep. Saying "They have gone away for a long time" causes anxiety that they caused this separation, and the phrase "They have gone to heaven" makes no sense to a child who has witnessed or knows about the body's disposition through burial or cremation.

- **Tell children the truth in a way they can understand.** Not doing this only delays understanding of what has occurred and the falsehood will lead to distrust of adults—particularly those who told these lies. As Rabbi Joshua Lieberman said in *Peace of Mind,* "A child can stand tears, but not treachery; sorrow, but not deceit."[8] Not disclosing any information to children leads them to believe that they are unimportant. Especially after a sudden death, such as from an accident, heart attack, or suicide, it is important to give children as many facts as they can handle—which is usually more than what adults want to divulge.

- **Answer the questions the child asks,** rather than the questions that you want to answer. Make sure they feel that their questions have been answered. Talking with them shows how much they understand about death, and demonstrates their misconceptions, fears, and worries, so these can be at least partly alleviated. When words fail, try giving children a hug—it answers their most burning question: Will they have physical and emotional support from now on?

- **A benefit of dealing honestly with children** about death may be a decrease in both accidents and suicidal behavior when they get older. Children who do not accept the finality of death may become either "death defiers," who have a higher risk of accidents and death, or adolescents with common suicide "gestures."[9]

- **Accept the child's behavior and methods of displaying grief.** We cannot prevent it and shouldn't try. Many children grieve intermittently, so do not be disturbed by intervals of normal behavior during the adult mourning period. At times, younger children may even seem uncaring or callous, but it is only their way of dealing with an uncomfortable and unusual event. They usually can only tolerate small doses of emotional pain, so have short "sadness spans" before resuming their normal activities. They may, for example, quickly resume playing with toys after seeing adults expressing remorse. Often, they repeatedly ask why the individual died.

- **Establish a safe environment immediately,** with consistent adult caregivers and the presence of their own toys, bed, and "stuff." If the caregivers leave the child for any reason, carefully explain the absence. When they must visit their pediatrician (or be with caregivers when they visit their doctor), carefully explain what the visit is for, since these contacts may be highly traumatic. Especially after having seen many doctors treat the deceased during a prolonged illness, children associate physicians with death.

- **Give children a chance to express their feelings** by asking them to share memories of the decedent. Allow them to "say good-bye" to the person in their own way: by making a card or picture of or "for" the decedent, or by attending the funeral or memorial service. One father, for example, whose son died suddenly of sepsis following a kidney infection, announced to his three surviving children that "everyone should mourn as they felt they wanted to. None of us should feel shy about weeping for Josh, male or female, young or old, but at the same time, we shouldn't feel obliged to cry if we did not need to."[10]

- **If the child asks to attend the funeral or memorial service,** it generally signals that they are old enough to do so. These rites are reality markers, special events with which to acknowledge the death and a future memory marking a significant life passage. Carefully explain what will happen in advance so that they are not surprised at any of the activities. Just as with adults, this ceremony may afford the child a sense of closure and a chance to openly express grief with the adult mourners. A common memory of this for Americans is that of John-John, John F. Kennedy's son, saluting at his father's funeral to show his respect. Although some believe that children under six years do not benefit from attending funerals or memorial services, experience has shown that is not always true. For example, one mother wrote that she chose not to let her four-year-old daughter attend her son's funeral. Years later, the daughter expressed resentment that she had not been permitted to attend.[11] If an alternative to burial is used, such as cremation or organ or whole-body donation, explain that to the child as "special soft ashes" or "letting the doctors use parts of his body to help others."

- **If older children want to grieve with the adults,** that should be permitted. Allowing them to see adult grief reactions makes them feel less concerned about expressing their own feelings.
- **Children's attitudes toward body decomposition and spiritual continuation** of the individual depend upon their religious background.[12]
- **High school students** see an infinite time separating them from old age, disease, and death.[13]
- **Subsequently, all family members, but especially children, have difficulty with "firsts,"** such as the first anniversary of the death, or their first birthday or holiday without a parent.

Some children never adjust well, especially to the death of a parent. One study found that when children lost their mother before 4 years of age, they experienced more than twice the incidence of psychoneurosis as adults and 2½ times the incidence of depression than did the general population. A similar pattern for adult depression occurred when children up to age 14 lost their mothers or if their fathers died when the children were between ages 5 and 9. If their fathers died when they were between ages 10 and 14, they had about a six-times-greater chance of having adult depression.[14,15]

Protocol for Delivering News of Sudden, Unexpected Death to Children

The protocol used for notifying a child of a death may depend, in part, on the child's age. The suggested death-telling methods below (table 13-2) closely parallel the three developmental stages suggested by Piaget and Kane. An adult close to the child should always be entrusted with the job. If the parent feels that he or she cannot tell their child immediately, another trusted adult should take the lead. Yet the parents should at least be present to share their grief with their child. *At all stages, the adults must immediately tell and show the child that they will continue to provide them with love and security.* Then adults must follow through, providing positive signals of love and demonstrating the solidity of the parent-child relationship, even (especially) through the mourning period.

Table 13-2: Protocol to Notify Children of Sudden, Unexpected Death

Age: Years	Method	Kane's Stages	Piaget's Stages
Infant	Younger than 2 years of age, children have no concept of death. They react to parents' emotional states and separation anxiety. Providing physical security for these children, rather than explaining the death, is most important: hold them, wrap them in a favorite blanket, keep their routine as normal as possible.		
2-7	Explain the death as "the end of life" or "no longer living." It is vital to say that death is permanent and was not because of anything they did or thought.	I. Death is concrete: in the immediate here and now. Magical or egocentric thinking exists; they can make someone dead by wishing it so. Can relate death to demise of pets.	*Pre-operational thought*: The child focuses on a single dimension of comparative objects at a time, such as height or width.
7-11	Explain that the person has died. Answer any questions. Make sure that they know that open expressions of grief and discussing their feelings are encouraged and expected.	II. Death explains why a person no longer functions. They recognize death is universal, with various causes.	*Concrete operational thought:* The child can think about the entire object as well as its component parts, such as the body's organs.
11 and up	Discuss the death, the rituals, and partici-pants' behavior as you would with an adult. Include them in the family's entire grieving process.	III. Children can think of death in abstract terms. Logical thinking recognizing reality, sometimes considering existential issues of life and death.	*Formal operations:* Children think about possibilities beyond reality—of what *might* happen.

Adapted, in part, from: Kane B: Children's concepts of death. *J Genet Psychol*. 1979 Mar; 134(1):141-153.

Saving a Parent in Memory

One of the greatest fears small children have when a parent dies is that they won't remember the parent when they are older. Feeling that they don't remember a parent or don't remember enough about a dead parent is also a major stressor for older children. These fears and stresses can be at least partly alleviated by preparing a special memory package about the parent for the child or children to keep. Some of the items that can be included are:

- Videotapes of the parent.
- Videotaped recollections of anecdotes that characterize the person, key events in the parent's life, and a description of how s/he acted toward and felt about the family. Include small details about the person, such as a favorite food, quirky expressions, or hobbies. Friends can help the surviving spouse make the video by including their memories also.
- Pictures of the parent—especially those with the child(ren).
- Letters from other friends and relatives to the child(ren) describing details about the parent, especially personality traits characterized by specific anecdotes.
- Mementos from the parent's life.

Like the memory boxes for the parents of dead children, this will be a treasured keepsake. Children often keep some of these items or the entire box of memorabilia near their beds as a security symbol. Many children (and other survivors) of Vietnam veterans, in lieu of such memorabilia, now use the Vietnam Memorial Wall in Washington, D.C., as a symbol of their deceased parent.

References

1. Wolfe B: Center helps individuals, families cope with loved one's death. *Health Prog*. 1998 May; 69(4):74-7.
2. Drotar D, Irvin N: Disturbed maternal bereavement following infant death. *Child Care Health Dev*. 1979 Jul-Aug;5(4):239-47.
3. Mandell F, McAnulty EH, Carlson A: Unexpected death of an infant sibling. *Pediatrics*. 1983 Nov;72(5):652-7.
4. Brown P: Children and death. saying goodbye. *Nurs Times*. 1993 Jan 27-Feb 2;89(4):26-9.
5. Cain AC, Fast I, Erickson ME: Children's disturbed reactions to the death of a sibling. *Am J Orthopsychiatry*. 1964;34:741-54.
6. Siegel K, Mesagno FP, Christ G: A prevention program for bereaved children. *Am J Orthopsychiatry*. 1990 Apr;60(2):168-75.

7. Furman R: The child's reaction to a death in the family. In: Schoenberg B, Carr AC, Peretz D, et al.: *Loss and Grief: Psychological Management in Medical Practice*. New York: Columbia Univ. Press, 1970, pp. 70-86.

8. Wessel MA: A death in the family. the impact on children. *JAMA*. 1975 Nov 24;234(8):865-6.

9. McIntire MS, Angle CR, Struempler LJ: The concept of death in midwestern children and youth. *Am J Dis Child*. 1972 Jun;123(6):527-32.

10. Brown P: "Children and death."

11. Sarnoff-Schiff H: *The Bereaved Parent*. New York: Crown, 1977.

12. McIntire MS, Angle CR, Struempler LJ: "Midwestern children and youth."

13. Kastenbaum RL: Time and death in adolescence. In: Feifel HL, ed.: *The Meaning of Death*. New York: McGraw-Hill, 1965, pp. 99-113.

14. Barry H, Lindermann E: Critical ages for maternal bereavement in the psychoneuroses. *Psychosom Med*. 1960 May-June;22(3):166-81.

15. Brown F: Depression and childhood bereavement. *J Ment Sci*. 1961 July;107(449):754-77.

14: Notifying Friends, Lovers, Co-Workers, and Students

Nearly everyone is, at one time or another, placed in the role of making death notifications to their own family members or friends. Even professionals who do this routinely as part of their job can suddenly find themselves in the uncomfortable position of "amateur"—one who has difficulty maintaining distance between himself and the survivors. But, as this ancient story illustrates, bereavement is universal.

> A woman was overwhelmed by sorrow after her son's death. Despite attempts to console her, she remained grief-stricken, crying about her misfortune, "Oh, why did this have to happen to me?" As her depression deepened, she was told of a wise man who helped suffering people and rushed to plead for his assistance. He offered to help if she would first bring him a pea, which seemed to present no problem until he added that it must come from a house where death had not been.
>
> She began her search, knocking on every door, asking if there had been a death in the home. In each case, she learned that someone in that home had died at some time. She returned to the wise man and told of her fruitless journey. But, as she related her adventures, she realized that death was a part of everyone's experience and that it touched all in many different ways. She left feeling the pain of her loss but less isolated and ill-favored. She returned home more willing to experience the process of grief.[1]

Ripples of Notification

The news about an individual's death spreads to others in a predictable pattern, sometimes described as being similar to the concentric circles that spread when a pebble is tossed into a pond. A death causes similar ripples in life's fabric. Those closest to the person (relatives or close friends) and geographically close to the event (medical personnel, police, and clergy) learn of the death first. Only later do co-workers, other friends, and distant (personally or geographically) relatives hear of the loss. As the ripples spread out, it is up to different groups to pass the message.

The wider community learns of the death slowly through word-of-mouth, death notices, and obituaries. In some cases, this notification may take years. Some people acquainted with the decedent may never learn of the death. A new method to distribute the news of a death is via listservers and news groups on the Internet. In this way, large numbers of associates learn of the death in a very impersonal way, usually in the privacy of their offices or homes.

When individuals are well-known, whether locally, nationally, or internationally, the word spreads much faster. The deaths of media stars (e.g., Rock Hudson), politicians (e.g., John F. Kennedy), or celebrities (e.g., Princess Diana) engender extensive coverage in the media, causing notification "ripples" much closer together as people learn of the death more quickly than usual. Deaths of local personalities or prominent professionals within a field have that effect within the area in which they were prominent, although the rest of the world may pay little attention.

Notifying Friends

Even among close friends, the pall of sudden death can raise a barrier to communication just when it is most needed. People feel uncomfortable around survivors; they often don't know how to act and, especially, don't know how to deliver the bad news. Even professionals who regularly perform such notifications in their work find notifying friends of a sudden death very difficult. This is amply demonstrated in this vignette that happened to Vicki Alexander, a trauma center charge nurse.

> I go on a houseboat trip every year with eleven other nurses I work with. It's an all-woman trip and we have more fun than you can imagine. This particular year, my friend Sarah went for the first time. She was a little nervous because she doesn't swim well, but she had started to relax and have fun.
>
> Every day, two or three of us would go back to the marina in the ski boat to get ice. On our second day on the lake, the girls who went got a message to call home. When we called, we were told that Sarah's mother had been killed in an automobile accident. She was 58 years old and Sarah was very close to her—actually fairly dependent on her.
>
> Several of us talked about what to do. Meg and I were the only people who really knew Sarah, so we decided that we would tell her and then Meg would drive her home. Having worked in the ICU with Meg for years, I knew she wasn't going to handle the notification part well, so I braced myself to do it basically alone.
>
> I asked Sarah if I could talk to her at the rear of the houseboat. Meg and I were both there. I didn't really have a plan. I knew it had to be done and I just let it happen. I told her, "There's been a serious accident." Knowing she had kids, I

> wanted to move quickly to the next part because the fear of your child being hurt is torturous. I said, "It's your momma, she's gone."
>
> I will never forget her reaction. She wailed, collapsed into my arms and starting vomiting. We lowered her to the floor and held her for awhile. She eventually was able to get to her feet and get in the ski boat so we could get to the marina to drive her home. I remained calm until they left the boat. Then I broke down and felt numb the rest of the night.
>
> Interestingly, Sarah doesn't remember anything about me telling her. I was afraid being around me would cause her pain, but she can't remember the notification at all.
>
> I never want to have to do something like that again, but I'm glad, under the circumstances, that it was me who told her. Just writing this causes my heart rate to increase and a knot to form in my stomach—and it's been seven years since it happened.[2]

Even more difficult for both the notifier and the survivor is when the survivor is not a friend, but an "acquaintance," as happened in the following case:

> A couple was visiting Flagstaff (Ariz.) from someplace back East. Someone from a hospital called the hotel to tell the couple that their son had been killed. However, the couple was out and the message was left with the front-desk clerk. Not knowing what to do, he told his manager. Getting up his nerve, the manager told the couple when they returned to the hotel. They were very upset, and the manager ended up driving them to Phoenix so they could catch a plane for home.[3]

One way to help friends and family cope with a loved one's death is to encourage them to deal with and seek closure for any unresolved issues they may have with the person. Specific suggestions are listed in table 14-1.

Notifying Lovers

In our society, the legitimacy of grief is based on kinship, with secondary mourners legitimized as friends. Yet both heterosexual lovers outside a formal marriage (and especially while formal marriage bonds exist) and homosexual lovers (especially if one or both partners are not openly gay) are often excluded from the mourning process. These individuals have been termed the "secret survivors."[4] The special problems they face begin with the notification, which can occur in any manner, including a casual conversation, a newspaper obituary, a notice at work, and over the Internet. These survivors cannot reveal shock or grieve openly when they get this news for fear that their liaison will be discovered (even if it is postmortem). They also may not be permitted to participate in the societal mourning rituals such as funerals or memorial services, depending upon their known relationship with their deceased lover. Few people will know enough to comfort these survivors. Others, believing that the relationship was primarily sexual, will offer inappropriate forms of comfort. Yet these survivors may face not only the loss of a close emotional tie, but also of possibly important financial support.

Table 14-1: How to Help Friends after a Death

Before the Funeral/Memorial Service

- Get in touch immediately by telephone, if not able to go in person.
- Say little during the initial visit. Be there and *listen*, even if the survivor is rambling or repetitive.
- Do not probe for details about the death.
- Write a letter to the decedent or record on tape some of your memories of the decedent to give to your friend.
- Offer to help out (only help if they agree) with specific tasks, for example:

  Serve as or arrange ushers for funeral/memorial service.

  House-sit to prevent burglaries during funeral/memorial service/visitations.

  Help to notify other friends/family about funeral arrangements.

  Provide food.

  Help coordinate the food and drink supply.

  Pick up friends and family at the airport.

  Arrange housing and transportation for out-of-town family members.

  Help arrange funeral or memorial service.

  Clean the house.

During the Funeral/Memorial Service

- Write a letter to the decedent expressing thoughts and concerns—and place it in the casket or with the body for cremation.
- Attend the funeral or memorial service. Stay afterward to help and console the family.

After the Funeral/Memorial Service

- At work, offer to share the person's workload.
- Share memories of the decedent.
- Mention the decedent's name often in conversations.
- Listen carefully and accept silent periods. Don't be in a hurry.
- Talk about thoughts, feelings, and memories.
- Avoid talking about trivia in front of survivors.
- Avoid clichés; use helpful comments (see chapter 4).
- Be yourself and show the concern you really feel.

Table 14-1: continued

After the Funeral/Memorial Service, cont.

- Offer to help out (only help if they agree) with specific tasks, for example:
  - Run errands.
  - Arrange childcare schedules.
  - Transport family or children, as needed.
  - Arrange housekeeping chores.
  - Grocery shop, do yard work, pick up laundry and mail.
  - Care for pets.
  - Mow the lawn, shovel the sidewalk, water or prune the shrubbery.
  - Help obtain information about problems that they are facing.
  - Be there to answer phones and greet visitors.
  - Keep a record of everyone that calls, visits, or has been contacted.
  - Help with the Thank You notes and other correspondence.
- Don't simply say: "Call me if you need anything." Survivors rarely call.
- Continue contact with the survivor to lessen their inevitable isolation.
- Prepare or provide dinner on a mutually acceptable day every week for two to three months.
- Offer to drive or accompany him or her to the cemetery regularly.
- Encourage others to visit or help out. (Many people who would like to do this feel uncomfortable and need some reassurance that their presence is wanted and needed.)
- Explain clearly what is expected of the survivors and what they can expect of others.
- Gently draw the survivor into low-key outside activities.
- Treat the survivor as a normal person when s/he returns to social activities. (Avoid pity.)
- Offer to house-sit so s/he can get away or visit out-of-town family.
- Keep any promises made to the decedent, if possible.
- Anticipate difficult periods, such as anniversaries (including of the day of death), birthdays, and holidays.

The only ones who can assist these survivors are those who knew of the relationship. Their caring attitude and sensitive assistance during this period may help the surviving partner. However, many of these survivors are more stoic than are others. As one said, "I got myself into this, I will have to handle the loss by myself, too."[5]

Openly lesbian or gay couples do not have quite as many difficulties after a partner's death. Friends, and often family, support them as they would a married couple. Notifications are frequently made to the partner, although unfortunately, in some circumstances, the notifiers' prejudices may not allow them to offer the same level of support and kindness they show to other survivors. That AIDS contributes to many deaths of gay men further taints many notifiers' reactions. Luckily, attitudes are changing, both about AIDS and about non-standard relationships. Hopefully, this will positively affect professional death notifiers.

Notifying Co-workers

While co-workers may not be classed among one's "friends," their deaths may greatly affect both individuals and an organization. The effect is greatest with the death of a key person within the organization, of a co-worker with whom a person worked closely, or when multiple employees die at one time or within a short time period.

It is uncertain whether these types of deaths affect health care workers more than others because of their attitude of invincibility. This may be especially true of people in "rescue" specialties that work in teams, such as emergency medicine, intensive care and operating room personnel, and paramedics. Because of the danger inherent in their jobs, firemen and policemen often have ritualized methods of dealing with these deaths—but may also, unlike other co-workers, have to deliver the initial news of the death to survivors (see chapter 19).

The organizational response to such events is often non-existent or inadequate. Surviving co-workers often must deal with their emotions alone or in small groups. Even with the best of intentions, managers are often uncertain how to proceed after sudden unexpected deaths. The first step is to see to the needs of the worker's(s') family(ies). Knowledge that co-workers or employers care after such an event helps survivors cope. More practically, managers can also bring a "package of assistance" with specific items to immediately help survivors. This could include:

- Manager's phone, fax, and pager numbers.
- Phone and pager numbers of other company personnel who will be able to assist survivors, such as by arranging transportation, helping make funeral arrangements, or contacting the decedent's friends about funeral or memorial services.
- Money to cover unexpected immediate expenses.
- A brief summary of the funeral and other insurance benefits provided by the employer, and the telephone number of the person to contact about this.

- The keys to an extra car or minivan to help transport out-of-town relatives.

Managers should use the general protocols in this book to help them interact with survivors. This is especially important if the death occurred on-the-job or was job-related, since the potential for negative interactions can be increased. Additionally, managers should ask survivors if they would like (or would permit) them to hold a memorial service at the workplace. If one is held, they must be sure to notify survivors so that they can attend and to arrange transportation for them, if necessary. Such memorial services are often held after the formal funerary rites. It is helpful to co-workers if the managers find out the details about these rites, ask survivors if co-workers can attend, and then advise the co-workers. The survivors then don't have to answer multiple inquiries and the co-workers don't have to make awkward calls to the survivors.

Some companies that have experienced tragic losses bring in professionals to help co-workers through their grief. A rapid response can start with altering the work environment, as happened in this case:

> Without warning, a bank employee began shooting fellow employees with a .357 Magnum. Although we thought that he had snapped, it turned out that he had a history of mental illness and had picked his victims from among those who had rejected his amorous advances. Three people died and one was badly injured before the shooter killed himself. Everyone was understandably upset. The bank had fortuitously contracted, only three days before, with a crisis intervention group from a local psychiatric hospital to help handle untoward incidents. They were called in to assist with the stress debriefing and follow-up.
>
> At their direction, all the bloodstained carpet, wallboard, etc. were replaced overnight. The "knockdown" furniture was disassembled and then reassembled so that the office layout was totally different when co-workers returned to their "new" office environment the next day. The conference room where most of the shootings took place no longer existed and the only smell was of fresh paint.
>
> Administrators held a series of meetings to talk with everyone involved. The crisis team had briefed them on what topics to cover and how to handle the sessions. Although scheduled for 1 to 1 ½ hours, each session lasted as long as employees wanted to talk. The crisis team subsequently counseled the most severely affected employees.[6]

Such professionals may then counsel some people individually, but more often they use group discussions with expert facilitators to help workers express their emotions, gain insight into the grieving process, and learn specific ways they can help themselves and each other. At one company, which lost several key people in an airline crash, employees' (90% men) reactions during these sessions ranged from wondering when their crying would stop to speaking of physical ills and insomnia since the crash. Many questioned their vocational choice, since being on the plane was related to their work. Suggestions to co-workers during these sessions included:[7]

- Face the reality of the loss by attending memorial services.

- Acknowledge their emotional pain. Do not avoid it by abusing substances or avoiding their thoughts and feelings.
- Use personal spiritual resources to deal with and gain a perspective on the tragedy.
- Garner support by sharing thoughts and feelings with social resources, such as friends, spouses, and co-workers.
- Believe they will get through this ordeal intact.
- Encourage those with profound, abnormal, or sustained grief reactions to seek professional help.

After these sessions, if there is interest, an organizational support group can be established. Professional leadership from outside the group affected should be obtained, since internal experts may also be affected by the tragedy.

Student Deaths

More than 14.7 million students attend U.S. colleges.[8] With estimates of between 4 and 15 deaths each year per 10,000 college students enrolled, this equates to between 6,000 and 22,000 deaths annually! Three-fourths of these deaths are due to unintentional trauma, homicide, or suicide.[9] Yet few schools have protocols to follow in the case of student deaths. Some college administrators are brash enough to say, "Students don't die here."[10]

The response to student deaths encompasses two aspects: telling survivors and dealing with the notification and subsequent grief reactions of fellow students. (A significant number of deaths occur during the pre-college years. Information about notification and grief for these groups can be found in chapters 12 and 13.) Deaths of college students are somewhat unique because they are usually living apart from their families (often in other cities or regions of the country), are rarely children, and often have very close interactions with fellow students.

Students' deaths represent a complex mixture, with similarities to deaths of co-workers and to deaths in families. The school's ability to handle the multiple aspects of the situation will determine how well survivors handle it. As W. R. Donahue said: "Whether death occurred on or off campus, in a large or small community, by foul play or accident, the dean's readiness to cope can result either in a series of painful, confusing, albeit unintentional blunders or in effective, considerate institutional service which minimizes unnecessary grief for friends, relatives, and the campus community."[11]

One way to handle these occurrences is to prepare a checklist to follow when deaths happen in the middle of the night or on weekends, as is invariably the case. Use the *Student-Death Protocol* (table 14-2) to make such a checklist. By doing so, college administrators can assure that foolish, avoidable, and potentially harmful errors that may hurt survivors are not made.

Table 14-2: Student-Death Protocol

Prepare
• Appoint a coordinator and alternates. Give their names to campus police/ security, residence hall directors, campus health, and other administrators.
• Make prior arrangements to access information from local hospitals, police departments, and the media. They often learn of the death before campus officials, especially if it occurs off campus. Without these arrangements, it may be very difficult to obtain information from these sources once a death occurs.
• Educate the staff about the procedures.
• Train at least one media spokesperson.
• Design a checklist for the coordinator and others to use.
Clarify Policies
• Refine the withdrawal process. This should be rapid and include all elements of the school's system, so that inappropriate mailings and requests are not sent in the student's name to the next of kin or other survivors.
• Tuition refunds. Whether 100% of the current term's tuition is refunded (as in 25% of all schools) or a prorated amount is refunded, it should be done quickly.
• Room/board fees are usually refunded on a prorated basis.
• Posthumous degrees. A very sticky issue on many campuses (why, I'm not sure), especially for those early in their academic careers.
• Donations to memorial funds. If small amounts are given in a student's name after the family requests it in an obituary or funeral notice, the administrative costs may be more than the amount donated. Generally, donations in the student's name to the general scholarship fund are recommended.
• Shipment of personal items. Who will pack these and pay for shipment? This should be predetermined.
• Funeral costs. Determine if there are any circumstances when the school will pay funeral costs or the costs of returning the body to the family (which usually involves embalming costs).
• Memorial services. Will they be permitted, paid for, or led by the campus? When and where can they be held?
Crisis Management
• Get correct information. A coordinator may need to go to the death scene (on campus) or make multiple calls to the police, hospital, or coroner's office.

Continued on next page

Table 14-2: continued

Crisis Management, cont.
• Contact campus police/security. They can often obtain necessary information from the police. • Correctly identify student by name and ID number. Do not confuse two students with the same names. • If there is a student with the same or a similar name, contact that student and ask him or her to call their relatives to assure them that the student is fine, despite the news reports. • Obtain student's campus address. • Obtain student's permanent address. • Obtain next of kin information. • Use telephone contact protocol. (See table 5-1.)
Notify
• Next of kin. The "coordinator" should make this notification. • Boyfriend/girlfriend/spouse. • Roommate(s). • Campus news and public affairs office. When deaths occur on campus or will attract notoriety because multiple students died or due to the method of death, one office should handle all news inquiries. That way, the information released is consistent—and more likely to be valid. It is the best way to stop unfounded rumors from spreading. • President of student's clubs and fraternity or sorority. • Chaplain to assist with survivor counseling and, where appropriate, to contact the survivors' clergy. • Campus health and counseling services and director of residential life to assist with survivor counseling. Experience shows that counselors should support students but not give encouragement or reassurance when they are in the immediate shock or subsequent depressed stages of grieving. • Academic dean, president, student's advisor, and other university officials. • University's risk manager/legal counsel if death was on campus. While the school may not be culpable, they may need to make that determination. • Student's instructors. • Registrar.

Continued on next page

Table 14-2: continued

Notify, cont.
• Safety/insurance officer. • International student services (in appropriate cases). • Scholarship office.
Subsequent Duties
• Meet with and arrange accommodations for the family if they wish to visit the campus. • Have a public recognition of the death on campus, for example, fly the flag at half-mast or have a campus-wide moment of silence. • Will the school, friends, or family arrange campus or other memorial services? • Notify students, faculty, staff, and administrators of the time and place for memorial and funeral services. The presence of senior school officials demonstrates to the family that the student was important and respected. • Send letters or framed certificates of recognition, appreciation, or accomplishments to the family. • Send diploma, if indicated. • Letter of condolences from dean or president. • Yearbook memorial section arranged. • Arrange for long-term psychological intervention and support for those on campus who were most affected by the student's death.

Adapted from References 12 through 15.

The exact people to be notified and the methods of notification (telephone, in person) will vary. If the notification is made in person, use the protocol in table 3-1, and if by telephone, use table 5-1. Dr. Richard Nelson describes one of his experiences calling parents about a student's death.

> One of the toughest parts of my job as an emergency physician is breaking the news by phone that a loved one has died. It's bad enough to do this in person, but to call someone you don't know and give them news that will forever change their life is very difficult. Of these phone calls, none are worse than informing a parent about the death of their son or daughter. Since our medical center sits on a large Midwestern college's campus, I have performed this unfortunate task a number of times.

Probably the worst such situation occurred when a 20-year-old male student was brought to the emergency department in full cardiac arrest. After an unsuccessful attempt at resuscitation, I called his mother who lived 110 miles away. I explained the situation to the mother and she was obviously heartbroken, as were the other family members who subsequently came to the phone. Several others phoned me later to confirm the tragedy. Especially poignant was that the son had called his mother less than one hour earlier complaining of feeling his heart racing. She suggested that he go to the hospital to have it checked out. He apparently collapsed in cardiac arrest as he was getting ready to do this; his roommate called 911.[16]

The coordinator should notify the student's immediate next of kin and his or her closest campus contacts. Others can be notified according to the school's plan. School administrators should be prepared to explain any or all campus policies. If next of kin or others don't ask immediately, they will ask soon after. They may also want to discuss other issues surrounding the death (see chapter 27 for some questions and their answers). Some people do not have to be contacted immediately, since they primarily need the information for administrative purposes (e.g., registrar, scholarship office).

Student survivors may require significant and immediate counseling. A "ripple effect" often spreads through the campus community, affecting many more students and faculty than just the dead student's immediate cohorts. The school's chaplain and health or counseling services should be prepared to offer assistance to them. Those most affected will also need administrative excuses to miss classes, and a few may need permission to withdraw from school for the balance of the term.

Grade School and High School

Deaths also occur among grade school and high school students and their families. Unlike college students, deaths normally occur away from school and the aftermath is notifying the school body and dealing with their grief response. Pre-planning for these events can help make the school's response smoother and more appropriate. Much of the protocol for university planning applies. In addition, appropriate school district or outside resources should be identified to assist the school's administrators, since sufficient counseling services will rarely be found within an individual school. Just as campus health services play a role in colleges, the school nurse can assist at these schools. Unlike college deaths, after a grade school or high school student's or teacher's sudden death, administrators may need to send letters to the parents of many children affected by the tragedy.[17]

When the death occurs at the school or when traveling to or from school, outside counselors are usually needed. When school disasters occur, as has been happening too often recently with mass murders on school campuses, students, faculty, and the community usually require various levels of post-traumatic stress counseling. (See chapter 26 for more information about this type of counseling.)

Teachers' Deaths

Teachers' deaths may traumatize entire schools or school systems. Students' reactions should be anticipated and handled using the protocol in table 14-2. The students in closest contact with the deceased teacher (e.g., students in her/his class and extracurricular activities s/he supervised) may be most affected. In primary grades where one teacher teaches a class for most of the day, those students may be profoundly affected. Likewise, the death of a teacher-coach who has acted as both advisor and mentor may greatly disturb those who were closest to the teacher. Supervisors should work with other school staff members, using the information in this chapter's previous sections: "Friends" and "Co-workers."

References

1. Davidowitz M, Myrick RD: Responding to the bereaved. an analysis of "helping" statements. *Death Educ.* 1984;8(1):1-10.
2. Alexander V: Personal communication with author, February 1999.
3. Rossano JW: Personal communication with author, December 1998.
4. Weinbach RW: Sudden death and secret survivors. helping those who grieve alone. *Soc Work.* 1989 Jan;34(1):57-60.
5. *Ibid.*
6. Iserson, AR and Silvers, M: Personal communication with author, March 1999.
7. Klompeen D: Company managers should be prepared to deal with grief following tragedy. *Occup Health Saf.* 1991 Apr;60(4):64-7.
8. U.S. Dept. of Commerce, Bureau of the Census, 1996.
9. Knott JE, Crafts R: The realities of college student death. *NASPA J.* 1980;18(2):29-34.
10. Wrenn R: College student death: postvention issues for educators and counselors. In: Papadatos D, Papadatos C, eds.: *Children and Death—Series in Death Education, Aging, and Health Care.* New York: Hemisphere, 1991, pp. 53-64.
11. Donahue WR: Student death. what do we do? *NASPA J.* 1977;14(4):29-32.
12. Crafts R: Student affairs response to student death. In: Zinner ES, ed.: *Coping with Death on Campus: New Dimensions for Student Services.* San Francisco: Jossey-Bass, 1985, pp. 29-38.
13. Halberg LJ: Death of a college student: response by student services professionals on one campus. *J Counseling Dev.* 1986 Feb;64(6):411-12.
14. Wrenn R: "College student death." In: Papadatos: "*Children and Death,*" pp. 53-64.
15. Knott JE, Crafts R: "The realities of college student death."
16. Nelson R: Personal communication with author, February 1999.
17. Kamins J, Lipton H: Crisis intervention teams: a model for schools. In Stevenson RG, Stevenson EP: *Teaching Students about Death: A Comprehensive Resource for Educators and Parents.* Philadelphia: Charles Press, 1996, pp. 92-9.

15: Notifying Other Incident Survivors

One group who can be considered survivors of a fatal incident is the patients who witness the resuscitative efforts and the death. These witnesses are found in intensive care units, emergency departments, and hospital wards. Experience shows that rather than experiencing fear, these patents often feel initial irritation followed by amazement at the medical team's efficiency.[1] Patients in nursing homes and hospices may see only the death and its aftermath, since resuscitative efforts may not be instituted or may be limited. Another group is those patients injured in the same incident in which, sometimes unbeknownst to the patient, their loved ones or friends died.

It is not unusual for physicians, nurses, and EMS personnel to be faced with questions from survivors still in critical condition. The dilemma then arises whether they should inform their patient about the death, if asked. The answer depends on what is in the patient's best interest. If the patient is stable and wants to know, then he or she should be told. This conforms to the ethical principle of truth-telling (veracity), and to the practical matter that it would be nearly impossible to keep this information from an awake patient who is interacting with multiple members of the medical team, family, friends, and, often, the police. However, there are instances where the patient clearly does not want to be told, as in the case below. This too should be respected.

> After a major disaster, a woman who had been in a terrible fire with her husband and others had recovered from her injuries. She "suspended all inquiry about the details of her husband's fate for more than four weeks, deliberately occupying her thoughts with personal friends and pleasant fantasies and recollections. When, however, her relatives visited her, they became more and more uneasy because the range of topics discussed in conversation was

> necessarily small. Any reference to the lost person and any attempt at planning the future had to be avoided. It finally became the psychiatrist's task to confront the patient with the sad news."[2]

This woman suffered from a pathological grief reaction. Yet some people do not want to immediately learn about their loved one's death, even when they suspect or "know" the truth.

In cases where the patient's medical condition is unstable, their welfare must come first. Notifiers should delay imparting the news until the patient is awake, stable, and able to understand this information. This often means telling them after they awaken from any emergency surgery. That may be many hours after they return from the recovery room, since notifiers should be certain that the patient has recovered sufficiently from the anesthetic to remember what is said. It is doubly painful to have to go back and repeat this message if it was told too soon after surgery and thus forgotten a few hours later.

The same strategies apply to telling children. In a moving series of interviews with an 8-year-old girl who survived the January 1990 crash of Avianca Flight 052 in Long Island, New York, a physician described how he advised the girl's father to tell her that her mother and brother were dead. Since she had been seriously injured, they waited until one week after the crash when she was awake, alert, and off major pain medications. She had already described seeing her mother and brother in the same condition after the crash as those she said were "dead," but had not yet accepted that they too had died.

> "When do we tell her?" asked the father.
>
> "Do you think that she doesn't know already?" answered Dr. Fornari. "You will not have to tell her with words. Sit with her, and she will tell you. Cry together."
>
> Replied the father, "I was thinking of telling her that I just found out, so she isn't angry that I haven't told her yet."
>
> Later, after he told her of the deaths, her father told Dr. Fornari, "It was as you said. Few words. I said, 'I have just learned that your mother and brother have died.' She exclaimed, 'Oh, Daddy—this is so painful.' Then we cried together on and off all night."[3]

"When you are thinking of telling a lie," said a teacher at Harvard Medical School in the late nineteenth century, "ask yourself whether it is simply and solely for the patient's benefit that you are going to tell it. If you are sure that you are acting for his good and not for your own profit, you can go ahead with a clear conscience."[4] We must be careful, however, since lying can all too easily become a habit—especially when it is used to make situations easier for caregivers.

References

1. Hackett TP, Cassem NH, Wishnie HA: The coronary-care unit. an appraisal of its psychologic hazards. *N Engl J Med*. 1968 Dec 19;279(25):1365-70.

2. Cobb S, Lindemann E: Neuropsychiatric observations. *Ann Surg*. 1943;117(6):814-24.

3. Fornari V: The aftermath of a plane crash—helping a survivor cope with deaths of mother and sibling—Case of Mary, age 8. In: Webb NB, ed.: *Play Therapy with Children in Crisis: A Casebook for Practitioners*. New York: Guilford, 1991, pp. 416-34.

4. Cabot RC: Truth and falsehood in medicine. *Am Med*. 1903;5:344-9.

SECTION 3: The Notifiers

"None love the messenger who brings bad news."

Sophocles, *Antigone*

16: Physicians

Physicians have two responsibilities when dealing with death—pronouncing the person dead and telling and comforting the survivors. They have struggled mightily to save a life, as often happens when death is sudden and unexpected; orchestrated a team of other physicians, nurses, technicians, and aides in a resuscitation ballet; and declared the finale when no more could be done. All activity ceases without a sense of completion—only of finality. The atmosphere changes. All efforts have been expended on the patient and the physician is exhausted, often both mentally and physically. Yet once they pronounce their patient dead, physicians must transition from technical interventions to social support by delivering the news of death in a compassionate and caring manner. As one author describes the process, "Objectivity must now be tempered by empathic sensitivity; role responses are replaced by interactional [*sic*] responses, and mechanical manipulation must give way to concerned involvement."[1] This is not easy to do.

According to the American Medical Association's Council on Ethical and Judicial Affairs, notification is a major physician responsibility that should not be delegated to others and should be taught. (See chapter 29 for information on teaching death notification.)

> Disclosing the death of a patient to the patient's family is a duty which goes to the very heart of the physician-patient relationship and should not be readily delegated to others by the attending physician. The emotional needs of the family and the integrity of the physician-patient relationship must at all times be given foremost consideration.
>
> Physicians in residency training may be asked to participate in the communication of information about a patient's death, if that request is

commensurate with the physician's prior training or experience and previous close personal relationship with the family.

It would not be appropriate for the attending physicians or resident to request that a medical student notify family members of a patient's death. Medical students should be trained in issues of death and dying, and should be encouraged to accompany attending physicians when news of a patient's death is conveyed to the family members.[2]

There is evidence that doctors give bad news badly. This may be due to their various fears: of being blamed, of the unknown, of expressing emotions, of not having all the answers, and of death.[3,4] This leads some to use an apologetic approach that has been called "a plea for mercy." The physician implicitly asks survivors, in their time of grief, for nurture and support. "The physician walks in, sinks into a chair and sighs heavily. Hesitantly, he says, 'This is one of the most difficult things I have to do as a physician . . .' or 'I really hate having to be the one to tell you this but . . ..'"[5] Or even worse, they use the blunt approach, typified by entering the room with survivors, shaking their head, and saying, "I'm not going to pull any punches—he's dead."

Some physicians—and one must wonder why they ever entered this "helping" profession—are crass to the point of stupidity, as this survivor's story illustrates.

Two people came laughing down the hospital corridor wearing scrubs. One even tripped over her feet. They passed by me in the waiting room, then turned back. One stood behind me and tapped me on the shoulder. I had to twist around to see her as she said, "Are you Tim's wife?" "Yes," I replied. "He expired," [she said.]

"Who are you?" I asked, since she had no identification and hadn't bothered to introduce herself. "I'm the doctor," she replied.

"Well, that was an awfully rude way to tell me." She frowned, shot me a dirty look, and said with obvious indignation in her voice, "Well, he's dead, Ma'am. Expired."

"Like a goddamn milk carton!" I thought. She made my husband's life seem so trivial. I was in such shock I started wandering around the halls, and the doctor walked off without a word.[6]

It's no wonder, though, that physicians learn to be somewhat distant when dealing with death and its aftermath, including the survivors. Medical students are intentionally given experiences that desensitize them to death. On their first day of medical school, they begin handling and dissecting an anatomical cadaver. This is meant not only to teach them anatomy, but also to depersonalize death.[7] This is followed by a year of pathology, handling tissues and organs of the dead, and occasionally observing autopsies on the recently deceased.

Many physicians must deal with death on a daily basis, especially those in primary care, emergency medicine, oncology, trauma surgery, geriatrics (including hospice and nursing home medicine), and critical care. But at some point in their careers, all physicians encounter their patients' deaths. There are no "deathless" specialties, except administration and, ironically, pathology. More than one-fourth of all in-hospital deaths are unanticipated, with more than one-third unexpected in intensive care units and two-thirds in emergency departments.[8]

For many physicians, death becomes so routine that they think less about it than do non-physicians. Those seeing death most commonly, such as those in emergency departments, trauma surgery, oncology, and intensive care, may be somewhat less stressed than their counterparts who experience patient deaths less often, but this is not always the case.[9] Some blame these emotions on a sense of eternal optimism in the face of death. As one experienced ICU nurse explained, "This often prevents physicians from helping patients achieve an optimal or peaceful death."[10]

Yet physicians may be more afraid of death than the average person and may have entered the medical profession to govern their above-average death fears.[11] In general, female physicians have more death anxiety than male physicians do, while some specialists (e.g., psychiatrists) have more than others (e.g., surgeons) do.[12] This anxiety may explain why there is very little discussion of the not-uncommon deaths by suicide among psychiatric patients. Psychiatrists rarely have to notify survivors; rather, they are recipients of the news. In general, they react to these deaths with self-blame and self-doubt.[13]

These different levels of death anxiety relate to physicians' methods of delivering the news about unexpected deaths to survivors. To overcome this anxiety, many physicians consciously or unconsciously follow a preparation process to construct the calm demeanor of professionalism most feel is important. Many follow a pattern similar to this physician's routine:

> I just take a deep breath and say, "I have to do it." I think everybody has to calm themselves down, just take a deep breath . . . and say, "Hey, you've got to start someplace." I usually sit down and think about it before I do it . . . I don't know what I do to prepare myself mentally. I guess I just psych myself up.[14]

Some anxiety may be due to the sense of guilt some physicians have after a death. Traditionally (although hopefully it is an idea that is on the wane), physicians treated death as the enemy, using all their skills, medications, and equipment to stave it off. If they "lost" this battle, they were taught to have the same feelings as one does after losing a military clash. Since it is physicians who usually make the decisions during, and decide when to stop, resuscitative efforts, they have the opportunity to shoulder as much blame as they want for "not saving" a life (even though it usually cannot be saved). One physician described that feeling, saying:

> Yes, absolutely. I do feel guilty whenever someone dies, especially if there is any element in there that could have possibly been reversed. You always wonder, "could someone else have picked that up earlier than I did?" No way around that. Anybody who says they don't has got to be a fool or the most incredible person in the world. Because I don't think anybody can say "I did everything." That's impossible.[15]

Once they become acculturated as a physician, they may feel a professional reluctance to demonstrate any emotion when sudden unexpected death occurs. As Tolle and Girard said,

> Unfortunately, we as physicians do not expect that we should grieve when patients die. We are regarded as counselors and support figures who are resistant to the emotional impact of death. Outwardly, physicians meet those expectations—we are rarely observed to demonstrate emotions . . . and we do not discuss our feelings, even with unexpected death. . . . [T]he reasons why physicians seem less affected by death are complex, but they include, for one, our own perceived needs to meet assumed professional and personal expectations. Still, there is every reason to believe that death adversely affects the physician's sense of accomplishment and satisfaction, and foments feelings of guilt, failure, and unworthiness. To ignore these feelings or allow them to go unaddressed is unacceptable.[16]

Medical Errors

Medical errors occur, and they sometimes cause deaths. How often is uncertain. Deaths from surgical and anesthetic errors are more identifiable and quantifiable, so surgeons and anesthesiologists may be not only more aware of the deaths they cause, but also the ones to interact with survivors. A 1987 British study found that 1 in 2,600 patients undergoing surgery died from an error in surgical technique, 1 in 185,000 from an error solely due to the administration of anesthesia, and 1 in 1,351 were partly related to the anesthetic.[17] When errors occur, those involved may be devastated, feel a need to defend themselves against legal charges, and be tempted to deny blame—all while having to notify and comfort survivors. (Also see "How did s/he die?" in chapter 27.)

Despite any unresolved feelings physicians may have after unexpected operating room deaths, survivors must be notified of all the facts. As one physician wrote, "The effect of this news is devastating. Place yourself in their position. Your own relative has gone into hospital for a minor operation and now there is a telephone call to say she is dead."[18] Three approaches have been suggested for notifying survivors after an operating room tragedy that similarly apply to other fatal medical errors: (1) Using a limited number of on-site people; (2) Using a larger team; or (3) Using a management group led by an uninvolved senior physician. The on-site group consists of the anesthesiologist or surgeon (or the physicians involved in a non-surgical case) and an uninvolved helper, such as the chaplain or nursing supervisor.

Notification about Deaths due to Medical Errors

A notification team should consist of at least the primary physicians involved (in surgical cases, it should include both the surgeon and the anesthesiologist), a nurse, and a chaplain, social worker, or interpreter. While its mission is to be mutually supportive, the team is also a risk-management tool that can overwhelm and intimidate survivors. Part of the reason for using a team is so that no one team member blames the others.

Others suggest that an uninvolved senior physician, as part of the risk-management process, do the initial notification as well as the continuing delivery of all facts in the case.[19] Yet this system can rarely be activated quickly. Therefore, the "numb and shattered" physicians involved in the death are usually the ones to deliver the news.[20]

Follow essentially the same notification protocol for deaths due to identifiable medical errors and for operating room errors. Remember these basic rules:

- Either cancel the remainder of the day's surgeries or have another team do them. For non-operating room cases, relieve all involved staff of responsibilities for that shift.
- Call survivors, if they are not present. Use the telephone protocol in table 5-1.
- Gather survivors in a separate room to deliver the news.
- Brief the members of the group, whether they are a few people or the structured "team."
- Use the notification protocol in table 3-1 to deliver the news.
- Give survivors all the facts as clearly as they are known. Do not hide or alter known information.
- Do not exaggerate the team or individual's blame or assume blame based on supposition.
- Give the family a 24-hour contact number for the person leading the in-hospital investigation.
- Be certain that working contact numbers are available for the key survivors.
- Debrief the notification personnel or team.
- Inform the medical examiner or coroner. (These cases generally fall under their jurisdiction.)
- Inform the hospital's risk manager.
- Debrief the operating room or other clinical team who themselves will be suffering stress.
- Arrange for subsequent stress/psychological follow-up for the personnel involved.

References

1. Robinson MA: Informing the family of sudden death. *Am Fam Phys.* 1981 Apr;23(4):115-8.

2. American Medical Association Council on Ethical and Judicial Affairs: Opinion 8.18: Informing Families of a Patient's Death. In: *Code of Medical Ethics: Current Opinions with Annotations.* Chicago: The Association, 1997, pp. 134-5.

3. Buckman R: Breaking bad news: why is it still so difficult? *Br Med J (Clin Res Ed).* 1984 May 26;288(6430):1597-9.

4. Eggly S, Afonso N, Rojas G, et al.: An assessment of residents' competence in the delivery of bad news to patients. *Acad Med.* 1997 May;72(5):397-9.
5. Robinson MA: "Informing the family."
6. Anon. Posted on WidowNet <www.fortnet.org/WidowNet/faqs/>.
7. Iserson KV: *Death to Dust: What Happens to Dead Bodies?* Tucson, AZ: Galen Press, Ltd., 1994, pp. 89-96.
8. Tolle SW, Girard DE: The physician's role in the events surrounding patient death. *Arch Int Med.* 1983 Jul;143(7):1447-9.
9. Tolle SW, Elliot DL, Hickam DH: Physician attitudes and practices at the time of patient death. *Arch Intern Med.* 1984 Dec;144(12):2389-91.
10. Began, V: Personal communication with author, 1 April 1999.
11. Feifel HL: The functions of attitudes toward death. In: *Death and Dying: Attitudes of Patient and Doctor.* New York: Group for the Advancement of Psychiatry, 1965, pp. 632-41.
12. Viswanathan R: Death anxiety, locus of control, and purpose in life of physicians. their relationship to patient death notification. *Psychosomatics.* 1996 Jul-Aug;37(4):339-45.
13. Litman RE: When patients commit suicide. *Am J Psychother.* 1965 Oct;19:570-6.
14. Clark RE, LaBeff EE: Death telling: managing the delivery of bad news. *J Health Soc Behav.* 1982 Dec;23(4):366-80.
15. *Ibid.*
16. Tolle SW, Girard DE: "The physician's role."
17. Lunn JN, Devlin HB: Lessons from the confidential enquiry into perioperative death in three NHS regions. *Lancet.* 1987 Dec 12;2(8572):1384-6.
18. Bacon AK: Death on the table. some thoughts on how to handle an anaesthetic-related death. *Anaesthesia.* 1989 Mar;44(3):245-8.
19. Davies JM: On-site risk management. *Can J Anesth.* 1991 Nov;38(8):1029-30.
20. Bacon AK: "Death on the table."

17: Emergency Departments, Critical Care, and Trauma

In recent years, about 300,000 people died in emergency departments (EDs), or about 3 per 1000 ED visits.[1] Only oncologists and hospice physicians see more deaths than emergency physicians do. Although emergency personnel commonly see sudden death and notify survivors, it remains emotionally draining—70% of emergency physicians find death notifications to be personally difficult. Perhaps this is because only one-half received any type of death-notification education in medical school and only one-third received any such training during residency.[2] Few have protocols to assist them in making these notifications.

In our emergency department/trauma center, sudden death arrives all too often. I normally buzz around the department in a scrub suit (jazzed-up pajamas) embroidered with my name. I only put on my white coat when I have to deliver the news about a death to survivors. I count it a good shift when I haven't had to don the coat.

The "Family Room"

Those who initially meet survivors usually are not involved in the resuscitative effort. While they may be nurses, they also may be chaplains, social workers, or specially trained volunteers. They should have an introductory message memorized to deliver to these survivors. The format will always be the same, only the specific information changes. One example is:

> Mr. and Mrs. Smith? I'm [greeter's name and position]. The paramedics brought your son to the emergency department after he was involved in a bad car crash. The trauma team that has been working on him tells me that he was found

> unconscious and has not awakened. I'm not sure about his other injuries. We're going to go to a quieter area and I'll get someone from the team to speak with you.

The key points to remember when delivering this message are to identify the survivors, identify the emergency department (or ICU, labor and delivery, operating room) representative, give very basic information, and guide the survivors to a quiet place. This quiet room is where survivors can be located if someone needs them, for example to give them updates or the news about the death, and where they can have some privacy to grieve.

After they arrive at the emergency department, relatives often feel isolated from the events, the ED personnel, and the activities surrounding them. They are often put in a "family room" away from the mainstream of activity. Often these rooms are in the interior of the ED and have been criticized by survivors for their lack of natural light. In fact, one survivor symbolically told me, "The room doesn't seem to have any light at all." Others complain, if asked afterwards, that the room where they waited didn't have decorations, any comfortable furniture, or that it was far too small. It is still better to supply this type of room than have survivors grieve in the waiting room, in the hall, or in an empty patient room. One British chaplain described their situation.

> Although longing to "do something," they were unable to focus their minds sufficiently to make any positive response to this urge, and thus sat passive but frustrated behind closed doors, acutely aware of every footfall and clatter of equipment outside. The nursing staff is acutely aware that someone ought to be with the relatives, but they are restricted in two ways. First, there is often simply no time for a nurse to sit and talk to relatives when her colleagues are under additional pressure because of the redirection of staff to the resuscitation room. In most cases, a five-minute chat and a cup of tea are woefully inadequate, anyway, and serve only to frustrate the nurse, who wishes she had more time, and further unsettle the relatives, who need the minimum of interruption if they are to remain in control of their emotions. Secondly, and more subtly, there is the thorny problem of emotional involvement.[3]

Viewing Resuscitations

There seems to be no good answer to the question of whether family members who have arrived during the resuscitation should be permitted in the resuscitation area. Many people encourage this practice, but the answer seems to lie in what is best for the patient, rather than for the family. If a resuscitation effort is in progress, then some hope may exist that the patient's life can still be saved. In that case, anything that distracts from the effort cannot and should not be tolerated.

The argument against allowing survivor onlookers is that for resuscitations using a large team, there are constant problems involving having too many people, having unclear communications, and not having a clear leader or one who is willing to make firm, timely, and rational decisions.[4] Having family members present simply adds another complication, and introduces the possibility of an onlooker fainting (as they sometimes do even while watching a laceration being sutured or an injection being given) or otherwise becoming another patient—at a very inopportune time. This is aside from any misinterpretation of the team's discussions or actions, which is a likely occurrence. Team members may also feel uncomfortable being judged in their actions by the family. (Emergency medical systems personnel, however, routinely experience this during resuscitative attempts.)

Yet Doyle et al. found that of those survivors who witnessed resuscitative efforts in the ED while accompanied by a staff member, 94% believed that they would participate again. A chaplain or ED nurse asked the relatives if they wanted to witness their relative's on-going ED resuscitation. They were brought into the resuscitation room after being quickly briefed on what they would see. An attempt was made to cover as much of the patient as possible. They were given a chair (if elderly) and permitted to leave and reenter if they wanted to. They were asked to step out if additional invasive procedures were necessary. When present, they were encouraged to talk to and touch the patient. Decisions to pronounce the patient dead were sometimes discussed with the family, although in some cases they were simply asked to leave the room. Many (76%) thought that their grieving was facilitated by their witnessing the resuscitation and 64% felt that their presence was helpful to their dying family member. The presence of these survivors did not seem to hinder the resuscitative efforts.[5]

The British had the same results when they asked relatives accompanying patients with heart attacks or in need of trauma resuscitations if they wanted to stay during the procedures. Most did, accompanied by a hospital chaperone. None disrupted the resuscitative efforts and all appreciated being able to be there. Subsequent psychological tests at three and nine months after the event showed that this group had fewer episodes of "intrusive imagery," such as flashbacks of the events leading to the death, than did those not present at the resuscitation (relatives in the control group). They also had lower levels of anxiety, depression, post-traumatic avoidance behavior, and grief.[6]

Dr. Ken Mattox, a trauma surgeon in Houston, Texas, responded to these findings, saying that this does not reflect the feelings of the "vast majority of the people in the trenches. . . I am not opposed to the bonding that I think is necessary in many instances, when the patient is moving toward the operating room or a specialized procedure, and you're finished with those activities that have the potential to cause a great impression and result in misinterpretation [by relatives]. That's the time for hand-holding, communicating, bonding, saying 'I love you.'"[7]

The best compromise solution comes from Drs. Ahrens and Hart, who surveyed the parents of children who died unexpectedly in emergency departments. They suggest that if relatives (parents in their cases) arrive before the resuscitation is terminated and wish to observe the resuscitation, they be permitted to do so after the key procedures have been accomplished. In pediatric cases, as with most adult "medical" cases, these procedures include establishing the airway, defibrillating, and placing central (into the large veins in the neck or groin) intravenous lines.[8] Serious trauma cases may be more difficult, since invasive procedures may be performed up until the patient is pronounced dead or is rushed to the operating room. In any case where families enter the room while resuscitation attempts are in progress, they must understand that they may be asked to leave (or may voluntarily leave) at any point, depending upon their reactions and what the team leader feels is best for the patient.

Experience shows that the process of having key survivors view resuscitations often works best if EMS personnel notify the receiving hospital in advance of this request. This allows them to decide whether they will permit it (if it is not policy), to advise team members, and to have a smooth way of escorting the relative to the resuscitation room at the appropriate time.

If the family is present when it is clear that resuscitative efforts should cease, this should be explained to the family before supportive measures are discontinued. This provides them with a chance to "say good-bye" before death is pronounced.

Survivors may not understand how much the medical team did for the patient before he or she was declared dead. This is not uncommon, as evidenced by the common statement from the news media that a person "was pronounced dead on arrival," when there were actually ten or more medical professionals working for an hour or more to save the patient's life. Survivors need to hear this in understandable language, so they can be assured that everything possible was done for their loved one.

Barriers to Effective ED Notifications

Emergency department personnel are at a distinct disadvantage when dealing with survivors of sudden unexpected deaths. First, the physicians and nurses in emergency medicine are usually aggressive, action-oriented people who wish to see an instantaneous return for their expended energies. They often see death as a personal failure—an assault on their sense of accomplishment and satisfaction—and respond accordingly.[9,10] Also, except in rare, and usually uncomfortably memorable, instances, they do not know either the deceased patient or the survivors. Other barriers are listed in table 17-1.

Resuscitative efforts effectively halt most other activity in an emergency department. Once resuscitation is terminated, the clinicians are crushed by the onslaught of other patients whose problems demand their immediate attention. Because of this backlog of sick patients who have been ignored during the resuscitative attempt, survivors are often given too little attention.

Notifying Survivors in the ED

Unlike the situation for many in-hospital deaths, emergency physicians and nurses will not have had any chance to bond with the family and so must quickly establish survivors' confidence in them while at the same time delivering devastating news. The authority of their positions should be projected as one "who knows," rather than as one "who acts" authoritatively or coercively. Racial, social, and cultural differences between the emergency department staff and the survivors may lead to a sense of distrust. Table 17-2 is a protocol for notifying survivors about deaths in the emergency department.

Table 17-1: Potential Barriers to Effective ED Notification

- **No preexisting relationship** with medical staff.
- **Survivor stress:** fear, grief, remorse, anxiety, panic.
- **Time:** staff has limited time, needs to treat other patients/crises, and may be interrupted to make other decisions.
- **Strange environment:** surroundings, noise, smells, lack of privacy.
- **Survivor status/behavior:** anger, inebriation, disbelief, not available.
- **Cultural or language differences.**
- **Medical staff stress:** must deliver bad news, ask for autopsy (or notify about medical examiner requirements), ask for organ/tissue donation, and allow time in the midst of other patients' emergencies.
- **Medical staff anger:** decedent caused other injuries or deaths.
- **Uncertainty:** often not clear about the exact cause or manner of death.
- **Sense of failure:** "losing" a patient often pervades discussions.

One technique medical personnel often use to deliver the news about sudden unexpected death is that of "presaging," or leading up to this news by dribbling out bits and pieces of bad information over a very short period of time. (This is also called "hanging crepe.") This technique allows survivors to gradually understand that something very bad has occurred.

"How much emotion should I show when delivering the news?" is a frequently asked question. During resuscitative attempts, caregivers' emotions must be put on hold to perform their duties in the most effective way for the patient. If the attempt is unsuccessful, it is okay to express some emotion when delivering the news of the death to survivors, but the notifiers must retain enough control to help and support the family.

Table 17-2: Protocol for Notification of Death in the Emergency Department

(See table 3-1 for a more complete list.)

PREPARE	
Anticipate	• If the ED has a written protocol to follow, get a copy and review it. • Have a non-clinical room available near the emergency department for bereaved survivors. In the room, have comfortable places to sit, a telephone, tissues, and a "panic button" staff can use to summon help. • If possible, have a special room near the emergency department in which survivors can view the body. Have tasteful, non-denominational décor. • Have a policy regarding relatives being present during resuscitation. This may vary, depending upon whether the patient is an adult or child, and whether it is a medical or trauma resuscitation. • Have a policy regarding how to handle media inquiries. • Have a policy about how, when, and to whom to return the patient's possessions, including clothes and valuables. • Have a list of agencies (and 24-hour telephone numbers) who must be notified in different types of death, such as medical examiner or coroner, organ/tissue procurement organizations, public health department, police, medical school anatomy department (for bodies that have been donated), child welfare agencies, etc. • Have a written list of procedures to follow in various types of death available to both staff and survivors. • Write down the decedent's name and a list of the key elements of the events surrounding death and during the resuscitation. Refer to this, as necessary, when speaking with survivors.
Identify	• Identify the survivors as being for the (proper) deceased patient. • Have a staff member meet the survivors when they arrive and escort them to a private area. • If you cannot be certain of the decedent's identity, say so immediately. • Are there other survivors who must be told? When will they arrive? • Find out what the relatives already know.

Continued on next page

Table 17-2: continued

	PREPARE, cont.
Notify	• If the patient is dying or resuscitation is continuing, inform survivors of the severity of the patient's condition and prepare them for a possible (probable, inevitable) death. • Update them frequently during the resuscitation attempt as to the patient's condition. Make this a part of the resuscitation protocol.
Organize	• Arrange for enough time so that you do not appear rushed and won't be disturbed for at least the initial notification. • Clean up! Change any soiled clothes. Have someone else help you identify any soiled areas you may have missed. Wear a white coat with your name on it (or an ID badge), if possible.
	INFORM
Identify	• If still not 100% sure of decedent's identity, describe the identifying characteristics or show them a photograph (of cleaned face only). • Identify yourself and those accompanying you, include your positions in the department and your roles, if any, in treating the patient.
Tell	• Prepare to remain in the room with the survivors for at least a few minutes. Don't dash in and out of the room or hang by the half-open door as if preparing to flee. • Use clear, non-technical language to explain what occurred. • Use a "D" word: "Died," "Death," or "Dead," to make sure that survivors clearly receive the information. • Pause for a moment and remain quiet so survivors have time to react. • Clearly explain any visible injuries from trauma or the resuscitation attempt and any postmortem changes (e.g., facial blueness or *livor mortis*) before they see the body. • Do not apologize for the death, since this may make survivors incorrectly think that more could have been done. • Offer a Polaroid® photograph of the decedent to survivors. If not desired, keep it with the medical records in case they want it later. • If the relatives want to speak, *listen*. Do not simply continue your prepared remarks. • If there are complex issues surrounding family housing and basic support, contact social services.

Continued on next page

Table 17-2: continued

	INFORM, cont.
Tell, cont.	• Survivors, especially parents of deceased children, may want to describe their version of the circumstances surrounding the death to demonstrate (to themselves or others) that they were not negligent. • Mild sedation for a key survivor may be necessary. This requires physician evaluation of the survivor, rather than simply a request by another survivor. • Be prepared for violence, although interpersonal violence is unusual. Property damage (hitting a wall, for example) and subsequent survivor injury is more common. • Following the initial meeting with the family, tell them that you will return after a short period to answer any additional questions.
	SUPPORT
Reassure	• Tell them that all reasonable efforts were made to resuscitate the patient (unless s/he was not supposed to have been resuscitated).
Relieve	• Assuage the family's guilt and mental anguish. State (unless it is very obvious that this is not true) that the event was not their fault. • If it is possibly true, reassure them that the patient did not suffer. Couch the information in phrases such as "Most people with a bad head injury never have a memory of the accident." or "Death comes almost immediately after . . .."
Assist	• Support the survivors, but give them privacy if they desire it. (Whether they can be left alone with a body that is a medical examiner's case depends upon the situation and local rules.) • Arrange transportation home for survivors, if needed. • Arrange overnight accommodations for survivors, if necessary. • Have a simplified procedure for survivors to register as patients in case of exacerbations of medical conditions. • If survivors are seriously hurt, consult the family or other survivors as to the timing of notifying them. Generally, if they are awake enough to ask, it is best to tell them. • Have a written list of the local and national numbers and addresses for various support groups, such as SIDS, murder victims, elderly survivors, etc. (See chapter 11 for some of these contacts.)

Continued on next page

Table 17-2: continued

	SUPPORT, cont.
Assist, cont.	• Contact the patient's physician as soon as possible. • Help protect them from the media, or brief them in advance (if they need it) if they will speak to the media. • Supply contact numbers survivors can call for additional information in the next few days, preferably for the physician or nurse with whom they best interacted in the emergency department. • Get phone numbers and addresses for recontacting survivors over the next few days or weeks. • Allow families to cut a lock of hair or take a photograph if requested. • Do not permit violence. Protect the survivor and the staff from harm. Use the security staff or police, as needed. • If a survivor is suicidal or homicidal, get a formal psychiatric consultation.
Conclude	• Be prepared to supply limited amounts of survivors' prescription medications—especially if they are from outside of the local area. • Ask survivors if they have any further questions. • Accompany survivors to the exit.
	AFTERWARDS
Debrief	• Notify the staff that they can release information of the death to appropriate callers.
Follow Up	• Be prepared to answer survivors' common questions (see chapter 27). • Be prepared for any possible reaction to the news, including disbelief, guilt, anger (at the patient, those responsible for the death, or the medical staff), exacerbation of medical conditions (such as angina), and behavior suggesting the need for psychiatric intervention (such as absolute denial). • Hold a debriefing for staff where they can share both medical information and personal feelings about the resuscitation and death. • Call or write the family with condolences and to offer any additional information about the patient (e.g., autopsy results), support groups or resources, and to answer any questions they may have.

Some information adapted from References 11 and 12.

The Stress of Notifications

The topics discussed during emergency department death notifications cause varying degrees of stress in the physician-notifiers.

One highly stressful topic is resuscitations. Whether it is because physicians must later describe their efforts to survivors, because they are uncomfortable with death, or because they are "caught up in the moment," many patients, especially trauma patients, who have little or no chance of survival continue to receive resuscitative procedures. Emergency personnel and trauma team members need to accept that some patients arrive "DOA" and cannot be resuscitated. These include any normothermic adult (>12 years old) with unsuccessful prehospital CPR for longer than 5 minutes (or more than 15 minutes with penetrating chest trauma).[13] The same holds true for cardiac arrests from "medical" causes. Adult (normothermic) patients whose hearts stop outside of the hospital and have not restarted by the time they arrive at the emergency department are nearly always dead—even if restarting them in the emergency department makes the dying process longer and more costly.[14] Medical personnel must be willing to say, "We did everything possible"—which is true. They must also be willing describe to survivors their criteria for not performing resuscitative procedures on patients.

Emergency physicians tend to avoid high-stress subjects (e.g., organ donation, autopsy permission) when they can. Table 17-3 shows the relationship between the stressfulness of common topics and how often emergency physicians discuss them during death notifications.

One stressor that is not included in the table, probably because it rarely occurs, is the aftermath of the death of someone known to the physician or ED staff. In the incident below, the father and mother were well-known to most members of the team. (This was one of three cases that prompted me to write this book.)

> An 11-year-old boy died after an ATV (all-terrain vehicle) accident. His mother, a former PICU nurse, wanted to see the body. She climbed into the bed and held the body for more than an hour. Another nurse, intermittently a chaplain, and later her husband stayed in the room. I spoke with her first when I told her that her son was dead and later when speaking with her 16-year-old son and a group of friends. The second time, after she had held, spoken to, and said her good-byes to her son, she seemed much more composed, and able to accept the reality of the death and to help support her other son.
>
> In the above case, I had to relate news of the child's condition, after a difficult attempted resuscitation (including having to do a formal tracheotomy), four separate times. The first time, I related the news of the death to the boy's mother and grandmother. I then had to tell the father, who I knew, that his son "was critical and might not live." (Someone else subsequently contacted him and told him of the death before he arrived at the ED.) I then spoke with the boy's 16-year-old brother when he arrived, although he both parents were present to support him. (He had already been told of the death, although I didn't know that at the time.) Soon thereafter, for the fourth and possibly most difficult time, I carefully

explained what happened (they already knew of the death) to a large group of friends who were with the family at the time the accident occurred. The group included several children from 8 to 14 years old, their parents, and others. Some had been with the boy at the accident site and others had stayed with him for a prolonged period until help could be summoned. I knew that whatever I said and how I said it would stay with the children, at least, for a long time.

A perceptive chaplain watched me relate news of the death. During it, I said "I will be happy to provide you with any information that you may need," as I gave them my card with my contact information. He later pointed out that "happy" was clearly the wrong word. Subsequently I used "willing," "available," or a similar term.

Table 17-3: Emergency Physician Stress and the Frequency of Topic Discussions during Death Notifications

Topics	Stressfulness For Physicians (1=Highest Stress)	Frequency in Death Notifications (Ranked 1-11)
Cause of death unknown	1	2*
Organ donation permission	2*	10
Autopsy permission	2*	6
Cause of death known	4	2*
Prepare family for viewing body	5	3
Emergency dept. care	6*	1
Family responsibilities	6*	5
Assessing survivor social supports	8	8
Definitive closure	9	7
Prehospital care	10	4
Referral to social services	11	11
Suggesting a liaison	12	9

*This topic tied with one other topic in causing stress for physicians delivering death notifications.

Adapted from: Swisher LA, Nieman LZ, Nilsen GJ, et al.: Death notification in the emergency department: a survey of residents & attending physicians. *Ann Emerg Med*. 1993;22(8):1319-23.

The Nurse's, Resident's, and Student's Roles

Emergency department nurses may be involved as the telephone caller, as the "crepe hanger" in the ED before notification, as the survivors' companion during and after notification, or as the person delivering the death notification. The survivors' reactions that nurses have the most difficulty coping with are (in decreasing order): withdrawal (inaccessible, mute, refuses to listen), denial (of fact, feelings, reality), anger (directed at nurse, doctor, self), isolation (feelings of aloneness), bargaining ("I'll pay anything not to have . . ."), inappropriate responses, guilt, and crying.[15] Nurses also frequently follow up with survivors, sometimes in coordination with the chaplain or social worker.

Occasionally, physicians give the job of death notification to residents, medical students, or nurses. While all three groups should be present to learn the techniques involved, to have an opportunity to hear what is said and how it is said, and to observe an attending physician showing some sensitivity, they should not be left to do death notifications on their own. That is a form of professional abandonment and, in a teaching hospital, the worst form of student abuse.

Identifying the patient can be very difficult in some cases. Many patients needing resuscitation arrive in the emergency department without identification, usually either because they have none or because the police have it. Care must be taken to corroborate the decedent's identity before any survivors are notified. To do this, emergency personnel or the investigating officers may have to ask survivors about their relative's general characteristics (height, skin and hair color), identifying marks (scars, tattoos, birthmarks), or deformities (prior amputations).

Dr. Richard Nelson, an emergency physician, describes a death notification complicated by an unusual identification problem:

> A 52-year-old patient was brought to the emergency department in full cardiac arrest. Standard resuscitation efforts were continued despite similar efforts having been unsuccessful in the field. During the resuscitation, it was noted that, despite having a very masculine appearance, male name, male identity driver's license, and male VA identification card, the victim had breasts and a vagina. After pronouncing the patient dead, I spoke to the wife and stepdaughter. Besides trying to break the news of the death as gently as I could, I also wanted to make sure the deceased was the correct person. Speaking to the wife in private, I asked about the possibility that her "husband" was actually female. She indicated there were certain things she did not know about her husband, and did not want to go into more details. She and her daughter later made a positive identification.
>
> The only follow-up I ever received on this case were the numerous calls I got from the coroner's office over the next few days asking me to confirm that they had the right body, since the deceased had male identification but was clearly a female.[16]

If still in doubt, it may be useful to show survivors a Polaroid of the decedent's face. (On occasion, even this method has proved erroneous, leading to misidentifications, burials under a wrong name, and relatives holding bedside vigils when their relative had actually died.)

References

1. Stussman BJ: National hospital ambulatory medical care survey: 1995 emergency department summary. *Advance Data from Vital & Health Statistics of the National Center for Health Statistics*. 1997 Apr 15;285.

2. Schmidt TA, Tolle SW: Emergency physicians' responses to families following patient death. *Ann Emerg Med*. 1990 Feb;19(2):125-8.

3. Lapwood R: Chaplain to casualty. *Br Med J Clin Res*. 1982 Jul 17;285(6336):194-5.

4. Iserson KV: Critical leadership. *J Emerg Med*. 1986;4(4):335-340.

5. Doyle CJ, Post H, Burney RE, et al.: Family participation during resuscitation: an option. *Ann Emerg Med*. 1987 Jun;16(6):673-5.

6. Robinson S, Mackenzie-Ross S, Hewson GLC, et al.: Psychological effect of witnessed resuscitation on bereaved relatives. *Lancet*. 1998 Aug 22;352(9128):614-7.

7. Bankhead C: New study supports presence of family at resuscitations. *Emerg Med News*. 1998;20(11):41-2.

8. Ahrens WR, Hart RG, Maruyama N: Pediatric death: managing the aftermath in the emergency department. *J Emerg Med*. 1997 Sep-Oct;15(5):601-3.

9. Honigman B, Armstrong J: Life and death. In: Rosen P, Barkin R, Danzl DF, eds.: *Emergency Medicine: Concepts and Clinical Practice*, 4th ed. St. Louis: Mosby, 1998, pp. 197-212.

10. Walters DT, Tupin JP: Family grief in the emergency department. *Emerg Med Clin North Am*. 1991 Feb;9(1):189-206.

11. Marrow J: Telling relatives that a family member has died suddenly. *Postgrad Med J*. 1996 Jul;72(849):413-8.

12. Holland L, Rogich LE: Dealing with grief in the emergency room. *Health Soc Work*. 1980 May;5(2):12-17.

13. Pasquale MD, Rhodes M, Cipolle MD, et al.: Defining "dead on arrival": impact on a level I trauma center. *J Trauma*. 1996 Oct;41(4):726-30.

14. Gray WA, Capone RJ, Most AS: Unsuccessful emergency medical resuscitation: are continued efforts in the emergency department justified? *N Engl J Med*. 1991 Nov 14;325(20):1393-8.

15. Wright B: Sudden death: aspects which incapacitate the carer. *Nursing (Lond)*. 1988 Nov;3(31):12-5.

16. Nelson R: Personal communication with author, February 1999.

18: Obstetrics

Obstetrics is a medical specialty of life, not death. Yet a normal part of any obstetric practice is treating women who have miscarriages or, are carrying fetuses that have died, and delivering babies too premature or deformed to survive very long or who are stillborn. Yet experience shows that obstetric residents receive very little education on how to deal with these situations.[1]

The death of a baby is one of the most stressful events in any obstetrician's professional life. Part of obstetric training, according to one obstetrician-social anthropologist, is that they are taught not to show emotion, and progressively learn to deal with births from a technological, rather than from a humanistic, perspective. In some training programs, despite faculty statements that residents "should show concern and compassion for patients with dead or anomalous babies," they are given the message that obstetricians may not have unresolved emotional issues or show their emotions to patients. In actual situations, students are told they "must be in control" and "act more like a doctor." [2]

Miscarriages (Spontaneous Abortions)

As the number of pregnancies rises, so does the incidence of miscarriages (what physicians call "spontaneous abortions"). This is the delivery of a fetus, usually during the first three months of pregnancy and always before 20-weeks gestation. (After that, it is considered a live birth.) Up to 18% of pregnancies, nearly one in five, end in miscarriages, which are the most common untoward events in obstetric practice. Since miscarriage is so common, many health care workers treat it not as a loss and a cause for mourning but, rather, as a medical problem. As one obstetrician said, "It's as common as drawing blood."

Parents experiencing miscarriages, however, are often devastated by the loss. Women typically feel sadness, guilt, anger, disbelief, and anxiety—which are all typical of acute grief reactions. In addition, they experience helplessness, hopelessness, self-doubt, and a changing relationship with their partner, family, and friends.[3] Their family and friends often fail both to recognize this impact and to provide the needed emotional support. This may be because they didn't even know about the pregnancy, since it was so early that it had not been announced. Or because they see it as a normal event while the parents may view it as a major crisis.

The havoc wreaked on and the grief felt by the parents depends more on the context of the pregnancy than upon how far along the pregnancy is, as is commonly believed. The difficulty of getting pregnant, whether it was a planned pregnancy, and whether prior miscarriages have occurred may all influence the grief parents feel. As with other deaths, mothers may question whether their own actions or inactions caused the miscarriage. Nearly 30% feel anger toward themselves. This, of course, is not helped by unsolicited and nearly always wrong advice from friends and family about how to avoid miscarriages the next time. (Except in unusual cases, miscarriages cannot be prevented by the mother's actions.)

Simply acknowledging the parents' grief can help alleviate the pain and isolation they often feel after a miscarriage. But when they then turn to their obstetrician, he or she often either cannot recognize the family's distress or has been trained not to shift roles from "healer" to "counselor-consoler." Typically, physicians are taught to view miscarriages as a physiological problem with a mechanical solution. That may be why, in one study, more than half the mothers interviewed after the death of an infant or fetus perceived their doctor as being insensitive, aloof, and unconcerned.[4] Mirroring this, a young obstetrician told me, "We don't have any sudden or unexpected OB deaths." Wow! How narrow is his vision?

One technique for helping parents grieve after a miscarriage is to show the fetus to them if they desire to see it. This can either be done in a sensitive or a crass manner. One 24-year-old woman had a very negative experience:

> I was taken to the Emergency Room after I miscarried, and the doctor and the nurse were working on me and he asked for a pan. I had no idea what was going on, only that I was bleeding very badly. Then all of a sudden the doctor held up, for me to see, a mass of flesh about four or five inches long and an inch or two wide, all bloody and dripping, and said rather dryly, "Well there's your baby, lady; you lost it." I still can't talk to anyone about this and it happened over two years ago.[5]

Totally inappropriate statements, meant to be helpful to parents, are commonly heard from medical personnel and the family's friends and relatives. These include: "Forget about this," "You're young enough to have another child," and "You now have a little angel in heaven." An inexperienced pediatrician demonstrated one reason not to use these phrases after a woman gave birth to infants too young to survive.

> When Mrs. Lee delivered very premature twins (less than 24-weeks gestation), a pediatric resident physician was at her bedside. Before the birth, Mrs. Lee and her husband made a decision that extraordinary resuscitation efforts would not be made. When the twins were born, they were allowed to die peacefully with their parents holding them and saying their good-byes. The resident pronounced the babies dead and, before leaving Mrs. Lee's room, laid her hand on Mrs. Lee's knee and said, "Don't worry honey, you are still young enough to have more children." An experienced neonatal ICU nurse who had accompanied the resident was appalled at what had been said. She explained to the resident that what she said was not something you say to a mom who has just lost her babies. Also, the resident didn't know enough about the patient to counsel her in this way. As it happened, Mrs. Lee had undergone several years of infertility treatments before she had finally gotten pregnant.[6]

Grief from miscarriages can carry over into parents' behavior in subsequent pregnancies and with subsequent children. It is common for parents to feel great stress in subsequent pregnancies until after "M Day"—the day in the prior pregnancy when the miscarriage occurred. In some cases, even twenty years after the event, parents may feel a sense of loss.

Mothers, because of their constant awareness of the pregnancy, may feel a greater loss than the father may. Pregnant women usually begin to fantasize about the child as soon as they become pregnant. The potential realization of this fantasy evaporates with the miscarriage. It can be somewhat alleviated, and the grieving process enhanced, if the parents are given a memento. In more advanced pregnancies, this might be a blanket, hospital bracelet, or lock of hair. With a first-trimester miscarriage, a memorial service may help. Caregivers should also assist parents in contacting one of the support groups for miscarriages or stillbirths. (See chapter 11 for a list of groups.)

The keys for health care professionals when dealing with parents during and immediately after a miscarriage are to listen to their concerns, help them express their grief, and provide them with sound information to lessen their guilt and to reassure them about subsequent pregnancies.

Intrauterine Deaths and Stillbirths

A physician I cared for while she was having a miscarriage probably characterized the feelings of most women who have a stillborn child when she inadvertently called it a "still life." The sensitivity the medical staff shows to women after stillbirths may affect them their entire lives.

> A mother of two children suffered for two weeks with the knowledge of an intrauterine death. The experience was particularly distressing for her because she had had a prior pregnancy termination that was quick and easy, yet with a dead

> baby inside her she had to wait. Her doctor suggested [before the delivery] that after the delivery she might want to look at her stillborn. She declined, as bereaved mothers often do.
>
> The doctor arrived after the delivery and found the baby wrapped in a sheet. He had to steel himself to unwrap and look at the slightly macerated baby; he re-wrapped the baby and laid it next to the mother. He encouraged her to feel the baby's feet through the sheet. The mother touched a foot and then gradually all of her baby through the sheet. Then she was able to look at and hold her stillborn. Later, the doctor met the parents to discuss the stillbirth, how to help their two children understand the death, and how to arrange a death certificate and the funeral.
>
> The management was upsetting for the doctor, who afterwards had gastrointestinal symptoms. His involvement with this patient throughout the period of the intrauterine death, during which he shared her distress and pain, was probably responsible; nevertheless, it was an experience that he valued. Actually seeing and holding the baby focused both the mother's and the doctor's grief and facilitated their mourning. The mother was grateful to have had this experience.[7]

Obstetricians, especially when they have recently seen the mother with an apparently healthy pregnancy, may feel their own sense of guilt, failure, helplessness, and some responsibility if there is a subsequent bad outcome. It is not always the obstetricians, but also others involved with the parents' care who may make the most impact—for better or for worse. Steve Kohler, M.D., an emergency physician in San Diego, Calif., related this sad tale:

> Before I went to medical school, my wife and I were expecting our first child. At term, my wife went into labor and we went to the hospital. On fetal monitoring, the obstetric nurse was unable to obtain a fetal heartbeat. Initially, we though this was equipment related, but soon she returned and announced coldly, "I'm sorry, but your baby is dead. I think you should know that over half of the couples whose first child dies get divorced." Attempting to process the sudden loss of our baby combined with this ominous warning was almost too much to handle. Shortly thereafter, a radiologist arrived with an ultrasound machine, stating, "I've been asked to do an ultrasound on you." Upon completion of this, he left without any word of his findings and no mention of the baby's condition. Only later did the obstetrician arrive and sensitively tell us that our child had died *in utero*. Yet it is the abrupt and unfeeling nurse and the silent macabre radiologist who haunt our memories to this day, ten years later.[8]

Intrauterine and perinatal deaths of a twin can be particularly devastating to parents. This raises questions about how soon after the ultrasound diagnosis of twins parents should be told, since as many as half of twin conceptions end up being single deliveries (known as "vanishing twin syndrome").[9] Parents of multiple births in which one or more deaths occurred often have difficulty resolving their grief—both at the loss of a child and the loss of their position as the parents of these multiple siblings. Commonly, the parents will continue to refer to themselves as "having twins," even though one died *in utero* or at birth.

Unfeeling comments such as "At least you have a healthy baby" cause pain and resentment. One mother who had lost one of her triplets made particular efforts never to look harassed or untidy, as she dreaded people saying "Well, three would have been too much to cope with."[10] This attitude also seems to prevail with parents who must have fetuses killed *in utero* in order to produce one or more healthy children (selective abortions).

When possible, especially in the case of stillbirths, photographs or other mementos of the child may later help the parents to successfully cope with and grieve for this loss. Several photographs should be taken and kept with the medical record. Parents who initially either refuse or destroy the photographs may want them later. As two London physicians wrote, "Photographs should be as natural a part of death as they are of life."[11] They found, however, that other medical professionals were not too comfortable with this idea.

Protocol for Obstetric Deaths

Obstetricians can help their patients by following the guidelines below that apply to all sudden unexpected deaths in obstetric practice. Table 18-1 contains additional techniques to use in the special circumstances that confront obstetricians.

- The primary physician should deliver the news.
- Tell the parents together, when possible.
- If possible, have another family member present who may retain more of the information and repeat it for the parents.
- Use a quiet, secluded setting.
- Do not be afraid to show your emotions.
- Use clear language to explain the facts, not medical jargon.
- Offer a subsequent meeting to answer any additional questions the parents may have. Give them contact information, if they don't already have it.
- Reassure, don't argue with the parents.

Table 18-1: Protocol for Obstetric Deaths

Miscarriage (Spontaneous abortion)
• Sensitively tell the woman (and spouse/partner) that she is having a miscarriage. • Identify and legitimize the grief she is feeling by raising the subject. • Explain the procedures as they are being done, including the examination, lab tests, and intravenous fluids. • Gently explain the reasons for any procedure, such as a dilation and curettage (D&C) or dilation and evacuation (D&E). • Ask the parents if they want to see the fetus. • Answer any questions the parents have, including the frequency of miscarriages (15% to 20% of all pregnancies) and the chances of having a subsequent normal pregnancy. • Reassure mother that there is nothing that she could have done to prevent the miscarriage. • Explain that the tissue (fetus) must be sent to pathology for testing. • If they ask about disposition, say that the fetus is then cremated. • Offer information about death certificates if required in your locale. • Offer genetic testing, if indicated. • Refer parents to a perinatal support group.
Woman carrying dead fetus/infant **(Death *in utero*, ectopic pregnancy,* or fetal demise)**
• Unless it is a surprise to the parents, gently confirm their suspicions. If they do not suspect that anything is wrong, use the general protocol in table 3-1. • Identify and legitimize the grief the mother is feeling by raising the subject. • Show the parents the ultrasound and the abnormality. • Offer a method for terminating the pregnancy as quickly as is compatible with the mother's safety. • Offer genetic testing, if indicated. • Give them information about obtaining copies of the death certificate, if indicated. • Refer parents to a perinatal support group. †

Continued on next page

Table 18-1: continued

Ultrasound diagnosis of severely deformed infant (Incompatible with life)
• Use the general protocol in table 3-1. • Explain why these events can occur and reassure the parents that they were not at fault. • Offer the opportunity for a second physician's opinion, if desired. • Show them the ultrasound and the abnormality. • Offer genetic testing, if indicated. • If appropriate and requested, refer them to groups that accept an anencephalic's organs for transplantation. (At present no U.S. center obtains organs from anencephalics, although it is done elsewhere.) • Refer parents to a perinatal support group.
Delivery of stillborn infant
• If the mother is sedated, explain first to the father and other family members. • Tell the mother, with other family present, when she is in a condition to understand. • Say that there is about one stillbirth for every 80 live births. Explain why this can occur and reassure parents that they were not at fault. • Ask the parents if they want to see the infant. • Identify and legitimize the grief the mother is feeling by raising the subject. • Offer information about funerary options. • Explain how they can obtain copies of the death certificate. • Refer parents to a perinatal support group.
Delivery of severely premature or deformed infant that will not live very long
• See chapter 12 on telling parents, since this task most often falls to the pediatrician.

* The fetus in an ectopic, or tubal, pregnancy is often not dead when found, but is in a position where it must be removed to save the mother's life.

† Perinatal support groups exist in many communities for parents who have suffered through fetal or infant deaths. Parents seem to relate better to these groups than they do to more general support groups for child deaths.[12]

References

1. Graham SB: When babies die: death and the education of obstetrical residents. *Med Teacher*. 1991;13(2):171-5.

2. *Ibid.*

3. Stirtzinger R, Robinson GE: The psychological effects of spontaneous abortion. *CMAJ*. 1989 Apr 1;140(7):799-801, 805.

4. Knapp RJ, Peppers LG: Doctor-patient relationships in fetal/infant death encounters. *J Med Educ*. 1979 Oct;54(10):775-80.

5. *Ibid.*

6. Began, V: Personal communication with author, April 1999.

7. Lewis E: The management of stillbirth: coping with an unreality. *Lancet*. 1976 Sep 18;2(7986):619-20.

8. Kohler S: Personal communication with author, May 1998.

9. Lewis E: "The management of stillbirth."

10. *Ibid.*

11. *Ibid.*

12. Wheeler SR, Limbo RK: Blueprint for a perinatal bereavement support group. *Pediatr Nurs*. 1990 Jul-Aug;16(4):341-4, 377.

19: Police

Within the scope of their work, police must perform death notifications during routine police activities. They also make death notifications while working with the medical examiner/coroner's office, in jail and detention work, in police-community relations, during probation and parole activities, and in cooperation with social service agencies, such as child and adult protective services. Police become involved with most families that experience deaths outside medical facilities. Nearly every officer has dealt with these situations. Thus, as a public service (available for house calls 24-hours a day), police departments may be able to offer psychological assistance to survivors without a major change in their structure or function.

Yet police do not routinely give high priority to human service work, often disparagingly calling such activities "social work." Although public service work takes up to 70% of their time, police officers view it as an addition to their primary task of law enforcement.[1] In fact, many police have developed an insensitivity to survivors' reactions as a defense mechanism to help them cope with their frequent exposure to death and dying. That probably gave rise to this cruel vignette:

> A squad car drives up in front of a policeman's home. Two officers get out and come to the door. The policeman's wife freezes in her tracks, knowing that this is how they do notifications when an officer is "down"—hurt or killed. They walk up to the door. She doesn't recognize them. One of them asks, "Are you the widow Jones?"[2]

However, with extra training in this area, police officers have the potential to successfully act as psychological paraprofessionals. They have the necessary qualities to function well in the face of family crises: cooperation, leadership, persuasiveness, group participation, and the ability to function under pressure.[3,4] Indeed, one study of pediatric deaths in Britain found that parents rated the police as "being more sympathetic than nurses or doctors, possibly because they have some formal training in breaking bad news."[5]

Police find performing death notifications one of the most stressful and difficult situations they routinely face.[6] For example, more than half of the Los Angeles, Calif., homicide detectives surveyed in one study found it to be moderately to extremely stressful and difficult. To deal with this, many officers separate themselves from the reality of death, such as the deputy who said, "That's not a body lying there—it's an investigation!"[7] One detective, perhaps not atypical, said that he usually went to a bar to get drunk after performing this task. Nearly all were concerned about the next of kin's reactions, especially the threat of physical violence to themselves or other family members. Most, especially those with the most experience, desired more training on this small, but emotionally powerful, part of their work.[8]

Police often rely on two key elements when delivering death notifications: their uniform and the setting. In most cases, they can rely upon their uniform (or at least their badge) and their title (e.g., officer, sheriff, deputy, detective, marshal, agent) to demonstrate a level of authority and to distance themselves from the survivors. Less frequently, they use their surroundings, such as police stations, courtrooms, or jails.[9] In hospitals, they can use the chapel, a family waiting room, or the special room in emergency departments reserved for families of very ill patients. When they must deliver the news at a person's home, they rarely have control of the setting.

A booklet that police departments and coroners often use to train for death notifications suggests that they be done (1) in person, (2) in time—with certainty, (3) in pairs, (4) in plain language, and (5) with compassion."[10] Excellent advice!

In Person

Death notification should be made in person whenever possible. This is much more feasible for police than for medical personnel assigned to hospitals. When possible, police should make these notifications in the company of relatives, legal representatives, or clergy who the family knows. Rather than delivering the news standing face-to-face in a doorway, it is more humane to first enter the survivor's residence and sit down. While most police officers usually are in uniform, which lends an air of authority to their presence and their words, this may not be true for detectives, officers called in after hours, and some federal officers. In those cases, a badge or ID may be their only symbol of authority, but it is usually sufficient.

Not to be recommended is the policy of some police agencies that are reluctant to take the responsibility for making death notifications: Officers remain outside the home to render any needed assistance while someone else makes a telephone notification.[11] In this impersonal scenario, others notify survivors "bluntly, by telephone" under the guise of not wanting to invade their privacy.[12]

In Time—with Certainty

Before making notification, it is vital to be certain of the decedent's identity. When trying to establish the identity of a decedent, be aware of the need to keep information confidential. Never take or broadcast information about a decedent or the death over the police radio. Even the slightest mistake can be devastating to both notifiers and survivors. Such information must be obtained in person or via the telephone.

Once there is absolute certainty about the decedent's identity, make notification as soon as possible. No matter what the time of day, survivors want to know. If there is a delay, survivors later wonder if there was some reason they were not notified immediately or if there was something that they could have done for the decedent in the interim. On the other hand, if the decedent's identity is not certain, follow departmental guidelines about when and to whom to make notifications. Also, if there has been an adrenaline-inducing event preceding the notification (such as a car chase or shooting), officers should wait a few minutes to "cool off" before making the notification.

In Pairs

Making death notifications in pairs gives notifiers flexibility (especially if they are in separate vehicles), safety in a potentially hostile situation, and the potential for increased empathy, especially if the pair is mixed (e.g., male/female, Black/White, or officer/chaplain). Police officers' most common concern when making death notifications is survivors' emotional reactions. The increased empathy of "mixed pairs" of notifiers helps when survivors become emotionally distraught, upsetting the officers, or in situations when they may be seen as not sufficiently sensitive, leading to complaints to their superiors.[13]

Occasionally, survivors confuse the messengers with their message, generating safety concerns, especially for younger officers. Although it infrequently occurs, many have fantasies that they will be physically attacked when they deliver bad news. More experienced officers often worry about subsequent violence among family members.[14] Some larger departments have family intervention or emergency psychology teams that can assist in these notifications. If they are available, officers should take advantage of these resources and learn from them.[15]

In Plain Language

All communications should be in plain language. In fact, it may be easier for police officers to do this, since they cannot hide behind the "medicalese" that hospital personnel commonly use. Officers do, however, need to use a "D" word ("Dead," "Died," or "Death") and avoid euphemisms such as "passed on," "left us," or "expired." Dancing around the truth won't help at this point. If the survivors don't seem to understand, repeat the message in a slightly different way. The plainest type of communication is non-verbal, such as touching their shoulder, arm, or hand and sitting next to the person when speaking.

With Compassion

The compassion that officers show toward survivors is their most important duty. It is all right to say, "I am sorry that this happened," but they should avoid platitudes, such as "It was God's will" or "Things happen for the best." These vague sayings only provoke anger and distrust.

Police officers most commonly deliver the news about sudden deaths directly, without fanfare or elaboration.[16] A common method is to use a prepared death announcement that imparts the same information in each case and is usually delivered in a monotone voice. This does nothing to inspire confidence in the officer or to help the survivor. Even worse is the blunt, uncaring approach typified by one Los Angeles, Calif., homicide detective who said, "I don't pull any punches." For example, finding no one at home when he went to make a notification, he left a note saying "Your son hanged himself in jail. For more information, call ______."[17] He viewed the survivors as distinctly different than himself, and showed this in the way that he delivered the news. Yet the majority of law enforcement officers who deliver death notifications in a blunt manner say that they feel heartless or cold when they do it.[18]

Find a relative or friend to help the survivor, if they are initially alone. If possible, stay at the location until they arrive. Some police officers, however, prefer to call a relative or religious advisor, since the reactions from neighbors may be unpredictable. The best guide is to follow the survivor's directions as to whom to call.

Officers will also be expected to answer basic questions about the body's location, viewing, the medical examiner's involvement and procedures, and how to notify a funeral home. If possible, assist the survivor to make a few essential telephone calls. A standard sheet listing the necessary phone numbers is a helpful tool for officers to distribute in these situations. (See the forms in tables 6-1 and 6-2.)

An officer's compassion may be put to the test when survivors respond in an unexpected manner to the notification, as did the woman notified by Larry Graham, a Deputy Sheriff with the Pima County (Ariz.) Sheriff's Department.

> I was dispatched to the mining town of Silverbell. It was after the mine had closed, but before the town ceased to exist. I was to notify John Doe that his sister had suddenly died. On arriving at the residence, a woman came out toward my car. We met in the driveway and I asked if she was Mrs. John Doe. She said she was. I said, "I am afraid I have some bad news. Your sister-in-law is dead."
>
> "Oh, thank God!" she replied. After a moment she said, "No, no, that is terrible news, but I thought you were going to tell me my *husband* was dead."
>
> Her husband, previously an open-pit (above ground) miner, was working in another state as an underground miner, which terrified her. When she saw me arrive, she was convinced I had come to tell her there had been a cave-in and that her husband had been killed. In that context, her reaction was understandable.[19]

Unusual Situations

Four specific death-notification situations increase police officers' stress: making tentative death announcements, delivering news after a homicide or suicide, notifying a possible suspect in a criminal act, and notifying survivors about line-of-duty police officer deaths.

Occasionally, police officers are called upon to make a notification when there is uncertainty about the identity of the decedent. This may be due to the condition of the body or because there are no means to readily identify the corpse. In those instances, it may be necessary to discuss with survivors the possibility that the remains may be those of a missing relative. These cases may be very stressful. If the body is intact, survivors can normally use pictures rather than morgue visits to identify the body. Other cases may be more complicated, requiring police to make "probable" identifications before DNA, forensic anthropology, and forensic dentistry identifications.

Police frequently make death notifications after homicides and suicides—especially when the victim has not been brought to the hospital. Counting in victims of drunk drivers, nearly 45,000 adults and children are murdered each year in the United States. While both types of notifications may be traumatic for survivors, police can be especially helpful in *homicides*, where multiple police and investigator interviews, media attention, and legal actions may prolong a family's suffering. If the initial police notifier informs the family of what they can expect, they may be better prepared, be aware that they should gather their support resources, and be a little less traumatized than they otherwise would be. They may also be able to defuse any potential violence that may be directed toward the assailant, if known. *Suicides* may be initially stressful for survivors, who may either blame themselves for the suicide or blame the decedent for abandoning them. It may be useful to arrange for professional follow-up for the survivors within 24 hours after the notification.[20] Teen suicides are of special concern to police because they can lead to copycat events within a community. Information about the decedent that police gain during their initial contact with survivors may prove useful in preventing subsequent suicides.

Occasionally, death notification must be made to someone who is also a suspect in the activity that resulted in the death. In these cases, the officers must achieve a balance between their roles as a compassionate notifier (this may not be the perpetrator) and as a criminal investigator. It is often best to split these roles between two teams that arrive simultaneously.

One of the saddest jobs an officer must do is to notify the relatives of a fellow police officer that he or she has died in the line of duty. Between 140 and 160 law enforcement officers are killed in the line of duty each year in the United States, although 269 died in 1974. Of these, about half are from accidents and the rest are from felonious causes.[21] Senior officers and officer friends of the family often handle these cases, with close follow-up by the police psychologist. This type of notification crosses the boundary between professional and family notifications, since the notifiers often know both the decedent and the family. But as seen in the protocols for in-line-of-duty deaths found in tables 19-1 and 19-2, the steps that must be taken are very similar to other notifications.

Death notification, although a small part of police work, may make a large contribution to job burnout. Education (especially dealing with the "how-to's"), providing specific "game plans," avoiding academic abstractions, and educational debriefings after specific events have proven useful.[22]

References

1. Hall MN: Law enforcement officers and death notification: a plea for relevant education. *J Police Sci Admin*. 1982 Jun;10(2):189-93.
2. Clark C: *Better, Not Bitter: The Story of Concerns of Police Survivors, Inc.* Camdenton, MO: Concerns of Police Survivors, 1992, p. 1.
3. Clark DB: A death in the family: providing consultation to the police on the psychological aspects of suicide and accidental death. *Death Educ.* 1981 Summer;5(2):143-55.
4. Snibbe JR, Snibbe HM: *The Urban Policeman in Transition: A Psychological and Sociological Review*. Springfield, IL: Thomas, 1973, pp. 489-91.
5. Finlay I, Dallimore D: Your child is dead. *Br Med J.* 1991 Jun 22;302(6791):1524-5.
6. Haglund WD, Reay DT, Fligner CL: Death notification. *Am J Forensic Med Pathol*. 1990 Dec;11(4):342-7.
7. Hall MN: "Law enforcement officers and death notification."
8. Eth S, Baron DA, Pynoos RS: Death notification. *Bull Am Acad Psychiatry Law*. 1987;15(3):275-81.
9. McClenahen L, Lofland J: Bearing bad news: tactics of the deputy U.S. Marshal. *Sociol Work Occupations*. 1976 Aug;3(3):251-72.
10. Brooks S, Conner R, Egan J, et al.: *In Person, In Time: Recommended Procedures for Death Notification*. Des Moines, IA: Crime Victim Assistance Division, Iowa Dept. of Justice, 1992.
11. Haglund WD, Reay DT, Fligner CL: "Death notification."
12. Hall MN: "Law enforcement officers and death notification."
13. McClenahen L, Lofland J: "Bearing bad news."
14. Eth S, Baron DA, Pynoos RS: "Death notification."
15. Everstine DS, Bodin AM, Everstine L: Emergency psychology: a mobile service for police crisis calls. *Fam Process*. 1977 Sep;16(3):281-92.
16. Clark RE, LaBeff EE: Death telling: managing the delivery of bad news. *J Health Soc Behav*. 1982 Dec;23(4):366-80.
17. Eth S, Baron DA, Pynoos RS: "Death notification."
18. Clark RE, LaBeff EE: "Death telling."
19. Graham L: Personal communication with author, January 1999.
20. Clark DB: "Providing consultation to the police."
21. Stillman FA: Line-of-duty deaths: survivor and departmental responses. National Institute of Justice, *Research in Brief*, August 1996.
22. Hall MN: "Law enforcement officers and death notification."

Table 19-1: Responding To Line-of-Duty Police Deaths

This was written by Roger C. Haddix, M. Ed., Chief of the Georgetown, South Carolina, Police Dept. His deputy chief died March 1994 in the line of duty.

An average of 143 law enforcement officers are killed in the line of duty annually in the United States.[1] Whether the result of an adversarial action or an accident, the trauma caused by each death is felt by family survivors and department personnel for many months, and even years, after the event. Still, most law enforcement agencies have not experienced a line-of-duty death. Perhaps for this reason, less than one-third of the agencies responding to a recent survey reported having any policy dealing with this sensitive issue.[2]

It is little wonder, then, that agencies dealing with a line-of-duty death for the first time often respond inadequately to the needs of survivors. This may stem from several factors, including the lack of information available regarding actions that agencies should take after the funeral. This article discusses some of the policy issues involved and recommends appropriate responses to family survivors and co-workers of officers who are killed in the line of duty.

Background

The subject of departmental response to survivors remained a largely uncharted and undocumented area until the mid-1980s. Before that time, only a few metropolitan agencies that had experienced line-of-duty deaths developed policies for such situations. This began to change on May 14, 1984, when 110 survivors formed Concerns of Police Survivors, Inc. (COPS), while attending a National Police Week seminar sponsored by the Fraternal Order of Police. This represented the first effort to form a national networking organization to aid survivors in the healing process and to provide guidance to agencies concerning line-of-duty death policies.[3]

Since that time, an increasing number of administrators have come to understand the importance of adopting line-of-duty death policies. As the threat to officers becomes more menacing and the list of police fatalities grows each year, the need for such policies becomes more apparent. The highly sensitive nature of on-duty deaths and the long-term response to survivors that agencies must provide underscores the need to formulate a policy before a tragedy occurs.

Preparing for Tragedy

No one wants to contemplate his or her own death. But, because law enforcement is a high-risk occupation and the very real possibility of death from accidents and felonious assaults exists, agencies have an obligation to their officers—and officers owe it to their families—to prepare for such tragedies.

Preparation should include educating officers about emergency notification of family members, funeral arrangements, survivor benefits, counseling options, and departmental support to survivors. Officers should take considerable comfort from knowing what benefits and support their families will receive in the event they are killed. Although the

Table 19-1: continued

tragedy of losing a loved one will not be lessened, with preparation and forethought, uncertainties and a lack of information will not aggravate the grieving process.

Emergency Notification Forms

Agencies should use employee emergency information forms not only to obtain critical personal information from their officers but also to record officers' desires for notification of family members in the event of serious injury or death. While departments commonly notify the spouse of an officer after injury or death, they usually fail to contact the parents or grown children of an officer simply because that information is not available. In the absence of prior instructions from the officer, agencies should provide official notification to surviving parents and grown children, or make arrangements with another department if distance prohibits notification by the officer's agency.

One of the procedural orders of the Charleston, South Carolina, Police Department, entitled *Handling a Law Enforcement Death or Serious Injury,* includes the "employee emergency information form," which is used to record notification information. The form also reserves space for special notification instructions and special family considerations. These forms are periodically updated and kept in the personnel section.

The National Association of Chiefs of Police publishes helpful line-of-duty death guidelines that contain a comprehensive officer questionnaire. The confidential questionnaire allows officers to record information about wills, insurance policies, funeral wishes, and the distribution of possessions. After the officer completes the questionnaire, it is sealed in an envelope to be opened only in the event of the officer's death or serious injury.[4]

Death Benefit Information

Agencies also should make sure to provide complete death benefit information to all officers so that they can prepare their families. This includes information about death benefit life insurance paid by the employing agency, survivor death benefits or annuities paid by a retirement plan, State and/or Federal death benefits, social security benefits, fraternal or labor group benefits, and financial benefits provided by civic organizations or special law enforcement support groups. Still, officers should review the benefits periodically because they may change over time.

The Mobile, Alabama, Police Department provides a comprehensive death benefits booklet for surviving family members. Officers who have this information possess an added degree of peace of mind knowing that their families will be provided for in the event of their death.

Family Support Team

Because of the complexity of issues surrounding a line-of-duty death, every agency needs to develop a family support team to provide a structured response to survivors. The Dallas, Texas, Police Department created such a team. The ten team members handle everything from family services to ceremonial considerations. Although few agencies require a team as large as the one in Dallas, every agency should develop a team to

Table 19-1: continued

address five critical areas. Team members should be designated by their specific roles: Command liaison, benefits coordinator, financial coordinator, chaplain or minister, and family liaison.

Command Liaison

A senior command officer should head the family support team. This officer ensures that team members receive an appropriate level of training in their duties and supervises the team response. The command liaison officer also keeps the department head informed of problems or needs of the family.

The command liaison officer must possess ample rank and authority to implement fully the department's response to the survivors. This officer also should maintain a log of actions and prepare a calendar of significant dates that should be observed. These include the officer's birthday, spouse's and children's birthdays, marriage anniversary, and graveside memorials.

Benefits Coordinator

The benefits coordinator may be a line officer, supervisor, or command officer from the administrative unit. As the title suggests, the benefits coordinator compiles all information on funeral payments and financial benefits provided to the family. This officer also explains other benefits and assistance programs that may be available. The benefits coordinator should meet with the primary survivor a day or two after the funeral.

Financial Coordinator

The financial coordinator may be an attorney or financial consultant who has been hired by the department or has volunteered to assist the officer's family. This person provides financial advice and assistance to family members so that they can make informed decisions concerning the amounts of money and benefits they will receive.

Chaplain or Minister

Chaplains or ministers provide comfort and support both to the family and to the department. Skilled in dealing with death and dying, they can offer insight and advice to survivors trying to cope with the trauma of loss. Many chaplains from larger agencies possess considerable experience with line-of-duty deaths and can provide invaluable assistance to chaplains of smaller departments.

Family Liaison Officers

Family liaison officers—assigned either permanently or on a rotating basis to this duty—maintain frequent scheduled contact with the family. They remain available on a standby basis to respond to any special request by family members. Administrators should grant them broad latitude and flexibility in the initial months of the grieving process. However, they should keep the command liaison and/or agency head fully apprised of the emotional state of the family and inform them of any problem that they have encountered. They also should maintain a record of activities that they perform for survivors.

Table 19-1: continued

The Survivors

Family

In the aftermath of an officer's death, agencies often ask, "Who are the survivors?" The answer is anyone in the immediate family—spouse, children, siblings, mother, and father. Too often, agencies focus on a married officer's spouse and children and forget the parents. Because of the unexpected circumstances involved in law enforcement deaths, agencies should give special attention to notifying all immediate family members, and especially to anyone listed on the officer's emergency notification documents.

Officers may leave instructions to exclude some immediate family members from the official notification process. While this leaves the task of notification to primary survivors, an agency representative still should contact these family members later with condolences and to offer assistance. Law enforcement agencies have only one opportunity to provide a proper and caring response to family members. Departments should spare no effort in assisting them.

Fellow Officers

In the wake of an officer's death, law enforcement agencies also must respond to another group of survivors—the police family. Officers spend a great portion of their lives on the job with fellow officers and employees. This close contact results in strong bonds of friendship and camaraderie among agency personnel.

The loss of an officer in the line of duty affects every department member. Without adequate support, some may develop emotional and performance problems that adversely impact the department.

Response Issues

Support to survivors—both family and departmental—includes regular contact by members of the family support team, members of the department who knew the deceased officer, and department commanders. These contacts should be both formal and informal, planned and spontaneous.

Studies show that in the months following an officer's death, survivors frequently feel abandoned by the department that was supposed to be so close to their loved one but now seems to have forgotten the officer after death.[5] Members of the family support team and agency officials should make special efforts to call, visit, or send cards on birthdays, anniversaries, and holidays. The agency also should give special attention to surviving children. While members of the department often make offers to get involved with the fallen officer's children, other obligations may soon take precedence. Officers must avoid making promises they cannot keep.

Counseling

In addition to a compassionate, understanding response from the department, some family and police survivors may require professional counseling. A report published by the National Institute of Justice (NIJ) states that the reactions of police survivors

Table 19-1: continued

(i.e., spouses, parents, siblings, friends, and co-workers) may be so profound as to be diagnosed as Post-Traumatic Stress Disorder.[6] This psychological disorder is associated with traumatic events considered outside the usual range of human experience.[7]

In the past, police survivors often suffered prolonged psychological stress because they did not seek help or agencies did not extend offers of assistance in this area. Traditionally, most law enforcement agencies have not considered the emotional and psychological needs of survivors to be a part of their responsibility. However, the NIJ report indicates that sensitivity and effective agency response procedures have a definite impact on the well-being of survivors.

Uniform Response

Research into police deaths also reveals that spouses of officers killed accidentally experience the same level of stress as do spouses of homicide victims. At the same time, research indicates that parents of officers killed accidentally respond differently than do parents of those who are murdered. The latter were found to be more traumatized, hostile, and depressed. Survivors also reported a difference in the response they received from departments. Researchers found that the survivors of homicide deaths received more preferential treatment than the survivors of officers who died as a result of accidents.

Although some insensitive observers may question the heroism of an officer's accidental death, the department's response must be identical regardless of the nature of the death. As with any memorial, it is the heroic life and the recognition of the supreme sacrifice made by the officer that is being honored, not the officer's death.

Court Proceedings

Deaths that result from adversarial actions create additional concerns, primarily relating to the attendance of family members at court proceedings. While the department should make every effort to honor the wishes of the family, agency commanders must address other considerations.

The media pose a particular concern because any appearance of family members in court will be recorded most likely in print and on film. Reporters understandably will seek interviews with survivors to capture their feelings and reactions. To deal with these possibilities, the prosecutor should be consulted and should help develop a plan for family members to attend hearings and trials.

A prearranged plan is essential to satisfy the family's need for representation at court, as well as the prosecution's concern that the jury pool not be unduly influenced by the family's attendance. If family members do attend the hearings and trial, the department should offer to provide transportation and escorts. The department and the prosecutor also must coordinate whether agency personnel should be present at hearings and the trial. Procedural rules in some states prevent involved officers from being present in the courtroom during testimony.

Table 19-1: continued

Whatever the case, some effort should be made to protect the officer's memory at trial. If neither the family nor the agency represent the fallen officer, who will? Considering the support groups that exist for other types of victims, it is an unacceptable irony that police officers may be forgotten victims when suspects come to trial.

Continued Support

For the family, the months following an officer's death become particularly traumatic and stressful. As the initial shock begins to wear off, the reality of loss sets in. The department's actions during this period—what it does and does not do—will greatly impact the long-term recovery process for survivors. No time limit exists for how long it should take a family to recover. Everyone deals with death and grieving differently. Perhaps the most important thing to remember is that the department now stands in the fallen officer's place.

Unfortunately, some agencies have done little or nothing for officers' families after the funeral. In contrast, other agencies have purchased and installed appliances, made arrangements for officers to mow the lawn, taken family members shopping, cared for children, provided transportation to and from school, or performed other simple inexpensive, but meaningful, tasks that the slain officer once did.

Of course, departments should not overwhelm survivors with attention. Nor should they devote an unreasonable amount of time and effort to providing support to survivors. No matter what a department does to assist the family and to compensate for the absence of the officer, a great feeling of loss remains inevitable. However, departments can and should take steps to provide an ongoing response to survivors. The following timeline incorporates aspects of policies and guidelines from several law enforcement agencies, as well as other sources.

First Month

For a month following the funeral, agency officials should make daily phone calls to check in with family members to see if they need anything. Family liaison officers should make regular visits; the command liaison officer, weekly visits. These visits need not be lengthy but are meant to reassure the family that they have not been forgotten.

The agency head also should place telephone calls and make personal contact with primary survivors when possible. In addition, department personnel might encourage their spouses to contact the surviving spouse or parents.

Second Through Sixth Month

The family liaison officers should continue to maintain regular contacts with the family. If the family indicates that the contacts can be reduced, the agency should honor their wishes, but the contacts should not be discontinued altogether.

Table 19-1: continued

Sixth Month and Beyond

Family liaison officers should continue to make calls and visits and provide any assistance necessary to the family. The agency should continue to invite family members to department functions and events. Research indicates that as time goes on, survivors take great comfort simply in knowing that the department will be there if they need assistance.[8]

Memorials

When an officer dies in the line of duty, the department, fraternal and civic organizations, friends, neighbors, and concerned and caring members of the community often feel the need to create a memorial in the officer's honor. Such acts of remembrance represent a fitting and lasting tribute to officers who have fallen in the service of their communities.

Law enforcement agencies can provide several appropriate memorials to an officer's family. The community also can provide a memorial by establishing a scholarship fund for the surviving children or for students of criminal justice at a local university. Departments can:

- Lobby for a special resolution from the state legislature or the city/county council.
- Arrange for special certificates from law enforcement-related organizations.
- Mount the officer's service weapon, handcuffs, badge, patches, and/or medals in a shadowbox for presentation to the family.
- Assemble a scrapbook of photos, articles, and personal stories about the officer. Children especially value such mementos in later years.

In addition, the department and local governing body can create more public memorials, such as:

- Renaming a street, building, park, or bridge after the fallen officer.
- Placing the officer's photograph in the lobby of police headquarters or another public building.
- Publishing, on the anniversary of the officer's death, a story of the officer's life.

Conclusion

After the line-of-duty death of an officer, citizens often ask the chief of police if the department has gotten "back to normal." The fact is, a department that experiences the line-of-duty loss of an officer will never be the same. As long as the fallen officer's co-workers remain with the agency, the memory of the officer will be kept alive.

On a daily basis, law enforcement officers must cope with an inordinate amount of stress brought on by constant conflicts with violators, complainants, irate citizens, and demanding supervisors. Compounding this burden is the fact that death could be just the next call away. All law enforcement officers deal with this burden every working day.

Table 19-1: continued

Officers should not have to bear the additional worry that their department will fail to care for their family adequately if a tragedy should occur. By developing a comprehensive response strategy, agencies can relieve officers of this burden.[9]

---

1. Flanigan TJ, Maguire K, eds.: *Sourcebook of Criminal Justice Statistics, 1991*. Albany, NY: Hindelang Criminal Justice Research Center: For sale by the Superintendent of Documents, U.S. Government Printing Office, 1992, pp. 413, 417.

2. Sawyer SF: *Support Services to Surviving Families of Line-of-Duty Death.* Concerns of Police Survivors, Inc., March 1994.

3. *Ibid.*

4. Arenberg GS: *Line-of-Duty Death of a Law Enforcement Officer: Easing the Pain for the Family and Fellow Officers.* Washington, DC: National Association of Chiefs of Police, 1988.

5. Stillman FA: *Line-of-Duty Deaths: Survivor and Departmental Responses.* Washington, DC: U.S. Dept. of Justice, National Institute of Justice, 1987.

6. *Ibid.*

7. American Psychiatric Association. *Diagnostic and Statistical Manual of Mental Disorders*, 3rd ed. Washington, DC: APA, 1980.

8. Radford P: Concerns of Police Survivors, Inc. (COPS) National Trustee, interviewed December 5, 1994.

Table 19-2: Police Line-of-Duty Death Policy

Modified from the policy developed by David T. Boyett et al., which was derived from: Sawyer, Suzanne F: *Support Services to Surviving Families of Line-of-duty Death.* COPS: 1989; and updated by Concerns of Police Survivors, Inc. (December 1995). Used with permission.

I. POLICY: It shall be the responsibility of the ____ Police Department to provide liaison assistance to the immediate survivors of an officer who dies in the line-of-duty, whether feloniously or accidentally, while an active member of the department, to include the clarification and comprehensive study of survivor benefits, and to provide tangible and intangible emotional support during this traumatic period of re-adjustment for the surviving family.

II. PURPOSE: The purpose of this policy is to direct the ____ Police Department to provide proper emotional care for the deceased officer's family. It should be remembered that the funeral arrangements are to be decided by the FAMILY, with their wishes taking precedence over the agency's.

III. DEFINITIONS:

Line-of-Duty Death: Any action felonious or accidental, which claims the life of a _____ Police officer who is performing work-related functions either while on or off duty.

Survivors: Immediate family members of the deceased officer: spouse, children, parents, siblings, fiancée, and/or significant others.

Beneficiary: Those designated by the officer as recipients of specific death benefits.

Benefits: Financial payments made to the family to insure financial stability following the loss of a loved one.

Funeral Payments: Financial payments made to the surviving families of an officer killed in the line-of-duty which are specifically earmarked for funeral expenses.

Death Notification

1. The name of the deceased officer WILL NEVER be released to the media before immediate survivors living in the area are notified.
2. If there is knowledge of a medical problem with an immediate survivor, medical personnel will be dispatched to the residence to coincide with the death notification.
3. Notification WILL ALWAYS be made in person and never alone. The Chief of Police (or his representative) or a Victim Witness member will act as the informing officer.

   Keep in mind, however, that if the above-suggested persons are not readily accessible, notification should not be delayed until these people can gather. If the opportunity to get the family to the hospital prior to the demise of the officer presents itself, DON'T wait for the appropriate delegation to gather.

Table 19-2: continued

As soon as most public safety families see you, they will know something is wrong. Ask to be admitted to the house. NEVER make a death notification on the doorstep. Gather everyone in the home and ask them to sit down. Inform them slowly and clearly of the information you have on the incident. Make sure you use the officer's name during the notification.

If the officer has already died, relay that information. NEVER give the family a false sense of hope. Use words like "died" and "dead" rather than "gone away" or "passed away."

If the person responsible for the death notification has been seriously affected by the death, he/she should understand that showing emotions is perfectly acceptable.

If specifics of the incident are known, the officer should relay as much information as possible to the family.

NOTE: *Reactions of the family may include hysteria, anger, fainting, physical violence, shock, etc.*

4. If the family wants to go to the hospital, they should be transported via department vehicle. It is highly recommended that the family NOT drive themselves to the hospital. Should there be serious resistance and the family insists on driving, have an officer accompany them in the car.

   The department should find out if there are any young children in the home. Victim Witness members will be responsible for arranging immediate baby-sitting needs.

   Because of the nature of possible radio transmissions, the officer making the transport should notify the officer-in-charge at the hospital that the family is en route.

   Surviving parents will be afforded this same courtesy of personal notification if they live in the same geographic area.

5. If immediate survivors are from out of town, request PERSONAL death notification from the public safety agency in that area. Logistical arrangements should enable simultaneous telephone contact with the _____ Police Department.

Assisting the Family at the Hospital

1. Arrangements regarding appropriate waiting and support facilities that have been donated for the family and fellow police officers after a line-of-duty death include: [transportation for family and relatives; sleeping accommodations for out-of-town relatives, local restaurants, child care, banking, funeral services, medical assistance, public affairs assistance, clergy, etc.]

   An Emergency Response Liaison (ERL) will be appointed to act as information liaison for medical personnel to the family of the officer and fellow police officers.

Table 19-2: continued

The ERL will ensure that pertinent information on the officer's condition is relayed on a timely basis. They shall also make the family and fellow police officers aware of hospital policy about visitation with the injured officer and/or visitation with the body following the demise, and explain why an autopsy is needed.

If it is possible for the family to visit their officer prior to death, they most certainly should be afforded that opportunity. IT IS THE FAMILY'S RIGHT to visit their loved one. The ERL should "prepare" the family for what they might see in the emergency department and accompany the family into the room for the visit if the family requests it. DO NOT BE OVERLY PROTECTIVE OF THE FAMILY. There is a definite need to touch and hold the body while there is still life, and being present when death occurs can be comforting to the family.

2. The ERL will see that the family is updated on the incident as soon as the family arrives at the hospital.
3. Victim Witness members will be present the entire time the family is at the hospital and should arrange whatever assistance the family may need at that time.
4. The people who made the initial notification should be among those at the hospital.
5. A survivor should not be sedated unless he or she requests the medication.
6. Idle promises should not be made to the family at this time, such as "We'll promote him/her posthumously" or "We'll retire his/her badge."
7. Arrangements will be made by Victim Witness members for transportation of the family back to their residence.
8. The ERL will be responsible for arrangements of the medical bills relating to the services rendered to the deceased officer and send them to the appropriate governmental agency for payment. The family should NOT receive any of these bills.

Support for the Family During the Wake or Funeral

1. A police officer will act as the liaison person. Although the liaison officer should know the deceased officer and be aware of the family relationships, the officer should not be so emotionally involved with the loss that he/she would become ineffective. The liaison officer must know that THIS IS NOT A DECISION-MAKING POSITION. THIS IS A ROLE OF 'FACILITATOR' BETWEEN THE FAMILY AND THE ______ POLICE DEPARTMENT. The liaison officer will:

   Ensure that the FAMILY'S NEEDS come before the wishes of the Department.

   Meet with the family and tell them what his/her responsibilities will be during this time.

Table 19-2: continued

Meet with the family regarding funeral arrangements. Since most officers have not prearranged their wishes for the handling of their own funeral, the family will most likely need to decide all aspects of the funeral. The Department should only make the family aware of what they can offer in the way of assistance if the family decides to have a "line-of-duty" funeral.

Be issued a pager immediately so there is an immediate line of communication.

Know all information concerning the death and the continuing investigation to answer family questions.

Be constantly available to the family throughout this traumatic process.

See that the surviving parents are afforded recognition and will have proper placement arranged for them during the funeral and funeral procession.

See that the family is briefed on the funeral procedure (i.e., 21-gun salute, presenting the flag, playing taps, etc.).

2. A commanding officer/public information officer will be designated to handle the media throughout this traumatic ordeal. In the unlikely event that the family should decide to accept an interview, this officer will attend and "screen" all questions presented to the family, so as not to jeopardize upcoming legal proceedings.
3. Victim Witness members will see that the home is prepared for the influx of visitors following the funeral, screen phone calls, and remain at the residence during the funeral and home visitations. Food and baby-sitting needs will be provided through the donating agencies (see #1 under "Assisting the Family at the Hospital").
4. The family should be made aware of local facilities large enough to accommodate attendance at the funeral. REMEMBER THAT THE DEPARTMENT SHOULD ONLY MAKE THE FAMILY AWARE OF THE ALTERNATIVES. IT'S THE FAMILY'S CHOICE.
5. Departmental vehicles will be made available to the family if they desire transportation to and from the funeral home. Any departmental vehicles used in the transportation of any family members will bear the "Honor Guard" magnetic signs.
6. Victim Witness members will be responsible for providing the family access to other public safety survivors or other support groups, such as Concerns of Police Survivors, Survivors of Homicide Victims, Compassionate Friends, Parents of Murdered Children, etc.
7. The _____ Police Department will send Victim Witness members on routine residence checks by the survivors' home for 6 to 8 weeks following the tragedy. This same member will ascertain from the survivor if any harassing phone calls are being received.

Table 19-2: continued

Providing Information and Assistance on Benefits to the Surviving Family

1. A Department benefits officer will gather information on ALL benefits/funeral payments available to the family. Ensure that this officer has the department's full support to fulfill the responsibility to the survivor to coordinate ALL death benefits/payments (i.e., insurance policies, outstanding debts, etc.). This officer should be completely responsible for filing appropriate paperwork and following through with the family to ensure that these benefits are being received.
2. The benefits officer should visit with the surviving family to discuss the benefits they receive within a few days following the funeral. A prepared printout of the benefits/funeral payments due the family listing named beneficiaries, contacts at various benefits offices, and when they can expect to receive the benefit should be given to the family. This same explanation should be repeated within a month following the death since the initial contact is often clouded by the emotional numbness the family experiences during the initial period after a death. Checks will be made every ____ months to be sure that the family is receiving or has received every possible payment.
3. If there are surviving children from a former marriage, the guardian of those children should also receive a printout of the benefits the child(ren) will receive.
4. The benefits officer should pay special attention to the problems with possible revocation of health benefits to the surviving family. There may be special rules for continuing this coverage they must comply with.
5. If criminal violations surround the death, the family will be informed of all new developments prior to any press release. Victim Witness members will act as a liaison with the court if there is a trial.
6. If there will be no court proceedings surrounding the circumstances of the officer's death, at the earliest opportunity, the Department will relay all details of the incident to the family.
7. The Chief and other high-ranking officials should be greatly visible during these days.
8. The public safety organization (FOP) or community support group should make an attorney/financial counselor available to the surviving family for whatever legal or financial counseling is necessary, such as establishing trust funds, educational funding, etc. The attorney should not be affiliated with the jurisdictional government and should work as an avid advocate for the family's interests.
9. Plaques or memorabilia given to the spouse will also be given to the parents.

20: In Prisons

Two types of death notifications involve prisons and prisoners. One is notifying prisoners of their friends and relatives' deaths. The second is notifying survivors about prisoners' deaths. While the second type of notification is well regulated, notifying prisoners of deaths seems to vary with correction officers' sensitivity.

Alan Taplow, who began an Alternatives to Violence Project at the New Jersey State Prison in Trenton, developed a workshop in which inmates described the typical way many are notified of their loved ones' deaths.

> A call came to the prison that an inmate's mother had died. The information was relayed to the corrections officer in charge of "block X," who simply yelled in the direction of the second level of cells, "Hey Anderson, your Mother croaked." According to prisoners who attended this workshop, inmates being notified of a death by an officer walking by the cell or calling up to the tier is not uncommon. They had no program to support inmates whose friends or relatives died.
>
> Distraught, the prisoner then had to traverse the difficult process of getting Social Services, the Chaplain, and the Warden to allow him to attend her funeral across the state line in Philadelphia. Since they would not allow him to leave the state, he had to persuade his relatives to ship his mother's body to New Jersey and also get them to pay for correction officers to accompany him to the funeral. Eventually, he went to the New Jersey funeral home in shackles, where he was only permitted to view the body. He was not allowed to communicate with any of his relatives, be in the room while they were there, or attend his mother's graveside service.

After Mr. Taplow left New Jersey, the prison chaplain staff was cut, so that even if they are promptly notified of a death, they now rarely have time to visit or counsel bereaved inmates.[1]

When deaths occur *in* prisons, many people in the prison system's chain of command must be notified in addition to next of kin. Depending on the information provided by the prisoner, their offense, the manner of their death, their citizenship, and other factors, the notification process can be quite complex. One example of the prison notification process is the protocol of the U.S. Federal Bureau of Prisons (see table 20-1).

Recently, some prisoners in both federal and state systems have been placed in private facilities, sometimes far from their homes. According to Dr. Tammy Kastre, who supervises the medical care in some of these prisons, when a death occurs, they use the state- or federal-agency-specific notification policy for that prisoner. In some cases, it is the facility warden who must notify survivors, while in others, such as Alaska, it is the state's prison commissioner. While the prisons that Dr. Kastre supervises have had only about one prisoner die per every 5 to 7 thousand inmates, they follow the same "rule" as do many hospital operating rooms: "No one actually dies in our prison!" They are all transferred to local hospitals for the actual death pronouncements.[2]

References

1. Taplow, A: Personal communication with author, 8 April 1999.

2. Kastre, T: Personal communication with author, 14 December 1998.

Table 20-1: U.S. Federal Bureau of Prisons' Death Notification Protocol

Deaths

A. Information Needed. Immediately upon the death of an inmate, the Warden (or designee) shall assemble the following information concerning the deceased inmate:

1. Name, register number, date of birth;
2. Offense and sentence;
3. Date, time, and location of death;
4. Apparent cause of death;
5. Investigative steps being taken, if necessary;
6. Name and address of survivor or designee;
7. Notification made;
8. Status of autopsy request; and
9. Brief medical history related to death.

B. Notification of Bureau Officials.

1. Immediate Notifications.
   (a) Death During Regular Workday. The Warden (or designee) shall immediately telephone the report to the Regional Director. The Warden confirms this notification by ensuring an electronic Report of Incident form is sent to the Regional Office, with an information copy to the Correctional Services Administrator, Central Office.
   (b) Death After Regular Workday. The Institution Duty Officer shall report the death in accordance with the Program Statement on Duty Officer Guidelines and Reporting Procedures. Generally, that Program Statement requires immediate telephonic notification of the Regional Duty Officer, except for deaths by natural causes that occur at a late hour. In any case, Correctional Services confirms this notification (ordinarily the next day) by sending an electronic Report of Incident form to the Regional Office, with an information copy to the Correctional Services Administrator, Central Office.
2. Verbal Report to Executive Staff. In addition to the above notifications, the Warden (or designee) shall notify the Regional Director by telephone or telemessage and note any circumstances about the death that may be cause for special concern. The Director is to be notified of all deaths, even if there are no significant findings. After reviewing the preliminary death information, the Regional Director shall directly notify the Director by telephone or telemessage and note any circumstances about the death that may be cause for special concern. The Regional Director shall also notify the General Counsel, the Medical Director and the Assistant Director of Correctional Programs by telephone or telemessage.

Table 20-1: continued

3. Medical Reports. As soon as possible, the Warden shall send the required medical reports to the Medical Director, with a copy to the Regional Health Systems Administrator.

C. Notification of Family and Friends.

1. Immediate Telephonic Notification. The Warden (or designee) shall immediately telephone the person named in the Acknowledgment of Inmate (Continuation Sheet) form (BP-408) to communicate the circumstances surrounding the death. The BP-408 is found in the inmate's central file. When the inmate has not named a next of kin on the BP-408, the employee must attempt to locate and notify the next of kin, since only the next of kin may determine the disposition of the decedent's remains and property. The employee may have to consult other parts of the inmate's central file or contact the inmate's unit team for next of kin information. The Chaplain is also available to assist in notifying the inmate's family.
2. Letter of Condolences. As soon as practical, the Warden shall mail a letter of condolence to the next of kin and advise that person of the circumstances of the death
   - If the death was by natural causes, a summary of the cause of death is to be given.
   - If the death was accidental and not by foul play, a reference to the nature of the accident and the cause of death is appropriate.
   - If the death occurred under suspicious circumstances or by foul play, the cause of death may be given but with a statement that the matter is under investigation and that, for that reason, details of the case may not be provided.
3. Disposition of Property and Remains. The disposition of the deceased inmate's property and remains shall follow either the provisions of a properly probated will or the local state intestate procedures. If the inmate dies without a will, the Bureau shall abide by the rules of the state in which the death occurred. If, after a reasonable period of investigation, surviving next of kin cannot be identified, the deceased inmate's property and remains shall be released to other persons named in the BP-408. A review of the inmate's central file, visiting list, telephone list, or past correspondence may be useful to obtain the necessary information.
4. Death Certificate. When the Death Certificate is received, the Warden shall send a copy to the person who received the decedent's remains.

Table 20-1: continued

D. Notification of Other Federal Officials. The Warden shall send a letter to the appropriate U.S. District Judge(s) explaining the circumstances of the death, with copies to the U.S. Attorney, Chief U.S. Probation Officer, and Regional Director. All correspondence to federal courts must contain the federal docket number and register number of the offender.

E. Notification of a Victim or Witness. Staff are required to provide written notification to the victims and/or witnesses within 30 days of the death of an inmate with a Victim/Witness Program assignment. Further notification information is in the Program Statement on Victim and Witness Notification.

F. Notification of State Officials. If a state boarder dies, the Warden shall notify the director of the appropriate state department of corrections by telephone, ordinarily no later than the next work day. The Warden confirms the notification by a letter that explains the circumstances of the death, with a copy to the Regional Director.

G. Notification of Consulate Officials. If a non-U.S. citizen dies, the Warden shall notify the appropriate consulate official by telephone, ordinarily no later than the next work day. The Warden confirms the notification by a letter that explains the circumstances of the death, with a copy to the Regional Director.

H. Exceptions

1. Death of WITSEC Case.
2. Death of Inmate Housed in a Contract Facility.

Reprinted from the U.S. Federal Bureau of Prisons. (Part PS 5553.05), September 17, 1997.

21: Medical Examiners and Coroners

Medical examiners (physicians who are usually trained as forensic pathologists) and coroners (appointed or elected officials who may not be physicians) often work with the police to notify survivors about deaths. They are responsible, with the police, for investigating death scenes, and are solely responsible for performing medicolegal autopsies and other postmortem examinations. Depending upon the jurisdiction, they may also be responsible for establishing the decedent's identity (when it is not obvious to the police), protecting the decedent's property, or discovering the identities of all relatives to whom notification must be made.

The King County (Seattle, Wash.) Medical Examiner's Office investigators leave the following letter with survivors. It explains the often confusing roles and responsibilities of the investigators and medical examiners. Something similar might be useful for others.

> We recognize that the loss of a loved one brings deep sorrow. We wish to express sincere sympathy to you in your loss.
>
> The King County Medical Examiner's Office is authorized by the laws of the State of Washington and King County to conduct investigations of sudden, unexpected, unnatural, suspicious, or violent deaths.
>
> The investigation includes taking pictures at the scene of death, gathering any evidence at the scene, and questioning the family or next of kin. Some questions asked of the family provide medical information for the Medical Examiner; others are for death certificate information. If you did not understand why a question was asked, please feel free to ask the investigator.
>
> From the scene of death, the body is taken to the Medical Examiner's Office at 850 Alder Street (part of Harborview Medical Center). There the investigation

will continue, including the examination of the decedent which may or may not include an autopsy. If an autopsy is performed, it is done by a qualified physician in order to establish accurately the cause and manner of death. If you specifically want an autopsy, please make this request to the investigator and every effort will be made to accommodate your request. If you do not want an autopsy performed, tell the investigator and your feelings will be taken into account. Keep in mind, however, that the state of Washington authorizes us to perform autopsies and permission from the family is not required.

In most cases, the decedent is examined in the morning after the day of death. When you have decided on a funeral home, please notify us and we will make the necessary arrangements for transfer.

Generally, the next of kin can pick up all personal effects that accompany the body to our office on the afternoon after the day of death. For this office to release the personal effects to someone other than the next of kin, *written permission* from the next of kin is needed. In some cases, the police department takes some of the personal effects as evidence. These items will then be made available to you only after all legal proceedings have been completed.

If an autopsy is performed, the report is confidential. The Medical Examiner will discuss it with you or, if you prefer, you may obtain a copy of it by request.

Again, we would like to express to you our sympathy. If you have any questions or if we can be of any help to you, please feel free to call us at (telephone number).

Used with permission of the King County Medical Examiner's Office, Seattle, Wash.

Depending upon the locale, individuals working for the coroner or medical examiner may need to notify survivors of deaths. When they do, unlike other notifiers, they may have three goals: (1) beginning the death investigation, (2) persuading the next of kin to arrange for the body's disposition, and (3) informing survivors about the death. While the goals of notification and death investigation may be obvious, the importance of survivors assuming the cost of body disposal may be paramount for some departments. These departments often work on limited budgets and can ill-afford to assume the costs for many burials or cremations.

Medical examiner's and coroner's offices perform death notifications either in person or via telephone, depending upon their policies. In one comparison of neighboring departments, the decision about which to use was as much based on the need to persuade relatives to assume burial costs as it was based on their philosophy about which notification method was most humane and effective. Those departments that could get inexpensive body dispositions were more likely to use telephone notifications. On occasion, they left this job for their office clerks or simply notified the survivor's employer so that he could make the notification.[1]

Where costs for county burials are inexpensive, distant relatives are sometimes spared the expense. Said one supervisor, "If it is some bum who died and you have to call back in Ohio to people who haven't seen him for years—I tell them: 'If you don't have money, don't do it.' Why should they get stuck with an expensive funeral . . . even an inexpensive one is too much for some families."[2]

When medical examiner's investigators make in-person notifications, they face one problem not encountered by police or chaplains making in-home notifications. Since they do not have the obvious identity or authority of a uniform (e.g., doctor, police, priest) or place (e.g., hospital), they must first establish their authenticity. Sometimes they do this by enlisting the help of a neighbor. This helps establish their bona fides, helps them gain entrance into the home, and allows them to quickly leave once they have made their announcement and have been assured that the relative will assume the costs of body disposition. (These costs can often be quite substantial and relatives may agree to assume these costs without realizing it. See chapter 27 for more information.)

Investigators use self-protection strategies to maintain their distance from the deaths they see daily and from the survivors with whom they interact. They think of death as an external event, almost completely separate from their everyday world. To them, the investigation is their "real" job. As one said, "That's not a body lying there. It's an *investigation*. You have to look at it as an investigation, not as a person lying there."[3]

When they deal with survivors, however, investigators must raise other defenses. They generally try to maintain the appearance of polite, sincere, authoritative, but disinterested, officials. They often view survivors' overt expressions of grief as being related to selfishness and fear rather than to sorrow. As one coroner said, "We have a saying around here that 'Grief lasts as long as the flowers take to wilt.' The other is display." Or, as others explained, "people take it well, as long as they have no audience; as soon as somebody enters the scene, weeping and wailing rapidly ensue."[4]

In some cases, families coming to the morgue may request to touch or hold a body, especially those of infants or children. While usually not permitted, it may be worth considering, since, as this vignette demonstrates, it can be therapeutic.

> An adolescent girl, her mother, and her aunt came to the medical examiner's office to identify her baby. They all expressed the desire to hold the baby again. After I [a nurse coordinator accompanying the family] explained to them that the baby would no longer look or feel the same, they still wanted to do this. Therefore, I prepared the child and accompanied the family to view their child. They spent a half-hour with their baby, holding her, rocking her, and talking to her. All four of us were crying as the mother talked to her baby about all the things she wanted for her and what she thought she would be when she grew up. What impressed me the most about the situation was that initially, as she was talking to her baby, she said things like, "You know Mummy loves you, don't you, Sweetheart? You know I take good care of you." And then as time went on, she changed to the past tense and said to us, "I took such good care of her, and I loved her so much." It was as though she finally realized the reality of the situation. They all then kissed the baby good-bye, hugged me, and went home. (After it was over, a pathologist asked the nurse coordinator not to "do that again; it is too hard on the family.")[5]

After disasters, medical examiners can play an important role by sensitively and quickly relaying information to victims' families. Such was the case, for example, after the September 1998 crash of Swissair Flight 111 in Nova Scotia, Canada, as reported by *USA Today:*

> The grim business of identifying remains continued. The medical examiner leading the 200-person team trying to identify the shattered remains of passengers said that a second person had been identified, through fingerprints and personal effects. [He] would not release details until the family had been notified . . . [The medical examiner] continues to meet with victims' families to tell them of efforts to identify the remains, but also "to say what I had to say, which is that the remains were fragmented." . . . . He met with families individually, "touching them and looking them in the eye. They needed that . . . I just feel somebody has to do this, and I couldn't send somebody else." Many families hugged him in response, he said.[6]

Others in the funeral industry, such as funeral directors, rarely deliver the initial news about a death. According to the National Funeral Directors Association, there is no protocol for them to follow.[7] They generally concentrate on grief-related counseling and services.

References

1. Charmaz KC: The coroner's strategies for announcing death. *Urban Life*. 1975 Oct; 4(3):296-316.
2. *Ibid.*
3. *Ibid.*
4. *Ibid.*
5. Smialek Z: Observations on immediate reactions of families to sudden infant death. *Pediatrics*. 1978 Aug;62(2):160-5.
6. Moore MT: Flight transcript gives more details of jet crew's plight. *USA Today*. 1998 Sep 9; Sect. A:4.
7. Pafford ME: Letter to author, dated 24 October 1997.

22: Nurses

Nurses play a large role when dealing with survivors after sudden unexpected deaths. In smaller hospitals, they may be the only medical personnel in attendance when family members arrive. In all hospitals, they have the duties of attending to the body and of keeping the unit functioning.

When one hears about a sudden unexpected death, the first reaction is to flee. Nurses have more opportunities to flee than most. They have responsibilities to clean and restock the resuscitation area, prepare and often transport the body to the morgue, and continue to deal with other patients. In a busy emergency department, trauma unit, operating or delivery room, or intensive care unit, nurses can often find many valid excuses not to deal with survivors. Yet, because of their training, they may be better prepared to do so than other members of the medical team.

The events surrounding a sudden unexpected death remain with survivors their entire lives. They vividly remember their interactions with the medical staff, for better . . .

> A doctor and nurse came in together to tell me my husband had died. They were both very considerate and kind. They both stayed with me several minutes and talked to me, which I think helped a lot. The nurse also brought a warm blanket and wrapped it around me; it seemed to calm me down.[1]

or for worse . . .

> The attention was terrible. The whole atmosphere was very cold as if all these people were used to seeing people dead and families hurt and crying. We could get no clear answers as to what happened and why she died or when she died.[2]

Most nurses use a "conditional" method of delivering the news of a sudden death. That is, they wait for survivors to provide them with cues as to how they should proceed. Their delivery method is then based on those cues. One nurse explained it this way,

> Just go in and start to tell them. And, if they get more upset, then you . . . change and get more supportive. Or you change your pattern of what you're going to say, and you . . . you just ad-lib it. I don't think you can ever go out on the stage with a script. How they react to the first thing you say determines how you react.[3]

An emergency department nurse echoed these sentiments, saying,

> Well, I guess I just wait and let the family set the guidelines. You have to judge each family differently. Sometimes your approach works, and sometimes it doesn't . . . Just kind of say the least amount possible. Just tell them what's happened, and ask if there's anything you can do and so forth. You know, let them either verbalize or not verbalize, and go from there. Some people you have to reassure and talk and talk; and some people, it's best just not to say very much of anything.[4]

In general, nurses develop "composure tactics" in order to maintain a professional demeanor in work situations that might cause them to become upset or to lose control.[5] Faced with sudden unexpected deaths, nurses' reactions vary. About one-third feel calm and another third describe their feelings as compassionate toward survivors. One-fifth, though, feel stressed. These feelings usually arise with nurses' first exposures to sudden death and remain constant throughout their careers.[6] The most difficult deaths to deal with, and that cause the most distress, are those that carry "high social loss," such as children's deaths. Many nurses avoid pediatrics for that reason.[7] Among emergency department nurses, the incidents that cause them the most stress are deaths in children and deaths in co-workers.[8] One nurse who is also a nun says, "After I lose a patient, I go to a special place where I sit and watch the sunset. I write a letter to that person, telling them how they have touched my life and that I will miss them. Later I put the letter in a scrapbook full of such notes—preserving my memories and enabling me to move on."[9]

In the emergency department, the nurse manning triage or the emergency medical system radio is the first to hear about an impending death (cardiac arrest, trauma code, etc.) that will arrive. The nurse should notify the appropriate systems, not only for the resuscitative effort but also for those people necessary to support the family. In institutions where "codes" or "trauma alerts" are gang paged, support personnel such as chaplains, social workers, or nursing supervisors can be part of that notification system.

A useful role nurses can play in any institution is to be the liaison between the family and other medical and administrative personnel. They are in the unique position of being able to understand and interpret for the family the events, terminology, and roles of the people with whom they come in contact. In this role, the nurse can be a consistent presence during the hectic, stressful, and emotionally wearing experience surrounding a loved one's death. The most helpful interventions nurses make with survivors in the emergency department setting are to provide emotional support, reassure them that the

Table 22-1: Nurse Interactions that Survivors Find Helpful

Action	Number Finding It Helpful
• Provided a separate room for survivors. • Told of death in clear language. • Provided comfort measures. • Given information about decedent's care. • Allowed to view the body. • Made to feel comfortable expressing grief.	More than 75%
• Given follow-up name and telephone number. • Nurse showed caring and concern. • Assisted in completion of forms. • Given opportunity to grieve. • Told when it was okay to leave. • Received follow-up telephone call.	66% to 74%
• Given opportunity to call their religious leader. • Allowed to see their loved one before death. • Given opportunity to ask questions. • Told in advance that loved one might die. • Given opportunity to call other family members. • Told what to expect before viewing body.	50% to 65%

Adapted from: Fraser S, Atkins J: Survivors' recollections of helpful and unhelpful emergency nurse activities surrounding sudden death of a loved one. *J Emerg Nurs*. 1990 Jan-Feb;16(1):13-16.

medical treatment was optimal, give the family an opportunity to view the body, and assure their privacy when they need it. Two to three weeks after the death, a telephone follow-up call from the nurse provides the family a chance to ask additional questions.[10] Two out of three families appreciate this gesture (table 22-1).

Nursing is often called the "caring profession." Nowhere is that more evident than when a nurse spends time listening to survivors, offers them emotional support, and provides comfort measures, such as drinks, blankets, and access to bathrooms and telephones. Nurses feel that these actions are important to survivors, and survivors agree.[11]

Once the patient has been pronounced dead, staff refer to it as "the body" or "the corpse," emotionally separating it from the "patients" for whom they must continue caring. In most health care facilities, nurses have another role—preparing bodies for the morgue. A little-discussed element of this job is to clean and remove extraneous medical equipment from the body (if it is not a medical examiner's case, when all disposable medical equipment must stay in place until the forensic examination is completed). Nurses or other staff then may tie the mouth closed, secure the hands so that they do not flop around, and shroud the body. Once placed on a covered stretcher, the lowest members of the nursing-team hierarchy (usually aids or orderlies)[12] transport "the package," "bundle," or "body" to the morgue via the freight or service elevator. Every effort is made to keep knowledge of these procedures out of the sight and minds of other patients, survivors, and visitors. (For more details, see Iserson KV: *Death to Dust: What Happens To Dead Bodies?* Tucson, AZ: Galen Press, Ltd., 1994.)

Outside of health care facilities, school nurses sometimes play a role in notifying children of sudden deaths. They can assist relatives who come to the school to get a child after a sudden death, help teachers notify classes or the school about a classmate's or a teacher's death, and help students and teachers deal with their subsequent grief.[13]

References

1. Fraser S, Atkins J: Survivors' recollections of helpful and unhelpful emergency nurse activities surrounding sudden death of a loved one. *J Emerg Nurs.* 1990 Jan-Feb;16(1):13-6.
2. *Ibid.*
3. Clark RE, LaBeff EE: Death telling: managing the delivery of bad news. *J Health Soc Behav.* 1982 Dec;23(4):366-80.
4. *Ibid.*
5. Quint JC: Awareness of death and the nurse's composure. *Nurs Res.* 1966 Winter;15(1):49-55.
6. McGuinness S: Coping with death. death rites. *Nurs Times.* 1986;82(12):28-31.
7. Glaser BG, Strauss AL: Temporal aspects of dying as a nonscheduled status passage. *Am J Sociol.* 1965 Jul;71(1):48-59.
8. Burns C, Harm NJ: Emergency nurses' perceptions of critical incidents and stress debriefing. *J Emerg Nurs.* 1993 Oct;19(5):431-6.
9. McIntier TM: Nursing the family when a child dies. *RN.* 1995 Feb;58(2):50-5; quiz 55.
10. Mian P: Sudden bereavement: nursing interventions in the ED. *Crit Care Nurs.* 1990;10(1):30-41.
11. Tye C: Qualified nurses' perceptions of the needs of suddenly bereaved family members in the accident and emergency department. *J Adv Nurs.* 1993 Jun;18(6):948-56.
12. Cohen FS: Removal of the dead: from room to morgue. *J Nurs Educ.* 1978;17(3):36-41.
13. Stevenson EP: The school nurse as a student bereavement counselor. In: Stevenson RG, Stevenson EP: *Teaching Students about Death—A Comprehensive Resource for Educators and Parents.* Philadelphia: Charles Press, 1996, pp. 76-81.

23: Chaplains and Clergy

Chaplains are clergy who work in hospitals, nursing homes, or prisons, or with the armed forces, police, or fire and emergency medical services. The role of chaplain seems to have been created to help mute the impact of death. When appropriate, the rituals of religion spare some bereaved (as well as the chaplains) part of the anguish that surrounds acute unexpected deaths. Yet chaplains carry a heavy burden, because people expect them "to understand what is ineffable (indescribable), and to do something about it."[1] While they frequently counsel patients, families, parishioners, and staff about death and dying, sudden-death notifications are usually their most difficult job. In these situations, they have no time to counsel or console the family in advance, and no time to "orchestrate" all the functions and rituals that surround a death. Yet they can still provide an "island of calm and sustenance" in the midst of the grief and distress that accompany sudden unexpected deaths.[2]

Besides being able to convey their empathy through non-verbal communication, chaplains typically learn to say their words of comfort "in a soothing and melodious way, while their facial expressions and eyes convey 'I may not know you but my heart goes out for you.'"[3] Chaplains have a high-stress job and must take care, especially in positions with frequent sudden-death notifications, to protect their own mental well-being, as the following vignette demonstrates.

> An experienced Air Force chaplain, who had just come from a grisly aircraft crash, told a novice: "Chaplain, if you haven't been used to death, get set. And don't be too upset if your theology takes a turn, changes. It's going to. I've buried a great number of men whose entire body I could have carried in the palm of my hand. There are times when you have to go out and search an area a mile square

and pick up as many pieces as you can find. Yet the man isn't dead until the flight surgeon says he's dead. Then you have to go see the wife . . . and you have to tell the woman her husband is not coming home any more . . ." He fell silent.[4]

The Chaplain's Role

Chaplains generally provide death notifications in two sites: health care facilities and homes. In hospitals, they often work as a part of the medical team, helping to gather survivors and assisting medical personnel during the actual notification. They may support the family after the medical team has left to perform other tasks. They also often assist the police, military, Red Cross, and others to make death notifications at survivors' homes. Table 23-1 provides a protocol to help chaplains make death notifications.

The chaplain's job is somewhat different than that of other notifiers. As one chaplain said, "Our task is not only to deliver the news of death, but also many times to help a broken family—physically, emotionally, and spiritually . . . In most cases, this death came without any warning whatsoever—with no opportunity to modify relationships, express a final 'I love you,' resolve a conflict."[5] Another saw the chaplain's role as distinctly different from that of other clergy, saying that in circumstances surrounding death, "Most people don't want religion, they want spirituality."[6] Not only do chaplains aid survivors, but they also help the primary staff, especially hospital staff, to accept their own limitations, relieving the guilt that often overtakes them when they inevitably lose patients.

Unlike many other notifiers, chaplains often need to say little. Their presence both signifies a critical situation and imparts a sense of comfort, as happened after a police officer's wife heard that her husband had been shot.

> "It took about 45 minutes to get to the hospital," she remembers. "They took me to the back and I spoke with the doctor. He had to admit that it didn't look very good, but I just assumed they always have to say that. I was sitting in the hospital—an hour and a half at most—and then the chaplain came in and he knelt down and he said, 'I'm sorry. They did everything they could.'"[7]

Sometimes, however, their presence suggests bad news when there isn't any, as Chaplain Pat Andresen explains:

> After her teenage son had been in a car crash, a woman was called to come to the emergency department. By the time she arrived, her son had been treated and was ready for discharge. Since the rest of the ED team was busy, the chaplain met her when she arrived. When she saw his nametag said "Chaplain," she collapsed on the floor, screaming "He's dead! My son is dead." Even when her son spoke to her, she wouldn't calm down. Only after about 30 minutes, when her son, in frustration, asked her for money for a soda, did she come to her senses.[8]

Table 23-1: Protocol for Death Notification by Chaplains

Preparation
• Dress professionally, even if called out in the middle of the night. • Say a prayer to guide you through the experience.
In the Hospital
• Introduce yourself to the charge nurse or physician. • Locate the telephones, bathrooms, patient's room, and nurse-physician work area if you are not familiar with facility. • Speak with the nurse or physician who will accompany you to meet survivors. • See table 3-1 for additional information about in-hospital notifications. • Find out which survivors are present and which are still en route.
Gather Information
• Decedent's name and address? Marital status? How did the death occur? • Is identification of the decedent positive or tentative? If tentative, why, and what does the family need to do now (make a photo- or an in-person identification, supply a photograph, etc.)? • Is the decedent's (and family's) religious affiliation known? Do they belong to a particular church or temple? • Where is the body now? • Who should the family contact for further information (medical examiner, police officer, hospital, funeral director, etc.)? • Identify the next of kin who need to be initially notified. • Obtain any available advance information about these surviving relatives. • Locate the home on a map. • Consider making a "test" phone call only to determine if you have the correct address. (Later, explain to family why this call was made.)
Go To Home
• Go with a partner (police officer, neighbor, or other relative). • On the way to the home, discuss your reactions to this incident and the importance of correctly informing survivors.

Continued on next page

Table 23-1: continued

Go To Home, cont.
• Decide who will be the primary spokesperson. • Confirm that you are speaking to the correct people. Ask the person answering the door, "Is this the home of (person you want to speak with)?" • Identify yourself and your partner. An ID card, clerical garb, or a partner in uniform helps to establish your credentials. • When they ask, "What's wrong?" say, "It is better if we speak inside." Then, enter the home and sit down.
Break the News
• *Option #1:* Speak only with the key survivor first. Then speak, or have them speak, with everyone else. • *Option #2:* Gather the entire group together before breaking the news. • Break the news gently, but quickly and clearly. Avoid stilted professional language and euphemisms. They already know something is very wrong and they want to know *now*. (Foreign-born individuals may want a little more time leading up to the announcement. Be sensitive to what they want.) • Guide the survivors through the initial stages of grieving. Don't fear showing your emotions. • May use phrases such as "He's in God's hands" or "He's with the Lord." • Do not fall into the trap of trying to explain God's actions or defend God for what happened. • Do not use statements that attempt to explain God's will, such as "God must have needed him" or "God has a reason for this." They only anger most survivors. • You don't have to say a lot. Think of yourself as a silently present ministry. That is what most helps survivors. • Ask survivors "Tell me about Mary." or "When did you last see Sam?" This helps them emote and begin to grieve. • Spouses can be asked "How did you meet Bob?" or "What will you remember the most about Sue?" • Obtain medical assistance, if required. • Maintain control and the direction of the situation. The chaplain represents order, stability, and structure to the survivors. Adapt to your surroundings in dress (e.g., take off your jacket), speech, and mannerisms.

Continued on next page

Table 23-1: continued

Notify Others
• If possible, do not leave a person alone after making the notification. • If your partner (such as a police officer) needs to leave immediately after the notification, for safety reasons, have a cellular phone or radio available to summon police or medical assistance if later required. • If the family has their own clergy, ask him or her to come to the home. • Ask the family if they want to share a prayer or read scripture, especially if they are from the same or a similar religious background as yours. • Ask if there is anything else you can do for the family, especially if they are from a religious or cultural group that is not familiar to you. • Help the family notify other relatives and special friends. They may also need to contact their lawyer or accountant. • Help family identify specific helping agencies, such as bereavement or other support groups and social service agencies. • If appropriate, prepare family to see "death scene" photographs in the media.
Information and Reports
• Obtain any additional information needed for body disposition, such as the name of the funeral home or crematoria. • Provide the family with the written information they will need to proceed with further arrangements or to obtain additional information. (See table 6-1.) • Leave your chaplain's card (not your church card). • Tell the agency that you represent that you have made notification and have left the home. This is a safety measure. It also ensures that a second notification won't be made inadvertently. • Do not discuss any of the events that transpired with anyone in the media. • Follow up on any commitments you made to the family. • If possible, make a second visit to the family within the week. • Attend the funeral or memorial service, if possible.

Modified from: De Revere DW, Cunningham WA, Mobley T, et al.: Death notifications. In: *Chaplaincy in Law Enforcement: What It Is and How to Do It*. Springfield, IL: Thomas, 1989; and International Chaplains' Ministry. *Introduction . . . Death Notification for Emergency Service Chaplaincy*. Edmonds, WA: ICM, 1993.

Chaplains may also become involved in death notifications after disasters involving many victims. In community-wide disasters, chaplains have been seen to react differently, depending upon how close they were to the incident, whether their parishioners or friends were involved, and their own state of mind. In one review of how ministers (not all acted in a capacity of chaplain, although many did) reacted to a local natural disaster—a series of devastating tornadoes resulting in many deaths—the ministers did many things in addition to death notifications. Among the activities they performed were attending the mass funeral service, visiting the injured in the hospitals, sitting with or counseling survivors, using their church for the suddenly homeless, distributing food, raising money to help survivors, helping at the temporary morgue, assisting at the clinic, helping to rebuild homes, and providing other disaster relief.[9]

With decreasing hospital budgets and an increasing role for social workers, chaplains are often either not available (some pastoral care services have been eliminated) or not called upon as often as they should be to comfort and assist survivors after sudden deaths. Sometimes chaplains are not called because the survivors are of a different faith. However, in many cases, an initial contact by the hospital chaplain can ease the burden on the family, on the family's personal minister, and on the hospital staff.

Most often, though, the burden of comforting survivors, helping them to make subsequent notifications, funeral arrangements, and provisions for short-term, daily-living needs is left to the already-overburdened medical staff, "though they retain a calm veneer, the time which they can spend with the bereaved is limited, for they have more than enough to do to fight for the living."[10]

Religious and Cultural Beliefs

Often the chaplain's job is to "make sense" of a tragedy. This works best for survivors whose religious beliefs play a large part in their lives. Although identifying a patient's religious affiliation may not seem important in the face of a medical emergency, spending a moment to try to ascertain this information may avoid a bizarre occurrence, such as the one that happened during the Piper Alpha offshore oil-rig disaster.

> When survivors were rushed into hospital, those responsible for obtaining and recording information about them failed to include religious affiliation. It was apparently felt to be of too minor importance to question critically ill men recently rescued from the sea about. [*sic*] Consequently, to fulfill the chaplain's responsibilities, one had the unenviable task of inquiring from overworked intensive care staff, "Is he one of mine?" This was an intrusion the staff hardly appreciated while busy with patients . . . As a consequence, representatives from several different denominations each intruded with a word of sympathy to each patient.[11]

Knowledge of different religious (table 23-2) and cultural attitudes toward death may facilitate communication with those of different faiths or backgrounds. If contact information forms are used for reference during notifications, they should also list on-call clergy for each faith.

Table 23-2: Religions' Beliefs about, Rituals for, and Attitudes toward Death

Adventist (Seventh Day Adventist, Church of God, Advent, Christian Church)	Individuals are not dead, only asleep. Resurrection will occur, with rewards and punishments, upon the return of Jesus Christ.
Baha'i	No official last rites.
Baptist	Clergy seek to minister by counsel and prayer with the family.
Buddhist	Bedside chanting is common after a death. A Buddhist priest should be contacted.
Church of Christ	No official last rites.
Church of Christ Scientist (Christian Scientist)	No official last rites.
Church of God	No official last rites.
Church of Jesus Christ of Latter Day Saints (Mormons)	No official last rites.
Eastern Orthodox Church	Last rites are performed.
Episcopalian	Last rites ("Rite for the Anointing of the Sick" or "Litany at the Time of Death") are usually performed. Aborted fetuses and stillbirths are not baptized.
Friends (Quakers)	Generally arrange simple body disposition: donation to science or cheapest cremation. Memorial service to remember the decedent's life and spirit. Belief in subsequent life is individual choice.
Grace Brethren	No official last rites.
Greek Orthodox	If the dying can swallow, they are given the "Sacrament of Holy Communion." If not, they receive "Holy Unction," anointing with Holy (or blessed) Oil. Death must be properly mourned to prevent harm to the living.
Hindu	Priest may tie thread around the body's neck or wrist signifying a blessing (should not be removed) and pour water into the mouth. Family will want to wash the body. Non-Hindus should use gloves if they must handle the body. The body is normally covered with a plain white sheet; married women may be covered by red fabric.

Continued on next page

Table 23-2: continued

Islam (Muslim)	Family washes and prepares body, then turns it facing Mecca. Non-Muslims should use gloves if they must handle the body. Miscarriages of more than 130 days gestation are treated as dead people. If resuscitation is still in progress, a family member may want to be present to read from the Koran.
Jehovah's Witness	No official last rites.
Judaism	Relatives traditionally want to be present and recite special prayers at the time of death. A *Shomer* (watcher) stays with the body until it is buried. Rapid burials are common. The Orthodox branch may refuse an autopsy and, sometimes, organ donation.
Lutheran	No official last rites.
Mennonite	No official last rites.
Methodist, United	Believe good will be rewarded and evil punished after death.
Pentecostal (Assembly of God, Foursquare Church)	No official last rites.
Presbyterian	Rather than "last rites," scripture and prayer are common following deaths.
Roman Catholic	No specific sacrament after death, although prayers are common. If a priest is not available, anyone with reason and the proper intention can baptize a person in an emergency by pouring water on person's head while saying "I baptize you in the name of the Father and the Son and of the Holy Spirit." (Then notify a priest.) Since Vatican II, "Anointing of the Sick" has replaced "Last Rites."
Russian Orthodox	Traditionally, after death the arms are crossed and fingers are set in a cross.
Sikhism	No objection to the body being handled by non-Sikhs. Family usually washes the body themselves. Bodies are normally taken to the family home for a last viewing and then to the funeral home.
Unitarian Universalist	Widely varying beliefs.

Adapted from References 12 through 14.

References

1. Weisman AD: On the value of denying death. *Pastoral Psychol.* 1972;23:24-32.
2. Soreff SM: Sudden death in the emergency department: a comprehensive approach for families, emergency medical technicians, and emergency department staff. *Crit Care Med.* 1979 Jul;7(7):321-3.
3. Thompson J: A chaplain's personal view of intensive care. *Intens Care Nurs.* 1990 Dec; 6(4):192-5.
4. Tarr H: *The Conversion of Chaplain Cohen.* New York: Avon, 1963, p. 118.
5. International Chaplains' Ministry. *Introduction . . . Death Notification for Emergency Service Chaplaincy.* Edmonds, WA: ICM, 1993.
6. Weber R: Quoted in: Elias M: Few would turn to clergy for help if they were dying. *USA Today*, 9 December 1997; Sect. A:1.
7. Clark C: *Better, Not Bitter: The Story of Concerns of Police Survivors, Inc.* Camdenton, MO: Concerns of Police Survivors, 1992, p. 6.
8. Andresen, P: Personal communication with author, March 1999.
9. Chinnici R: Pastoral care following a natural disaster. *Pastoral Psychol.* 1985;33(4):245-54.
10. Thompson J: "A chaplain's personal view."
11. *Ibid.*
12. McQuay JE: Cross-cultural customs and beliefs related to health crises, death, and organ donation/transplantation: a guide to assist health care professionals understand different responses and provide cross-cultural assistance. *Crit Care Nurs Clin North Am.* 1995 Sep;7(3):581-94.
13. Black J: Broaden your mind about death and bereavement in certain ethnic groups in Britain. *Br Med J Clin Res.* 1987 Aug 29;295(6597):536-9.
14. Walker C: Attitudes to death and bereavement among cultural minority groups. *Nurs Times.* 1982 Dec 15-21;78(50):2106-9.

24: Medics, Firefighters, and Search and Rescue

Unlike physicians and nurses, those working in emergency medical systems (EMS) have the unique experience of trying to save lives and having to pronounce death with family members present—and often observing. Like emergency department staff, they rarely know the patient or the survivors prior to their arrival and, once the patient has been pronounced dead, feel time pressure to quickly put their emergency vehicle back in service.

The key purpose for beginning the paramedic profession was to implement new cardiac resuscitation methods and "to 'raise' the clinically dead from cardiac arrest."[1] Yet for patients on whom medics perform out-of-hospital CPR, only about 1 to 7 patients per 100, on average, are discharged from hospitals alive.[2,3] In those who have a cardiac arrest after trauma and who are brought to the hospital, only about 5 per 200 survive, with only about 3 per 200 being able to function.[4] That means that many patients are pronounced dead on the scene, either after failed resuscitative efforts or where CPR was not begun because it would have been futile. As one medic said, "No matter how quickly we are summoned or how well we perform, the usual outcome of a CPR call is the same: Death."[5]

Most medics find that notifying families of a death is emotionally difficult. Medics who work the fewest hours, and thus have the least experience, have the most problems coping. The situations they find the most stressful include sudden unexpected deaths, children's deaths, and deaths when the family is present or there are no prehospital advance directives.[6] Table 24-1 contains a protocol for in-home death notifications by EMS personnel.

Table 24-1: Protocol for Emergency Medical Services In-home Death Notification

Prepare
• Know how to recognize and use prehospital advance directives and prehospital do-not-resuscitate orders. Be prepared to discuss with survivors why you did or did not follow them.
Interact
• Interact with family during the resuscitative effort. Supply them with an easily understandable update (not in "medic-speak") about how things are going and what your options are. Let them watch if they wish to and they aren't hindering patient care. If they wish to speak to the patient, even if the patient is unconscious, allow that. • Don't give false hope if there is no response to the interventions. • Interpret for the family any radio messages from the base station. • If a composed family member can help the resuscitative effort (usually by helping bring things to the team), allow them to do so. • Balance treating the family's grief reaction with the resuscitative effort.
For Resuscitations in Progress
• Notify receiving hospital if key survivors (especially parents) have asked to stay with the patient during the hospital resuscitative attempt. • Allow at least one key survivor to ride in the ambulance (usually in front) to the hospital.
Notify
• Know and be prepared to explain your system's death-pronouncement criteria to answer their question "Why did you stop?" • Look at the survivors as you talk with them. • Do not use euphemisms, such as "passed on," "expired," or "left us." Use one of the "D" words: "Died," "Death," or "Dead."
Comfort
• Primary medic should spend adequate time with the family while the second medic prepares the emergency unit to go back in service. • Direct your information to and take your lead from the spouse, parent, or significant other. Include others in your gaze and answer their questions appropriately.

Continued on next page

Table 24-1: continued

Comfort, cont.
• After the fact, interact in a "softer" way than during the resuscitation—indicating that you are responding to the survivor's feelings, as well as to their stated concerns. • Second medic can also obtain necessary identifying information for EMS report from the most composed survivor. • Sit or crouch beside the survivors rather than standing over them as an intimidating figure. Make frequent eye contact, but do not stare. • Touch the back of the arm, the shoulder, or hold their hand (usually for people of the opposite sex). However, be culturally sensitive and back off if they give you signals that touch is not desired. Occasionally, when it is clear that it is appropriate, a brief hug or an arm around the shoulder may show them that you care.
Inform
• Describe simply and clearly what you did and why you did it. • Listen to how the person feels and what they want to know. • Tell them what they want to know in an honest (not brutal) and non-judgmental manner. Omit clichés. • Do not reinforce survivors' denials that death has occurred. • Restrain angry survivors only enough to protect them. • Supply only the medical information that you have clearly observed. Do not make any judgments about what caused the death, even if it seems obvious. For example, an adult who drowned may actually have died from a heart attack or stroke. • Refer to the deceased person as "him," "her," or, if possible, by name. • Review chapter 27 to learn how to respond to some typical queries. • Do not feel that you must keep talking. Being there is often sufficient.
Support
• Have available a list of resources and referrals that can provide additional support and assistance to the survivors. • Do not leave family members stranded and alone if you transport the patient. Arrange a ride for them, and be sure that anyone driving is in a condition to do so safely.

Prehospital Advance Directives

Medics must be aware of their region's prehospital advance directive laws or protocols that limit the need to perform unnecessary and unwanted resuscitations. Often referred to by their color (e.g., "orange forms" in Arizona, "pink forms" in Oregon, different colored bracelets and necklaces in other states), they allow medics to not begin resuscitative measures in cases of cardiac arrest. They are most commonly used for homebound, hospice, and nursing home patients.[7,8]

In some less-advanced EMS systems that lack prehospital do-not-resuscitate directives for hospice and other chronically ill patients, medics often have to do resuscitative procedures even when survivors already know that their loved one has died. In these instances, rather than hoping that medics will perform a miracle, family members may be distraught when medics begin to do procedures on their loved one.[9-11] They may even approach arriving medics, saying, "There's nothing you can do. Her doctor said to wait an hour after she died before calling you." Survivors feel anger in these situations, especially when responders arrive using lights and sirens, when many personnel show up, and if they are disrespectful.[12] In some instances, homebound terminally ill patients may be "dragged through a bizarre yet uninterruptable sequence of events if the family happened to call 911. . . . The paramedics [are] required to resuscitate the patient on the way to the hospital, and the emergency room staff would have to continue working on the patient after arrival."[13]

Death Pronouncements

Medics also need to know, and be prepared to explain to survivors, their region's death-pronouncement protocol/criteria. These vary from region to region depending upon those supervising the emergency medical system. When a medic pronounces someone dead in the field, either with or without concurrence, via radio, with their base-station physician, survivors usually want to know why and how it was done. (To avoid having to make this explanation, especially if families seem at all hostile, medics often begin to transport the patient in their ambulance before pronouncing them dead.)

Medics have less medical background and less authority than do their white-jacketed colleagues. Yet, since they are present when death occurs, medics must deliver the news to survivors. Their authority in these circumstances stems from their uniform, the trust the public places on those summoned through the 911 system, and, when resuscitative efforts have been attempted, the family's observation of their efforts. Observing CPR, for example, sends a very powerful message about caring, as Dr. John Lantos described after he performed CPR on his sister-in-law.

> It is perverse to imagine that this dramatic, ritual power is morally irrelevant, that CPR is "just" a medical therapy. Among other things, CPR is our culture's desperate dance around the bed of a dying loved one. It is brutal, but that is part of the reason it works. It has strange elements of human sacrifice, of ritual

mutilation, and that is another part of why it works. It is used profligately in cases where it is unlikely to be beneficial, because we have so little else to offer, and because it feels so right.[14]

Nearly all survivors are satisfied with the medics' decisions to terminate resuscitative efforts in the field.[15] Occasionally, though, these terminations may come unexpectedly to both the EMS providers and the families. Ken Briggs, while working with the Groton Rescue Squad in Brown County, South Dakota, had an unnerving experience soon after local ambulances were equipped with automatic voice-prompted external defibrillators (AED) for use during resuscitations.

On the scene with a cardiac arrest patient, we were doing CPR and were told by our base station to continue until one of the advanced ambulances carrying one of the area's first AEDs arrived. On their arrival, they placed electrodes on our patient so the internal computer could assess the patient's heart rhythm. When the machine was set to assess the rhythm, it loudly announced in its mechanical voice, "STOP CPR."

When the patient's wife heard this, she assumed that the machine had told us to stop resuscitative efforts. (It hadn't. It only instructed us to cease for a few seconds so it could assess the rhythm.) Suddenly, she began shouting, "Don't stop! Don't stop!" One of my partners took her aside and explained the situation. Although her husband was in very critical condition (and was later pronounced dead at the hospital), she appreciated that we were continuing our efforts and would not stop on the orders of a machine.

Medics should have a preprinted list of referral sources to give to survivors once a death pronouncement is made. Often they use the list given out by their base-station hospital or modify the information form in table 6-1.

The EMS Demeanor

How medics relate to survivors is vital, since at this pivotal moment, memories are seared into their minds and their behavior patterns may be radically altered. Even years after the event, many survivors recall not only the tone of voice and manner of speaking, but also the exact words medics said to them. Most of these survivors do relatively well. But in one study, 20% had increased their visits to physicians and 10% still used tranquilizers to help them cope.[16]

Sometimes EMS personnel don't have to say anything. Their attitude and non-verbal behavior say it all. This is especially true during rescues or body recoveries such as this one remembered by Fran Kunz, of the Pima County (Ariz.) Search and Recovery Divers.

We responded for a body recovery of a mentally challenged Native American from a large cattle pond on the Sells Indian Reservation. In other recoveries on the reservation, we seldom had contact with the families as they choose to remain in the background. This particular mother, though, stood at one end of the cattle pond and watched us closely. We entered the water from the other end and completed a

> couple of search patterns before locating her son. We brought him up and turned his body over to authorities. At that point his mother, a small frail women obviously feeling sorrow for the loss of her son, came over to us and thanked us for "bringing back her son." Still in my wetsuit and muddy from the cattle pond, I gave her a hug and we both cried.[17]

Since emergency personnel are often in the survivors' homes, the interactions may be a bit out of the ordinary. Richard Judd, an EMT, recalls a 5 A.M. call for an 82-year-old woman's husband who had obviously died during the night:

> Her husband was in the kitchen, on the floor. He was clearly dead. He was cold. He was cyanotic. He was morbid. He had rigidity. All of the things were there. I did my examination, checked the pulse, checked the body, and I looked up and she said, "He's dead, isn't he?" "Yes, he is," I said. "Yeah, I thought so," she said. We sat there for a few minutes, and she asked, "Well, what do I do now?" I asked her if she had any friends or relatives. She didn't. So I asked if she had a minister we could call. She did, so we called him.
>
> While Judd and his partner waited for the minister, the woman asked if she could prepare breakfast for them. They hesitantly accepted. "As her husband lay covered on the kitchen floor, she fixed us eggs, home-fries, and toast." They sat with her for 1½ hours. "What we did during the time we had with her was to make sure she was OK . . . By the time we left she had some support . . . She was all by herself . . . We didn't have anywhere to go, so we sat there and had some coffee with her, and some toast and eggs. You might say, "Gee, wasn't that a little macabre for you to sit there?" Well, no. She needed something to do and, reasonably, she wanted to be with people.[18]

In general, survivors believe that medics deliver the news about sudden, unexpected deaths in a professional, gentle, and supportive manner. Medics spend nearly half an hour with survivors if they have not begun resuscitative efforts and slightly longer if they have made a resuscitation attempt.[19]

Resuscitations in Progress

Being left behind when an ambulance leaves carrying a loved one undergoing resuscitative procedures can be one of the most devastating events of a survivor's life. They often feel a sense of responsibility to do what they can to "watch over" their loved one, or at least to feel that they are a part of the effort. Being left to make their own way to the hospital denigrates their position and disempowers them. A nurse, who flew with her critically injured son in the air ambulance, had this reaction when she was abruptly left at the airport:

> The fire crew said there was no room for me in the ambulance with my son. Why couldn't I have ridden in front? I had promised him that I would not leave him. All I could think of was that they were going to get him to help, so I wasn't about to be the one to slow them down. But looking back, it was awful. I was

driven to the ED *very slowly.* Was that because they already knew he was gone and they wanted to stall me? From the looks on everyone's face when I got to the ED, it was pretty apparent. I felt like everyone had been kept abreast of his status but me, *because I was not there*.[20]

When key survivors are transported in the ambulance, EMS personnel can assist both them and the hospital team by advising ED personnel in advance (via radio) that the survivor(s) want to stay with the patient during the resuscitative attempt. Based on the nature of the case and the patient's needs, the ED team can then make a decision about permitting this, arrange for an escort for the survivor, and advise the rest of the team. This situation most commonly occurs with infant and child resuscitations.

References

1. Meoli M: Supporting the bereaved: field notification of death. *J Emerg Med Serv JEMS*. 1993 Dec;18(12):39-46.

2. Lombardi G, Gallagher EJ, Gennis P: Outcome of out-of-hospital cardiac arrest in New York City: The Pre-Hospital Arrest Survival Evaluation (PHASE) Study. *JAMA*. 1994 Mar 2; 271(9):678-83.

3. Schwab TM, Callaham ML, Madsen CD, et al.: A randomized clinical trial of active compression-decompression CPR vs. standard CPR in out-of-hospital cardiac arrest in two cities. *JAMA*. 1995 Apr 26;273(16):1261-8.

4. Shimazu S, Shatney CH: Outcomes of trauma patients with no vital signs on hospital admission. *J Trauma*. 1983 Mar;23(3):213-6.

5. Meoli M: "Supporting the bereaved."

6. Norton RL, Bartkus EA, Schmidt TA, et al.: Survey of emergency medical technicians' ability to cope with the deaths of patients during prehospital care. *Prehospital Disaster Med*. 1992 Jul-Sep;7(3):235-42.

7. Iserson KV: Foregoing prehospital care: should ambulance staff always resuscitate? *J Med Ethics*. 1991 Mar;17:19-24.

8. Iserson KV: A simplified prehospital advance directive law: Arizona's approach. *Ann Emerg Med*. 1993 Nov;22(11):1703-10.

9. *Ibid.*

10. Iserson KV: "Foregoing prehospital care."

11. Iserson KV: If we don't learn from history . . . : ethical failings in a new prehospital directive. *Am J Emerg Med*. 1995 Mar;13(2):241-2.

12. Critz SH: The attitudes and experiences of families with death determination in the home. *Am J Hospice Care*. 1989 Sep-Oct;6(5):38-43.

13. Jones-Bey H: The face of death. *J Minority Med Stud*. 1997;49-55,78.

14. Lantos JD: Bethann's death. *Hastings Cent Rep*. 1995 Mar-Apr;25(2):22-23.

15. Fosnocht DE, Delbridge TR, Garrison HG, et al.: Surviving relatives' acceptance of the decision to terminate resuscitation in the field (abstract). *Ann Emerg Med.* 1993;22:919.

16. Schmidt TA, Harrahill MA: Family response to out-of-hospital death. *Acad Emerg Med.* 1995 Jun;2(6):513-8.

17. Kunz FD: Personal communication with author, December 1998.

18. Costello L: Death & dying. *Emerg Med Serv.* 1989;18(8):17, 25-28, 33-4.

19. Schmidt TA, Harrahill MA: "Family response to out-of-hospital death."

20. Ogden, S: Personal communication with author, 18 March 1999.

25: Military

Military notifiers have three groups to notify when a member of the military dies: the military command, the surviving members of the decedent's working group, and the next of kin. Similar to disaster situations, military notifiers must often inform other surviving unit members of multiple simultaneous deaths. The protocol for military in-line-of-duty death notifications in table 25-1 or the protocol for U.S. Navy death notification in table 25-2 can be used when notifying team members or the next of kin.

Brief History of Military Death Notification

The earliest systematic next of kin notification in the U.S. military occurred during World War I (1914-18). Before that, the reporting of military deaths was haphazard. Official casualty procedures entailed only an entry into the unit reports or notification within the military chain of command. During the Civil War (1861-65), the U.S. Army regulations only stated

> After any action or affair, a report of the killed, wounded and missing will be made, in which the name, rank, and regiment of each officer and soldier will be specified, with such remarks and explanations as may be requisite for the records of the Department of War, or be necessary to establish the just claims of any individual who may have been wounded or of the heirs and representatives of any killed in action.[1]

During the Spanish-American War (1898), there was increasing pressure for the U.S. military to provide lists of dead soldiers, as evidenced by this official wire to the Army:

> We receive dozens inquiries every day from mothers and fathers of Philippine troopers. They are almost crazed by the uncertainty. Can you not induce War Department to get by cable list of dead to date and have daily list cabled hereafter the same as from Cuba? That would be a small favor for the Government to render the families of its volunteer soldiers. [*sic*]

The U.S. Adjutant General responded two days later: "Secretary War directs names and regiments be furnished by cable of the dead of your command, from leaving San Francisco to date. Hereafter weekly list will be cabled."[2] [*sic*]

Occasionally during this period, notifications were rather terse, as when Dr. Jesse W. Lazear died. He was part of the military-sponsored medical team investigating the cause of the deadly Yellow Fever epidemic in Cuba in 1900. Under Walter Reed's leadership, he used himself as a guinea pig, quickly contracted the disease, sickened, and died. His wife, who had returned to Washington, D.C., to give birth to their second child, learned of his illness and the death simultaneously through a curt telegram from the Surgeon General: "Doctor Lazear died at eight P.M. this evening."[3]

During World War I, General Order Number 89 specified that "In order that the families of deceased officers and soldiers of the American Expeditionary Force [A.E.F.] may receive promptly all information possible concerning those who are killed in action, or die of wounds, injuries or disease, chaplains and Red Cross searchers and others of the A.E.F. will, when writing letters of sympathy in case of death of a member of the A.E.F., conform to the following rule:

> "Such letters, unsealed and marked in the upper right-hand corner with a small cross, will be forwarded under other cover addressed Central Records Office, Adjutant General's Department, A.E.F. The letters will there be examined by a representative of the Base Censor, and forwarded to destination after verification of the death by the Casualty Section, Central Records Office."[4]

By the end of World War II, the War Department was processing about 3,300 casualty and "change in status" reports from the European Theater of Operations each day and, presumably, an equal number from the Pacific Theater. Overall, they processed over 1 million casualty reports between D-day and the end of the European war. [5] These included not only those killed, but also those who were wounded, missing in action, and captured. Before the D-day invasion, the U.S. Army held conferences and mock exercises to improve their casualty reporting, although field commanders were reluctant to assign soldiers to this task. Perhaps because of their lack of manpower and experience, there were a large number of inaccurate reports during and immediately after the invasion, "causing embarrassment to the Theater and the War Department and unnecessary suffering to next of kin."[6] Because of reporting errors, in 1945 the War Department redefined those who should be reported "dead" by saying, "Any person will be reported dead when there is reasonably conclusive evidence of death or where there are circumstances that lead to no other logical conclusion."[7]

Letters of condolence from the decedent's commanding officer are now standard. But prior to October 1944 (at least in Europe), they were optional. Initially, the letters only stated that the person had died. Later, after public appeals from relatives, who wanted all possible information, they included all the details that wouldn't compromise security. Many of these letters had to be returned for correction before they could be forwarded to the next of kin.[8] Yet once they were received, they were greatly appreciated, as shown by this message distributed by the Women's Volunteer Committee, Moore General Hospital, Swannanoa, N.C.:

> I feel strongly that the proper authorities should be thanked, officially, for the splendid letters received by the next of kin of war casualties from Chaplains and Commanding Officers. The letters, with a very few exceptions, show great thought, personal interest and sympathy, and they bring almost unfailing comfort and help to the bereaved families. There is usually an enormous improvement in the morale of those bereaved members after such a letter is received, although comparatively few of the recipients seem to think of acknowledging them, deep though their gratitude is. These letters must often represent almost superhuman effort on the part of these busy men, and it seems only right that they should know, from own personal experience and contact, how worthwhile is their task. It must be hard to keep on writing, yet rarely learning of the effect or reaction. As a member of the Women's Volunteer committee engaged in making condolence visits to the next of kin of war casualties to extend the sympathy of the Army, I personally think such letters are the most merciful and morale-building of all the Army efforts in this connection.[9]

However, once again during the Korean War, the casualty reporting system was so bad as to put the U.S. Army in "a very embarrassing position."[10]

Current Notification Procedures

By the Vietnam War, the U.S. military had greatly improved their casualty reporting system. The military now uses multispecialty casualty notification teams to notify survivors about service-related deaths.

An example of a typical military notification process is that of the U.S. Air Force. They use a Casualty Notification Team, consisting of a Casualty Notification Officer (CNO), a chaplain, and a medical officer (flight surgeon, family physician, physician assistant, or nurse). The CNO is either the member's commander or a "standby designate" (selected from a rotating list) who is a field grade officer whose rank is equal to or higher than that of the decedent. The notification process consists of three parts: pre-notification, notification, and post-notification. The CNO has the primary duty to assemble and brief the team, type a letter to the survivor, report active duty deaths to the command, and render assistance to the family. The team members wear their dress uniforms to reflect a good image. The team cannot make the notification until the death is actually confirmed.

They deliver the notification, with the CNO telling the survivor by reading the official death-notification letter. The chaplain offers comfort and prayer while the medical officer is "attending to any reaction of the NOK [survivor]."[11] The chaplain also provides pre-notification counseling to the notification team; usually determines how long the notification team should stay with survivors; provides follow-up counseling, as needed, for the family and military unit; and arranges for religious services.

When notification teams, chaplains, or military medical personnel must deal with other unit members, they are intervening in a unique situation with a variety of potential responses. The reaction of unit members varies with their proximity to the decedent(s) and to the event that caused the death. Their overt reactions may be muted due to peer pressure, their personal expectations, and their need to over-control their environment, a maladaptive syndrome called "inhibited grief." Within flying units, the denial is nearly universal, bolstered by such bravado that the official U.S. Air Force song celebrates that fact that "we live in fame and go down in flame." A bit more macabre is an Air Force song toasting "Here's to the dead already, and hurrah for the next man to die." Eventually, though, even the most stalwart men usually experience the classic acute responses to trauma: anxiety, sleep disturbances, irritability, increased alcohol use, and somatic complaints. Unit survivors are particularly prone to inappropriately accepting responsibility for events they did not control.[12] Table 25-1 outlines the process the Casualty Notification teams generally follow.

The International Red Cross has a worldwide network for notifying surviving family members of deaths in the armed forces. Notification is initiated by first contacting the local Red Cross Duty Officer. They require the decedent's name, birth date, and branch of service in order to notify relatives. If possible, they also want the decedent's social security number and last military address. In the United States, the American Red Cross has long provided this service for many military members and families. Occasionally, Murphy's Law intervenes, short-circuiting the system, as Larry Graham relates:

> I was stationed stateside with the U.S. Army. Serving as the non-commissioned officer in charge at brigade headquarters for the weekend, I had already spoken with a Red Cross representative several times concerning notifications to brigade members of deaths and serious illnesses in their families. When he called again, I answered the phone, as usual, "Sergeant Graham speaking, sir." The man identified himself and then paused. "Are you Larry Graham?" he asked. He was shocked and flustered that the person who needed to be notified was, by coincidence, the base contact person. Nevertheless, he informed me that my sister had been killed in an auto accident. The system normally worked much better than this.[13]

Due to improved communications, many survivors now know the news as soon as the Red Cross does. Therefore, their caseworkers have recently focused more on helping survivors than on notification. According to the American Red Cross, they have no standard protocol for making these notifications, although they do provide more general education through their "Art of Helping" course.[14]

Table 25-1: Protocol for Military In-Line-of-Duty Death Notifications

Pre-notification
• Brief the notification team members. Be sensitive to their anxieties, since they may not have done this before. • Get accurate directions to where you are going. Have a map available, if necessary. • Determine the religious affiliation of the decedent and survivors, if possible. Provide a chaplain of the same faith, if possible.
Notification
• Support survivors. • Provide resource list. • Help contact family's personal religious minister. • Help contact individuals who the survivors identify as their personal supports. • Expect the unexpected. The family may have already been informed of the death—or of the probability that the death has occurred. • Help survivors make decisions, but don't make the decisions for them. • In military unit, identify those in need of special or additional counseling.
Post-notification
• Arrange family support, if needed. • Help arrange funerary observances. • Attend the funeral(s), if possible. • Arrange counseling for military unit, if needed. • Identify unit members in need of additional counseling. • Work within the unit's mission needs to continue to assist members with readjustment.

Military Notifications—Survivors' Reactions

In many situations, however, military death notifications still occur, and are unique. One flight surgeon described how the families on an air base respond to official death notification procedures.

> This quiet network begins because of the policy that notification of a death is made through official channels. The result is that, after a crash, every wife whose

> husband is unaccounted for is a potential widow until she hears differently. The wives let each other know whose husbands are accounted for, so that the circle of potential widows is lessened. Since the death notification is generally made by a team consisting of the Wing Commander, the Flight Surgeon, and the Chaplain, any one of these individuals in a staff car in a housing area is watched from behind the windows by wives waiting to see where the dreaded vehicle will stop. These anxious moments are an ongoing part of their lives.[15]

Sometimes, however, it doesn't work like that, as one Air Force chaplain described.

> After asking God for guidance, I went to the home of this young wife. It was 9:30 in the morning, an unorthodox time for a chaplain to be making a call. However, Mary stopped her housework, apologized for her appearance, and asked me to sit down. Her looks plainly said, "What a time for a chaplain to be calling!"
>
> Opening the conversation, I remarked, "As a pilot's wife, you undoubtedly have thought of the risks a pilot takes every time he flies. There is always an element of uncertainty." I said this seriously so that it would not be taken for just a casual remark. Mary looked at me for a moment without replying, then she said, "I have thought of that."
>
> A second or two later, she asked, "Are you trying to tell me something?" to which I answered "I have sad news for you. There was a fatal accident this morning."
>
> She replied quickly, "Come to the point . . . was Harry killed?" To which I had but one reply, "Yes."
>
> The girl cried out, "I can't believe it. It was just a few hours ago that he left me. Are you sure there is no mistake?" she began to cry quietly. I went to the door and her friends came in. The time for pastoral consolation and prayer would come later.[16]

The story below describes the devastating effect military deaths have on some families, especially children.

> Only last year I learned that, for years, one of my daughters reacted with very real anxiety to any summons from a classroom. She mentioned that it was common knowledge among her schoolmates on the fighter base that a flier's child could be called out of class, would disappear, and would never be seen again by their classmates. Later, the other children would learn that the father had died and that the family was packing to leave the base. Thus, any summons out of class was a potential death notification.[17]

Once the military member dies, their family is entitled to on-base housing for only a limited time (until recently they were immediately evicted), since they are no longer connected to the military. Thus many major life stressors occur simultaneously: the losses of a loved one, their home and surroundings, the family's primary income producer, the children's school and friends, and their immediate support system. These types of losses have few civilian counterparts outside of war or devastating widespread disasters.

Yet families of career military members "know the system" of death notification and response. Harry Spiller, as a Marine Corps Sergeant, performed this duty for the Marine Corps during the Vietnam War. He described one example of a military death notification to family outside the military culture. In the episode below, Marine Gunnery Sergeant Jack Pierce accompanied him.

> Pierce turned onto Route D. They passed the first house, then the second, and finally pulled into the driveway of the Simmons's family . . . "Can I help you?" a voice echoed from behind them. "Are you Mr. Simmons?" Pierce inquired. "Sure am," he replied.
>
> "Mr. Simmons, as a Representative of the President of the United States and the Commandant of the Marine Corps, it is my duty to inform you that your son, Lance Corporal Jack Simmons, was killed in action on May 5, 1967, in the defense of the United States of America."
>
> Simmons eyes narrowed as he quickly chewed his tobacco then spit. After a moment he spoke up, "You must be mistaken. My boy just got there."
>
> "I'm sorry, Mr. Simmons. There's no mistake."
>
> The farmer reached for his hat, removed it from his head, then wiped his brow. Placing the hat back on his head, he mumbled, "We'd better go in the house and tell the wife." The three walked across the yard to the back door and into the house. A heavy-set woman stood in the middle of the room, wiping her hands on a dishtowel. She glanced at her husband's disturbed face. "What's the matter?" she asked.
>
> Mr. Simmons looked up with tear-filled eyes. "It's Jack, Mom. It's Jack." Mr. Simmons grabbed her. They embraced each other as Mrs. Simmons cried, "Oh, God, no! Not my baby!"
>
> Suddenly the kitchen door opened and a teenage girl entered the room. "Dad? Mom?" Seeing the strangers, she asked, "What's going on here?"
>
> "It's Jack, honey. He's been killed in action." The young girl stood horrified. "No, not Jack, not Jack!" Her screams filled the room as she turned and ran out of the room. Mrs. Simmons followed closely behind. [The men then discussed the known details of how their son died.]
>
> "When will they send him home?" he asked. "It'll be 10 to 14 days, sir," replied Pierce. "We'll have your son sent to whatever funeral home you request. If you'd like, we'll give your son a full military funeral."
>
> "He'd like that," Mr. Simmons said in a low voice.
>
> "We also provide a military escort, if you like. We'll send the telegram today, sir. Shortly, you'll be receiving a telegram confirming your son's death from Marine Corps headquarters. Now, if you have no further questions, we'll be leaving." Spiller handed Mr. Simmons a business card. "If you need us for anything, just call."
>
> "Thank you, Sergeant. Thank you both for being so kind."[18]

Table 25-2: Protocol for U.S. Navy Death Notification

(From *Navy Casualty Assistance Calls Manual*, Bureau of Naval Personnel Instruction 1770.3)

The Responsibilities of the Casualty Assistance Call Officer (CACO):

- To make personal notification to the next of kin that their relative is dead, unaccounted for—Duty Status-Whereabouts Unknown (DUSTWUN), or reported missing.
- To provide a brief explanation of the circumstances.
- To provide updated information regarding remains of deceased or search efforts for a DUSTWUN person.
- To express, to the next of kin of those who have died, the Navy's condolences, concern in the case of members in a DUSTWUN or missing status, and continued support for next of kin during their adjustment to their unfortunate circumstances.
- To extend assistance to the next of kin by assessing the need for immediate financial assistance and follow-up arrangements as necessary.

Within 24 hours of next of kin notification, you will carry out the following duties:

- Visit Primary Next Of Kin (PNOK); relay family decision on allowing Navy preparation/private funeral home preparation of remains; extend assistance with funeral arrangements/memorial service.
- Counsel PNOK on Navy funeral expense allowances on preparation (embalming), shipment, and casketing of remains; determine their decision and obtain name and telephone number of local receiving funeral home.
- Relay PNOK decision to Naval Office of Medical/Dental Affairs, (MEDDEN Affairs), Great Lakes, IL.
- Advise that CO's letter of circumstances/condolences is to be prepared within 48 hours of casualty incident.
- Liaison with casualty's command for additional details of casualty incident.
- Assist dependents in arranging travel to/from funeral site.
- Monitor personal effects shipment through casualty's command representative listed on item BRAVO, Personnel Casualty Report.
- Offer assistance in planning funeral/memorial service/military funeral, honors and chaplain for pastoral care.
- Liaison with receiving funeral director, arrange the funeral honors, and attend funeral.

Table 25-2: continued

- Remain available to further assist with difficulties that may arise during the family's adjustment to the tragic event.
- Arrange for dependents' continued occupancy in government quarters or Basic Allowance for Quarters (BAQ) equivalent for 180-day period following member's death.
- Provide information and assistance in applying for survivor benefits.
- Monitor progress of transport of remains and keep next of kin informed.
- Apprise next of kin via CACO Call Card of next of kin 24-hour toll-free telephone numbers in Washington, D.C.
- Contact Fleet Hometown News Center, Norfolk, Va., to ensure no impending Navy originated news articles appear hereafter in family's hometown newspapers.

You will report to your Casualty Assistance Calls/Funeral Honors Support (CAC/FHS) Program Coordinator:

- (1) when you need assistance or support; and/or (2) always to advise the Program Coordinator of problems, complaints, or next of kin dissatisfaction.
- The CACO is the "team leader" in assisting the next of kin. There are numerous resources available to assist you in this endeavor (listed in Manual's appendix).
- The CACO's role is varied: a leader, a messenger, a resource coordinator and an administrator. You will find it helpful to be organized and to keep accurate and complete written records of your duties and activities. In preparation for CACO duty, you should thoroughly familiarize yourself with the (CACP) Manual, BUPERSINST 1770.3.

The following represents the usual order of events once the program is initiated:

- CAC/FHS Coordinator tasks the CACO to personally notify next of kin and provides the CACO with details on the casualty incident and next of kin information, etc.
- The CACO liaisons with duty chaplain or other Navy representative, (e.g., Hospital Corpsman); the two proceed immediately to residence of next of kin.
- Personal notification occurs between 0600-2400 under most circumstances. Immediate need of primary next of kin for financial assistance is assessed; contact Pers-663 for arranging payment of Death Gratuity.

Table 25-2: continued

Responsibilities Checklist

- ❐ Receive Personnel Casualty Report data; tasking from CAC/FHS Coordinator.
- ❐ Coordinate initial visit with Chaplain, if possible.
- ❐ Identify and make contact with next of kin immediately.
- ❐ Make a clear factual statement about the casualty, and offer the Navy's condolences/concerns.
- ❐ Inform next of kin of current location of remains.
- ❐ Inform family of Navy's primary care of remains, if appropriate.
- ❐ Inform that letter of circumstances is forthcoming from Commanding Officer.
- ❐ Determine if emergency financial assistance is needed.
- ❐ Advise family if Judge Advocate General (JAG) Manual investigation is conducted.
- ❐ Advise family if aircraft mishap investigation is conducted.
- ❐ Advise family if Naval Criminal Investigative Service (CIS) investigation is conducted.
- ❐ Before departing residence, identify and coordinate a family support group (e.g., friends, minister/priest, and relatives).
- ❐ Assure next of kin of your continued availability.
- ❐ Leave completed CACO Call Card and toll-free telephone number with family.

Follow-up Notification Checklist

- ❐ Call CAC/FHS Coordinator immediately upon completion of notification visit.
- ❐ Ensure naval message is sent stating notification has been made and confirming next of kin name and address.
- ❐ Contact Fleet Hometown News Center, Norfolk to stop all Navy originated news articles from appearing in hometown news.
- ❐ As appropriate, provide primary next of kin's desires regarding care of remains/local receiving funeral home (name/address/telephone number) to MEDDEN Affairs.
- ❐ Determine from casualty CO or MEDDEN Affairs current location of remains and expected itinerary.
- ❐ Contact PERS-621/BUPERS Duty Officer regarding Death Gratuity ($6,000) payment procedure.
- ❐ Assist next of kin in completion of letter of request for copy of releasable portions of JAG, Aircraft Mishap investigations, as appropriate, if requested.

References

1. U.S. War Department: *Revised Regulations for the Army of the United States, 1861*. Washington, DC: U.S. Army, AR 465, p. 70.
2. U.S. War Department Adjutant General's Office: *Correspondence Relating to the War with Spain and Conditions Growing out of the Same*. Washington, DC: Government Printing Office, 1902, pp. 800-1.
3. Altman LK: *Who Goes First? The Story of Self-Experimentation in Medicine*. Berkeley, CA: Univ. of California Press, 1998, pp. 148-9.
4. Center of Military History: *United States Army in the World War, 1917-1919, Vol. 16*. General Orders, GHQ, AEF, General Order Number 89, June 7, 1918, France. Washington, DC: U.S. Army, p. 339.
5. U.S. Army Forces in the European Theater, General Board: *Casualty Reporting in the European Theater of Operations*. Study Number 44, Bad Nauheim, Germany, 1945-46. [Dy69A5no44].
6. *Ibid.*
7. Circular 2, War Department, 1945, paragraph 5a.
8. *Ibid.*
9. *Ibid.*
10. Cleaver CG: *History of the Korean War, Vol. III, Part 2—Personnel Problems.* U.S. Army Far East Command, Tokyo: Office of the Chief of Military History, 1952, p. 46.
11. U.S. Air Force Instruction 36-3002, Sec 3.10.12.
12. Young SA, Holden MS: The formation and application of an overseas mental health crisis intervention team, Part II: Application. *Mil Med*. 1991 Sep;156(9):445-7.
13. Graham, L: Personal communication with author, March 1999.
14. American Red Cross. *Art of Helping—Case Management Training: Instructor's Course Outline*. Falls Church, VA: American Red Cross, 1996.
15. Jones DR: Emotional reactions to military aircraft accidents. *Aviat Space Environ Med*. 1982 Jun;53(6):595-98.
16. Shea N: *The Air Force Wife*. New York: Harper & Brothers, 1951, p. 309.
17. Jones DR: "Emotional reactions to military aircraft accidents."
18. Spiller H: *Death Angel: A Vietnam Memoir of a Bearer of Death Messages to Families*. Jefferson, N.C.: McFarland, 1992, pp. 176-8.

26: Disasters: Survivors and Workers

Catastrophic events with scores of deaths can lead survivors to shut down their emotional capacity. This has been demonstrated after both natural and man-made disasters. Robert J. Lifton provides one of the best descriptions—the reaction of the survivors after the atomic bomb was dropped at Hiroshima (the "Hibakusha").

> Very quickly—sometimes within minutes or even seconds—Hibakusha began to undergo a process of "psychic closing off"; that is, they simply ceased to feel. They had a clear sense of what was happening around them, but their emotional reactions were unconsciously turned off. Others' immersion in larger responsibilities was accompanied by a greater form of closing off, which might be termed "psychic numbing."[1]

Disasters also increase many survivors' despondency to dangerous levels. For example, suicide rates among survivors increased nearly 14% in the four years after a serious flood, 31% in the two years after a hurricane, and by nearly 63% in the year following an earthquake.[2]

War-generated and natural disasters often produce the greatest number of casualties, and survivor assistance must often come from outside the immediate area. Death notification and psychological assistance for survivors, however, follow the same principles as outlined in the protocol in table 26-1. Commercial airline crashes consistently produce the next greatest numbers of simultaneous victims. The less-common train and bus crashes are functionally similar, with the same need for survivor assistance as in plane crashes. In the relatively rare passenger ship disaster, survivors may have additional stress if the victims' bodies are not recovered.

Table 26-1: Protocol to Support Disaster Survivors

- Meet survivors as they arrive at the morgue waiting (or other gathering) area. Staff should wear identification: Armbands color-coded to an individual's job, such as support, medical, counselor, clergy, etc., are optimal.
- After identifying the survivors, give them all the information currently available. (Accurate information is priceless in disaster situations.)
- If there are enough counselors on each shift, assign them specific survivor family groups to follow.
- Keep track of which survivors are there or where they have gone.
- Give survivors an overview of the identification process, the forms they need to complete, and required autopsy or other forensic investigations. Assist them with the necessary formalities and paperwork.
- Assess survivors involved in the disaster for injuries.
- Provide comfortable rest areas, bathrooms, communication, and eating facilities while survivors wait to hear news of their loved ones. (This may require logistical support from local hospitals, the National Guard, Red Cross, Salvation Army, or similar local agencies.)
- Have a staffed play area for small children. (Surviving children's need for immediate psychological support is often neglected.)
- Support emotionally distressed relatives who are waiting to identify bodies.
- Provide a liaison with the disaster scene and local hospitals.
- Accompany survivors to any mass briefings held for them.
- Protect survivors from the media and, when desired, act as their spokesperson or intermediary. (The media can help publicize that mental health services are available for survivors who were not at the morgue.)
- Support survivors through the process of identification. Assure them that they have not misidentified their loved one or have otherwise made an error (a common fear). This may be particularly stressful, since the bodies are often burned, dismembered, or mutilated and may have begun decomposing for lack of refrigeration.
- Give survivors information about available funerary facilities, if asked.
- Provide crisis psychiatric intervention, as necessary.
- Help identify the survivor's normal support system to further assist them.
- Collect survivors' identifying information so follow-up can be done.
- During the event (usually at each change of shift) and after the event, the notifier/mental health team should hold debriefings to share information and to relieve their own stress.

Airline Crashes

As a rather insensitive official commented after an airline crash, "As long as planes fly, planes will crash." A statistic commonly cited by disaster planners is that in 80% of commercial airline crashes, at least 80% of the passengers die. Thousands of people can become bereaved survivors in a moment.

Airlines have protocols they follow when deaths occur. In a major disaster, however, even when the protocol is used, notifications don't always go smoothly. Here is one survivor's story after Air Florida Flight 90 from Washington, D.C. to Tampa, Fla., crashed into the Potomac River, killing most of those aboard, including her brother. The combination of mass media coverage and poorly trained personnel led to this distraught relative's struggle through a macabre game of Twenty Questions.

> "Someone called Mom and said a plane had crashed, and she thought they said something about Tampa . . . they said it was Flight 90 . . .That's his flight number, but Mom probably just got the number wrong . . . I just heard the number myself on the radio . . . Oh, God, I'll call the airline and call you right back."
>
> I get a busy signal a couple of times before an Air Florida agent responds, "Air Florida, may I help you?" The familiar greeting comforts me. See, there's nothing wrong, I reassure myself. "Yes, I want information on an arrival time." "Certainly. What is the flight number?" he asks cheerfully. "Flight 90." Now his voice takes on a business-like quality as he quickly replies, "We cannot give out information on that flight." "What do you mean you can't give out information on that flight?" "We can't give out information on that flight," he repeats. My heart pounds, as I calmly ask, "Did an Air Florida plane crash today?" "Yes." "Was it going from Washington to Tampa?" "Yes," he says, seeming relieved to answer my questions. "How many flights do you have going from Washington to Tampa today?" "Two." "When were they scheduled?" "One this morning. One this afternoon." "Did the one this morning make it?" "Yes." "Thank you very much," I say softly and hang up the phone, my heart pounding . . .
>
> It is announced on TV that relatives who are waiting at Tampa International Airport have been taken to a special room. They suggest that other relatives come there for up-to-date information and counseling. "Do you want to go?" asks Gene [her partner]. "I'll take you." My impulse to go is short-lived. "No, what good will it do? We're getting current information here. Why do I want to be around other upset people I don't know? What can counseling do? I want to be here with you, and where I can talk to Art [her older brother]."
>
> Every half-hour, I am on the phone with Art. It takes at least 10 attempts to get through the busy circuits. The Tampa-Virginia lines are being overworked by all the grieving people soothing each other, seeking information, and refusing to believe their worst fears are true. Just like us. The news is spreading through Luray, and the phone is constantly busy with people who want to know, "Is it true?" and "What's the latest?" . . .

"We are sitting around looking at each other, too," Art says when he calls at 10 P.M. "The airline will let me know when it's official." "Why are you assuming he's dead?" I ask. "Because Bev (our cousin) went to the Marriott Hotel in Washington where they announced the list of survivors. He wasn't on there, Susie," he says reverently. Did I hear him right? It is hard to hear from inside the fog, with my heart beating so loudly . . .

Art calls early the next morning, and says Air Florida finally called at 3 A.M. to tell us officially that Rex was dead. "It's been horrible," he says. "I lay awake all night waiting for the call I knew would come . . . I answered knowing what they would say. Mom and Dad stood around me like little kids, waiting for the news. They knew by my voice. Everyone started sobbing."[3]

On October 1, 1998, in response to problems with victim identification after commercial airline crashes, the U.S. Transportation Department began requiring all airlines flying into or departing from the United States to ask American citizens for the name and phone number of someone to notify in the event of an accident. The State Department pressed for this rule after they encountered difficulty notifying the next of kin after the Pan Am Flight 103 bombing over Lockerbie, Scotland. Since it was an international flight, they had the responsibility of notifying next of kin. Pan Am took seven hours to provide a passenger manifest, and then it often gave only initials for first names or incomplete last names for the passengers. While the rule was included in the 1990 Aviation Security Improvement Act, it wasn't until the TWA Flight 800 crash in July 1996 that relatives, frustrated by the delays in being notified, pressured the government into enacting the provision.

Under the Act, airlines must request specific information from passengers. Passengers must provide their own full names before being allowed to board. Providing contact information is voluntary, and the information is supposed to be destroyed once the flight reaches its destination. Airlines are prohibited from using this information for marketing. Eventually this rule may be expanded to include domestic flights.

Major air carriers are training their personnel to deal with grieving relatives more effectively. (See the emergency response protocol for United Airlines in table 26-2 and the federal plan for aviation disasters in table 26-3.) Some, such as TWA, have a "Trauma Response Program" that sends people to the scene of an airline crash to help survivors.[4] Airlines must also notify survivors once an individual crash victim has been identified (they used to wait until the entire passenger manifest was assembled before they notified anyone). Airlines have also implemented procedures to more quickly transport family members to the crash site or memorial service. Federal law now prohibits "ambulance-chasing" lawyers from seeking business from victims' families for forty-five days after a crash.[5]

Helping Disaster Survivors

To effectively notify and provide support for survivors after major disasters, an emergency multidisciplinary mental health team must be set up and educated on their roles in advance of the event. As with other components of disaster management, it helps if members practice their roles in as close to a real scenario as possible. Based on this experience, they may have to modify their procedures, since they may find that expected communication, supplies, and transportation would be absent.

The National Organization for Victim Assistance (NOVA) has developed guidelines for crisis intervention with disaster survivors. Immediately after the crisis, such interventions:

- Help survivors reestablish their sense of safety and security. May need to provide physical safety, shelter, food, and clothing. Commonly, survivors must also be protected from invasions of their personal space, such as by reporters. Those assisting them must remember that survivors must *feel* safe, not only be safe.
- Provide an opportunity for ventilation and validation. Survivors may feel intense, often-conflicting emotions. Helpers should encourage them to describe the incident, their part in it, and their reactions to it (similar to the CISD debriefing described for disaster workers, below).
- Help them to predict and prepare to deal with problems and their concerns arising from the incident. These are the practical steps survivors need to put their lives back on track. A checklist of things they need to do and a discussion (and list for them to take) about people and agencies that can assist them are essential.[6]

One key to the success of these groups is to have recognized experienced leadership. The lack of on-site coordinators has seriously hampered many mental health crisis teams, leading to dysfunction and ineffectiveness.[7] Coordinators should participate in regularly scheduled disaster drills to become familiar with their role and that of other component groups within the disaster system. They also must develop policies to guide their team, such as how to use the volunteers who inevitably arrive after a disaster. (In general, they should only be made part of the team if they meet specific requirements.) Team leaders should be prepared to schedule shifts so that the service can be provided 24-hours per day for a prolonged period. Shifts must be formalized and strictly adhered to. This is because all disaster workers tend to work long beyond their capacity and then burn out.

If the disaster occurs where most victims live, workers are often based at whatever temporary morgue has been established. This is where survivors usually become certain that their loved one is dead.[8] In transportation accidents, survivors may gather at all the places where the airplane, bus, ship, or train on-loaded or was to off-load passengers. In some cases, such as after the 1985 Gander, Newfoundland, plane crash and the Dallas-Fort Worth, Texas, crash the same year, survivors gathered at area hotels. These sites provided survivors with a "libidinal cocoon" where they did not have to meet or react with the outside world and could provide mutual support.[9] Each site may need to provide varying levels of support. When victims are part of a larger group, such as a military unit, a college, or a company, these "survivor communities" will also need support.

Disaster workers themselves seldom want immediate counseling, since they do not see themselves as victims or survivors. The importance of post-traumatic stress debriefing for this group is now recognized, and is widely utilized among fire, police, and

EMS groups. Medical personnel rarely participate in these debriefing sessions. They believe (incorrectly) that these incidents are simply an extension of their normal work, so they will have no trouble "handling it."

"Handling" Disasters: Critical Incident Stress Debriefing (CISD)

In addition to disaster survivors, those rendering aid also need support. They can be thought of as the "hidden victims" of these incidents. Most professionals "handle" the situation while it is ongoing. Disaster workers often use group support systems and "gallows" humor to support each other through the harrowing ordeal. Some of the U.S. Air Force personnel who had to handle and help identify hundreds of decomposing bodies after the mass suicide at Jonestown, Guyana, in November 1978, said:

> To tell the truth, the only way me and my friends found to keep one sane was to joke around so much and to keep laughing, even if it meant making fun of the bodies.. . . a joke, good or bad, breaks the tension, and takes people's minds off of what they are doing. During the Jonestown detail, the grosser the joke, the better . . . Personnel working with the remains tend to make what would normally be distasteful jokes . . . about the remains.[10]

However, once the acute event is over, most disaster workers benefit from at least some immediate guided discussion, formally called Critical Incident Stress Debriefing (CISD)—but perhaps more appropriately termed "psychological first aid." CISD was developed to reduce the number of "psychological casualties" among emergency service personnel when situations they were involved in overwhelmed their normal coping mechanisms. It is designed to provide a forum in which individuals can ventilate their emotions, gain support and encouragement, and identify and learn to deal with post-traumatic stress disorder symptoms. CISD can also be used for survivor groups.

CISD is thought to alleviate the acute stress response immediately after the event, and it eliminates or ameliorates delayed stress reactions. Such a reaction, once called "battle fatigue," is now termed "Post-Traumatic Stress Disorder" (PTSD). After very traumatic events, team members may have difficulty sleeping with recurrent nightmares revisiting the incident, waking hallucinations similar to nightmares, repeated anxiety attacks with shaking and crying spells, and suffer unjustified severe self-doubt about their performance level during the episode.[11] The symptoms that often last the longest are avoiding any thoughts, feelings, activities, or situations that remind them of the event. (Also see table 10-3 for symptoms of psychological reactions to combat.)

"Critical incidents" may not be of disaster magnitude. They all, however, are outside the range of the emergency workers' usual experiences and can generate unusually strong feelings. These incidents include:

- Mass casualty events.
- The death of a team member.
- Personnel-caused deaths (including police-involved shootings).
- Cases evoking profound emotions (e.g., infant or child deaths).

- Cases that attract significant media attention.
- Loss of life after a prolonged rescue effort.
- Highly dangerous events.
- Other unusual events in which the emotional response may exceed the normal coping mechanism.[12]

CISD—The Method for Workers

As originally described, there are four sequential aspects to CISD. These are the on-scene debriefing, the initial defusing, the formal CISD, and the follow-up CISD.[13] All four aspects are not always employed, however.

On-scene or Near-scene Debriefing

This is performed by an officer, chaplain, or health professional knowledgeable in both CISD and the team's operations. This individual primarily watches for the development of any signs of acute stress reactions. Rather than a formal debriefing, it is mainly a period of aware observation.

Initial Defusing

Performed within a few hours of the incident, this is a situation in which participants have an opportunity to discuss their feelings and reactions in a positive and supportive atmosphere. This discussion may be led by a senior officer or health professional familiar with CISD who has good interpersonal skills, or may have no leader at all and be a spontaneous interaction among team members. It is best done through a mandatory team meeting. The key to success at this stage is to maintain a supportive rather than a critical atmosphere, to keep comments confidential, and to ban comments that are tough, insensitive, or could be construed as "gallows humor." If this is not done, it will quickly end any shared feelings among team members.

Formal CISD

Typically led by a mental health professional familiar with CISD, these formal sessions are held within 24 to 48 hours after the incident. Specially trained public and private CISD teams now exist throughout the United States, Canada, and in many other countries. Many of these are associated with local or regional police or fire departments (who can also be contacted to locate other competent teams). These sessions often follow a standard format by first laying out the non-critique and confidentiality ground rules. Then the participants are asked to describe themselves and key activities during the incident, their feelings during the incident and at present, and any unusual symptoms they experienced or are experiencing. Participants may be asked to explore linkages between the event and past events, non-judgmentally describe others' actions (to help describe their own actions), and describe their own and the group's successes during the incident. The facilitator then describes typical PTSD symptoms and finally suggests an activity to help them regain a sense of purpose and unity (such as attending the memorial service for the victims). During this session, the leader also tries to identify those who may need more intensive counseling.

Follow-up CISD

Not always or even frequently done, these sessions are held from several weeks to months after the incident. They are can be held to resolve specific group issues or, more often, to help specific individuals. (When held on an individual basis, these are essentially psychological counseling sessions). Groups who will encounter events triggering PTSD in the course of their work must have this service available *before* it is needed. Individuals providing these counseling services may themselves be subject to PTSD, and, if so, should also undergo debriefing.[14]

Additional Resources

For more information to assist professionals working with PTSD victims, contact the National Center of PTSD: tel. (802) 296-5132; E-mail: ptsd@dartmouth.edu; web site: http://www.dartmouth.edu/dms/ptsd/Clinicians.htm or the Post Traumatic Stress Resources web page at http://www.long-beach.va.gov/ptsd/stress.htm.

References

1. Lifton R: *Death In Life: Survivors of Hiroshima*. New York: Vintage Books, 1969.
2. Krug EG, Kresnow M, Peddicord JP, et al.: Suicide after natural disasters. *N Engl J Med.* 1998;338:373-8.
3. Ellis C: "There are survivors": telling a story of sudden death. *Sociol Quart*. 1993 Nov;34(4):711-30. © 1993 by JAI Press, Inc.
4. Anon: TWA's trauma response team. *Emerg Med Serv*. Jan. 1997, p. 56.
5. Zoroya G: Aviation task force makes strides for victims. *USA Today*. 1998 Sep 28;Sect. D:1.
6. Young MA: Crisis response teams in the aftermath of disasters. In: Roberts AR: *Crisis Intervention and Time-limited Cognitive Treatment.* Thousand Oaks: Sage, 1995, pp. 151-87.
7. Xenakis SN, Marcum JM, Maury JL, et al.: Consultation in the aftermath of an air tragedy. *Mil Med*. 1991 Jan;156(1):23-6.
8. Raphael B: A primary prevention action programme: psychiatric involvement following a major rail disaster. *Omega*. 1979; 10(3):211-26.
9. Black JW Jr.: The libidinal cocoon: a nurturing retreat for the families of plane crash victims. *Hosp Community Psychiatry*. 1987 Dec;38(12):1322-6.
10. Jones DR: Secondary disaster victims: the emotional effects of recovering and identifying human remains. *Am J Psychiatry.* 1985;142:303-7.
11. Sokol RJ: Early mental health intervention in combat situations: the USS Stark. *Mil Med.* 1989;154:407-9.
12. Mitchell J: When disaster strikes . . . the critical incident stress debriefing process. *JEMS*. 1983;8(1):36-9.
13. *Ibid.*
14. Lesaca T: Symptoms of stress disorder and depression among trauma counselors after an airline disaster. *Psychiatric Serv.* 1996;47(4):424-6.

Table 26-2: United Airlines' Emergency Response Protocol
(Selected Portions)

Family Assistance Representative's Tasks

Onboard Acknowledgment

After a disaster it may be your job to communicate with a family and advise them that their relative has been involved in the incident. (Please note that the Family Assistance Representative does not make a death notification, as this task is the responsibility of the Medical Examiner's office. The acknowledgment you will make involves only information that United Airlines has confirmed.) This may take the form of a phone call within a few hours of the incident when it has been confirmed that a particular passenger was involved in the disaster and that there are no survivors. Or it may take the form of an in-person contact with family members who have traveled to the scene of the incident seeking information about their loved one. This kind of communication with a family is a difficult and emotionally charged task, whether it is carried out on the phone or in person. The following suggestions may be helpful in talking to families.

Acknowledgment by Phone

A. Preparing yourself for the call.

- Read the Onboard Acknowledgment Checklist included in this manual.
- The call should be made only after you have been given the "go-ahead" by your team leader.
- Regardless of the circumstances, it's best that you get prepared for the call, prior to ever picking up the phone, so take your time . . . to make sure that you're ready. Remember that you're probably nervous, so it's best to collect your thoughts; and it may be a good idea to make notes for yourself, in order to make sure that you give clear information to the person you're calling.
- While it's obvious that this first call will be hard for the family, remember that it will also be hard for you.
- Have a short meeting with the EAP to clarify what you'll say and how you'll say it.
- In many cases you'll know who the legal next of kin is, as this person may have already called United for information about their loved one. These are situations in which the family is anticipating a call from United. It may also happen that a family member or friend has called United on behalf of the next of kin, who may be too distressed to call themselves.
- In some cases your call may be to a family that as yet has had no contact with United. (It's possible that such a family is not yet aware that a disaster has happened.)
- Expect that your first call will be brief. It's probably best to not try to link other tasks (e.g., requesting dental records) to the initial phone call.

Table 26-2: continued

B. Making the call.

The content of the call should include:

- Your name.
- The fact that you are calling from United Airlines.
- Verification by you that you are talking to the appropriate person, whether it's the spouse, the parent, or the adult child of the passenger. (Never make an acknowledgment to a child.) It's possible that you may get an answering machine—it's best to not leave any message at all. Just call back later.
- Specific facts that have been confirmed; namely that one of our flights has crashed at a particular location—and that to the best of our knowledge their loved one was onboard; and that there are no survivors. (This is only an example, the actual circumstances could be quite different.) Another possibility is that you might have to tell a relative that the status of the passenger is unknown at this time, but that you will call them back with information as soon as possible.
- Your offer to assist them in getting other relatives or close friends to their home to support them.
- Your assurance that you or a colleague will be available 24 hours a day to give information, answer questions, etc.
- Your offer of Red Cross assistance.
- A phone number where you can be reached. Even though it seems that the task of writing down your phone number may be an easy one, in fact it might be very difficult, if not impossible, for the family to accomplish it.
- It's probably a good idea for you to ask the family's permission to call them back within the next hour with more information as you get it.
- The immediate reaction of a family member to your phone call is very unpredictable, and you should be prepared for a large variety of reactions from them. Intense reactions are normal, not abnormal. They will be in shock. They may insist that a mistake has been made, and you should acknowledge with them how hard it is to hear this information. You should also be prepared for the possibility that the family member may express intense anger toward you.

C. After the acknowledgment call.

- Read and use the Onboard Acknowledgment Checklist. Please note that the checklist has a place on the bottom where you can record the date and time of the call. It's important for you to fill this in—we don't want another Family Assistance Representative to make the mistake of calling a second time to do the initial acknowledgment.
- After you make the call, it's a good idea to talk to an EAP representative about how it went.

Table 26-2: continued

Samples of Initial Onboard Acknowledgment

Please note that the following is only example that may give you some direction as you prepare to make your first very difficult call to the family of a passenger. The real words that you speak into the phone should come from within you.

> Hello, Mrs. Smith? My name is _____, and I work for United Airlines. I'm very sorry to tell you that to the best of our knowledge your husband and son were both on United Flight # ____, which crashed at _____.
>
> I'm sorry to tell you that we've been advised that there are no survivors . . .
>
> Do you have family near by? Will you call them and have them come over? Let me get off your phone and give you a chance to call them, but I'd like to call you back in the next 15 to 20 minutes. Would that be OK? Can I give you my phone number? Do you have a pen & paper handy? My name is _________ and I'll call you back very soon.

Another possibility might be as follows:

> Hello, Mrs. Smith? My name is ________ and I work for United Airlines. I'm very sorry to tell you that to the best of our knowledge your husband and son were both on United Flight # ____, which crashed at _________.
>
> I'm sorry that at this moment we don't have word on the status of your husband and son, but we're trying to get that information as quickly as possible. As soon as we find out their status I'll let you know. Do you have family near by? Will you call them and have them come over? Let me get off your phone and give you a chance to call them, but I'd like to call you back in the next 15 to 20 minutes. Would that be OK? My name is ______________ and I'll call you back very soon.

At some point after the initial call the family may ask you how we confirmed that their loved one was onboard the flight. If so, explain the process to them without using airline jargon.

Onboard Acknowledgment Checklist

Your team leader has given you the clear go-ahead to make the call. _______

In advance, you've identified the appropriate family member to call. _______

Now that you've called, you have verified that the person on the line is the appropriate family member/next of kin. _______

You've given your name. _______

You've said that you're calling from United Airlines. _______

You've given the specific facts that have been confirmed. _______

Table 26-2: continued

Onboard Acknowledgment Checklist, cont.

You've offered to provide assistance in transporting relatives to the family's home, or to the site. _______

You've said that you or a colleague will be available 24 hours a day to give information, answer questions, etc. _______

You've given the phone number where you can be reached.

You've asked the family's permission to call back within the next hour. _______

You've talked to the EAP about how the call went. _______

DATE OF INITIAL CONTACT_______________

TIME OF INITIAL CONTACT_______________

YOUR NAME _______________

In Person Notification

After a disaster it's common for family members of our passengers to travel to the site of the disaster. (It's also important to remember that with some disasters very few families may travel to the site.) They will arrive at the site seeking information about their loved one, but they may arrive before the status of their loved one is confirmed. They will seek information at local hospitals where injured survivors are being treated, but with the passage of time (hours or days), with no word from their loved one, they are likely to arrive at the conclusion that their loved one is among the deceased. At some point the Medical Examiner will reach a confirmed identification of their loved one's remains, and it may be your job to notify the family.

Please note that in the changing political environment of aircraft disasters it's very difficult to predict precisely the types of situations in which a Family Assistance Representative may be asked to do a notification. In some incidents you won't perform this difficult task at all, as someone from the Red Cross or the Medical Examiner's office may be given responsibility for the notification. Unfortunately there may be other circumstances in which you will be asked to do the job. An international incident, for example, is one in which no Red Cross assistance will be available on site, leaving only the UAL Family Assistance Representative as the responsible person.

A. Preparation for the notification.

Notification should be made only after you've been given the go-ahead by your team leader.

- If the notification is to be done at the Relative Center, arrange for a room or private area in which you can meet with the family members. In most circumstances it would never be appropriate to make the notification in a public area.

Table 26-2: continued

- Don't make the notification alone. Have another employee accompany you while carrying out this task. Ideally you will also have a working relationship with a volunteer Red Cross mental health professional at the site who is working in partnership with you in meeting the family's needs.
- Have a short meeting with the EAP or the Red Cross mental health volunteer to clarify what you'll say and how you'll say it. (The EAP may not always be available.)
- Arrange to have all the family members who have come on site to be present at the same time. They can support each other-, and you don't want to perform this difficult task more than once.

B. Making the notification.

- Inform the family that you have important information and invite them to go with you to the room or private area you've already made available.
- When you get to the meeting room, ask the family to sit down with you, which may help them accept this difficult information. (Even though the family may have already supplied the dental records of their relative, and therefore may be expecting this meeting, the actual confirmation of death will still be a very difficult moment for them.)
- Be as direct as possible when notifying a family. For example: "I'm sorry to tell you that the medical examiner's office has confirmed the identification of your daughter." Try to give the message in as few sentences as possible, but make the message as clear as possible. Don't use euphemisms about death, such as "expired", since this could lead to doubt or confusion. Use the words "dead" or "died," so that there will be no misconception about what is being said. Avoid using words like "body" or corpse" or "remains" instead, refer to the deceased person by *name*.
- The immediate reaction of a family member to this news is very unpredictable, and you should be prepared for a large variety of reactions from them. They may insist that a mistake has been made, and you should acknowledge with them how hard it is to hear this information. Intense reactions are normal, not abnormal.
- After you've made the notification, you may feel an impulse to "escape" from the family, which is a rather understandable reaction. It's probably best, though, to stay with them for at least a few minutes, to let them know that you're there for them. Your own good judgment will help you to decide when the family needs to grieve on their own. By the time you make the notification you may have developed the kind of relationship with the family in which it's appropriate for you to stay with them in their grief.

Table 26-2: continued

- You may not have all the information the family wants when you make a notification. For example, the family may want to know the exact circumstances of their relative's death, but this is information that may never be known. Let the family know where you got your information; write down any questions they may have; let them know that you will try to get answers for them; and that you will give them more information as it becomes available.
- The family may ask how the Coroner/Medical Examiner arrived at a positive identification of their relative's remains. Even if you think you know the answer to this question, it's probably best to not offer information, but instead to ask the family if they would like to meet with a representative of the Coroner/Medical Examiner's office. Your job will be to help set up such a meeting if the family so desires.
- The family may ask to view the remains of their loved one. In general, this is not a good idea, but it's another issue that the family should discuss with a representative of the Coroner/Medical Examiner's office.
- Don't discuss funeral arrangements with the family immediately after notifying them unless they initiate the subject.
- After making the notification you may find it helpful to talk with an EAP representative.

Table 26-3: Federal Family Assistance Plan for Aviation Disasters
(9 April 1997, Abridged)

1. REFERENCES. (Drafts of prior plans omitted)

2. PURPOSE. This plan assigns responsibilities and describes the airline and federal response to an aviation crash involving a significant number of passenger fatalities and/or injuries. It is the basic document for organizations which have been given responsibilities under this plan to develop supporting plans and establish procedures.

3. IMPLEMENTATION. This plan will be put into execution, in full or part, by the Director, Family Support Services (FSS), at the direction of the Chairman, National Transportation Safety Board (NTSB).

a. The Director, FSS will make a recommendation to the Chairman, NTSB whether to activate the plan or portions thereof.

b. Federal agencies that have responsibilities under this plan maintain control of their resources while supporting the NTSB in accordance with the above references. (For purposes of this document the terms "federal agencies" and "federal staff" includes the American Red Cross.)

c. The NTSB, through its communications center, will initiate notification of federal agencies to activate planning and coordinating with the airline an appropriate response based upon the magnitude of the aviation crash. Additional requirements will normally follow as the incident situation becomes better known. Upon direction from Director, FSS, the NTSB communications center will notify some or all of the following operations centers:

(1.) American Red Cross (ARC) (703) 206-8822

(2) Department of State (DOS) (202) 647-1512

(3) Department of Health and Human Services (DHHS)
(301) 443-1167 Ext 0 or 1-800- 872-6367

(4) FBI Operations Center (202) 324-6700

(5) Federal Emergency Management Agency (FEMA) (202) 898-6100

(6) Department of Defense (DOD) (703) 697-0218

(7) Department of Justice (DOJ) (202) 514-5000

d. The role of the NTSB can generally be described as a coordinator to integrate the resources of the Federal Government and other organizations to support the efforts of the local and state government and the airline to meet the needs of aviation disaster victims and their families. The NTSB assists in making available federal resources to local authorities and the airlines. Family counseling, victim identification and forensic services, communicating with foreign governments, and translation services, are just a few of the areas in which the federal government can help local authorities and the airlines deal with a major aviation disaster. It is recommended that the local government emergency services provide a liaison officer to the joint family support operations center to participate in the local,

Table 26-3: continued

airline, and federal response.. . . It is recognized that the joint family support operations center layout is dependent on the facilities and rooms available at the time.

e. Local authorities will maintain the same jurisdiction they had prior to Reference A and B, such as accident response, recovery, security, cleanup, and medical examiner operations. As in the past the NTSB will still lead the aviation crash investigation. If the aviation crash is determined to have been caused by a criminal act, the FBI will then become the lead investigation agency.

f. The airline continues to have a fundamental responsibility to the victims and their families affected by an aviation crash. The airline is still primarily responsible for family notification and all aspects of victim and family logistical support. Although their major responsibilities have not changed, "The Aviation Disaster Family Assistance Act of 1996" places the airline in a more collaborative relationship with families, the NTSB, and other supporting organizations.

g. All personnel involved in providing services to assist the victims and their family members should be trained in crisis response and must demonstrate compassion, sympathy, technical expertise, and professionalism. Information provided by family members and victims through discussions, interviews, counseling, and any other form of exchange of personal information must remain confidential and used only for the intended purpose. Combined with common sense and teamwork, everyone's efforts in the end, will be greatly appreciated by those served.

4. SCOPE.

a. This plan pertains to any domestic or foreign aviation crash that occurs within the United States, its territories and possessions of the United States, and territorial seas.

b. This plan is written with three possible crash scales supporting organizations should consider in their development of supporting plans and asset allocation calculations.

(1) Crash scale 1. This involves an aviation crash that involves 100 or fewer passengers and crew who are either fatalities or require medical assistance.

(2) Crash scale 2. This involves an aviation crash that involves 101 to 200 passengers and crew who are either fatalities or require medical assistance.

(3) Crash scale 3. This involves an aviation crash that involves 201 or more passengers and crew who are either fatalities or require medical assistance.

5. ASSUMPTIONS.

a. The Chairman, NTSB will request federal agencies to support the NTSB in accordance with the above references.

b. Local and state officials having jurisdiction will allow the federal government to provide assistance.

Table 26-3: continued

c. There will be fatalities and seriously injured passengers and crew for each of the above three scenarios.

d. Large numbers of families of fatalities will travel to the city closest to the incident and will utilize the accommodations provided by the airline. The remainder of families of fatalities will remain at their local residence.

e. Many families of seriously injured personnel will travel to the location where the injured are hospitalized and once released from the hospital will return home.

6. GENERAL. The family assistance mission tasks that follow an aviation crash are:

a. Make initial notification to family members of victims involved in the aviation crash based on manifest documents and other available information.

b. Monitor search and recovery operations conducted by the local jurisdiction and offer assistance where needed.

c. Determine the status and location of victims.

d. Obtain approval of local jurisdiction to provide federal assistance, where appropriate.

e. Assist the local medical examiner in the identification of fatalities and the notification of their families. (It is noted that there are differences between a medical examiner and coroner. For purposes of this document the term "medical examiner" is used interchangeably with "coroner".)

f. Provide psychological and logistical support and services to victims and their family members.

g. Provide daily briefings to families on the progress of recovery efforts; identification of victims; the investigation; and other areas of concern.

h. Arrange for a memorial service for victims and their family members.

i. Provide for the return of personal effects.

j. Maintain contact with victims and their families to provide updates on the progress of the investigation and other related matters.

7. RESPONSIBILITIES. There are seven Victim Support Tasks (VSTs). VSTs are tasks that participating organizations may be required to perform based upon the size and circumstances of the actual incident. The seven VSTs are: NTSB Tasks; Airline Tasks; Family Care and Mental Health; Victim Identification, Forensic and Medical Services; Assisting Families of Foreign Victims; Communications; and Assisting Victims of Crime. Due to each aviation crash being unique all of the following responsibilities may or may not be employed. Agencies and organizations should consider this and the various crash level scales when developing their supporting plans.

Table 26-3: continued

a. NTSB: VST 1, "NTSB Tasks."

(1) Coordinate federal assistance and serve as liaison between airline and family members.

(2) Provide NTSB toll free number to family members to obtain information on the recovery and identification effort, accident investigation, and other concerns. This number will normally be provided to families on site during the initial family briefing and repeated in subsequent briefings. The NTSB will coordinate with the airline to have airline family representatives provide the toll free number to the families that do not travel to the site.

(3) Request a copy of the passenger manifest from the airline.

(4) Coordinate with Department of Transportation for marine search and rescue.

(5) Review with the airline family support logistics with special consideration toward security, quality of rooms and facilities, and privacy for family members.

(6) Integrate federal and airline staff to form a joint family-support operations center to facilitate close coordination of services and activities.

(7) Coordinate assistance effort with local and state authorities, to include the medical examiner, local law enforcement, emergency management, hospitals, and other emergency support personnel.

(8) Maintain communications with the airline involved to receive frequent updates on the status of notification of victims' families.

(9) Conduct daily coordination meetings with the airline and federal staff to review daily activities, resolve problem areas, and to synchronize future family support operations and activities.

(10) Provide and coordinate family briefings to those at the site and those who decide not to be at the site.

(11) Discuss with the medical examiner the subject of DNA testing: under what conditions would it be used; what extent would it be used; whom the medical examiner would use to collect and test samples; and whom would pay for testing of samples.

(12) Coordinate with investigator in charge for a possible visit to the crash site for family members. Liability release forms from family members should be considered in the planning process.

(13) Provide information releases to the media pertaining to family support areas of interest.

(14) Maintain contact with family members to keep them informed about the progress of the investigation as well as to continue to meet their future needs.

Table 26-3: continued

a) Generally, about 2 to 4 months after the date of the crash, factual reports written by the NTSB investigators are made available in a public docket. Families should be informed approximately 4 weeks prior to the factual report being made public that they may request the NTSB provide a copy of the report to them. The report will be provided to them at no cost.

b) Families will also be notified of the public hearing concerning the crash, if the NTSB decides a public hearing is necessary. The hearing is designed to gather additional facts and selected individuals are subpoenaed to testify. Travel and lodging to the hearing is at the family's expense. Families will be provided seating and copies of official exhibits discussed at the hearing.

c) Families will be invited to attend at their own expense the public meeting at NTSB's Washington, D.C. headquarters. The NTSB investigative staff presents to the full five Member Board a draft accident report for member discussion and approval at this public hearing. This report results in the NTSB's probable cause of the crash and recommendations on how to prevent future aviation crashes.

(15) Consolidate and review after action reports to resolve problem areas and update operating plans and procedures.

b) Airline: VST 2, "Airline Tasks."

(1) In addition to accident notification required by 49 CFR 830.5, notify the NTSB communications center at (202) 314- 6290 immediately upon knowledge of a crash.

a) Provide place of incident, number of passengers and crew, and number of injured and fatalities (if known).

b) Provide origination, connection points and final destination (if known), and whether the flight was domestic or international.

c) Provide name and telephone number of the person who is in overall charge of the incident site.

d) Provide name, telephone number and location of the hotel that has been designated as the joint family support operations center.

e) Provide name and telephone number of the person responsible for the passenger manifest.

f) Provide name and telephone number of the person responsible for family notification.

(2) Provide the public a reliable publicized toll free number with sufficient telephone capacity.

(3) Provide timely notification to family members of passengers which may consist of a continuous process of updates based upon manifest reconciliation with boarding documents. Personnel should be trained in crisis response and death notification.

Table 26-3: continued

(4) Provide the NTSB, upon request, the most current reconciled copy of the passenger manifest. Each copy should be numbered or annotated so it can be distinguished from previous copies.

(5) Secure facilities at departure, arrival and connecting airports where family members may be initially gathered to protect them from unwelcome media and solicitors, as well as to receive continuous updates on the reconciliation of the passenger manifest and other information on the crash. If at a secured facility, family members will be notified personally and privately by personnel trained in crisis response and death notification that their loved one was on the plane.

(6) Provide logistical support to family members that desire to travel to the incident site (or to a hospital location), which includes, but is not limited to, transportation, lodging, meals, security, communications, and incidentals. Factors to consider in selecting a facility are quality of rooms and size of facilities, privacy for family members, and relative location to medical examiner's office, temporary morgue, airport operations, crash site, NTSB investigation HQs, and medical treatment facilities.

(7) Inform family members (or family friends or clergy who are with the family) at an appropriate time, but as early as possible after being notified, that it is critical that they contact their family dentist to obtain the dental records and dental x-rays of their loved one. Ask the family to have the records and x-rays overnight expressed to the address of the hotel where the joint family support operations center will be located. Packages should be addressed to the Director, Family Support Services, NTSB. If the family is coming to the site the next day, the family may arrange to hand carry these documents. It is important to explain that dental records and x-rays are critical in the victim identification process. If the family is already at the site or arrives without making arrangements with their dentist, Disaster Mortuary (D-MORT) Team personnel will coordinate with the family's dentist to obtain dental records and dental x-rays.

(8) Make provisions for a joint family support operations center to include space, communication and logistical support for the assisting federal staff.

(9) Make provisions for private areas within the hotel for D-MORT and medical examiner personnel to collect antemortem questionnaire information from families that are at the site. Also provide quiet space and communications for D-MORT and medical examiner personnel to telephonically collect antemortem questionnaire information from families that decide to stay away from the site. Additionally, plan to provide ARC with two private rooms for crisis counseling. These facilities will also be used to inform families when positive identification has been made by the medical examiner. By having the D-MORT/medical examiner team liaison officer located within the joint family

Table 26-3: continued

support operations center, transportation of victim's remains and other logistical considerations can be better coordinated without having an airline reservation specialist at the morgue location.

(10) Provide DOS liaison officer necessary information on foreign passengers to facilitate interaction with appropriate foreign government embassies.

(11) Provide notification of family members prior to releasing passenger names to the public. Family members should be given appropriate time to notify other family members and friends prior to public release of the victim's name.

(12) Provide the public with continuous updates on the progress of the notification process, such as providing the numbers of victims' families notified as of a certain time and the number remaining to be notified. This process will continue until all victims' families have been notified.

(13) Provide contact person to meet family members as they arrive and while at the incident site. This person will be responsible for assisting the family while at the site and should continue to be the airline interface with the family after the family returns to their residence.

(14) Maintain daily contact with family members that do not travel to the incident site by providing a contact person from the airline. This person will be responsible for assisting the family until no longer needed.

(15) Inquire at the time of notification or soon after, if family members desire ARC crisis assistance or an ARC person just to talk to. If they are undecided or say no, let them know if they change their mind to inform their airline representative. Pass all requests for assistance to the ARC liaison officer who will coordinate for an ARC staff member in the family member's local area to contact the family.

(16) Establish a joint liaison with ARC at each supporting medical treatment facility to track the status of injured victims and to provide assistance to their families.

(17) Develop procedures for the handling of personal effects not being held as evidence for purposes of a criminal or accident investigation. Utilizing a third party that has experience in the return of personal effects associated with aviation disasters should be considered. Done properly it is time consuming and resource intensive. Consideration should also be given to protecting airline employees from re-experiencing the crash and possible future psychological and physical health effects. Provisions will be made for unclaimed possessions to be retained for at least 18 months from the date of the crash as required by law.

(18) Assist family members as they depart the incident site and provide a contact person who will continue to be the airline interface with the family after the family returns to their residence.

Table 26-3: continued

(19) Consult with family members about any airline sponsored monument, including any inscriptions.

(20) Provide reasonable reimbursement to the ARC for the services it provided to the family, airline, and supporting personnel.

(21) Coordinate with Department of Justice in arranging meetings with family members to explain their rights under the victim of crime legislation should the crash be declared a crime.

(22) Provide the same support and treatment of families of non-revenue passengers (and any other victim of the accident) as for revenue passengers.

(23) Participate in daily coordination meetings to review daily activities, resolve problem areas, and to synchronize future family support operations and activities. Information that is needed to be presented at the daily coordination meeting is . . . needed to plan logistical requirements, such as food, lodging, and transportation, as well as providing everyone with an overall picture of current and future support operations.

c. American Red Cross (ARC): VST 3, "Family Care & Mental Health."

(1) Provide a liaison officer to the joint family support operations center to coordinate with other members of the operations center staff ARC related issues and family requests for assistance. Additional personnel may be needed for crash scale 2 or 3 scenarios.

(2) Coordinate and manage the numerous organizations and personnel that will offer their counseling and support services to the operation. It is important to monitor and manage this area so that families are not outnumbered and overwhelmed by well-intentioned organizations and individuals.

(3) Employ an accounting system to accurately record cost data for specific cost categories for later reimbursement.

(4) Activate local, state, and national ARC personnel to provide crisis and grief counseling to family members and support personnel. This includes coordinating with the airline to contact and set up an appointment, if appropriate, with family members that do not travel to the site.

(5) Assess the needs and available resources of other agencies and coordinate with them to ensure ongoing emotional support for workers during the operation and provide debriefings before departure.

(6) Establish a joint liaison with the airline at each supporting medical treatment facility to track the status of injured victims and to provide assistance to their families.

(7) Coordinate with the airline to establish areas for families to grieve privately.

(8) Coordinate on site child care services for families that bring young children.

(9) Arrange a suitable non-denominational memorial service days following the crash and a memorial service for any future burial of unidentified remains.

Table 26-3: continued

(10) Provide families, at their request, referrals to mental health professionals and support groups that are in the family member's local area.

d. Department of Health & Human Services (DHHS): VST 4, "Victim Identification, Forensic, and Medical Services."

(1) Provide a liaison officer to the joint family support operations center to coordinate with other members of the operations center staff DHHS related issues and family requests for assistance. Additional personnel may be needed for crash scale 2 or 3 scenarios.

(2) Provide a D-MORT assessment team to the crash site location within six hours of being notified by NTSB to assess the capabilities of the local medical examiner. After the assessment NTSB and DHHS will make their recommendation to the local medical examiner and seek his/her approval of receiving federal assistance in the identification and mortuary service effort, to include site location of a temporary morgue.

(3) Provide necessary D-MORT team members to assist the medical examiner in victim identification and mortuary services. Configuration of team and skills required will be determined by details of the crash, medical examiner's request for assistance, and crash scale 1, 2, or 3 factors reviewed by the assessment team.

(4) Provide, if appropriate, a portable morgue facility and the necessary equipment and supplies to augment the local medical examiner's capabilities.

(5) Monitor the status of incoming dental records and x-rays to insure that all records have been received. If not, take steps to obtain the records and x-rays. Request assistance from DOS for acquiring necessary records for foreign passengers and crew.

(6) Develop a standard antemortem questionnaire and disposition of remains form that can be adapted to meet local medical examiner and state requirements. The disposition of remains form will be used to obtain directions from the lawfully authorized next of kin on what he/she desires the medical examiner to do with remains that may later be identified as those of their family member. Information collected from family members is strictly confidential and will be used only for medical examiner purposes.

(7) Interview family members who are both on site and off site for ante-mortem identification information and disposition of remains information.

(8) Coordinate with the medical examiner to integrate non-D-MORT personnel, who are providing assistance to the medical examiner's office, into the D-MORT team.

(9) Assist the medical examiner in notifying family members of positive identification, to include explanation of how identification was determined. Notification team may include, if appropriate, ARC crisis counselor and airline family escort.

Table 26-3: continued

(10) Check remains and associated personal effects being returned with the remains prior to release to local funeral director. Insure that all documentation is correct, chain of custody is established, and returned personal effects are cleaned.

(11) Provide NTSB names of victims and their NOK, NOK relationship to victim, and addresses and telephone numbers of NOK. A source for this information is the antemortem questionnaire.

(12) Assist the airlines, if requested, with finding next of kin to be notified by use of established cooperative relationships with local, state, and federal law enforcement agencies.

(13) Provide, if requested, professional medical staff and technicians to assist in the care and recovery of injured victims.

(14) Assist the ARC, if requested, with additional trained and experienced crisis counselors.

e. Department of Defense (DOD): DOD supports DHHS in VST 4, "Victim Identification, Forensic, and Medical Services." If required:

(1) Provide the use of a military installation, such as Dover Air Force Base, for mortuary support operations.

(2) Provide personnel from the Armed Forces Institute Pathology (AFIP), Office of the Armed Forces Medical Examiner (OAFME), to assist in the identification effort and also conduct appropriate DNA comparison testing on specimens submitted by the medical examiner.

(3) Provide assets from the US Navy's Support Salvage (SUPSALV) for the purposes of offshore search, salvage, and recovery of non-military aircraft wreckage, when these services are not locally available. SUPSALV is delegated the responsibility for technical and, when tasked operational control of aircraft search, identification, and/or underwater recovery operations. NTSB and SUPSALV will jointly determine if assets should be deployed and SUPSALV will advise the NTSB on alternate search and recovery methods which may be employed.

(4) Provide within 24 hours a trained Graves Registration and Recovery Team to assist in the recovery efforts at the crash site.

(5) Provide within 24 hours, requested dental records and x-rays of military fatalities that are active duty, retired, veteran, or reserve.

(6) Provide pouches and transfer cases for human remains.

Table 26-3: continued

f. Department of State (DOS): VST 5, "Assisting Families of Foreign Victims." If required:

(1) Provide a liaison officer to the joint family support operations center to coordinate with other members of the operations center staff DOS related issues, such obtaining dental records and dental x-rays from foreign families and responding to family requests for assistance. Additional personnel may be needed for crash scale 2 or 3 scenarios involving international flights.

(2) Provide official notification to foreign governments that have citizens involved in the aviation incident after obtaining necessary information on foreign passengers from the airline.

(3) Assist the airline in notifying US citizens who may reside or are traveling outside the United States that a member of their family has been involved in an aviation crash.

(4) Provide translation services to facilitate communications with the victim's family and all interested parties.

(5) Assist the airline, the federal support staff, and others in maintaining daily contact with foreign families that do not travel to the United States.

(6) Assist families of foreign victims with entry into the United States and extend or grant visas.

(7) Facilitate necessary consulate and customs services for the return of remains and personal effects into the country of destination.

(8) Assist in the effort to provide the medical examiner the necessary information on foreign victims to complete death certificates.

g. Federal Emergency Management Agency (FEMA): VST 6, "Communications." If required:

(1) Provide a liaison officer to the joint family support operations center to coordinate with other members of the operations center staff and local and state officials emergency management related issues. Additional personnel may be needed for crash scale 2 or 3 scenarios involving a major city emergency response.

(2) Provide personnel, upon request of the NTSB, to assist in public information dissemination, to include assistance in establishing and staffing external media support centers, such as the crash site, wreckage hanger, family support operations center, airport, and other areas that may attract media interest.

(3) Provide voice and data communication assets to communicate from the incident site to the NTSB communications center.

Table 26-3: continued

h. Department of Justice (DOJ): VST 7, "Assisting Victims of Crime." If required:

(1) Provide, upon NTSB request, a FBI Disaster Squad with sufficient personnel to obtain fingerprint identification of aviation crash fatalities. This team will work with the medical examiner and the D-MORT personnel at the morgue location.

(2) The following responsibilities will only be implemented if the airline disaster is officially declared a criminal act:

a) Provide a liaison officer to the joint family support operations center to coordinate with other members of the operations center on DOJ related issues.

b) Provide information to victims and their family members, on site and off site, as required under the Victims of Crime Act of 1984, as amended, the Victim and Witness Protection Act of 1982, other relevant statutes, and the 1995 Attorney General Guidelines for Victim and Witness Assistance.

c) Assist the ARC, if requested, with additional trained and experienced crisis counselors through the Office for Victims of Crime's Community Crisis Response Program.

d) Provide updates to victims and their family members on the progress of the criminal investigation.

8. COORDINATING INSTRUCTIONS.

a. The point of contact for this plan is the Director, FSS, NTSB. The telephone number is (202) 314-6100. The office fax number is (202) 314-6110.

b. Upon implementation and until the NTSB FSS staff is situated at the joint family support operations center, calls should be directed to the NTSB communications center: (202) 314-6290 (voice) or (202) 314- 6293 (fax). The communications center will pass any information or messages to the appropriate NTSB family support staff member.

c. DHHS, ARC, and DOS have major and critical responsibilities under this plan. These agencies are to develop formal supporting plans. Coordinating drafts of plans are to be submitted to the Director, FSS NLT June 30, 1997. The remaining federal agencies, DOD, FEMA, DOT and DOJ, are not required to submit formal supporting plans, but should develop procedures to fulfill their responsibilities under this plan. Coordination with the airline industry is encouraged.

d. It is recommended that supporting agencies provide the same individual or individuals to each aviation crash as their liaison to the joint family support operations center. Fortunately, major aviation incidents do not occur frequently. Unfortunately, when they do occur, people and organizations in the past have had very little or no experience dealing with the many sensitive issues of an aviation disaster. By developing a core group of experienced staff, operational procedures

Table 26-3: continued

will continually improve and individual and group experiential bases will increase, all culminating in the better delivery of support services to victims and their families. This does not preclude agencies from designating and training alternate personnel.

e. It is strongly recommended that federal personnel involved at the incident site wear clothing articles, such as hats, shirts, and/or jackets that identify the agency or group with which they are associated. This will be helpful for families, as well as for all those involved in supporting the operation.

f. Agencies that are activated and participate in supporting victims and their family members under this plan are requested to submit an after action report to the Director, FSS, within 30 days of completion of their tasks. This information must be captured so appropriate lessons can be derived, corrective actions taken, and plans changed accordingly.

g. Other than the media releases by the airline on the progress of family notification and release of passenger names described in paragraph 7b, all media inquiries and releases that pertain to the family support operation will be referred to the NTSB family support public affairs officer. The NTSB will advise and assist the local medical examiner on any media affairs in his or her area of responsibility. There are no restrictions on victims or family members meeting with the media, if they so desire.

h. Due to differences in individual airline and airline underwriter policies, as well as the aviation crash itself, reimbursement of costs associated with participation in an aviation disaster will be made after discussions with the airline and their insurance underwriter.

SECTION 4: Important Information

The worst thing about grief is the length of time during which the experience lasts. For the first weeks one is in a state of shock. But the agony lasts long after the state of shock comes to an end. After a year, or about two, the agony gives way to a dull ache, a sort of void. During the night in one's dreams, and in the morning when one wakes, one is vaguely aware that something is wrong and, when waking, is complete, one knows exactly what is.

Lord Halisham of St. Marylebone: *A Sparrow's Flight—the memoirs of Lord Hailsham of St. Marylebone Quintin Hogg*, Baron, 1907. Collins, 1990.

27: Survivors' Questions/ Some Answers

Survivors always have questions; some are more complicated than others are. The following are some questions notifiers commonly fumble when speaking with survivors. Many of the answers are modified from a much more extensive list of questions and answers found in another of my books, *Death to Dust: What Happens To Dead Bodies?* (Tucson, AZ: Galen Press, Ltd., 1994).

Are you sure s/he's dead? . . . it's him/her? . . . there's nothing else you can do?

After being told that their loved one is dead, the first question most survivors ask is "Are you sure?" The quick answer is "Yes, s/he's dead." But mistakes have been made. Clinicians should be certain that they have followed their normal protocol for determining death before notifying the family.

In the emergency medical (ambulances) system (EMS), up to one-third of survivors know the person is dead when they make the call. These are usually expected deaths, frequently home-hospice patients or their equivalent, and family members often say that they did not expect the dramatic response that ensued when they dialed 911. Some of these patients' physicians actually instruct the family to wait an hour or more after the death before calling—to ensure that it is obvious that resuscitative measures would be useless.[1] This most often occurs in areas without prehospital advance directives, which are instructions to EMS personnel, usually at the patient's bedside, not to perform life-supporting procedures.[2-4]

More frequently, notifiers make an error identifying either the deceased person or the decedent's family. In the rare cases involving multiple dead and unconscious victims with facial injuries and without identifying marks or papers, rescuers and medical personnel may misidentify both the dead and the living. When this occurs, the mistake may not be discovered until the misidentified survivor regains consciousness. Even identifications by relatives are not perfect, many survivors, including parents and spouses, have misidentified both their living and their dead relatives. These cases, stressful for all involved, are rare enough that they are usually widely publicized and, even in retrospect, could not have been avoided. If there is doubt about a victim's identity, notifiers should either not announce the death to survivors or state that the victim's identity is uncertain.

The decedent's relatives may also be misidentified. This occurs more often than many people would like to believe. It may occur due to negligence, but is usually due to poor information, inadequate communications, or a system that does not allow survivors to be properly identified.

> Several years ago, a new chaplain ushered me into the "Family Room" of our emergency department just after an unsuccessful resuscitation. This patient had been one of several critical trauma patients that had arrived simultaneously on a busy Friday night. The chaplain's comment was, "This is the family you have to talk with." I went in, sat down, and described to the patient's father, mother, and siblings the patient's injuries and our unsuccessful resuscitation attempts. The family members simply stared at each other without saying a word. They neither cried nor expressed any other emotion. Finally, the mother interrupted me to say, "But he only had a crushed foot." The chaplain had taken me to another patient's family who, thankfully, quickly understood what had happened. I, however, was quite upset. And I subsequently had to retell the news to the deceased patient's real family.

Sometimes, these types of mistakes are almost a routine, as described by Sam Keim, M.D., an emergency physician:

> I interned at a busy inner-city public hospital where, on Friday and Saturday nights, lines of people waited to enter the charge nurse's office—the only private place in the emergency department. They were the relatives and friends of the many patients we had pronounced dead that night. Usually they were so intermingled that we had a hard time identifying which people went with which deceased person—especially since we often did not have an accurate identification of the decedent. Many mistakes were made, as in, "I'm sorry to tell you that your son died." "But I only have three daughters," they responded. "I mean your daughter," we said. That wasn't a good situation.[5]

After the news has been broken to the correct survivors, they ask the inevitable question, "Isn't there anything else you can do?" While sitting next to the family and, usually, making physical contact, simply say, compassionately, "No, we (and the paramedics, bystanders, etc.) did everything we could. I'm sorry, there's nothing else we can do. S/He's dead."

How did s/he die? (medical, legal, circumstances)

After "Are you sure?" this is the next question survivors usually ask. It is tempting for those notifying the family to give details to assuage the survivors' curiosity, if not their grief. Yet this can be dangerous. While general information about the circumstances surrounding a death may be available to the physician, police officer, chaplain, or other notifiers, relatives quickly ask for additional details that may be, at present, hazy, incomplete, or simply wrong. For example, survivors often ask, "Who was driving?" and "Was anyone drunk?" after deaths from motor-vehicle collisions.

While initial information (which is usually all that is available in emergency departments, to notifying officers and to medical examiners' investigators) may indicate the answer, survivors should be counseled to await definitive answers from the investigating officers. In some cases, even these police officers may need to wait for more detailed information from specialized crime-scene or traffic investigators. Inaccurate responses may lead to increased grief and later legal difficulties for those reporting this information.

When asked about the medical cause of death, physicians can, if they have enough information, make a reasonable guess. If an autopsy will not be done, this "best guess" will probably be listed as the cause of death. However, if there will be an autopsy (as there often is following sudden, unexplained, criminally related, or traumatic deaths), physicians must emphasize that any suggestion about the cause of death is only a theory until the pathologists complete their report.

The question "How did s/he die?" takes on a different tone when a patient unexpectedly dies at a medical facility while undergoing medical treatment. The medical personnel involved in the patient's care usually must not only notify survivors but also try to answer this uncomfortable question. Adding to the stress of notifying survivors, the clinicians may experience guilt or puzzlement over what could have or should have been done for their patient. (See also "Medical Errors" in chapter 16.) In general, relating the events as they unfolded is best. These facts should be related by the most-senior attending clinician responsible for the patient's treatment. This individual should not attempt to hide information or blame others. In rare circumstances, and especially if it will help the notifier to face the family, the case should be quickly and immediately discussed with an appropriate attorney. This, though, should not delay talking with survivors. Under many state laws, the statute of limitations period for a potential malpractice claim does not start until the relevant people (generally the survivors who are notified first) have accurate information regarding the injury. In addition, any attempt to hide or cover-up facts will place the physicians' credibility in jeopardy. This seriously compromises any possible defense.

Did you, the staff, the medics do everything that they could?

Survivors wonder, even if they don't ask, "Did they (you) do everything they (you) could do?" This question may arise when survivors view the body, especially if medical equipment is still in, on, or around the body. Others may be hesitant to ask immediately. The question should be answered before it is asked. While some clinicians take this as an affront, it is a very reasonable question for survivors to ask. When informing the family about the death, part of the statement should be, "We (They) did everything we (they) could." This, however, is not sufficient for most survivors, whether they voice it or not.

At a later point in the discussion or during a repeat meeting with survivors (either soon after death or during a follow-up conversation), clinicians should be prepared to describe exactly what medical procedures were done for the decedent.

This question about whether "everything" possible was done may haunt many survivors who don't ask it, becoming part of their guilt. Notifiers should, therefore, try to impart this information to the family decisively, and with as much detail as they want. Some survivors, especially those with some medical knowledge, want extensive details. Others may only want sanitized generalities. After stating "I can tell you as much about the resuscitation attempt as you would like to hear," the notifier can decide how explicit to be. In some cases, the amount of information provided will be based on the questions survivors ask.

Non-clinician notifiers may not be able to answer survivors' technical questions. The survivors should be referred to the clinicians involved, the medical examiner's office, or the decedent's private physician. These individuals can use the medical records and autopsy reports to answer their questions.

Why did s/he die?

Metaphysical questions such as "How could God let this happen?" cause notifiers into more problems than any other type of question. The natural response for those who are deeply religious may be "It was God's will." However, unless you know that the grieving survivor shares the same deep and irrevocable belief in God's will, it is best to avoid this statement. This applies even for clergy, who are wont to emphasize faith in times of crisis, as happened in the following incident.

> Immediately after hearing my description of the tragic death of her young son in a motor vehicle collision, the mother turned to me and asked, "Did the priest give him last rites?" "Yes," I responded, since he had performed the rite during the resuscitative process. "Then keep him away from me," she continued. It turned out that the priest had been telling the mother that her son had died because it was "God's will." This gave her no comfort and, in fact, clashed with her understanding of God's role in her universe.

"Why did this have to happen?" is an attempt to find meaning in an event. Finding meaning is an individual process. What helps one person won't help another, so notifiers who don't know the decedent or the survivors may not be able to be very supportive in this context, at least initially, since we grieve by recalling shared memories.

In many instances, silence may be the only appropriate response to this question. In fact, many phrases anger survivors rather than comforting them. These include those that have been termed the "God clichés." A list of such phrases is provided in table 4-2.

What could I have done differently? "If only . . ."

Many, if not most, survivors play the "what if?" game based on their "survivors' guilt." They continually rebuke themselves for not preventing the death. Thinking back, they believe that they could have called for help sooner, recognized subtle or non-existent symptoms, or prevented the person from acting as he or she did. Nearly always, these actions would have been impossible, but, to distressed survivors, they seem to be reasonable actions they should have taken. Survivor guilt should be actively discouraged. It never helps the survivor and can lead to pathological grief or, even, to self-destructive behavior.

In virtually all cases, the notifier's answer to this question is "There was probably nothing anyone could have done to prevent this. It was a sudden unexpected tragedy." If a survivor called for emergency care, an additional statement is, "Calling for emergency help was the right thing to do, and you did it."

Sometimes they ask, "What if I knew CPR?" or "What if I had done CPR better?" The answer, as medical professionals know is, "In these cases, even if done correctly, CPR is rarely effective."

Occasionally, survivors did contribute to the person's death, such as not putting a child in the back seat of a car, not putting them in an adequate car seat, or not having them buckle their seat belt. In those instances, when they ask if you think they were at fault, respond by acknowledging how difficult this situation is for them. *Do not* be drawn into assigning blame. Preventive care and safety education save more lives than does acute intervention. Immediately after a sudden death, however, is not the time to do this education.

What happened to the other person (people) involved?

It's not unusual following car crashes, as well as other incidents involving multiple victims (fires, shootings, boating mishaps, etc.), for survivors to inquire about the other people involved in the event. When answering this question, first consider which of three scenarios applies.

The first, and most common situation, is when friends or other relatives of the survivors are involved. This can pose several problems for notifiers. Often, the notifiers do not have enough accurate information to relay news about others involved. If accurate information is available and the survivors have a right to know, inform them.

On occasion, the notifier knows the news, and it is not good. If the survivor asking for the information is in critical condition, the question becomes whether the news should be conveyed before their condition stabilizes. There has been some debate over this, but I favor acting in the patient's best interest, even if that seems somewhat paternalistic. If, however, they are stable enough to not need emergency interventions (such as immediate surgery) and are awake enough to cogently and repeatedly ask for the information, they should be told. These actions suggest that they need, and can absorb, the information immediately.

The second common scenario is when survivors do not know the others involved, but are both curious and generally concerned about the other people's welfare. In these cases, it is usually best to relay only general information such as "They're doing fine." or "They're not doing well." It is the notifier's responsibility to maintain confidentiality, and this is one time it comes into play.

The third scenario, thankfully less common, is when the survivors have ulterior motives for asking about the others involved. For example, they may feel that others precipitated the events leading to the death (a drunk driver, a rival gang member, the bus driver, etc.) and they want to seek revenge. It is best not to give out too much information in these cases. If these motivations are suspected, the police should also be notified.

What is SIDS?

Sudden Infant Death Syndrome (SIDS) is the leading cause of death in infants older than one month of age. It normally strikes children less than two years old. Although there have been many theories about what causes SIDS, no answer has been found.

Generally, children who die of SIDS have been healthy and without signs of disease. Factors that seem to partially protect against SIDS are breast-feeding or immunizing infants. Placing normal infants in a face-up (supine) position to sleep markedly reduces the risk of SIDS. Aggressive campaigns in some countries to have parents put their children to sleep facing up (the "Back to Sleep" movement) has reduced the numbers of SIDS deaths as much as 80 percent. In the United States, this reduced the SIDS death rate 43% between 1989 and 1995.

Twice as many of these deaths occur in the fall and winter months than at other times of the year, with more of these deaths occurring in extremely cold climates. Other risk factors associated with SIDS deaths include:

- Male children—twice as likely to die of SIDS as are females.
- Black infants—three times more likely to die of SIDS than are White infants.
- Native American and Alaskan Natives—three to five times more likely to die of SIDS than are White infants.
- Mother was less than twenty years old during her first pregnancy.
- Mother had a short interval between pregnancies.
- Mother obtained late or no prenatal care.
- Mother smoked during pregnancy.
- Child exposed to cigarette smoke.
- Low birth weight infant.

Diagnosing a death as being from SIDS is based on the five factors below plus an autopsy.

- An infant from one week to one year old (although normally between one and eight months old).
- The child is found dead after being fed, with death presumably occurring during sleep.
- No history of a potentially lethal condition.

- No history of abuse or neglect within the care setting in which the infant died.
- No prior infant deaths in the same family, at the same location where the infant died, or with the same caregiver.

Since the diagnosis is one of exclusion, SIDS deaths must be carefully investigated. Multidisciplinary SIDS investigators, including the police and medical examiner's investigators, usually take meticulous histories from caregivers and carefully examine the death scene. An autopsy almost invariably follows to rule out unknown illnesses or foul play.

Parents will inevitably react negatively to the scrutiny they receive. Those in the survivors' support system, the investigators, and any medical personnel involved can help the parents by treating them as grieving parents, not as criminals. Use all the normal death-notification and support procedures outlined for all other sudden unexpected deaths, especially those for child deaths.

Part of the support parents need is to know how to obtain their child's autopsy results. It is best, in these cases, if the medical examiner's office or the family pediatrician contacts them with the results. If there are findings that would influence decisions about future pregnancies, a knowledgeable physician should make this contact.

While multiple SIDS deaths can occur in one family, it is extremely rare. Recently, investigators around the world have re-opened many investigations that were initially presumed to be multiple SIDS deaths. In some cases, the caregivers were charged with murder.

With SIDS deaths possibly more than any others, it is important to help parents connect with special support groups. These groups, available nationally and in nearly every community, bring together parents with similar experiences. Sharing these experiences and information about their subsequent lives often helps survivors cope after this tragic loss. A list of SIDS support groups can be found in chapter 11. (Information in this section is from: Randall B: *Death Investigation: The Basics.* Tucson, AZ: Galen Press, Ltd., 1997, pp. 114-29. © 1997 by Galen Press, Ltd. Used with permission.)

What is "brain death"?

This question usually arises after prolonged resuscitation attempts or serious head injuries. Often it is in relation to a request for organ donation, since these are the non-related cadaver donors from whom most transplanted organs are obtained.

The common term "brain death," technically and more clearly stated as "death by brain criteria," means that the body has been physiologically decapitated. For survivors, it is important that they understand that their loved one is *dead*—medically and legally.

These criteria were developed both to allow survivors to donate their loved one's organs (which usually cannot be done if the heart has already stopped) and to tell physicians that their patient is dead and should be removed from the ventilator (respirator). In the 1960s, many totally unresponsive patients who had been kept on ventilators were found at autopsy to have "respirator brains," which had become soft, dark green, or totally liquefied after the cells had died days or weeks before.[6] French neurologists described these patients as being in a state beyond coma (coma dépassé). Indeed they were—they were dead.

In an anatomic decapitation, the head is actually lopped off, but the heart continues to beat for some time, spraying blood from the severed neck arteries. Yet despite the continued pumping of the heart, there is no question that the person is irreversibly dead. Even in ancient times, the Talmud said, "the death throes of a decapitated man are not signs of life any more than are the twitching of a lizard's amputated tail."[7] Likewise, in death by brain criteria, all brain functions cease. The person is dead, even though the head remains attached to the body.

The term "death by brain criteria" can be somewhat ambiguous, since it refers to at least three distinct types of brain malfunction: (1) death by *whole brain criteria*, in which both the upper brain and the brainstem have ceased functioning; (2) *cerebral death*, in which the upper brain has ceased functioning, but the lowest centers in the cerebellum (back of the brain) and brainstem still function; and (3) *neocortical death*, in which there is a lack of function in the "thinking" part of the brain.

The most widely accepted and only legal definition of death by brain criteria in the United States, Britain, Canada, and most other Western countries, is "death by whole brain criteria."

The upper brain (neocortex) contains thoughts, perceives pain and pleasure, and controls voluntary actions; it is the person. The brainstem, on the other hand, is a developmentally older organ. It controls basic biological functions without which the upper brain does not work. Found at the base of the brain, the brainstem directly controls wakefulness (reticular activating system), breathing (respiratory center), and blood pressure (vasomotor center). Passing through the brainstem are all of the brain's pathways to the rest of the body for movement, all receptors for conscious sensation, and all controls for integrating body functions (sympathetic and parasympathetic). It is a densely packed highway of nerves. Even minor damage to this area often results in death. *No matter what condition the upper brain is in, once the brainstem is inoperative, the whole brain is dead.*

The most common causes of "death by brain criteria" are:

1. Injuries or masses (lumps or swelling) in the upper part (supratentorial) of the brain, including blood clots, direct injuries, strokes, tumors and infections.
2. Injuries or masses in the lower part of the brain (infratentorial) that directly injure the brainstem.
3. Metabolic or chemical disorders, such as a persistent lack of oxygen (anoxia), lack of blood flow (ischemia), absence of glucose (sugar), or the presence of intrinsic or extrinsic poisons that destroy the brain cells' functions.[8]

Most Christian scholars strongly support the concept of death by brain criteria, based on the doctrine that the soul departs the body at the moment of death. Most Jews likewise accept the concept of death by brain criteria, as do many other non-Christian religious groups. Yet religions that stress the integration of mind and body, such as Taoism, Confucianism, Zen Buddhism, and Shintoism, have difficulty accepting death by brain criteria. Less than one-fourth of all Japanese, for example, favor national "brain death" criteria.[9,10]

In most cases, physicians make the diagnosis of death by brain criteria on purely clinical grounds. Not every brain cell need be dead, and in fact all cells are usually not dead when examined by positron emission (PET) scanning. Rather, the physician attempts to establish the fact that there is irreversible loss of brainstem function. Physicians specializing in neurology, neurosurgery, or critical care medicine who are neither the patient's primary physicians nor members of a transplant team usually do this. They normally follow these steps:

1. Determine the cause of coma.
2. Decide whether irremediable structural brain damage has occurred.
3. Rule out reversible causes of coma such as an extremely low body temperature, drug intoxication, or a severe chemical imbalance.
4. Demonstrate that all brainstem reflexes, including breathing, are absent.

The reflexes physicians look for are those that tell whether the vital connections in the brainstem are still intact. They test a patient's ability to breathe on his own by first supplying the patient with 100% oxygen for several minutes while he is still connected to a ventilator. They then continue the oxygen but remove the ventilator just long enough to see if an increase in the body's chemicals (carbon dioxide) will stimulate breathing. This is normally tested twice.

Next, they test other reflexes corresponding to connections between various (cranial) nerves originating in the brainstem. Among these are: coughing or gagging in response to suctioning the airway, constriction of the pupil in response to light, blinking in response to touching the cornea, grimacing or movement in response to pressure above the eye, and moving the eyes when the head is rotated (doll's eyes phenomenon) or the ears are flushed with ice water. No patient who failed all these tests to determine brain activity has *ever* regained consciousness. In the rare cases in which individuals have been mistakenly declared dead by brain criteria, some of these procedural safeguards were not followed.

Physicians can only tenuously apply death-by-brain-criteria guidelines to children, especially those younger than two years old. The criteria for this age group are still being formalized. Physicians specializing in the care of very young children with brain injuries will normally help make a determination of death by brain criteria.

A unique and confusing group who seem not to fit the guidelines are infants born with very little brain substance and with no skin or bone covering what brain tissue does exist—called "anencephalics." These infants are not dead by brain criteria since their brainstem functions, but they will normally not live more than a week without external support (ventilators) and can never interact meaningfully with their environment. Many of their parents wish for them to be transplant donors, but, although some European countries permit this, it is not currently possible in the United States.

I'm sure there will be a miracle. Okay, when is s/he coming home?

This statement of faith, denial, or naiveté happens more often than most people realize. Most commonly, it is heard when "brain dead" patients are on ventilators. Although they may look like they are asleep or are only in a coma, they are, in fact, dead.

> A 32-year-old woman was declared dead by brain criteria ("brain dead") following a severe head injury in a high-speed rollover car crash. Her extended family gathered from across the country at her bedside. They varied in age, level of medical knowledge, and religious perspective. "During the four days following the brain death, the patient's family questioned housestaff, nurses, and consultants about the significance of each change in vital signs, and the persisting spinal reflexes. They waited with hopeful countenances and would measure carefully each of the physician's words. Despite unchanging pronouncements, the family trusted that tomorrow would bring some improvement." Only four days after she was declared brain dead would the family accept that the ventilator had to be removed and the body buried.[11]

While the above scenario is common and repeated daily at major medical centers, the following is a bit more bizarre. After a 35-year-old man was declared "brain dead" following a motor vehicle crash, the victim's widow was asked for permission to turn off the ventilator and if his organs could be donated. She refused both requests, stating that she wished to take the patient home and maintain him on a ventilator. She was referred for psychiatric care.[12]

As the long-time chair of our medical center's bioethics committee, I am no longer surprised at how often survivors simply do not believe that their loved one is dead. Rarely is there an overt denial of physicians' conclusions or tests, only an abiding belief that the person will rise from their hospital bed. Our bioethics committee normally turns these "faith" situations over to our very competent pastoral care staff.

While our chaplains deal with these situations with a "wait until they come to terms with the death" approach, others deal with it more directly. One well-known bioethicist–Jesuit priest, John Paris, told me, "I just ask them if they have lost their faith in God's ability to do miracles. When they answer that that is what they are awaiting, I tell them that I will disconnect the ventilator. If God wants to do a miracle, He can do it then and the patient will breathe." Few chaplains (or bioethicists) handle this situation in as direct a manner.

What caregivers can do in these situations is to carefully explain the nature of "brain death," focus on one or two of the survivors who seem to understand, and encourage them to discuss the situation with others.

If all else fails, since these patients are legally and medically dead, clinicians can simply sign the death certificate, disconnect these patients' ventilators (breathing machines), and their heart will stop shortly afterwards. Without survivors' support for this action, however, this can result in a very ticklish situation. In such situations, and generally after consulting with the institution's attorney, many clinicians who plan to do this also have on hand their chaplains, social workers, bioethicists, and if necessary, their security staff.

Can we see the body? When?

Yes, they can view the body. Most often, survivors will feel a little uncomfortable about asking to see the body. Caregivers must verbalize permission with statements such as, "Would you like to view (decedent's name)? I (or one of the staff or chaplain) will go with you."

Generally, survivors will view the body after it and the resuscitation areas are suitably prepared. After being told of the death, there will generally be a period before the body can be viewed. During this time, the family can sort out whom among them wishes to, and should, view the decedent. They should be warned that there will still be some equipment (such as an endotracheal tube) in place and the body may look different because of the injury, the resuscitative effort, or the body's postmortem changes (cold, discolored, stiff).

In the hospital, and even in the home setting after a resuscitative event, medical personnel should do everything possible to make the body presentable before the relatives view it. When permitted by law (medical examiner or coroner's rules must be observed in some cases), the body should be cleaned and covered for modesty, medical equipment removed, and the area should be cleansed.

Family members may have a strong need to see, touch, or hold the body. This permits them to eventually have some closure, putting the death behind them. Yet they usually feel that they need permission to do this. The staff person accompanying them can demonstrate his or her acceptance by touching the body first. If it is a small child, the staff person can pick the body up and hold it, offering it to the parent. Clarice Schultz, a nurse, described how her mother was given such "permission" when her baby brother died.

> As was the custom in that area, my parents were going to transport his body to the funeral home themselves after he had been examined at our home by the physician and pronounced dead. Dad brought the car to the door and Mom carried the baby. When she got to the car, she became confused and said to my sister, "Should I put him in the back seat?" My sister responded by touching Mom's shoulder and saying, "No, Mom, why don't you hold the baby?" Mom cuddled the baby for the entire fifteen-mile trip. Afterward, when she talked about the incident she said these memories gave her so much comfort.[13]

During the grieving process, survivors often visualize the body, especially if there has been an accident, wondering how badly the body was damaged—and usually imagining the worst. If there are large damaged areas, it often helps to cover them or even apply bandages. When a body, especially the face, is badly mutilated, advise survivors of this in advance. They will probably only want to view an unaffected part. If they see and touch the body, even if only an undamaged part, such as a hand or foot, they can begin to grieve. If the body is covered, as it usually is postmortem, the family usually will not disturb the covering. However, if they do, they should not be stopped.

Parents may get into the bed with their child's body and hold it for a period of time. Medical personnel are becoming used to this and permitting it, even in busy emergency departments. Initially, a staff member should accompany survivors. Once the situation is stable, especially if survivors wish to conduct a religious or special family ritual and ask to be left alone, the staff member should depart. (In potential legal situations, it may be necessary to have a police officer remain in attendance. When this is explained, most families understand.)

What happens to miscarried fetuses and stillborn infants?

Nearly all U.S. hospitals still routinely cremate fetal remains with other tissue specimens. If asked, however, they will usually return fetal remains to the parents for burial. Some institutions now have special burials for fetuses, whether they were from miscarriages, abortions, or the result of ectopic pregnancies. On occasion, however, these fetuses have been used for political purposes. In October 1998, the Los Angeles County coroner released to religious groups the remains of fifty-four discarded fetuses from a closed abortion clinic for "a Christian burial." The ACLU threatened to sue.[14]

Miscarried fetuses (known medically as "spontaneous abortions") are usually smaller than the end of an adult's little finger and occasionally as long as an index finger. Most other tissue passed in a miscarriage is placenta and blood clots. This tissue is normally sent to the pathologist for examination. If any congenital defects are found, the parents should be told about them. In many places, the parents may see the aborted fetus before it goes to the pathologist; most do not avail themselves of this privilege.

In the United States, all but two states require a death certificate for fetal deaths, although most only require it if the fetus was older than 20-weeks gestation.[15] In Britain, a developing fetus that dies before 28-weeks gestation is considered an *abortus*, but if it is 28 weeks or more, it is a *stillborn* and a death certificate must be completed. Both pathologists and parents treat stillborn infants as they would any infant death.[16]

Since the establishment of fetal tissue banks, some women who abort spontaneously may be asked or ask to donate their fetus. Unfortunately, the fetus will often be at too early a stage or be too deformed to be used.

Over the past few years, some medical centers have developed burial sites for the results of these "failed pregnancies." One example is the communal burial site developed at the Milton S. Hershey Medical Center in Pennsylvania. They hold quarterly services over a common grave that holds the remains of miscarriages, ectopic pregnancies, and stillborn babies. (Stillborns are not usually buried in such sites but often in regular graves.) These sites provide a focal point for grieving parents attempting to achieve closure. As Norman Foster, chief of mortician services at Hershey, said, "We'd get letters, calls from parents, weeks to years after the birth, sometimes up to twenty years later. These are unresolved grief feelings that people can carry for decades, and they wish they knew where their baby was regardless of how early the pregnancy." Or as one woman, who miscarried twins after a two-month pregnancy, said, "So many people don't acknowledge this as a true loss. It's comforting to know there's a symbol—an acknowledgment to our loss."[17]

Is an autopsy required? Possible?

Whether or not the body is autopsied depends mainly on the circumstances surrounding the death, where the death occurs, and the survivor's sentiments about autopsies. In some circumstances, it may also hinge upon wishes expressed in the decedent's advance directive or upon their insurance policy. Relatively few non-medicolegal autopsies are now done in the United States.

Most U.S. jurisdictions have "medical examiner laws" that require a pathologist or coroner to determine whether or not an autopsy will be performed for

- Cases of sudden or unexpected deaths.
- Deaths when the decedent has not been seen by a physician in the past 24 hours.
- Mysterious or unusual deaths.
- Deaths in prisons or jails.
- Unnatural or unexplained deaths.
- Violent deaths (including motor vehicle deaths).
- Deaths that might pose a public health hazard.
- Deaths within 24 hours of general anesthesia.
- Sudden infant deaths (most jurisdictions).
- Executed prisoners (some jurisdictions).
- Where a body will become permanently unavailable due to cremation or burial at sea (some jurisdictions).
- Deaths from malnutrition (some jurisdictions).
- Deaths associated with child or sexual abuse (most jurisdictions).

Even if death from violence is delayed many years, such as when an individual finally succumbs to infection after being paralyzed by a gunshot wound, it falls within the medical examiner's domain.

Medical examiner cases require no consent for an autopsy. Medical examiners are not required to perform autopsies in all of these cases and their budgets usually don't allow them to autopsy all bodies in these categories. They decide whether to do so after an initial examination of the scene, medical records, personal effects, and the body. In some areas, a local health officer, judge, district or county attorney, or director of a state mental hospital may also order autopsies.[18]

What is an autopsy? How do I get the report? How much does it cost?

An autopsy, also known as necropsy or postmortem examination, is where pathologists, physicians who specialize in the anatomy of the human body, dissect the body to determine, if possible, a cause of death. Autopsies also help to ensure quality control in medical practice, help confirm the presence of new diseases or the recurrence of old and unsuspected diseases, educate new physicians, and enhance the investigation of criminal activity.

In the modern autopsy, pathologists not only remove and inspect the major organs, but also use all the sophisticated tools of modern medicine to analyze body fluids, tissues, and cellular components.

There are three levels of autopsy: (1) *Complete:* in which all body cavities, including the head, are exposed for examination; (2) *Limited:* which generally excludes the head; and (3) *Selective:* in which the physician examines only one or more organs of special interest. Medical examiner autopsies are at least "limited," and most often "complete."

After an autopsy, the major organs are usually put in plastic bags and stored in the chest and abdomen, unless pathologists have written permission to keep them.[19] When permitted to do so, many teaching hospitals will keep most of the organs for later study and teaching.[20] The pathologist routinely keeps small pieces of organs (about the size of a crouton) that show, or might show. evidence of disease or injury for subsequent microscopic and chemical analysis. They may also keep and analyze fluid from the eye, heart, gallbladder, stomach, urinary bladder, spinal canal, vagina, and other sources. National standards require that "wet tissue" from autopsies be held for six months after issuing a final autopsy report, tissue in paraffin blocks (from which microscope slides are made) must be kept five years, and the slides themselves along with the autopsy reports must be retained for twenty years.[21]

Determining the cause of death can help a family's grief process or assuage guilt. Autopsy results can sometimes reassure the family that nothing else really could have been done to save the decedent, that they were not the cause of their loved one's death, or that there was no known familial disease. They can also feel reassured that tissues removed or findings discovered at autopsy will help other people.

Survivors must usually give their permission before pathologists perform a non-medicolegal autopsy. State statutes clearly specify who has legal custody of the corpse and the right to authorize an autopsy. In most states, this is the next of kin, but in a few states, the individual who assumes custody of the corpse for burial may give autopsy permission.[22]

The order in which next of kin may authorize an autopsy is usually: surviving spouse, adult children, adult grandchildren, parents, siblings, and others per statute.[23] Sometimes even a minor may authorize the autopsy.[24]

If the autopsy was done at the family's request or with the family's permission at a hospital, the person who signed the authorization needs only to request a copy of the report. It is probably best to request the report in writing at the time that the authorization for the autopsy is given. Getting these results is worthwhile, since family members often learn unexpected and valuable information from these reports that can help them or their children. Yet at least half of surviving spouses do not receive the report. Of those who do, two-thirds feel the findings benefit themselves or others.[25] A physician may be needed, however, to interpret the report.

If a medical examiner performs the autopsy, the nature of the case will determine how a copy of the report is obtained. In routine cases of sudden or accidental death where no foul play is suspected, the next of kin can usually obtain a copy by requesting it in writing from the medical examiner's (or coroner's) office. In cases where the autopsy results will be introduced into court records as evidence, a lawyer involved in the case may need to request the report.

Postmortem results may not be completed for a month or more after the examination of the body. Some tests and examinations take considerable time; some tissues, such as the brain, require prolonged periods in preservatives before they can be adequately examined. In unusual cases, small tissue or fluid specimens may be sent to outside laboratories or to consultants for their review before a final report can be generated. Ultimately, the autopsy report goes into the patient's medical record. Normally the patient's physician also receives a copy.

Neither the family nor the decedent's estate is charged for an autopsy performed by a medical examiner, since the government pays the cost of medicolegal autopsies. Modern autopsies for medical, rather than medicolegal, purposes cost more than $1,000 in the mid-1980s and are higher now.[26] If the autopsy is done at a hospital, they may "eat" the cost, since the charge is not reimbursed by either Medicare or insurance companies.[27] Many of these hospitals now actively discourage autopsies. Others now simply charge the family when they do them. Some private hospitals no longer do autopsies, sending the bodies of deceased patients to teaching hospitals if the family requests that an autopsy be done. In that case, the family must pay for the procedure.

If there is an autopsy, can there be an open casket? When can we hold the funeral?

Autopsies, like organ or tissue donations, do not prevent embalming or open-casket funerals. Modern funeral directors know how to embalm autopsied bodies, and they will generally look no different than they would have without an autopsy. Funeral directors and pathologists, however, generally have poor relationships. For that reason and because embalming after autopsies may be more difficult than usual, they may discourage autopsies.

The timing of funerals may be uncertain if there is an autopsy. Funeral directors and families sometimes complain that autopsies have delayed funerals. If the autopsy is non-medicolegal, this should be discussed with the pathologist or in-hospital mortician. If it is a medicolegal autopsy, making contact with the medical examiner, coroner, or on-scene investigator may help expedite release of the body. The funeral director should also make the survivor's wishes known. Bodies autopsied outside the United States or Canada will rarely be in a condition to have an open-casket funeral.

Do I have to speak to or notify the police?

Police will usually need to investigate sudden, violent, or unexpected deaths that occur outside of a hospital or in the emergency department. They will need to speak with anyone with information pertaining to the case. The more complicated it is, or the more the death seems to be the result of a criminal act, the more investigation they will do. Survivors may need to speak not only with the initial investigating officers, but also to detectives.

If these types of deaths occur at home, the ambulance dispatcher will generally notify the police. They, in turn, will notify the medical examiner or coroner's office if the individual is pronounced dead at the scene. If the death occurs in the emergency department and the police have not yet been notified, ED personnel will notify both law enforcement and the medical examiner or coroner.

What forms do I have to sign?

Governmental and institutional regulations require survivors to sign a number of documents after a death. Many require some decisions. Some survivors claim that they do not remember signing any forms—probably a result of their acute grief response. A good policy is to give survivors a copy of all papers they sign.

The "Death Pack" for University Medical Center, Tucson, Ariz., contains a typical set of forms, including:

- **Authorization for the release of the deceased patient's body.** This authorizes the hospital to release the body to a specified funeral home or similar agency. In cases referred to the coroner or medical examiner, that office signs the form when they complete their investigation or autopsy.
- **Itemization and acknowledgment of receipt of the deceased patient's clothes and personal effects, including valuables.** If there is an ongoing investigation, many of these may be collected by the medical examiner or police, so survivors do not immediately receive them.
- **Record for donation of anatomical gift.** This is explicit permission for the regional organ procurement organization to remove those organs and tissues that are useable for transplant, research, or educational purposes. The survivor specifies which organs and tissues may be taken and for what purposes they may be used. (A person must usually arrange whole body donation with a medical or dental school or similar institution before death. Copies of these forms and information about body preservation and transport can be obtained from that school's anatomy department (usually on-call 24 hours a day). Many people carry this contact information in their wallets.)
- **Request for autopsy.** In cases not automatically referred to the coroner or medical examiner, survivors are asked if they wish to authorize an autopsy. The hospital's pathologists may perform this non-forensic autopsy at no cost to survivors. The form includes a section specifying restrictions on the parts that may be examined.

What forms do I need to find?

Survivors must find several forms as soon after a death as possible. Many will be in the family's safe deposit box or another secure place. Although this is not what key survivors wish to do immediately after a tragedy, they are usually the only ones who can locate or retrieve these documents. Some of the most important documents to find are:

- **Prearranged funeral, burial, or cremation policy.** This may be the first thing that needs to be located. If all or part of the funerary costs have been prepaid, it is important to know immediately who is supposed to perform the body disposition and what other costs are involved. If this isn't found in time, the costs for the policy have been wasted and a lot more money than necessary has been spent.

- **Deed to a cemetery lot.** Cemetery lots are often presold. These policies need to be found immediately to discover where the cemetery is and what services are covered. Cemeteries nearly always charge extra for opening and closing the grave, placing the marker, and a vault.
- **Donation agreements.** If the decedent made an agreement to donate his or her whole body to science, it is important to locate it. Although the medical school (usually the recipient) will have records, the agreement specifies who pays for transporting the body, how to contact them, and other relevant details.
- **Wills.** If a will exists (or might exist), check in all the logical places: safe deposit box, lawyer's office, and desk drawer with other important papers. If no will exists, contact a lawyer to see if probate is necessary and what it entails.
- **Insurance policies (life, health, disability, travel, organizational***).* Check all policies to be sure that coverage still exists. For life insurance, make certain that all potential claims are identified. The decedent may have belonged to some organizations that offer automatic life insurance coverage. (To identify these organizations, go through the decedent's membership cards and check the magazines that he or she receives during the next several months. Then ask these organizations about such coverage.)
- **Bank account records (checking, savings, CD).** If the accounts are held jointly, there should be no problems with gaining access to them. If they are in only the decedent's name, ask a lawyer. An executor for the estate may need to be appointed to get access to the accounts.
- **Stock, bond, and mutual fund records**. As with bank accounts, how the title to these assets passes to heirs depends on how and where they were set up.
- **Annuity payment records.** If the decedent was receiving annuity payments, they usually cease at the time of death. The payer must be notified and any checks issued after the date of death should be returned, unless the estate's or the survivor's lawyer says otherwise.
- **Mortgages.** If mortgage insurance was purchased, the mortgage will be paid in full at the time of death. The lender must be notified to obtain this benefit.
- **Marriage certificate.** This is necessary to obtain Social Security survivor benefits.
- **Birth certificates of surviving minor children.** This is necessary to obtain Social Security benefits.
- **Military discharge or VA claim papers.** Necessary to obtain benefits if the decedent was a veteran or was covered under Veterans Administration benefits.
- **Death certificate.** Necessary for social security benefits, insurance settlements, and other legal or financial matters that require proof of death.

What alternatives are there for disposing of the body?

Most commonly, corpses are either buried (usually with prior embalming if in the United States or Canada) or cremated. Body parts may be removed for transplantation or study prior to either embalming or cremation. A few bodies are donated to science, usually with arrangements made prior to death. Even fewer are buried at sea (whole), cryonically preserved, or have other dispositions. (For a complete discussion of all possible dispositions across cultures and time, see Iserson KV: *Death to Dust: What Happens To Dead Bodies?* Tucson, AZ: Galen Press, Ltd., 1994.)

It is primarily custom, rather than religious requirements, that dictates how survivors dispose of a loved one's body. Contrary to popular belief, neither embalming nor a funeral is mandatory prior to burial or cremation. In the United States and Canada, most bodies are buried. Of the more than 2 million funerals annually in the United States, nearly 65% have open caskets, 16% have closed caskets, 14% are cremated, and 5% have other dispositions.[28, 29]

Cremation is a worldwide custom and the primary form of corpse disposition for several religions. It is an ancient practice that has waxed and waned in popularity over the millennia. Its use in Western countries has been increasing since the mid-twentieth century. Since cremation is considered the final legal disposition of a body, the resulting "ashes" can be scattered, buried, or otherwise distributed in nearly any manner. Yet survivors should take care where they scatter them, since if they are scattered on the lawn or in gardens around a house, it may later become very uncomfortable to sell it and move elsewhere.

"Direct (or immediate) burial" or "direct cremation" is the less-expensive alternative of going directly from death to burial or ashes, without detouring for embalming or a funeral, viewing, wake, or other ritual with the body present. Memorial services, essentially funerals without the decedent's body present, are becoming more common—especially following cremations. They are used to remember individuals whose bodies have been cremated, buried, or lost in accidents.

Can we donate organs and tissues?

The living can arrange to donate their organs and tissues, or their whole body after death. Relatives (as surrogates or executors for the decedent) can usually only donate the organs and tissues.

The need for transplantable organs and tissues continues to grow. Americans generally applaud organ donations, but are reluctant to donate. The number of people dying in the United States while awaiting transplants has been *increasing by 20% each year,* with a new person joining this hapless waiting list every fifteen minutes. Yet the rate of organ donation has not increased. Fewer than one in five adult Americans have completed organ/tissue donor cards. Postmortem organ and tissue donation involves three steps:

1. Determining that death has occurred.
2. Requesting the donation from relatives.
3. Removing the organs and tissue.

Survivors must first agree to donate the deceased individual's organs or tissues. They will have usually discussed this with an adult decedent who, if possible, signed an organ/tissue donor card (or specified organ donation on their driver's license if that is official or in an advance directive). Persons under 18 years of age may sign a donor card with their parent's permission, but it is the parents or legal guardian who usually must consent to organ or tissue donation. (A protocol for making the request is in chapter 7.)

As donor cards make clear, a person may specify which of the more than 75 possible organs or tissues that can be used to help the living are to be donated. (All regions do not accept all types of organs and tissues, and making some donations may be incompatible with making others.) Medical personnel will comply with these wishes if they are aware of them, if it is feasible, and if the decision-making survivors also agree. Table 27-1 lists the criteria for some of the more common donations. Those who can give permission for donations are generally the same as they are for autopsy permission. (See "What is an autopsy?" above.) Medic Alert® or similar identification jewelry helps medical personnel identify individuals as potential donors, as do wallet cards—if they are carried.

Each year in the United States, relatives bury or cremate at least 5,000 human organs after refusing to donate them for transplantation.[30] Families feel more comfortable about donating a relative's organs if the decedent discussed this with them in advance.

Federal law requires medical personnel to approach all survivors after deaths to request organ and tissue donations. Many medical personnel remain reluctant to do so. They often justify not asking because the death was a medical examiner's case (35%), the family was not available (20%), the family was too upset (18%), the decedent was medically unsuitable to donate (14%), and the patient could not be identified (12%).[31] In many cases, however, survivors broach the subject of organ and tissue donation with the notifiers—either because the decedent had discussed this issue or because they are familiar with it from personal experiences.

If the death occurs at home, survivors must notify the appropriate agencies (for tissue donation only). If a family refuses permission for organ donation from a patient who has been declared dead by brain criteria, the hospital should remove "life supports" and release the body to the medical examiner or family, as appropriate.[32]

There are no age or medical restrictions for donating organs or tissues for biomedical research. Some organ procurement organizations allow an individual to specify what research they would like to support with an organ or tissue donation, and the surgical recovery team will take the appropriate material.

In situations that preclude organ, but not generally tissue, donation for transplantation, the organs may still be useful for research. Examples of such situations are those in which a person dies a cardiorespiratory death (the heart and lungs stop and the organs are no longer getting oxygen) or if a medical examiner feels that a medicolegal autopsy is mandatory because of the nature of the death. In some cases, a medicolegal autopsy may be performed after organ donation, especially when the cause of death is obviously from an isolated injury, such as a gunshot wound to the head. Generally, however, if a death falls under the medical examiner's jurisdiction, organs and tissues may be retrieved only if the body is released without an autopsy.

Table 27-1: Criteria for Organ and Tissue Donors

(Criteria change often and vary by region. Contact your local organ procurement organization for their most current criteria.)

All Tissue and Organ Donors

Death by brain or heart criteria. (Many centers accept only death by brain criteria.)

No malignancy other than localized treated basal cell carcinomas that have not recurred within the past six months, and carcinoma in situ of the uterus or cervix. (These do not apply to cornea donation.)

No body-wide infection or injury to tissue

No known neurological disease or AIDS risk factors.

Tissue Specific

Heart Valves

Full-term birth through 59 years of age with no prior heart surgery.

No disease of heart valves.

No injections into the heart.

Bone

Ages 15 through 65.

No steroid use. (Short-term steroid inhaler use *may* be acceptable.)

No collagen-vascular disease (e.g., lupus, rheumatoid arthritis).

No neurological disease.

Corneas

Ages 24 months to 85 years.

Must be retrieved within 16 hours after death.

(The above criteria vary widely among regional eye banks.)

No AIDS, HIV seropositivity, or high-risk behaviors for them or hepatitis C.

No Creutzfeldt-Jakob Disease.

No congenital Rubella.

No death from unknown cause.

No death from a undiagnosed neurological disease.

No active encephalitis or progressive encephalopathy.

No active endocarditis.

No active viral hepatitis.

Not a recipient of Human Pituitary-derived Growth Hormone prior to 1985.

No intrinsic eye disease.

No retinoblastoma.

No malignant tumors of the anterior ocular segment (eye).

Table 27-1: continued

Corneas, cont.

No known adenocarcinoma.

No active ocular or intraocular inflammation.

No active leukemia or lymphoma. (Other types of cancer are acceptable for eye donation.)

No progressive multifocal leukoencephalopathy.

No Rabies.

No Reye's Syndrome.

No active septicemia (bacteremia, fungemia, viremia).

No prior corneal transplant, radial keratotomy, or laser refractive procedures.

Organ Specific

Kidney

Less than 80 years old with normal kidney function.

Heart

Generally younger than 65 years old.

Liver

Generally younger than 80 years old.

Lung

Generally younger than 65 years old.

No lung infection.

Pancreas

Generally younger than 60 years old.

No pancreas malfunction

Small Bowel

Center-specific criteria.

Adapted from: Iserson KV: *Death to Dust: What Happens To Dead Bodies?* Tucson, AZ: Galen Press, Ltd., 1994. (Used with permission.) Revised with information from Donor Network of Arizona, Tucson, AZ: December 1998.

Organ donation after death is governed by state statutes, most of which are quite similar. Several states, including Arizona, have laws that allow physicians to remove organs or tissues, despite family objections, if the individual previously requested this using an organ donor card or an advance directive. At least fourteen states have "presumed consent" laws that automatically allow authorities to remove cadaver eyes for cornea transplants, and other therapeutic and research purposes, if there are no objections from the family or no written objections left by the decedent.[33]

With slight variations, every state in the United States, Washington, D.C., and Puerto Rico have adopted the Uniform Anatomical Gift Act, which has six key elements:

1. Persons 18 years or older who are of sound mind may give all or part of their bodies upon death for specific purposes.
2. Surviving relatives may donate an entire body or any parts of the body if the decedent left no instructions (the suggested order of decision making is: surviving spouse, adult child, parent, adult sibling, guardian).
3. Medical specialists may determine whether the anatomical gift is suitable for the intended purpose and may refuse to accept any or all parts.
4. Only specified parties may be recipients of anatomical gifts (any hospital, surgeon or physician, accredited medical and dental school, or tissue or organ bank) and the gifts may only be used for education, research, advancement of science, or therapy, including transplantation.
5. The donor has the right to revoke or amend a donor card at any time, simply by destroying the card.
6. The state continues to have the right to require an autopsy as stipulated in medical examiner or similar statutes.

Under the Act, hospitals, physicians, teaching institutions, storage banks, and a limited number of others can act as recipients of anatomical gifts. n Canada, the provinces of Alberta, British Columbia, Newfoundland, Nova Scotia, and Quebec have adopted a similar measure, the Human Tissue Gift Act. Similar guidelines for organ and tissue donation are available in most British Commonwealth and European countries.

Most major religions endorse organ and tissue donation and transplantation.[34] Muslims, Rastafarians, Shintos, and Zoroastrians are the major religious groups that oppose donation, although their bans are not observed by all members or in all countries. Many Native Americans and Gypsies will not permit organ donation. There is no religious objection to organ transplantation by the Sikhs, Hindus, Baha'is, Buddhists, Catholics, most mainstream Protestant denominations, and Jews (although some Orthodox Jews may question the concept of death by brain criteria).[35-38]

Organ donation costs the family nothing. This question arises most often with patients declared dead by brain criteria, since once they have been designated as organ donors, these cadavers must be kept on "life support" machines to keep blood and oxygen going to the organs until they are removed. Once a person has been declared dead and has been designated an organ donor, the organ-procurement organization covers all hospital and physician costs associated with maintaining the body and recovering the organs and tissues.[39] Hospitals bill these charges to the organ recipient. Hospital costs before the person was declared dead are, of course, still the family's responsibility, as are any funeral, burial, or cremation expenses once the body is returned to them.

How are organs and tissues obtained?

Organs and tissues can only be removed after a person is declared dead by either brain (the entire brain no longer functions) criteria or cardiorespiratory (the heart stops) criteria. It is best not use terms such as "brain death" (confusing), "life support" (if he's dead, why is it *life* support?), and "harvest" (a terrible term suggesting farming the dead rather than saving the living).

To avoid a conflict of interest, the physician treating a patient who is a potential donor is never involved in the transplant process. He or she can then concentrate on saving the patient's life. Likewise, the physician who determines death is not involved in either removing the organs/tissues or in transplanting them. Many people do not know this and believe that the medical care necessary for their relative's survival might be curtailed if they agree to organ donation. Not true! Only when the treating medical team declares a patient dead does the organ transplant team become involved.

Once a person has been declared dead by brain criteria and relatives agree to donate organs, the medical team must preserve the organs' functions until they are removed from the body. They keep the body on a respirator (ventilator) to oxygenate the lungs and give medications to keep the body functioning.

If the person is dead by cardiorespiratory (heart) criteria, most U.S. transplant centers will only remove tissues. After 1975, believing that kidney transplants had better success if removed from a donor while blood was still going through the organ, U.S. physicians began to avoid transplanting kidneys from patients whose heart had stopped, using only those from patients declared dead by brain criteria.[40] In some centers, surgeons have reverted to using cadaver kidneys because of the scarcity of donated organs.

The organ-procurement team follows a rigid protocol (table 27-2) determined by national standards that protects the donor, donor family, institutions at both ends of the procedure, and the recipient. The team verifies that death has been pronounced, ascertains that there is no medical reason why the organs should not be used, and runs additional laboratory tests to evaluate the organ's function before it is removed. The time taken to do these tests varies, since in some cases many of the necessary test results may already be available.

Organ procurement looks like any other surgical operation on a critically ill or injured person. In this case, though, the "patient" is a "heart-beating cadaver" and is already dead by brain criteria. All the normal surgical procedures are still followed, however, since it is vital to maintain sterility and to keep blood and oxygen flowing to the various organs until they are removed and preservation procedures begun. To accomplish this, an anesthesiologist monitors the heart rhythm, blood pressure, and other body systems; a ventilator pushes oxygen into the lungs; and intravenous fluids drip into the veins. (But, of course, no anesthesia is given, since the dead do not feel pain.) The surgical team scrubs, gowns, and prepares the corpse as in any other operation. Complete sterility is preserved, and normal instruments and procedures are used. Scrub nurses pass the instruments and a circulating nurse oversees the scene. When a cadaver will supply multiple organs, various surgical teams take turns removing the organs. There is some scientific disagreement on the order in which organs should be removed for their optimal survival, although the "life-preserving" organs, i.e., heart, lungs, liver, and, in a few centers, small intestines, are usually removed first.

Only when all of the organs are removed does the situation change dramatically. Once the heart is removed, the anesthesiologist simply disconnects the ventilator, since the cadaver can no longer be artificially oxygenated. The surgical teams, when finished with their procedures, sew up the cadaver and leave the room; the body now is in the mortician's realm.[41]

How are tissues donated? Which can be donated?

Unlike organs, which must be retrieved while the heart is still pumping oxygen-rich blood through them, tissues are generally removed after a person's heart stops. They survive quite well without oxygen for 12 to 24 hours. While every organ donor program accepts donations of eye tissue, the other organs listed below vary with the area of the country and the specific donation program.

Eyes are the most commonly donated tissue, because in fourteen states specific permission is not required, under so-called "presumed consent" laws. More than 35,000 corneal transplants were performed in the United States in 1997, with over 90% of those resulting in restored vision.[42] Technicians, who in some areas are also morticians, normally remove the eyes within four hours of death. These technicians are trained in the removal, handling, and preservation of the donated eyes through a short course given by the local ophthalmologists, eye hospital, or organ donor banks. Some morticians remove the eyes without charge, as a community service—whether or not they are involved with any of the burial or funeral arrangements.

After eye removal, a plastic ball is placed in the eye socket so that as long as the eyelids are closed, no one can tell the eyes have been removed. Although only the cornea, the clear part in the front of the eye, can be transplanted, ophthalmologists use other eye tissue (sclera) to attach muscles to false eyeballs in people who have lost their eyes and use the entire eye for research into eye disorders.

Skin is procured to help burn victims. If a cadaver has been refrigerated within 12 hours after death, skin can be recovered for up to 18 hours after cardiac death. If not refrigerated, it must be recovered within 15 hours.[43] In a sterile environment, often the operating room, technicians remove a layer of skin between .005 and .018 inches thick, about the same as the skin that peels after a sunburn. Most of the thirty United States tissue centers routinely remove donor skin from the lower chest, abdomen, back, and the front and back of the legs—all areas covered by clothes to allow an open-casket funeral. While only about five square feet of skin can be taken from each donor, about fifteen square feet is needed to cover a large child's burns one time—and each burn patient undergoes many such skin grafts.[44]

Table 27-2: Procedure for Organ Recovery Team

Donor Identification

1. Verify that death has been pronounced in accordance with state law or hospital policy.
2. Contact local organ procurement organization to determine patient's potential to donate.
3. Determine that none of the following medical conditions are present:
   a. Malignant tumor:
   For Organ Donations: Except primary brain tumor without a shunt in place.
   For Tissue Donations: No malignancy except localized treated basal cell carcinomas that have not recurred within the past six months and carcinoma in situ or the uterus or cervix.
   b. Repeated positive immunodeficiency virus (AIDS) tests.

Donor Evaluation

1. History and review of all organ systems.
2. Chart review.
3. Physical examination.
4. Vital signs.
5. Laboratory tests:
   a. Complete blood count (CBC).
   b. Electrolytes (sodium, potassium, chloride, bicarbonate).
   c. Blood typing.
   d. Hepatitis screen.
   e. Syphilis screen.
   f. AIDS screen.
   g. Other viral screens.
   h. Blood and urine cultures.
   i. Other tests are also required for donation of the kidneys, liver, heart and pancreas to assess their function.

Adapted from: Iserson KV: *Death to Dust: What Happens To Dead Bodies?* Tucson, AZ: Galen Press, Ltd., 1994. (Used with permission.) Revised with information from Donor Network of Arizona, Tucson, AZ: December 1998.

Physicians use bone grafts to replace bone lost because of tumor, injury or degenerative disease. They also use the minute bones of the ear (within the temporal bone) to restore hearing in people with specific types of deafness. Bone donations are routinely taken from above the hip (iliac crest), the large leg bones (femur, tibia and fibula), and the kneecap (patella). In some cases, portions of the ribs, upper arm bone (humerus), and jawbone (mandible) are also removed. The bones are replaced with plastic bracing so that there is no apparent disfigurement of the cadaver. If the body has been refrigerated within 12 hours after cardiac death, bone can be removed anytime in the subsequent 24 hours. If not cooled, the bone must be removed within 15 hours after death. After removal, the bone is cleaned, cut, air dried, packaged, and sterilized using freeze-drying or gamma radiation. It can then sit on a shelf for many years before use.[45]

Leg (saphenous and femoral) veins can also be taken in the subsequent 12 hours, and heart valves in the subsequent 24 hours.[46, 47]

What happens after donation?

Organs for transplant are sent to compatible recipients who are identified through the United Network for Organ Sharing (UNOS) national computer system. When an organ becomes available for transplant, UNOS ranks the pool of potential recipients by strict medical criteria and by the urgency of their need. A potential recipient's ranking may be affected by how well the tissues match, his blood type, his length of time on the waiting list, and his immune status. For hearts, livers, and lungs, matching the size of the organ with that of the recipient is often an important consideration. In most cases, the distance between the recipient and donor is an important factor since many organs cannot be preserved very long. UNOS has suggested beginning a national pool for some organs but, as of early 1999, federal courts had delayed, if not stopped, that proposal's implementation.

The tissues and solid organs removed from donors are transplanted whenever possible. If they are found to be unacceptable for transplant, they may be used in transplantation research. Any residual parts are cremated.

Although the transplant team may share some basic information with the donor family or recipient, such as the donor's or recipient's age and whether he or she had children, confidentiality is maintained at both ends. Anonymity forestalls the emotional excesses that have been seen from both the donor family and the recipient, as well as the rare incidents where donor families have requested money from the recipient.

After a donation, the surviving kin or those charged with disposal of the body get custody of the remains. The family is responsible for funeral arrangements. Relatives can still arrange for embalming and an open-casket funeral if the illness or injury that killed the person does not preclude it. According to the funeral industry, removing organs and tissues *does not* interfere with customary burial arrangements, "regardless of the type or extent of the donation."[48]

Can the whole body be donated to a medical school?

Yes, and it is generally quite simple if arrangements with a medical school have already been made before death. (In some locales, such as Illinois, bodies are donated to a central organization, which then randomly distributes the bodies among all the state's medical schools.) As a survivor, you must know about the arrangements. As with organ donation, the schools themselves normally require permission from the decedent's relatives. Most states consider donation of a body to a medical school for dissection its final legal disposition. More than 90% of the cadavers used by U.S. medical schools have been donated.

Some schools require that bodies come to them immediately; others allow a short delay for funeral services. Most schools do not pay transportation costs for an "out-of-town" body and some require that a mortician deliver the body to them. Others allow the body to be transported by an ambulance, relatives, or the school's own vehicle.

Most schools, however, will not allow people to donate a body for a specific purpose (e.g., dissection by orthopedic surgeons) since how a body is used will depend on its condition at the time of death. Though some schools will dispose of any body they receive that they cannot use, others may return it to the family. Virtually all bodies accepted by medical schools are used for anatomical teaching, generally within two years of donation.

If death occurs in another state, complying with the legal requirements necessary to transport the body back to the medical school where the donation has been arranged may take so much time that the body is no longer in a condition suitable for anatomical use. An alternative in such cases is for a relative to locate a nearby medical school that will accept the body.

Law prohibits the international shipping of bodies as anatomical specimens. But if someone should die in a foreign country, it is possible to donate a body to a foreign medical school for dissection. Many of these schools (due to legal, cultural, or religious restraints) desperately need anatomical specimens. After all, anatomy is the same around the world and all physicians must learn it.

The question frequently arises: Which takes priority, donating organs or using the body for anatomical dissection? In general, the removal of needed organs takes precedence, as these donations often will be immediately life saving. Since many fewer bodies are acceptable as organ donors than as anatomical cadavers (because of the mechanism of death or the diseases at the time of death), most donated bodies undergo anatomical dissection.

How do we select and contact a funeral director or funeral home?

While it is best to make a decision about a funeral home, crematoria, cemetery, etc., before death, few people do. Survivors may need to make a decision quickly. This is one area where close friends can help by gathering information for the ultimate decision-maker, usually the closest relative, to use.

Unless funerary services have been preselected, the name of a funeral home should not be picked "out of the air" when needed to complete forms in the emergency department. Survivors should say that they will wait and call the appropriate person with the information the next day. This allows time to choose the services desired and an acceptable provider.

The first thing to do is to decide exactly what services are desired. Will a funeral be simple, traditional, or elaborate? Will the body be buried or cremated? Do you want open-casket viewing or not? What is the budget? Once these decisions are made, choose a provider.

The easiest way to locate these services is to use two methods simultaneously. First, ask friends and other survivors about good experiences they have had with local funeral homes, cemeteries, and crematoria. Second, go through the telephone book and call the funeral homes or crematoria. Ask for their "general price list." Note whether they offer to fax or e-mail it, or if it is available on the Internet. Do they exert pressure on the caller to make quick decisions or more expensive purchases than desired? Recheck these items when making a visit in person.

Traditionally, funeral homes differentiate themselves by religious affiliation, cost, aggressiveness, and location. The services they offer may also vary, although most will arrange any service survivors desire. No religion bars its members from using any funeral home; the choice is merely local custom. Nonsectarian homes hold funerals for anyone. In the United States, those that cater to specific religious groups are usually classified as Christian or Jewish. African-American, Chinese-American and other ethnic communities also often use only specific funeral homes for their funerary rites. While repeated use of one funeral home by one group or faith allows the funeral home's personnel to become familiar with their rituals, funeral costs are usually higher due to the lack of competition.

Funeral homes also differ greatly by price. Funerals are one of life's most expensive functions (along with the cost of homes, cars, and weddings), so a funeral home should be selected with care. If preparations are made in advance, it is possible to join one of the more than 150 local non-profit memorial societies in the United States or in many Western countries. Memberships cost between $15 and $25 per year. The society directs members to local funeral homes or crematoria that will provide relatively inexpensive funerals, burials, and cremations. Contact the Continental Association of Funeral and Memorial Societies, (800) 458-5563, for more information.

What costs are involved in body disposition?

Funerary costs can be very expensive, especially after sudden, unexpected deaths. In this situation, survivors tend to over-spend because of their grief, dismay, guilt, and delegation of decisions to others. While most funeral directors charge a set professional fee, the other services are itemized and billed separately. Survivors may choose from (and pay for) a menu of available services.

Survivors normally pay for funerary costs through personal savings, or with the proceeds from burial or life insurance. There are six types of expenses included in the typical funeral and burial, some of which also apply to cremations.

1. Professional and staff fees for funeral directors.
2. The use of funeral home facilities and equipment.
3. Caskets and vaults (usually the most expensive items)

4. Expenses paid either through the funeral director or separately, such as minister fees, flowers, obituaries, limousines, burial clothing, and special transportation of the body.
5. Cemetery costs: grave and interment (opening and closing grave) or cremation charge, urn, and any formal disposition site, such as a columbarium niche.
6. Memorial monument or marker for a grave or niche.

The typical open-casket funeral in the United States now costs more than $5,500, and does not include burial costs such as those for opening and closing the grave; a cemetery plot, crypt or mausoleum; and monuments or markers.[49] These can add many thousands of dollars more, with the total often exceeding $10,000. Less-expensive alternatives include direct burial with or without a graveside service, funerary rites purchased through a non-profit memorial society (this must be pre-planned), and direct cremation. These may cost $2,000 or less.

Cremation and related services, if arranged at the time of death, generally cost $1,000 to $2,000 through a funeral home. If the person was a member of a memorial society having arrangements for direct cremation, the cost can be reduced substantially. Costs will also be much less if a cremation container, rather than a formal casket, is used.

Direct burial and cremation does not include a funeral. But both give survivors the flexibility of holding memorial services (funerals without the body and, often, without the strict formality) anywhere, in any manner, and at any time they choose.

The survivors of people who donate their whole body to science rarely have any expenses involved with disposition, except when they must pay to have the body transported to the medical school. After use, the medical schools pay to cremate the bodies.

The U.S. Federal Trade Commission (FTC) enacted its Funeral Rule in 1984 to protect consumers. Recently, because "funeral home compliance with the Rule was low" (only about 36% of funeral homes complied), it was strengthened and the FTC, in conjunction with state attorneys general, began enforcing it with proactive monitoring and fines.[50] The FTC now believes between 60 and 80% of funeral homes are complying with this consumer-oriented Rule.[51] Consumers should be aware of their rights under the Rule. Suggestions about the best way to shop for and purchase funerary services, and things to remember are listed below.

- Purchase services in advance, preferably from a non-profit memorial society. This avoids having to purchase them under duress. But find out . . .
    - * Where the money is kept?—some sites may not be as secure as others. (The rules are different in each state.)
    - * What happens to the interest earned on the money?
    - * Exactly what services are included in the package? What other services (at additional cost) will be needed?
    - * What happens if the firm goes bankrupt?
    - * Can the contract be canceled and the money returned?

* What happens if death occurs far away from the place where the contract was purchased?

- Shop for the services needed by telephone, rather than in person. Always ask for their "General Price List," containing all the services obtainable and their prices. Funeral facilities are required to have this available and to give complete and accurate prices to prospective purchasers. (But you must *ask* for it.)
- Funeral homes must get explicit permission before embalming a body, unless state law requires it in a particular circumstance. They are not permitted to state that the law requires embalming unless that is true (as it is in very limited circumstances). For example, it is not required when:
  * Direct cremation is desired.
  * Immediate (direct) burial is desired.
  * Refrigeration is available and a closed-casket funeral is desired.
- If funeral homes embalm bodies without getting prior approval, they cannot charge for the service (unless they could not contact survivors and did not have refrigeration available). This is in a written statement they must give consumers.
- Funeral homes are not permitted to state that funeral goods or services, such as embalming and caskets of any type, will delay the body's natural decomposition for the long term—since they won't.
- Funeral homes may not require the purchase of a casket if there is to be a direct cremation. They must offer an "alternative container" (an inexpensive non-metal receptacle often made of fiberboard, pressed wood, or composition materials, which most crematoria usually use for cremations).
- Funeral homes may not charge a "handling fee" if survivors choose to purchase a casket from someplace other than the funeral home. (There are many discount caskets available quickly from Internet and other vendors.)
- Funeral homes may not state that the law or a cemetery requires outer burial containers or vaults, if that is untrue. This must be written on the price list containing such items.

Once funerary services have been selected, check the itemized list to be sure that everything is included, that there are no extra items, that the prices are correct, and, if they say particular items are required by law, that the law is cited on the statement.[52, 53]

What will a funeral director do for us?

Among the services that funeral directors provide, at the survivors' behest, are to

- Coordinate and, sometimes, conduct funeral service.
- Assist the clergy who run the service.
- Supervise embalmers.
- Instruct and assist the pallbearers.

- Arrange transportation for the body from the morgue or place of death to the funeral parlor.
- Sell caskets, urns, burial clothes, or restoration services.
- Coordinate sales of cemetery plots, markers, and columbarium niches, as well as arranging for special disposition of cremains (such as scattering the ashes at sea).
- Provide death notification cards.
- Arrange transportation for the family, and orchestrate transportation for both the family and the body to the cemetery or crematorium.
- Help lodge members run separate funeral services.
- Seat mourners.
- Provide music.
- Maintain guest registers.
- Place death notices in newspapers.
- Offer bereavement counseling and follow-up.

These services are all costly, and most are itemized on the general price lists provided by the funeral director. A few are included as part of the "non-declinable" professional fee. The others are additional costs. Ask what is covered by the funeral home's basic fee and then decide whether anything additional is desired.

How can we transport the body to or from another city, state, or country?

With our highly mobile society, questions about transporting bodies "home" for funerary rites have become increasingly common. Most funeral directors are familiar with the procedures necessary to transport bodies within the United States. However, only funeral homes in larger or border cities have experience with international body transportation.

Bodies are usually shipped using a common carrier (airlines, trucking companies, and railroads) and each has their own shipping requirements. Most bodies transported any distance within the United States, and nearly all bodies transported internationally, go as cargo in commercial airliners. Funeral homes usually help make air travel arrangements, both for the body and for anyone who will accompany the remains. If notified, many airlines provide special waiting areas and preboarding for those accompanying a body. Some airlines provide the (live) passengers with discounted rates off their full-fare, last minute ticket prices. (This ticket price is generally far above what most fliers pay.).

Amtrak also transports human remains, providing station-to-station shipment. The railroad accepts human remains in caskets enclosed in carrying cases with handles; reused airtrays (the disposable standard packaging for bodies transported in commercial airliners) suffice. No special rates are available for those accompanying the body. Some bodies also travel by private vehicle.

Each state has its own rules about transporting corpses. However, embalming is not usually required unless the person died from a specific contagious disease, the transport time will be inordinately long (more than 18 to 72 hours after death, depending on the state laws), the body has decomposed, or it has been disinterred. Many states and carriers also require a permit to move a body. These are usually obtained from funeral homes or the local boards of health.

There is no problem with airline passengers transporting cremains (cremated remains) as carry-ons. A large number of cremains also travel via the postal service. Care must be taken that the box they are shipped in is not simply the container the cremains come in from the crematorium—they tend to leak. When funeral directors ship cremains, they normally place them within sturdy, pressure-resistant containers, which are tightly sealed and sent via a service that can track the packages. A signature upon receipt is usually required.

United States regulations for returning bodies from another country are relatively straightforward. In fact, the most difficult part of getting corpses back to the United States is meeting the local requirements in the country of death. Many foreign governments have elaborate requirements for shipping bodies out of their country. Over 300 steps, involving 100 or more contacts in two or more countries, may be required to ship a corpse back to the United States.[54] It is often best to let a funeral director in the receiving country who has experience in international shipments help make these arrangements.

The U.S. State Department estimates that it normally takes from ten to fifteen days following death for a body to be returned from western European countries and considerably longer from other parts of the world.[55] Transportation time from primitive areas may be very long, since containers in which to transport the body may have to be custom-made. If a person dies under suspicious circumstances, especially if the death is the subject of a court case, they may not release the body until the judicial process is complete. This could take months or years.

Even when bodies are returned to the United States relatively quickly, they will probably not arrive soon enough (before decomposition begins) to hold an open-casket funeral. American-style professional embalming rarely exists outside of Britain, former British colonies, former American protectorates, parts of Mexico, and southern France. By the time most bodies return to the United States, no embalmer may be able to restore them to a viewable condition. Returning ashes to the United States is very simple. It requires all of the following:

- A marker on the container stating that it holds cremated remains.
- A copy of the official death certificate.
- A cremation certificate.
- A certificate from the crematorium stating that the container holds only the cremated remains of the decedent.
- A permit to export the remains (if required by the country where the shipment originates).

For assistance or information from the U.S. State Department, families or funeral directors can call the Department of State Citizens Emergency Center. On Monday through Friday, 8:15 A.M. to 10 P.M. or Saturday 9 A.M. to 3 P.M. eastern time, call (202) 647-5225. At other times and on holidays, call (202) 634-3600 and ask for the overseas-citizens-services duty officer.

What is a death certificate? When can I get a copy?

A death certificate is the official document declaring a person dead. Death certificates serve two societal purposes: they prevent murder cover-ups and they provide public health statistics. In the United States, Britain, and most industrialized countries, physicians must now sign a death certificate listing the presumed *cause of death* (such as "automobile crash," or "gunshot wound") and the *manner of death* (such as "natural causes," "homicide," "accident," or "suicide").[56] Other significant conditions that do not directly contribute to death, such as chronic lung disease, diabetes, or heart disease are often listed separately. Many survivors do not understand the information on the death certificate.[57]

If the attending physician does not sign the death certificate, the coroner or medical examiner's office does an investigation and, if indicated, a forensic pathologist will perform an autopsy to decide the cause of death and to identify which deaths need police investigations.

Survivors need a death certificate to obtain a burial permit, make life insurance claims, settle the estate, get permission for family leave, obtain airline "bereavement" fares, and receive death benefits.[58] In the United States, there are three types of death certificates:

1. A standard death certificate.
2. Death certificates for fetal or stillborn deaths.
3. Medicolegal death certificates.

After the physician has completed the death certificate (with or without basing it on autopsy findings), it passes to the funeral director, local and state government offices, and finally, in the United States, to the Center for Health Statistics.

Funeral directors often struggle to obtain a physician's signature on a death certificate. In an age of managed care groups and multispecialty clinics, their problem is not only to snag the busy practitioner for his or her signature, but also to identify the correct physician to sign. Survivors cannot bury or otherwise dispose of a corpse until a licensed physician signs a permanent death certificate or a medical examiner signs a temporary death certificate. (Temporary certificates, which list the cause of death as "pending," are issued when further laboratory tests are needed to help determine the actual cause of death.) Except in unusual cases, disposition of the remains need not wait for the final autopsy reports, which may take weeks to complete.[59]

After the death certificate has been signed, local authorities usually issue a Certificate of Disposition of Remains, also known as a burial or cremation permit. Crematories and cemeteries require this form before they will cremate or bury a body. In some locales the form is combined with a transportation permit that allows survivors to move or ship the body.

American clinicians seem to think that accurately completing death certificates is not important.[60] Up to 29% of United States death certificates err both as to the cause of death and the decedent's age.[61 - 64] About the same number incorrectly state whether an autopsy was done.[65] Less significant discrepancies occur in listing the decedent's marital status, race, and place of birth. Death certificates of minority groups have the most errors.[66]

Many certificates are meaningless simply because physicians complete them without knowing the real cause of death. For example, listing "cardiopulmonary arrest" means nothing; everyone's heart and lungs eventually stop, the important point is *why?* An autopsy is often needed to determine this. Other certificates are obscured to protect families' reputations or incomes, with listings such as "pneumonia" for AIDS deaths or "accidental" for suicides. Disguising deaths from alcoholism, AIDS, and other stigmatizing causes on these certificates is widespread.[67 - 69] This practice appears to be exacerbated where medical examiners' autopsy reports are part of the public record.[70] For this reason, some states may eliminate the cause of death from publicly recorded death certificates.[71]

Death certificates and other standard legal papers surrounding a death normally cost between $1 and $5 each. Additional official copies cost the same amount. Funeral directors usually obtain these forms and include the cost on their bill. When a body must be shipped to a non-English-speaking country, the forms must often be translated (for an additional fee).

How does the decedent's name get in the newspaper?

Funeral homes place "death notices" (actually a form of advertising) when they handle a death. While some papers print death notices for free, most charge for mentioning the funeral home. Some newspapers, probably to avoid practical jokers, refuse to take death notices from anyone other than funeral directors. If a body is donated to a medical school, however, the family must arrange the death notice. The medical school's mortician can assist them in doing this.

Common mistakes funeral directors make when placing death notices include submitting inaccurate information, missing newspaper deadlines, failing to inform relatives that a notice has been placed, misspelling names, and omitting or giving incorrect information regarding visitations, flowers, or donations. It pays to double-check the funeral home's information before the notices are placed.

Unlike a death notice, an obituary is a news item about a notable person, informing the community that he or she has died. The newspaper's staff writes obituaries. If there is widespread interest about the person, the obituary may placed on the national or international news wires. Newspapers generally print obituaries for people who lived or were known within their circulation area or who were of nationally known or influential.

Unless a person is a major celebrity or the manner of death itself is noteworthy, obituaries rarely describe much about the circumstances of the death. In the past, phrases such as "died after a long illness" connoted cancer and "sudden death" meant heart attack. Today, the combination of a young age and the words "lingering" or "protracted illness" often means AIDS. Unless the circumstances are unmistakably clear, the word suicide is avoided. Instead, either nothing is said about the mechanism of death, or it may simply be labeled "an accident."

How can I get more help?

Survivors don't usually ask about how they can get additional help, even if they obviously need it. They may, however, ask for help for their children, spouse, friends, or relatives. Notifiers who are aware of community resources greatly facilitate survivors' grieving and healing by advising them of available appropriate grief support groups. Referral to an appropriate group is important, because experience shows that if survivors go to groups to which they cannot relate, they will quickly cease to attend.

Typical grief support groups may include those for adults (general), senior citizens, suicide survivors, homicide survivors, parents, young people (usually teenagers), children (often divided into ages 5 to 8 and 9 to 12), SIDS parents, and fetal or neonatal death survivors. Many resources and some grief "chat rooms" are now on the Internet. Chapter 11 lists some national support groups.

References

1. Schmidt TA, Harrahill MA: Family response to out-of-hospital death. *Acad Emerg Med.* 1995 Jun;2(6):513-8.
2. Iserson KV: Foregoing prehospital care: should ambulance staff always resuscitate? *J Med Ethics.* 1991 Mar;17(1):19-24.
3. Iserson KV: A simplified prehospital advance directive law: Arizona's approach. *Ann Emerg Med.* 1993 Nov;22(11):1703-10.
4. Iserson KV: If we don't learn from history . . . : ethical failings in a new prehospital directive. *Am J Emerg Med.* 1995 Mar;13(2):241-2.
5. Keim S: Personal communication with author, January 1999.
6. Eckert WG: Timing of death and injuries. *Medico-legal Insights* (from *Inform Letter*), 1991 Fall.
7. Bab. *Talmud*, tractate Chullin 21A: Mishna Oholoth 1: 6.
8. Cooper DK, De Villiers JC, Smith LS, et al.: Medical, legal and administrative aspects of cadaveric organ donation in the RSA. *S Afr Med J.* 1982 Dec 11;62(25):933-8.
9. Sass HM: Criteria for death: self-determination and public policy. *J Med Philos.* 1992 Aug;17(4):445-54.
10. Sass HM: Ethical arguments for accepting death by brain criteria criteria. In: Land W, ed.: *Organ Replacement Therapy: Ethics, Justice, Commerce: First Joint Meeting of ESOT and EDTA/ERA, Munich, December 1990.* Berlin: Springer Verlag, 1991, pp. 249-58.
11. Prichard JG, Bale RM, Abou-Samra M, et al.: Severe cerebral injury and brain death: management of the patient's family. *J Fam Pract.* 1985 Nov;21(5):341-8.
12. Perl M, Shelp EE: Sounding board. psychiatric consultation masking moral dilemmas in medicine. *N Engl J Med.* 1982 Sep 2;307(10):618-21.

13. Schultz CA: Sudden death crisis: prehospital and in the emergency department. *J Emerg Nurs*. 1980 May-Jun;6(3):46-50.

14. Associated Press: Religious burials for fetuses bring ACLU opposition. *Arizona Daily Star*. Tucson, AZ, 1998 Oct 10; Sect. A:14.

15. Carlson L: *Caring for Your Own Dead*. Hinesburg, VT: Upper Access, 1987, p. 52.

16. Kalkofen RW: After a child dies: a funeral director's perspective. *Issues Compr Pediatr Nurs*. 1989 Jul-Aug;12(4):285-97.

17. Associated Press: Medical center opens burial site for parents with failed pregnancies. *Observer-Reporter*. Washington, PA, 1998 Oct 29.

18. Schmidt S: Consent for autopsies. *JAMA*. 1983 Sep 2;250(9):1161-4.

19. Dept. of Pathology, Univ. Medical Center, Tucson, AZ: *Post Mortem Examination*. August 1990.

20. Univ. of Arizona Dept. of Pathology: *Autopsy procedures–how to do an autopsy: the twenty steps. Tucson, AZ,* 1992.

21. *CAP Today*, August 1988, p. 25, from: rules of the National Laboratory Accreditation Program.

22. *Ariz Rev Stat Ann* §36-382; *Hawaii Rev Stat* §453-165; *Md Ann Code* art 5, §501; *Mich Stat Ann* §14.45(2855); *Miss Code Ann* §41-37-25.

23. Ludwig J: *Current Methods of Autopsy Practice*. Philadelphia: Saunders, 1972, p. 299.

24. Schmidt S: "Consent for autopsies."

25. Tolle SW, Bascom PB, Hickam DH, et al.: Communication between physicians and surviving spouses following patient deaths. *J Gen Intern Med*. 1986 Sep-Oct;1(5):309-14.

26. Hill RB, Anderson RE: *The Autopsy: Medical Practice and Public Policy*. Boston: Butterworths, 1988, p. 15.

27. *Kan. State Ann.* §65-2438.

28. Daniel TP: *An Analysis of the Funeral Rule Using Consumer Survey Data on the Purchase of Funeral Goods and Services: Federal Trade Commission Bureau of Economics staff report*. Washington, DC: Federal Trade Commission, 1989, p. 6.

29. U.S. Federal Trade Commission: *Funerals: A Consumer Guide*. Washington, DC: Bureau of Consumer Protection, November 1996.

30. Evans RW, Orians CE, Ascher NL: The potential supply of organ donors. an assessment of the efficiency of organ procurement efforts in the United States. *JAMA*. 1992 Jan 8;267(2):239-46.

31. Olsen JC, Buenefe ML, Falco WD: Death in the emergency department. *Ann Emerg Med*. 1998 Jun;31(6):758-65.

32. Annas GJ: *The Rights of Patients: The Basic ACLU Guide to Patient Rights*, 2nd ed. Carbondale, IL: Southern Illinois Univ. Press, 1989, p. 232.

33. Mathieu D: *Organ Substitution Technology: Ethical, Legal, and Public Policy Issues*. Boulder, CO: Westview Press, 1988, p. 37.

34. UNOS: *Protocols*. June 1991.

35. Green J: Death with dignity: Baha'i Faith. *Nurs Times.* 1989 Mar 8-14;85(10):50-1.
36. Green J: Death with dignity: Sikhism. *Nurs Times.* 1989 Feb 15-21;85(7):56-7.
37. Sugunasiri SH: The Buddhist view concerning the dead body. *Transplant Proc.* 1990 Jun;22(3):947-949.
38. Green J: Death with dignity: Judaism. *Nurs Times.* 1989 Feb 22-28;85(8):64-5.
39. UNOS: *Protocols.* June 1991.
40. Anon: Brain death (editorial). *Br Med J.* 1975 Feb 15;1(5954):356.
41. Iserson KV: Organ procurement in the acute setting. In: Mathieu D: "*Organ Substitution Technology: Ethical, Legal, and Public Policy Issues.*" pp. 52-58.
42. Jones SP: Personal communication with author, January 1999.
43. *Ibid.*
44. Skolnick AA: Tissue bank expands facilities, efforts (news). *JAMA.* 1991 Sep 11; 266(10):1329-31.
45. *Ibid.*
46. Jones SP: Personal communication with author, January 1999.
47. Crescenzo D, et al.: Human cryopreserved valve conduits: a quantitative analysis of injury associated with variable warm ischemic time, antibiotic disinfection, and cryopreservation using transmission electron microscopy. 28th Annual Meeting, Soc Thoracic Surg. Orlando, FL: February 3-5, 1992.
48. NSM Resources: *A Helpful Guide to Funeral Planning* (pamphlet). Evanston, IL: National Selected Morticians, 1987, p. 10.
49. National Funeral Directors of America: *Funeral Price Information from the NFDA 1997 General Price List Survey.* NFDA Online (http://www.nfda.org/resources/funeralprice.html).
50. U.S. Federal Trade Commission: *Nationwide Crackdown on Funeral Homes that Fail to Provide Required Consumer Information Launched by FTC with State Attorneys General.* FTC press release: July 6, 1995.
51. U.S. Federal Trade Commission: *FTC Announces Results of the First Year of the Funeral Rule Offenders Program.* FTC press release: January 22, 1997 .
52. U.S. Federal Trade Commission: *Consumer Access to Price Information about Funerals to Get Major Boost Under New FTC/Industry Program.* FTC press release: January 19, 1996.
53. Funeral Industry Practices: *Trade Regulation Rule,* 16 C.F.R. Part 453 (1996).
54. Forgey WW: *Travelers' Medical Resource: A Guide to Health & Safety Worldwide.* Merrillville, IN: ICS Books, 1990, p. 26.
55. *Ibid.*
56. Randall B: *Death Investigation: The Basics.* Tucson, AZ: Galen Press, Ltd., 1997, pp. 96-113.
57. Watson E: An epidemiological and sociological study of unexpected death in infancy in nine areas of southern England. III. Bereavement. *Med Sci Law.* 1981 Apr;21(2):99-104.
58. Ludwig J: "*Current Methods of Autopsy Practice.*" p. 265.

59. Grollman EA, ed.: *Concerning Death: A Practical Guide for the Living*. Boston: Beacon Press, 1974, p. 182.

60. Hanzlick R: Improving accuracy of death certificates (letter). *JAMA.* 1993;269:22:2850.

61. American Medical Association Council on Ethical and Judicial Affairs: Opinions on confidentiality, advertising and communications media relations, 5.057: confidentiality of HIV status on autopsy reports. *Code of Medical Ethics: Current Opinions with Annotations*. Chicago: American Medical Association, 1994.

62. Kircher T, Nelson J, Burdo H: The autopsy as a measure of accuracy of the death certificate. *N Engl J Med*. 1985 Nov;313(20):1263-9.

63. Kircher T, Anderson RE: Cause of death: proper completion of the death certificate. *JAMA*. 1987;258:349-52.

64. Hunt LW, Silverstein MD, Reed CE, et al.: Accuracy of the death certificate in a population-based study of asthmatic patients. *JAMA*. 1993;269:15:1947-52.

65. Hanzlick R: "Improving accuracy of death certificates (letter)."

66. Wallace RB, Woolson RF: *The Epidemiologic Study of the Elderly*. New York: Oxford Univ. Press, 1992, pp. 263-4.

67. Maxwell JD: Accuracy of death certification for alcoholic liver disease. *Br J Addict*. 1986 Apr;81(2):168-9.

68. National Center for Health Statistics: Data line. *Pub Health Rep*. 1990;105:209-10.

69. King MD: AIDS on the death certificate: the final stigma. *Br Med J*. 1989;298:734-6.

70. American Medical Association Council on Ethical and Judicial Affairs: "Opinions on confidentiality, advertising and communications media relations, 5.057."

71. Proposed rule would remove cause of death from death certificates. *Forum*. 1992;58:6:11

28: Dealing With The Media

The media justifiably have been taken to task for distributing victims' names before their immediate relatives can be notified. Putting information "on the air" is often much easier and faster than is locating and informing survivors. The public seems to agree, with 73% in one poll feeling that news organizations invade people's privacy.[1] One example is how the media responded when terrorists bombed Pan Am Flight 103.

Pan Am Flight 103: The Media Response

After Pan Am Flight 103 exploded over Lockerbie, Scotland, in December 1988, the media responded on all fronts, accosting townspeople in Lockerbie, victims' families waiting at the Kennedy (New York) and Metropolitan (Detroit) Airports, and students at Syracuse University who lost many classmates. Members of the press also began calling families, friends, and possible acquaintances of those on board—often delivering the news of the death before anyone else had notified these survivors. The subsequent investigation of the media's involvement by two journalism professors at Syracuse University, Joan Deppa and Nancy Weatherly Sharp, provides one of the clearest pictures of the media's activity after such tragedies and how they put people who are suddenly distraught after a sudden loss into the media spotlight.[2]

At Kennedy Airport, photographers took pictures of a woman who collapsed to the floor screaming, "My baby! My baby!" The next day this woman would see herself in this position in a full-page picture in the *New York Daily News.* The authors also described these incidents:

- Photographers, television crews, and reporters focusing on crying Syracuse students at an all-faiths chapel service a few hours after the crash.
- A young student passing out after a reporter called her apartment to tell her that her friend had died in the crash.

- Reporters barging into homes uninvited and disparaging the families.
- Reporters physically restraining waiting families at JFK airport to ask them questions—and injuring some in the process.
- Repeatedly asking survivors, "How do you feel?" (The journalism professors say that this offends not only survivors, but also the media's audience, and should be relegated to the pile of journalistic relics.)

Lockerbie residents found ways to protect some helpless survivors. For example, when a reporter interviewed a group of teenagers, he was never told that a boy who had lost his parents and sister in the crash was sitting near him in the room. In another case, a Syracuse student shielded her best friend's mother by fielding all reporters' questions.

Eventually, after the sudden impact of the death passed, some families began to see reporters as valuable sources of information. One family who couldn't find out information about the crash from the airline, for example, was surprised when a reporter, whose questions they had answered, quickly got them what they wanted. Many survivors began to set rules to follow if reporters wanted to speak with them. They soon distinguished between those journalists who acted appropriately and those who didn't. Some eventually came to believe (in hindsight) that massive media attention was beneficial because it showed the world the extent of the tragedy and loss.

Similarly, after the Mount St. Helen's eruption, those who lost loved ones felt that the media's invasion of their privacy, inaccuracies in news reporting, and the extensive media attention prolonged their grieving.[3]

Planning for Media Interactions

The best way to deal with the media after sudden, unexpected deaths is to have a plan. While this is obviously impractical for the average individual suddenly thrust into the media spotlight, institutions such as hospitals, EMS agencies, police departments, schools, and public transportation agencies should develop plans for dealing with the media and practice implementing them. A few suggestions are listed below (some are taken from media sources).[4, 5]

Know that the media will usually ask:

- What happened?
- Where did it happen? Can we see where it happened?
- Were there other injuries?
- Was anyone else involved or hurt?
- Do you know why this happened?
- What did you do/are you doing to prevent this?
- Is anyone else in danger?

When interacting with the media:

- Use one trained "designated spokesperson" whenever possible.
- Plan a "message" before meeting reporters, and be certain that it is delivered.

- Don't answer the "Have you stopped beating your dog?" questions. (These are the no-win questions common to some sensationalistic elements of the press.)
- Watch your body language. Be comfortable, but not too relaxed. You don't want to give the impression that you don't care.
- Pay close attention to the questions and listen for feedback from the reporters.
- Remember your message.
- Don't "over-gesture," since the camera exaggerates these movements.
- If seated, don't swivel in the chair. Sit on only the front half of the chair, so your body position suggests interest and attention to the reporters.
- Use props as appropriate. They may better explain the situation and they give you something to do with your hands.

Candor is often the best tactic (but don't prematurely release the victims' names), since reporters can sense deceit and usually uncover the information anyway. If there is a reason that information cannot be released at that time, say so and give the reason. Use "no comment" only when:

- You aren't qualified to answer a question. (Don't speculate or make up answers.)
- You haven't had time to consider what your answer might mean to the public.
- You are angry or the question is inflammatory.

In cases of acute, unexpected deaths, some local media observe a four-hour period in which they do not release the decedent's name. This generally gives the hospitals, police, chaplains, or social services time to notify survivors. Unless all media sources observe this regional policy, don't rely on it. If the national media becomes involved, they won't stick to this type of agreement.

In some regions, officials have reversed their relationship with the media. If they do not know the decedent's identity, the officials may release information about a non-routine death to the media. They then hope that relatives who suspect that their loved one is the decedent will call and make an identification.[6]

References

1. Times Mirror Corp. Poll, 1988. Cited in: Deppa J, Sharp NW: Under international scrutiny: reaction of media targets. *Am Behavioral Sci.* 1991;35(2):150-65.
2. Deppa J, Sharp NW: "Under international scrutiny: reaction of media targets."
3. Murphy S: After Mount St. Helen's: disaster stress research. *J Psychosocial Nurs Ment Health Serv.* 1984;22(7):9-19.
4. Bremer R: Don't tense up. *Public Relations J.* 1976;29:27.
5. Detwiler RM: Crisis management and the Pearl Harbor syndrome. *Public Relations J.* 1979;32:26-31.
6. Charmaz KC: The coroner's strategies for announcing death. *Urban Life.* 1975;4(3):296-316.

29: Learning More/Educating Others

Clinicians who deal with sudden death on a daily basis must pass their knowledge of how to care for survivors on to the next generation. As Dr. Morris Kerstein aptly notes:

> Rushing off to save those who are alive and need help does not mean rushing past the grieving family. It is interesting how much less attention is given to the dying patient's family when actually more is needed. Death must not be a failure for the physician and care does not terminate with the patient . . . The physician dealing with death is then the one who can and must share his experiences with interns, residents, and young practicing physicians. It is right that psychiatrists and clergy guide in medical school, but education is a cooperative effort. It is also interesting that psychiatrists seem to be the most involved, yet, truly have the least experience. The clinician, be he internist or surgeon, sees death; it is he who must lead. He must be the teacher.[1]

The Problem

The Need to Learn

Professionals whose job includes delivering news about sudden unexpected deaths need to learn how to perform this task before doing it. As one grieving mother said after a bad experience with a pediatrician informing her about her child's death, "I think these doctors need the education, even if they have to go back to school."[2] Researchers echo this, saying, "Young pediatricians and obstetricians particularly may find it difficult to relate humanely to death and dying, not because they have no feelings or suffer no grief but because their training and personal attitudes do not permit them to deal effectively with death on the personal level. At times they do not really know what to do when the event occurs; therefore, they do nothing."[3]

Many medical students, not surprisingly, often try to "hide behind the facts" rather than deliver understandable and sympathetic information to the bereaved. While most do well, a few students resort to delivering bad news with "brutal frankness," a tendency (which can be discouraged through education) that only demonstrates these individuals' fear of death.[4] The results of a survey (table 29-1) of medical students and internal medicine residents about their fears, learning needs, and the best methods for learning about how to deliver bad news to patients can easily be adapted to notifying survivors about sudden unexpected deaths. Indeed, that was the one thing overwhelmingly cited as being thought of as "bad news."

Table 29-1 is by no means a complete list. Additional worries relate to health care providers' personal fears regarding mortality, their unresolved issues about grief and bereavement in their own lives, and the cumulative grief they have experienced as a result of numerous and continuous patient deaths. Providers must learn to acknowledge and process these personal fears, reflect on their own past experiences, and acknowledge and process their professionally acquired grief. To do this, introspective exercises combined with team debriefings often help. Some of these fears may be lessened by institution-wide rituals or services commemorating the dead (as often happens after disasters or at the end of anatomy classes at many medical schools).

This deficiency is not confined to any one medical specialty or to physicians alone. For example, one study of emergency department directors showed that most felt that the major part of improving the process was to train physicians.[5] Nurses also lack relevant education about sudden death and how to interact with survivors.[6,7] They are inadequately prepared for this stressful role and learn how to do it through repeated exposures, often without the benefit of any subsequent feedback.[8] The same holds true for chaplains, police, EMS personnel, social workers, and others who must notify survivors about sudden unexpected deaths.

The Absence of Learning

Even while death and dying education has proliferated over the last decade, few courses teach professionals how to deliver the news to survivors about sudden unexpected deaths.[9] As an experienced clinician-educator wrote, "Even though various health professionals encounter death on a regular basis, they are rarely trained to handle either the delivery of the news of death or the reactions of those receiving it."[10]

Since death notification is rarely included in the medical curriculum, some may feel that it "is not a 'proper' subject, and the feeling of venturing out beyond the pale of standard medical practice into an uncharted and unfamiliar area adds to the insecurity and anxiety."[11] This anxiety can only be diminished through education followed by experience.

Table 29-1: Notifying Survivors: Fears, Learning Needs, and Methods to Learn

Fears

- Survivor's reaction to news.
- Notifier reaction to news. (S)
- Survivor's reaction to the notifier. (S)
- Notifier reaction to survivor. (S)
- Communication issues. (S)
- Knowledge issues.

Learning Needs

- How to be sensitive.*
- Appropriate use of words and language.
- How to deal with survivor reactions.
- How to minimize harm and pain.
- How to read or predict survivor reactions.
- How to be clear and informative.
- How to approach the topic.
- Appropriate emotion to convey.
- How to help and support survivor.
- How to be direct.

Best Methods to Learn

- Observation.
- Hands-on experience in real situations.
- Practice in simulated situations.
- Discussion. (S)
- Classes, readings, case studies, own life experiences (as a survivor).**

(S) = Primarily a student concern.
* = The primary answer in this category. All others represent about 10% of respondents.
** = These were secondary responses mentioned by at least 10% of respondents.

Modified from: Makoul G: Medical student and resident perspectives on delivering bad news. *Acad Med.* 1998;73(10 Suppl.):S35-S37.

Unfortunately, most medical "short courses" dealing with resuscitation, such as Advanced Cardiac Life Support (ACLS), Advanced Trauma Life Support (ATLS), and Pediatric Advanced Life Support (PALS), have not incorporated death notification into their training programs or manuals. (It almost seems by implication that they think their resuscitation methods will always succeed!) Some educators, though, have unofficially inserted sudden-death notification into these courses.[12]

Most EMS personnel receive formal training in death and dying. This often does not include information on death notification, which nearly all EMS personnel believe they need. Training received at hospital-based conferences seems to be the most effective method for reducing the emotional difficulties that EMS personnel have with death notification.[13]

Training for the police, funeral directors, and chaplains may include didactic programs adapted from courses produced by Mothers Against Drunk Driving (M.A.D.D.).[14] Death notifiers in the military seem to be the only ones consistently trained in advance.

Wanting To Learn

Notifying survivors about an unexpected death is very stressful.[15] Therefore, individuals who are, or will be, involved in the process would like to learn it in a non-threatening environment before they have to "fly solo." Methods do exist to educate those who, as a part of their professional duties, will have to notify survivors about sudden, unexpected deaths.

Adult Learners and Uncomfortable Subjects

Adult learners, particularly when faced with uncomfortable subject matter, have certain requirements that educators must recognize. This is especially true for people who may view education about sudden-death notification as a "soft" topic, such as physicians or police. Any successful course on death notification must incorporate the basic principles of adult education. (See table 29-2.)

Developing Confidence

In addition to specific material, any course on death notification needs to convey a sense of confidence that the student will be able to do well when faced with a real notification situation. This confidence is crucial because confident notifiers transmit appropriate non-verbal cues, and, in addition, they are more successful in delivering the news. Robert Guttenberg describes an experiment that demonstrates this and which can be used in class:

> After asking one participant to leave the room, I instruct the other what to do when she comes back. When [the individual] returns, I ask her to hold a pitcher of water three feet above a small glass and pour water into the glass. The first time she tries to pour the water, the others convey their expectations that she'll fail—and comment on the humiliation she'll feel as a result: "That glass is too small." "You'll spill water all over the carpet." Invariably, she fails. Her hand trembling, she spills water all over the carpet. I then ask her to try again. This time, the others encourage her: 'You can do it." "Don't worry about it," they tell her. And, with their encouragement, she pours a steady stream of water into the glass, spilling only a few drops.[16]

The confidence that can be gained both through observation and role-playing lends a measure of authority, composure, and ability to notifiers.

Table 29-2: Principles of Effective Adult Education

- Students' expectations are very high, and if these expectations are not quickly met, they will withdraw from the activity.
- Students each come with different backgrounds and experiences.
- Information and skills must be taught in an obvious sequence.
- Tell students how the training will benefit them. (What's in it for me?)
- Students and instructors should have realistic goals for the course.
- Use stimulating material, but the amount should not overwhelm students.
- Learning should relate to the students' past experiences.
- Instructors should emphasize learning successes and minimize failures. (Make me feel good about myself.)
- It is best when students can set their own pace.
- Adults learn better if there is participation and interaction.
- Always treat them like adults.
- If possible, students should be able to use what they learn soon after the initial instruction (usually in simulations).

Adapted from: Billi JE, Cummins RO: *Advanced Cardiac Life Support: Instructor's Manual.* Dallas, TX: American Heart Association, 1997, pp. 4-5; and Lord JH: *Trauma, Death, and Death Notification: A Seminar for Professional Counselors and Victim Advocates.* Washington, DC: Mothers Against Drunk Driving and the U.S. Dept. of Justice for Victims of Crime, 1996, p. 5.

Sudden-Death Notification: A Course Outline

The following brief outline is included to provide educators with a basic structure for death notification courses.

Course Objectives

At the end of the course, participants will be able to:

- Use in-person death-notification protocols specific for their professional, institutional, or personal situation.
- Use age-appropriate methods for relaying the news of unexpected deaths to children.
- Use a telephone-notification protocol to request that survivors come to the hospital and to tell them about the death.
- Use facilitative listening when speaking with survivors.

- List at least five helpful phrases to use when speaking with survivors.
- Describe the systems for obtaining autopsy and organ/tissue donations in their area and the cases that come under the medical examiner's/coroner's auspices.
- Describe methods for assisting grieving survivors in the days after a death.

Course Length

The answer to "How much time is needed to introduce the topic of sudden, unexpected death notification?" is to use any time that is provided. While it may not be optimal, some education is always better than none—and in most schools, training programs, and facilities for professionals who must deliver this news, no death-notification education is provided.

An effective method for introducing this topic to a wide range of medical and EMS communities is to add it to existing short courses on resuscitation, such as ACLS, ATLS, and PALS. While this method will not generally allow enough time for in-depth discussions or hands-on practice, it will provide the basic information to the maximum number of health professionals. It also validates the topic and suggests that course participants need to learn more about it.

This material can be presented in a one-day course or broken into sections for several sessions. Some centers, such as the Oregon Health Sciences University, have found that they can successfully teach this material in a 2½-hour session.[17] Many instructors prefer to spread it out, presenting the material during regularly scheduled conferences over weeks or months. The problem with that approach is that a level of trust needs to be built up among the participants in the group for them to be willing to voice their experiences and feelings during simulation sessions. This trust will be lost if participants continually change, as naturally happens with non-concentrated presentations.

Smaller sessions with limited goals have been successfully used at different centers. The keys to one program's success were that it was held during the initial resident orientation, with "protected" time away from clinical activities, and was seen to have practical clinical relevance in an area with high stress and limited prior education.[18]

The other natural option would be to include this instruction in a "death and dying" class. While this seems a natural fit, both students and instructors should realize that there are large differences between death-notification materials and those normally presented in death and dying courses. For one thing, these skills are more similar to crisis counseling than to death and dying education. For another, the focus of attention in death notification is to work with the survivors rather than with the dying patient.

Course Outline

1. Introduction: Importance of notifying survivors correctly.
2. Realistic expectations about what notifiers can accomplish.
3. Using in-person notification protocols.
    a. In hospitals or other health care facilities.
    b. In the home.
    c. At the workplace or school.

4. Using telephone notification protocols.
   a. Local.
   b. Long-distance.
5. Communicating with survivors—overcoming awkwardness.
   a. Verbal, para-verbal, and non-verbal communication skills.
   b. Relaying the bad news.
   c. Expressing sadness and regrets.
   d. Immediate grief reactions.
   e. Interpreting verbal and non-verbal cues.
   f. Helpful communications.
   g. Requesting organ/tissue and autopsy permissions.
6. Frequently asked questions. (See list in chapter 27.)
7. Notifying parents.
   a. Complications surrounding SIDS deaths.
   b. Small and adult children's deaths.
8. Notifying children.
   a. Children's behavior following deaths.
   b. How much should they be told?
   c. Should they participate?
9. Viewing resuscitations and the body.
10. Additional roles for nurses, chaplains, social workers, and others.
    a. Chaperoning survivors (during and after resuscitation attempts).
    b. "Hanging crepe" during resuscitation attempts.
    c. Assisting with immediate social concerns.
    d. Following up with survivors.
11. Additional topics. (Depending upon the audience and the time available.)
    a. The tension between maintaining our necessary personal defenses (not showing too much emotion, "maintaining professionalism") and empathizing with survivors.
    b. Delayed grief reactions.
    c. Follow-up methods. Realistic expectations about what notifiers can accomplish.
    d. Cultural sensitivity and differences in the notification process.
    e. Differences in notifying adults, children, and groups.
    f. Preparing to make notifications (having important materials and people available when needed).
    g. Using a team approach to working with survivors.
    h. Local and national resources for survivors.

Course Format

The most effective teaching method for adults is a combination of didactic material with visual stimuli, quickly followed by "hands-on" experience.

Advance Readings

Written materials can introduce students to new concepts, deliver practical information in a concise and understandable manner, and reinforce knowledge the student already possesses. Providing advance reading materials allows students to begin the course with a basic level of knowledge (if they read it). Some students learn better using written materials than they do through lectures, discussions, and other less-structured activities.

Aside from the basic protocols, one subject that is excellent to introduce through written materials is methods of communicating with survivors, including the helpful and non-helpful phrases. These subjects can be reinforced later in lectures, discussions, videos, role-playing, and practical experience.

Advance Exercises

Awareness of the non-verbal signals we send is the easiest way to control this part of the message. A simple home exercise, which takes only a few moments (but many students will become intrigued and spend much longer doing it), is to simply stand before a mirror and test using various positions, expressions, etc. while simply saying, "I'm sorry." Students should note the enormously different messages they send depending on their facial expression, head position, and tone of voice.

Videotapes and Slides

A variety of videotapes on death and dying are available, although few concentrate on actually delivering the news about death to survivors. Short segments from commercial movies and television programs (especially soap operas) show physicians, nurses, chaplains, police, co-workers, military, friends, and relatives delivering news about death. Although they may not demonstrate the most elegant or sensitive death-telling methods, they can stimulate discussions about correct notification methods. Slide sets of the various protocols and other tables found in this book can be purchased from Galen Press, Ltd. See the order blank in the back of the book for information.

Group Sessions

Group sessions are most valuable for giving individuals an awareness of the possibilities and pitfalls surrounding sudden-death notifications, presenting general performance standards, and validating personal feelings about death and grief.

The teaching methods can either be applied to "large" groups (the entire set of attendees) or to "small" groups with two to five people participating (divide the attendees). With some methods, particularly when formulating lists of ideas for discussion, the entire group may help generate the list which smaller groups then discuss—or vice versa. Large group sessions can also be used successfully for imparting general information in didactic sessions and for general performance feedback.

Case Scenarios

The lecture or a modified-lecture format is a cost-effective way to educate large numbers of individuals. Those who have used this method for educating professionals about sudden-death notification usually use case-based interactive lectures. Some also include panel discussions and audience participation.[19] While these methods impart some concepts, their use alone seldom gives learners the emotional investment necessary to incorporate the information into their professional armamentarium.

The Oregon Health Sciences University uses the following three scenarios to teach residents how to compassionately inform families about emergency department deaths.[20]

1. The physician must tell the wife of a 55-year-old man that he died suddenly in the emergency department. The two had come to the ED together because he was experiencing chest pain. He had been in excellent health and had no prior heart disease. While he was away from his wife having tests, he suddenly went into cardiac arrest. Despite appropriate resuscitative measures, he died. She is awaiting his return and does not expect such tragic news.

2. The parents of an 8-year-old child have been notified by the school to go to the emergency department. The physician must tell them that the child died before they got there. She had been struck by a car in a hit-and-run accident on her way home from school and suffered a massive head injury, flail chest, and a femur fracture.

3. The third survivor lives fifty miles away from the hospital and must be contacted by telephone. Her husband left for work feeling ill and subsequently suffered a heart attack. He was brought into the ED in cardiac arrest and could not be resuscitated. The physician does not know how much, if anything, the spouse already knows. The options are to deliver "critical news" or the information about the death, depending on how the spouse responds.

Role-Playing

Role-playing is an educational method that is easily applied to death-notification education. To be most effective, participants should play all roles—survivor, notifier, and onlooker/friend. The scenarios should be representative of typical experiences when the communication is effective, and also when it goes awry.

It is most effective to videotape some of these sessions for immediate review. This allows common errors to be corrected and reinforces people's normal communication skills and empathy. Most importantly, it demonstrates to the trainees that they can perform effectively in these situations.

Simulated Survivors

A significant step up from simply role-playing is to use simulated survivors. Several groups of medical educators have developed programs based on volunteers portraying survivors and interacting with students. In all cases, the "survivors" are trained to simulate actual encounters under varying situations.

One of the earliest of these programs was developed at the Oregon Health Sciences Center for internal medicine and, subsequently, for emergency medicine residents. Using volunteers from a local hospice to play survivors, the program has two goals: (1) helping them focus on meeting survivors' needs rather than simply fulfilling the postmortem requirements (relating the news about death, getting information, having forms signed), and (2) reducing the physicians' sense of emotional isolation and anxiety following patients' deaths.

In this program, after a brief introductory meeting to describe the program, groups of four residents and a facilitator meet for two hours of simulation with a "survivor." The "survivor" bases his or her responses on the case of a patient who died shortly after arrival at the hospital. The "survivor" has information about the family background and medical facts, but has no script and is encouraged to respond spontaneously and be creative. (They may, for example, "leave" to "view the body" with all the accompanying necessary interactions.) The other participants are given information relevant to their role in the case. Facilitators assign roles to the residents, help direct their behavior, answer questions about hospital procedures, and ensure that all residents actively participate. Once the simulation ends, they help provide the residents with "gentle feedback," although the "survivors" provide most of this, relating their own needs, feelings, and real survivors' most likely responses to their actions.[21]

The Children's National Medical Center in Washington, D.C., subsequently developed a program with simulated surviving parents who residents needed to inform about their child's death. The residents' interactions were videotaped to provide the trainees with feedback on both the content of their interactions and on their interpersonal skills in dealing with the survivors.[22]

In many instances, it may often be easier and more educational to have students role-play as survivors. This gives them an opportunity to see what it is like "in the other chair."

Handouts

Handouts can reinforce course themes and give site-specific information to stimulate the students' interest—since they will need to use this very practical material. These handouts can then be distributed to other members of the students' clinical teams. Good handouts for this course include:

- A list of institutional or departmental procedures after a sudden death.
- A list of cases that come under the medical examiner's jurisdiction.
- Copies of the forms used by survivors and notifiers after sudden deaths.
- Regional organ and tissue donation criteria.
- Booklets containing notification protocols. (Available from Galen Press, Ltd.)
- Survivor Information Forms (see tables 6-1 and 6-2).

Individual Sessions

Individual sessions should take the form of counseling students in close proximity to actual notifications. When feasible, they are usually reserved for before, during, and after notifications in which an experienced mentor participates. The "during" sessions occur between their meetings with survivors such as after the initial notification and before returning to give them additional information or make requests. Otherwise, students can discuss the events surrounding notification with mentors soon after notifications. These sessions can even occur via telephone, and can also occur before, during, or immediately after the notification.

Even if the mentor does not participate, a notification that is either audio- or videotaped (the latter being best), can be reviewed for teaching purposes. As with videotapes of resuscitations and other videotapes used for teaching and quality control purposes, these should be erased shortly after use unless all parties agree in writing that the tapes can be used for future teaching.

Evaluating the Students and the Course

There are two elements to course evaluation. The most important is to test the students to see if they have the desired knowledge and abilities at the end of the course. The other is to test whether it was the course itself that imparted this knowledge.

The most effective (and generally most complex) evaluation methods are those which test whether students can successfully apply the course information. So the question after this course is, "Can students now advise survivors about sudden, unexpected deaths in a competent manner?" This can be evaluated in three ways: observation during real notifications, observation during simulated notifications, and written tests.

Observation

For training programs in which the instructors are on-site most, if not all, of the time, experienced observers should accompany students when they deliver the news of a sudden death. This method of evaluation may be limited to emergency medicine residencies and to short periods of time (or under special circumstances) in other training programs, (e.g., for chaplains early in their residencies, surgical deaths in the operating room, other in-hospital deaths when an instructor is present, and EMS programs when the instructor also responds to the call). Direct observation is rarely done, since it usually requires logistical support far outside the range of most training programs. As Tolle and Girard said after investigating the issue,

> Few medical faculty members have observed a house officer pronounce a patient dead and communicate the news to the family. Rarely do faculty encourage medical students to be involved in the process. Yet it is likely that inexperience increases anxiety for the young physician who is left to develop, primarily though personal experience, his or her own practices at the time of the patient's death. Because there is little direction in these matters, the emotional needs of the family are likely to be inadequately met.[23]

One excellent method that can be more easily employed in many clinical settings is to have trainees accompany experienced practitioners when they deliver bad news. There are two dangers when doing this. First, the notification must not appear to be done before an audience, so the number of trainees must be limited. Second, "experienced" practitioners, in different situations and at different times, typically demonstrate both good and bad methods of delivering news to survivors. The key is for the students to observe the good, rather than the bad, methods.

Simulation

A second way to test students is to use simulated survivors. Similar to the simulated patients used in medical training and testing (see "Simulated Survivors" above), this involves one or more "survivors" who react to a preset scenario. As with simulated patients, it helps if these "survivors" have gone through experiences similar to what they are doing for the test. These scenarios can vary to test student's basic and advanced abilities in death notification, to test them in the various circumstances they may encounter (hospital, home, on-scene), and be re-utilized in a standard manner for validation. If CD-ROM interactive programs were available for this, they could be more widely used, avoiding the need to locate and prepare simulated survivors.

Written Tests

The third method, less effective than the other two, but simpler, is to use a written test simulating several types of encounters. Either multiple-choice or fill-in-the-blank questions describing death-notification scenarios can be used, with a pause at critical steps for inquiries about how to proceed. For example, after describing an emergency department death notification and asking a number of test questions at each step, the following question could be asked:

1. The child's mother puts her head in her lap and begins crying uncontrollably. You put your hand on her shoulder, put some tissues in her hand and say:
   a. It was God's will.
   b. Be grateful that you still have your (can have) other children.
   c. Things always work out for the best.
   d. I know just how you feel.
   e. Time heals all wounds.
   f. Nothing. (correct answer)

While a written test can also be used to pre-test students for prior knowledge about death notification, it is inferior to the other methods when testing whether students can adequately function in death-notification situations. Only direct observation gives that information. Pre-testing students and comparing their level of knowledge against their post-course knowledge and ability also provides a rough guide to the course's effectiveness.

Course Evaluations

The typical student evaluation for these types of courses can be useful in telling whether the format and instructors meet the needs of adult learners (perceived relevance and the ability to use the material are most common). It does not show whether the course imparts an ability to use the information.

Continued Learning

Once the course is completed, the most effective way to further develop the principles learned and to reinforce their use is to incorporate discussions about death notification into normal educational activities. At health education sites, this should include discussions during major hospital conferences, such as morbidity and mortality rounds, case conferences, grand rounds on relevant diseases, etc. Even more commonly, this should be discussed on attending, nursing, and ethics rounds. Other professionals should review their death notifications during regular meetings where they report to supervisors, such as during police and EMS shift changes.

References

1. Kerstein MD: Help for the young physician with death and grieving. *Surg Gyn Obstet.* 1973;137:479-80.
2. Fischhoff J, O'Brien N: After the child dies. *J Pediatr.* 1976 Jan;88(1):140-6.
3. Knapp RJ, Peppers LG: Doctor-patient relationships in fetal/infant death encounters. *J Med Educ.* 1979 Oct;54(10):775-80.
4. Hoy AM: Breaking bad news to patients. *Br J Hosp Med.* 1985 Aug;34(2):96-9.
5. Greenberg LW, Ochsenschlager D, Cohen GJ, et al.: Counseling parents of a child dead on arrival: a survey of emergency departments. *Am J Emerg Med.* 1993 May;11(3):225-9.
6. Cooke MW, Cooke HM, Glucksman EE: Management of sudden bereavement in the accident and emergency department. *Br Med J.* 1992 May 9;304(6836):1207-9.
7. Eastham K: Dealing with bereavement in critical care. *Intens Care Nurs.* 1990 Dec;6(4):185-91.
8. Tye C: Qualified nurses' perceptions of the needs of suddenly bereaved family members in the accident and emergency department. *J Adv Nurs.* 1993 Jun;18(6):948-56.
9. American Medical Association: *Medical Education for End-of-Life Care.* Council on Medical Education, Report 4 (I-96), Chicago, IL: AMA.
10. Lasagna L: The doctor and the dying patient. *J Chron Dis.* 1969 Jul;22(2):65-8.
11. Buckman R: Breaking bad news: why is it still so difficult? *Br Med J (Clin Res Ed).* 1984 May 26;288(6430):1597-9.
12. Wolfram RW, Timmel DJ, Doyle CR, et al.: Incorporation of a "Coping with the Death of a Child" module into Pediatric Advanced Life Support (PALS) curriculum. *Acad Emerg Med.* 1998 Mar;5(3):242-6.
13. Norton RL, Bartkus EA, Schmidt TA, et al.: Survey of emergency medical technicians' ability to cope with the deaths of patients during prehospital care. *Prehospital Disaster Med.* 1992 Jul-Sep;7(3):235-42.

14. Lord JH: *Trauma, Death and Death Notification: A Seminar for Professional Counselors and Victim Advocates.* Washington, DC: Mothers Against Drunk Driving and U.S. Dept. of Justice, 1996.

15. Tolle SW, Hickam DH, Larson EB, et al.: Patient death and housestaff stress (abstr). *Clin Res.* 1987;35(3):762A.

16. Guttenberg R: Softening the blow: how to break bad news to a patient's family. *Nurs Life.* 1983 Jul-Aug;3(4):17-21.

17. Schmidt TA, Norton RL, Tolle SW: Sudden death in the ED: educating residents to compassionately inform families. *J Emerg Med.* 1992 Sep-Oct;10(5):643-7.

18. Tolle SW, Cooney TG, Hickam DH: A program to teach residents humanistic skills for notifying survivors of a patient's death. *Acad Med.* 1989 Sep;64(9):505-6.

19. Hart RG, Ahrens WR: Coping with pediatric death in the ED by learning from parental experience. *Am J Emerg Med.* 1998 Jan;16(1):67-8.

20. Schmidt TA, Norton RL, Tolle SW: "Sudden death in the ED."

21. Tolle SW, Cooney TG, Hickam DH: "A program to teach residents humanistic skills."

22. Greenberg LW: Death in the emergency department (letter, comment). *Pediatrics.* 1995 Feb.;95(2):321.

23. Tolle SW, Girard DE: The physician's role in the events surrounding patient death. *Arch Int Med.* 1983 Jul;143(7):1447-9.

Index

— V —

— W —

About the Author

Kenneth V. Iserson, M.D., M.B.A., FACEP, a Professor of Surgery and Director of the Arizona Bioethics Program at the University of Arizona College of Medicine, Tucson, AZ. Dr. Iserson practices emergency medicine and is the medical director of southern Arizona's search and rescue group. Over the years, he has counseled numerous survivors after their loved one's unexpected death. This book is the result of his investigation on the best ways to relate tragic news and to teach this knowledge to others. Dr. Iserson is also the author of: *Death to Dust: What Happens to Dead Bodies?*, *Ethics in Emergency Medicine*, *Getting into a Residency: A Guide for Medical Students*, and *Get Into Medical School: A Guide for the Perplexed.*

Galen

Galen of Pergamum (A.D. 130-201) the Greek physician whose writings guided medicine for more than a millennium after his death, inspired the name, Galen Press. As the father of modern anatomy and physiology, Galen wrote more than one hundred treatises while attempting to change medicine from an art form into a science. As a practicing physician, Galen first ministered to gladiators and then to Roman Emperor Marcus Aurelius. Far more than Hippocrates, Galen's work influenced Western physicians and was the "truth" until the late Middle Ages when physicians and scientists challenged his teachings. Galen Press, publishing non-clinical, health-related books, will follow Galen's advice that "the chief merit of language is clearness . . . nothing detracts so much from this as unfamiliar terms."

Also by Galen Press, Ltd.:

After-Death Planning Guide
by Kenneth V. Iserson, M.D.

Civil War Medicine *
by Alfred Jay Bollet, M. D.

The Cost-Effective Use of Leeches and Other Musings of a Medical School Survivor
by Jeffrey A. Drayer, M.D.

Death Investigation: The Basics
by Brad Randall, M.D.

Death To Dust: What Happens To Dead Bodies?
by Kenneth V. Iserson, M.D.

Ethics in Emergency Medicine, 2nd ed.
Edited by Kenneth V. Iserson, M.D. Arthur B. Sanders, M.D., and Deborah Mathieu, Ph.D.

Get Into Medical School! A Guide for the Perplexed
by Kenneth V. Iserson, M.D.

Getting Into A Residency: A Guide for Medical Students, 4th ed.
by Kenneth V. Iserson, M.D.

Getting Into A Residency Companion Disks
DOS and Windows™ versions

House Calls, Rounds, and Healings: A Poetry Casebook
by David Schiedermayer, M.D.

Non-Standard Medical Electives in the U.S. & Canada, 1998-1999
by Kenneth V. Iserson, M.D.

The International Medical Graduate's Guide to U.S. Medicine, 2nd ed.
by Gloria A. Goldman, J.D.

Resumes And Personal Statements for Health Professionals, 2nd ed.
by James W. Tysinger, Ph.D.

For more information, please contact:
Customer Service
Galen Press, Ltd.
P.O. Box 64400
Tucson, AZ 85728-4400 USA
Internet: Http://www.galenpress.com
Tel: (520) 577-8363 Fax: (520) 529-6459

* (call for information)

Order Form Order Form Order Form

Yes! .. . Please send me:

____ copies of ***Grave Words: Notifying Survivors about Sudden, Unexpected Deaths*** @ $38.95 each $ ________

____ copies of ***Grave Words: Pocket Protocols*** @ $ 6.95 each $ ________

____ copies of ***Death to Dust: What Happens to Dead Bodies?*** @ $ 41.95 each $ ________

____ copies of ***After-Death Planning Guide*** @ $ 3.00 each $ ________

____ copies of ***Ethics In Emergency Medicine, 2nd ed.*** @ $39.95 $ ________

____ copies of ***Résumés and Personal Statements for Health Professionals, 2nd ed.*** @ $18.95 each $ ________

____ copies of ***Death Investigation: The Basics*** @ $24.95 each $ ________

____ copies of ***Non-Standard Medical Electives in the U.S. & Canada, 1998-1999*** @ $31.95 each $ ________

____ copies of ***Get Into Medical School! A Guide for the Perplexed*** @ $34.95 each $ ________

____ copies of ***Getting Into A Residency: A Guide For Medical Students, 4th ed.*** and ***The Companion Disk*** @ $41.95 each $ ________

☐ **DOS version** ☐ **Windows® version**

____ copies of ***The International Medical Graduates' Guide to U.S. Medicine,*** @ $ 31.95 each $ ________

____ copies of ***House Calls, Rounds, and Healings: A Poetry Casebook*** @ $12.95 each $ ________

____ copies of ***The Cost-Effective Use of Leeches and other Musings of a Medical School Survivor*** @ $ 14.95 each $ ________

AZ RESIDENTS — ADD 7% Sales Tax $ ________

Shipping: $3.00 for 1st Book, $1.00 / each additional $ ________

Priority Mail: ADD $3.00 for 1st Book, $2.00 / each additional $ ________

TOTAL ENCLOSED (U.S. Funds Only) $ ________

[ ] Check [ ] Visa [ ] Mastercard [ ] Institutional Purchase Order

SHIP TO: Name: ________________________

Address: ________________________

____

City/State/Zip: ________________________

Phone: **(required)** (________) ________________________

CREDIT CARD: Number: ________________________

Expiration date: ____________ Signature: ________________________

Send completed form and payment to:

Galen Press, Ltd.
PO Box 64400-GW
Tucson, AZ 85728-4400 USA

Tel (520) 577-8363
Fax (520) 529-6459
Orders: 1-800-442-5369 (US/Canada)

Visit our Home Page at http://www.galenpress.com

Also available through your local bookstore.

Order Form Order Form Order Form

Yes! .. . Please send me:

____ copies of ***Grave Words: Notifying Survivors about Sudden, Unexpected Deaths*** @ $38.95 each $ ________

____ copies of ***Grave Words: Pocket Protocols*** @ $ 6.95 each $ ________

____ copies of ***Death to Dust: What Happens to Dead Bodies?*** @ $ 41.95 each $ ________

____ copies of ***After-Death Planning Guide*** @ $ 3.00 each $ ________

____ copies of ***Ethics In Emergency Medicine, 2nd ed.*** @ $39.95 $ ________

____ copies of ***Résumés and Personal Statements for Health Professionals, 2nd ed.*** @ $18.95 each $ ________

____ copies of ***Death Investigation: The Basics*** @ $24.95 each $ ________

____ copies of ***Non-Standard Medical Electives in the U.S. & Canada, 1998-1999*** @ $31.95 each $ ________

____ copies of ***Get Into Medical School! A Guide for the Perplexed*** @ $34.95 each $ ________

____ copies of ***Getting Into A Residency: A Guide For Medical Students, 4th ed.*** and ***The Companion Disk*** @ $41.95 each $ ________
☐ **DOS version** ☐ **Windows® version**

____ copies of ***The International Medical Graduates' Guide to U.S. Medicine,*** @ $ 31.95 each $ ________

____ copies of ***House Calls, Rounds, and Healings: A Poetry Casebook*** @ $12.95 each $ ________

____ copies of ***The Cost-Effective Use of Leeches and other Musings of a*** **Medical** ***School Survivor*** @ $ 14.95 each $ ________

AZ RESIDENTS — ADD 7% Sales Tax $ ________

Shipping: $3.00 for 1st Book, $1.00 / each additional $ ________

Priority Mail: ADD $3.00 for 1st Book, $2.00 / each additional $ ________

TOTAL ENCLOSED (U.S. Funds Only) $ ________

[ ] Check [ ] Visa [ ] Mastercard [ ] Institutional Purchase Order

SHIP TO: Name: ____________________
Address: ____________________
____
City/State/Zip: ____________________
Phone: **(required)** (________)____________________

CREDIT CARD: Number:____________________

Expiration date: ____________ Signature:____________________

Send completed form and payment to:

Galen Press, Ltd.
PO Box 64400-GW
Tucson, AZ 85728-4400 USA

Tel (520) 577-8363
Fax (520) 529-6459
Orders: 1-800-442-5369 (US/Canada)

Visit our Home Page at http://www.galenpress.com

Also available through your local bookstore.